D1565246

CRISIS INTERVENTION IN THE COMMUNITY

Richard K. McGee, Ph.D.,

Director, Center for Crisis Intervention Research,
and Associate Professor,
Department of Clinical Psychology,
University of Florida
Gainesville, Florida

UNIVERSITY PARK PRESS
Baltimore · London · Tokyo

To

CHARLOTTE ROSS and AUDREY BAKER

and to *all* of the founders of crisis intervention
services, whose courage and idealism have established
a new dimension in the treatment of the human condition

UNIVERSITY PARK PRESS
International Publishers in Science and Medicine
Chamber of Commerce Building
Baltimore, Maryland 21202

Library of Congress Cataloging in Publication Data

McGee, Richard K

    Crisis intervention in the community.

    1. Crisis intervention (Psychiatry) 2. Suicide—Prevention. I. Title.
RC480.5.M24   362.2'2   73-17489
ISBN 0-8391-0722-6

TABLE OF CONTENTS

FOREWORD

NORMAN L. FARBEROW

Crisis intervention is a relatively new field. Its beginnings appeared in the mid-1940's and early 1950's with the pioneer investigations of Lindemann into grief and bereavement following the disastrous Cocoanut Grove Club fire and the early work of Caplan at Harvard in his Wellesley project. The 1960's and 1970's extended crisis theory and intervention with the development of suicide prevention centers, crisis centers, "hot lines," and similar agencies. The prospects were exciting, for it appeared as though a new discipline had been initiated, with the community serving as the arena for active intervention and calling into play the skills of mental health professionals, public health officials, educational experts, the police, the ministry, and many others. The focus of concern was the everyday "normal" crisis, such as going to a different school, having a new baby in the house, or adjusting to a death in the family. New conceptualizations of services, discipline, and theory seemed imminent. However, the fulfillment of the early promises has been disappointing. Crisis intervention seems to have become the primary responsibility of either the mental health professional, who is operating from the traditional medical model point of view, or the public health official, who is concerned with natural catastrophes, such as hurricanes, floods, or disease epidemics. McGee's book identifies these regressive trends and attempts to bring us back to the initial excitement of innovative approaches and procedures.

McGee starts by putting crisis intervention back into the community, where individuals of all socioeconomic levels experience emergencies of all kinds. He sets no limits to crisis; it is self-defined; it occurs when a person feels himself to be in a crisis. McGee's contention is that this person must have someone to turn to; for the most important element in relieving crisis is not that information is available, but rather that there is some kind of immediate response at all. Crisis intervention, he states, is as necessary in the armamentarium of community services as police, hospitals, newspapers, and schools, and it should occupy its own rightful place as an available service, coordinated with all the other services of the community, but separate, unique, and independent.

Any such extensive program, if viable, also will require a large number of appropriate personnel to man it. McGee's answer to this problem is to point to the usefulness and the contribution of the nonprofessional. From the many examples in the whole development of new careers he has one of the best, for approximately 80 percent of the close to 200 suicide prevention and crisis intervention centers in this country are operating now with nonprofessionals as their primary staff resource. And they are doing very well. Perhaps they even bring something to the task which has been obliterated in the professional curricula of medical, psychology, and social work schools, that is, a readiness and willingness for personal involvement. Whatever it is, the nonprofessionals, coming from a great variety of backgrounds, are proving to be the essential element in the success of many new programs designed to meet service needs in the community. Of course, there are still problems of selection and evaluation, but then these exist for the professional disciplines as well; for being professionally trained does not qualify an applicant automatically for work in the field of crisis, as is so aptly pointed out. I agree with McGee wholeheartedly in eschewing the term "nonprofessional." It seems to me that this term is used too often in a pejorative and disparaging manner, as if "professional" were inherently better. We must find a more appropriate term which will apply to both the academically and the experientially trained person.

The crisis intervention model espoused by McGee is nonmedical. Adequate crisis intervention services cannot be offered with a medical model, according to McGee, for it immediately sets up restrictions and exclusions and adds diagnostic labels derived from psychopathology. Crisis is a universal phenomenon, found in every person in every culture, and as such is more of a behavioral event than a medical one. Thus, McGee actually predates the conclusions of the yet-to-be-released Part I of the Nader Report on the community mental health centers, in which one of the major criticisms has been their establishment and reliance on outmoded medical models.

McGee also performs an invaluable service in bringing system and order to the process of establishing a service in the community. He provides guidelines and "how to" information, heretofore completely unavailable in one place, not only for any community contemplating establishing a new service, but also for those already functioning, allowing them to analyze what they have and have not done and to change if they so desire.

It will be interesting to watch the next few decades to see if McGee's predictions about the development of crisis intervention and suicide prevention services will come true. His prophecies of face-to-face counseling by volunteers, mobile teams of crisis workers traveling into the community, aggressive follow-up of suicide attempters, immediate counseling for families of suicide victims, and others, have already appeared, but separately and scattered among different communities. All of these activities are best encompassed within one agency, a crisis intervention service complementing and supplementing the network of other services in the community.

PREFACE

Background of the Project

Beginning in 1964, many new programs were established in this country under the name of "Suicide Prevention Center." Most of them were initiated by mental health associations. They utilized lay volunteers to answer the telephone and to provide referral to other agencies. Some offered limited counseling service to people in acute distress. The programs varied greatly as to their quality of service, their philosophy and purposes, and most of all in the degree of acceptance they enjoyed among the professional resources already existing in the area.

As the movement began to spread, new program initiators would eagerly solicit help and advice from the directors of services which were already established. "How do you start a suicide prevention center?" or, "How could we start a center like yours in our community?" were the questions most frequently asked of directors, consultants, community mental health specialists, and even volunteers. There were very few answers to these questions. Most directors of the first suicide services had neglected to record their own early struggles. They had not kept a diary of their day-by-day activities. Most directors and founders could remember the major events in the history of their center, but they frequently could not keep them in proper sequence, nor could they recall the subtleties of interpersonal relationships which accompanied the negotiations. The professional chauvinism, the political power plays, the seductive manipulations and the influence peddling that had gone on behind the scenes were forgotten or repressed; some of the most important details of starting a new community program were lost.

In 1966, there were already some suicidologists who believed that it was possible to suggest a model format for suicide prevention services. However, most observers agreed that it was too early to formulate any model center for exportation to communities in general. There was too little known about the new programs. There was very little information about methods for training volunteers to work on the telephone, although there was fairly high agreement concerning the material they should learn. There was very little known about how to relate to the rest of the community, and it was apparent that many of the programs were not at all certain that they wanted to form such ties. There was a great deal of doubt in the minds of many people who surveyed the national scene as to whether or not the new suicide prevention movement should continue, and what form it should take. It was a time when systematic data collection and observation were very badly needed. There were many facts and experiences to sift through before any definitive statements could be made about establishing suicide prevention centers.

It was in this context that the present project was conceived. It was proposed that a careful look might be taken at what happens when spontaneous community action results in the development of a suicide prevention service. It was felt that by taking the same careful look at 10 very different centers, in nine equally different communities, it would be possible to draw some conclusions which would offer potential guidelines for those centers still to be developed. The goal was a thorough, in-depth study of each organization, its history, its functions, its personnel, its goals and aspirations, and its success. The latter—success of a program—is, of course, a difficult assessment to make. Criteria of success are nonexistent in terms of statistical measures. What makes a good center? The answer is a position statement expressing a value system of the evaluator.

It is certain that in 1966, no one was in a position to attempt to formulate such a position statement. Whether or not it is now possible may be a matter of some disagreement; there are at least some data with which to work. The 10 centers have been observed, studied, analyzed, impressionistically evaluated, and compared by on-the-site investigators, as well as through the reports of the center directors. Information concerning what went into making these 10 centers what they now are is available for contemplation and debate. It is accessible for duplicating or rejecting, all, or in part. The pages which follow are offered as the result of a three-year inquiry from January, 1967, to January, 1970. Presumptuous as it may seem to those who are more cautious, and perhaps more modest, the following chapters are intended to provide a set of guidelines for developing suicide and crisis intervention services, based upon the results of studying 10 of the brave pioneers who dared to sally forth and chart new courses without the luxury of knowing how to avoid previously discovered pitfalls and follies.

As the study period progressed through the data analysis and writing phases, maturational changes continued to occur in the subject of the investigation—the suicide prevention center movement. The most universal and general change has been in both the name of the programs and the concept of their mission. Although originally developed as *suicide prevention centers*, these 10 community services, and almost all of those that have followed them, slowly evolved into more general *crisis intervention* programs. This was demanded of them by the clients who called, 85 percent of whom had no suicidal intentions at the time of their call. Most callers suffered from an elevation of *perturbation* rather than of *lethality*. The shift to this broader scope of concern has several consequences, one of which is noted repeatedly throughout this book. *It is now impossible to distinguish, either conceptually or functionally, between suicide prevention centers, services, or programs and crisis intervention centers, services, or programs.* Both terms—suicide prevention and crisis intervention—denote a single type of helping system; they are used synonymously in the chapters which follow. It would be possible, of course, to force a literal definition for the two concepts which might distinguish them. To do so, however, would be a sterile intellectual exercise, void of meaning or relevance in relation to the nearly 200 programs which currently serve the population in 170 cities in 44 states of this country.

Furthermore, coexistent with the evolution of the suicide prevention center into a more general crisis intervention system has been the nationwide emergence of the comprehensive community mental health center. Under the provisions of the Community Mental Health Centers Acts (Public Laws 88-164 and 89-105), each community mental health center constructed and/or staffed with federal funds must include an emergency service as one of five essential program components. The definition of an acceptable emergency service was rendered by the National Institute of Mental Health in the *Bulletin of Suicidology* in 1971. It was evident immediately that the community crisis intervention system was the mechanism whereby emergency mental health services were to be delivered.

Thus, what began in 1967 as an interest in suicide prevention has evolved into an analysis of the mechanisms for providing emergency mental health services as one form of an even broader range of general crisis intervention services. The chapters of this book are intended to anticipate the needs and concerns of all who would engage in program planning and development in this still embryonic, yet increasingly universal, effort to meet the psychosocial needs of people in crisis.

METHODS AND PROCEDURES

There were two primary methods employed in this extended program. The first source of data for the study utilized self-reports. Once the cooperation of each of the 10 centers was secured, they were enjoined in a collaborative effort to undertake a self-study with the help of our research staff. Their descriptions of their own programs were solicited. An extensive, 118-page study guide was prepared to assist each program in undertaking the self-study. Its purpose was to stimulate the director to contemplate his program in ways which otherwise might not occur to him.

To facilitate the self-study, representatives of each of the 10 agencies were convened in two meetings to discuss the study, the data instrument, and the methodology. These meetings served to increase further their commitment to the project.

The second method of data collection was conducted through site visits to each agency. These visits permitted a variety of opportunities to observe the center and its personnel in an experiential way. There was always a period of time spent in just talking with the director. Data on the center's history, organizational structure, clinical procedures, and manpower were developed by use of this more informal interview method. During the site visits, there was usually a meeting of the staff or volunteer workers at which case material was presented and discussed. The research staff member was perceived as an "outside consultant" on programming and was able to learn much about the center from the questions raised by its director and workers. Some sections of the study questionnaire were left with the centers to be completed and returned by them at their convenience. Naturally, this procedure resulted in a great deal of difficulty in getting material from some agencies. Sections dealing with vital statistics and records were especially difficult to have returned because they asked the centers to make an accounting of their cases and their activity. Some had never done that in any systematic way. However, as a result of persistent effort, the research staff was able to elicit total response from all but two programs.

ACKNOWLEDGMENTS

The results of this project are the joint efforts of many people. Naturally, greatest among those who assisted were the directors and staff of the individual centers. Grateful appreciation is expressed to all of them: Charles Edwards, James Powell, and Ken Whittemore at the Fulton-DeKalb Emergency Mental Health Service in Atlanta; John Altrocchi at Duke University and Lois Batton at the Suicide Prevention Center in Halifax County, North Carolina; Ferd White, Leon Balch, Janet McMahon, and Howard Durham in Chattanooga; John Kandilakis and Ken Carpenter at the Knoxville Suicide Prevention Center; Nancy Grimm, Fred Likely, Tom Hegert, and Grete Haas at WE CARE in Orlando; Al Sanders, Irene Burnett, and Hal Frank in Brevard County, Florida; John Yeatts, Chuck Thomas, Jerry Mobley, and Rosemary Jones with LIFELINE in Miami; Chaim Rose, Lee Tanner, and Sol Zitter with FRIENDS in Miami; Al White, Ross Cameron, Ted Machler and Phillip Reed at the Pinellas County Emergency Mental Health Service in St. Petersburg; and Eleanor Jean, Marie Womack, Joyce Beuerlein, and Harriet Hall at the Nashville Crisis Call Center. All contributed immeasurably to the conduct of this investigation.

Analyzing the reports and writing the individual sections of the report were likewise joint efforts entered into by many fine associates. Judy Hasterok, Bobby Irving, Larry Levin, and Bryan Warren collated most of the individual study reports and wrote summaries of the major findings. The agency visits and initial reports were undertaken by Lee Drag and Nancy Lee Hixon, both of whom carried the project through its first two years. Also, the entire program of data collection, analysis, writing, and distribution rested upon the loyal and dedicated secretarial service of Patricia Reichert, without whom it could not have been accomplished.

Finally, I am forever grateful to Odette, Sam, Bob, and Leila for letting me live at Indian Springs.

RICHARD K. MCGEE
University of Florida
Gainesville, Florida

THE HISTORICAL AND CONCEPTUAL CONTEXT

1
THE ORIGIN OF CRISIS INTERVENTION SERVICES IN THE UNITED STATES

The past 50 years have witnessed the development of a national consciousness about suicide and its prevention. Understanding of the historical perspectives of this movement is facilitated by three distinct facts. First, there was a definite beginning. Secondly, there was a distinct turning point. Thirdly, the really significant history covers a very short span of time. For practical purposes, one can conceptualize two periods of time. There is an early period, from 1906 to 1960, and then there is the decade from 1960 to 1970. Conceptualized somewhat differently, there is the pre-Los Angeles era, and then there is the decade following the advent of the Los Angeles Suicide Prevention Center.

THE PRE-LOS ANGELES ERA

The earliest programs developed for suicide prevention have been described in a number of publications (Dublin, 1963; Farberow and Shneidman, 1961). Most of them were established in Europe during the first three decades of this century. The first recorded effort to develop a program for the prevention of suicide in this country occurred in 1906, with the formation of the National Save-A-Life League in New York City. The League continues in operation under the leadership of the founder's son, The Reverend Harry M. Warren, Jr. It spans the history of the suicide prevention movement in this country. While it has been largely untouched by the recent developments, it continues its daily efforts to intervene in individual cases of contemplated and threatened self-destruction. This program has been discussed in several reviews of the early history of the movement (Dublin, 1963; Farberow and Shneidman, 1961; Kobler, 1948), and because the League has played a relatively minor role in the recent developments, no effort will be made to enlarge upon these descriptions. It is, nevertheless, important to recognize the League as the early pioneer—at one time, the avant-garde—of suicide prevention centers in the United States.

Along with the Save-A-Life League, there was another early and potentially powerful influence who similarly spanned the entire history of the movement to date, and whose *early* influence made a relatively minor impact. Louis I. Dublin was a life insurance actuary, a public health programmer and demographer, and a great humanitarian who made the first attempt to stimulate a national awakening to the problem of suicide. Recently hailed as the "pioneer of suicidology" (McGee and McGee, 1970; Shneidman, 1964), Dublin published *To Be or Not To Be* in 1933. It was with this historic volume that Dublin first attempted to prick the conscience of the public health profession. In it he appealed to the local health department officials across the country to turn their attention to this major cause of death. He was completely frustrated in these attempts, and 30 years later, he minced no words in taking the public health profession to task for its apathy (Dublin, 1965). Dublin often reflected that he was "a voice crying in the wilderness" in these early days. But, eventually, his time for great leadership arrived, and he lived to see the fruition of many of his ideals. Ironically, it was not until his retirement from active pursuits that the movement could catch up with him during the decade of the 1960's.

There was, of course, a degree of academic and clinical interest in suicide during those early years. *The Bibliography on Suicide and Suicide Prevention* (Farberow, 1969) contains a total of 2202 entries for the 60-year period from 1897 to 1957. These were articles and papers which appeared in professsional journals. However, one reviewer of this literature has observed that they consisted largely of anecdotal speculations, parroting of previous findings which were uncritically accepted, or unsupported opinions and contentions. He concludes that articles which tested hypotheses were rare, and that those which offered a theoretical orientation were nearly nonexistent (Seiden, 1969). The especially striking fact which concerns the suicide prevention center movement is that of the 2202 entries in the 1897 to 1957 section of the *Bibliography*, only three are indexed under the heading of "prevention services, centers." By contrast, the section of the *Bibliography* covering the 10-year span from 1958 through 1967 lists 1267 items, of which 29 are related specifically to programs or centers established for suicide prevention. The distinct turning point in this history, which has in some way influenced nearly every subsequent development, was the establishment of the Los Angeles Suicide Prevention Center (LASPC).

THE LOS ANGELES SUICIDE PREVENTION CENTER

Accounts of the early beginnings of the LASPC have been told many times by those staff members who participated in them. They have been retold as often by admiring colleagues, to the point that, as Norman Farberow put it, they have become almost apocryphal, and many of the actual events have been lost in the telling. However one chooses to tell the story, certain elements must be included, such as the fortuitous discovery by two behavioral scientists of several hundred actual suicide notes filed in the office of the Los Angeles County Medical Examiner-Coroner. This discovery, together with the realization of its scientific worth, led Norman Farberow and Edwin Shneidman to make the first of many explorations into the psychological processes of a person about to take his own life. They analyzed the thinking processes and identified the "logic of suicide;" they looked into affective states and uncovered the ambivalence; they dissected the communications and discovered the clues which foretell an act of self-destruction. Thus, they became convinced that suicide could be prevented. Further investigations led them to search the emergency and surgical wards of the Los Angeles County Hospital for patients admitted because of recent suicide attempt. The initial intention was to get more data, but they immediately found themselves enmeshed in the treatment function.

The story might have gone no further than this if it were not for the support and confidence of Harold M. Hildreth, a friend and colleague from the Veterans Administration Psychology Service who had recently moved to the National Institute of Mental Health (NIMH). Hildreth recognized the potentially worldwide contribution which could be developed in this fertile research and clinical soil; he urged and guided the formulation of grant applications to the NIMH. The first of two major project grants was awarded in 1958 for a period of five years. With this grant, the LASPC was established and on its way. The second grant was for a period of seven years, from 1963 through 1969. Farberow (1968, 1970) has written comprehensive reviews of the LASPC, using the occasion of the 10th anniversary of the program to reflect upon its development and its role in stimulating the course of the suicide prevention center movement. It is relevant to discuss certain of these outstanding contributions here, for without them the spread of the movement beyond the Los Angeles area would have been doubtful, if not impossible.

In the years from 1958 to 1965, the LASPC staff developed concepts, procedures, and empirical data which formed the technology of suicide prevention. Their individual findings and contributions number into the hundreds, but the greatest of them merge into the categories listed below. It should be kept in mind that this technology, which was unknown prior to the LASPC, has been the basis upon which all of the new programs which have followed have been built.

24-Hour Telephone Intervention Service

The LASPC is unique among centers, in that it did not start with a telephone service. Only after the staff had been working in the County Hospital for several months did it become evident that they could function just as effectively away from the hospital ward. As the word about the program spread, more and more contacts came through the telephone during office hours. Months later, the staff realized that they could no longer ignore the ringing of the telephone while they were working in their offices at night and on weekends. Thus, the "night watch" corps was established, and a 24-hour service was instituted. It may be in the interest of fairness to note that nearly 60 years earlier, the National Save-A-Life League had also established a 24-hour telephone answering service for suicidal people. It was not just the act of sitting by the telephone with a staff of trained personnel which was the LASPC contribution; it was the fact that this seemingly simple procedure became the focus of thoughtful analysis, careful evaluation, and extensive description. The LASPC staff not only performed the task, they took the lead in describing the program publicly for the benefit of others to follow (Farberow, Shneidman et al., 1966; Kramer, 1964; Randell, 1970).

Technology of Telephone Intervention and Therapy

A number of suicide prevention programs have prepared advertising or publicity brochures describing *what* their program does for the person who calls seeking help. Only the LASPC has taken the initiative in developing techniques and in describing *how* to perform these life-saving functions. It was entirely from within the Los Angeles center that the technology of telephone crisis work developed. One of the most significant of these developments is the concept of lethality and the rudimentary psychometric method for making an assessment of that important variable (Litman and Farberow, 1961; Tabachnick and Farberow, 1961). This became one of the key functions identified for the telephone therapist; but the LASPC staff also enunciated two other roles for the worker, namely, establishing the communication and formulating a mobilization or action plan to transfer the caller to other helping resources for longer term care if necessary (Litman, 1963; Litman, Farberow et al., 1965). Finally, the technology of telephone intervention was placed into a methodological format with the description of the style, or the attitudinal stance, which maximizes the use of authority, extensive activity, and the help of significant other people (Farberow, 1967). By 1963, the LASPC had demonstrated that a telephone service around the clock was feasible, and they had developed a set of methods and procedures for using the telephone effectively. Thus, the LASPC laid the foundation for the developing movement which was soon to begin spreading across the country.

Development of Volunteer Personnel

Everyone who pauses to reflect on the development of the suicide prevention services in this country may arrive at his own personal opinion regarding that which was the single most important sine qua non of the movement. In the opinion of many, it was the demonstration of the effectiveness of the nonprofessional volunteer that was the most important factor permitting the development of new programs. This demonstration had its roots in the changing zeitgeist exemplified by the final report of the Joint Commission on Mental Illness and Health (1961). In its report, the Commission called attention to the unrelenting manpower shortage, and it advanced the idea of the "mental health counselor with access to consultation" as the solution to the increasing lack of traditional professional personnel. Appropriately, on the heels of this report, the National Institute of Mental Health sponsored a demonstration training program for turning housewives into psychotherapists, under the direction of Margaret Rioch (Rioch et al., 1963). One of the early presentations of the Rioch program was made at the American Psychological Association meeting, held in Los Angeles in 1964 (Rioch, 1964). Most of the LASPC staff went to hear that symposium; they were impressed, but most of all, they were challenged. The idea of possibly training volunteer housewives for telephone duty was not new. In his role as Senior Consultant, Louis Dublin had been advising the Los Angeles staff to adopt the nonprofessional worker, as Chad Varah (1965) had done in organizing the Samaritans in London. But it seemed that the risks were great, and the resistance had been strong. Under the potency of Rioch's results, the resistance weakened, and a cautious experimentation began. The outcome has been observed across the nation as the descriptions of the LASPC volunteers have reached the hands of people who wanted to establish a suicide prevention service in their own community. The success of the volunteers in Los Angeles has been documented repeatedly in the literature of suicidology (Farberow, 1966; Heilig, 1967; Heilig et al., 1968).

Training Institutes

Although the Los Angeles center had done more than its share toward launching the new era of suicide prevention by developing the technology and demonstrating the feasibility of the telephone service and the volunteer manpower, there was still the need for a vehicle by which the new culture of practical suicidology could be disseminated. The means by which this was accomplished was a series of semiannual Training Institutes held at the LASPC. Initially, these were week-long programs, but they eventually became condensed into three-day intensive seminars. Participants came from all over the country during the years from 1964 to 1967. There probably is no way of knowing for certain, but a conservative guess is that over 60 percent of the suicide and crisis intervention services which were established after 1965 had at least one representative of their program attend one of the LASPC Training Institutes. Many more of those centers which could not send a participant to Los Angeles found a valuable resource in the packets of reprints, manuscripts, and other training materials which were distributed by the center.

The LASPC has not confined its training functions to just community personnel responsible for the establishment of new programs. In addition, there have been many clinical psychology interns, social work and medical students, and psychiatric residents who have spent assigned rotations as preprofessional members of the clinical team. Further, through the years, a number of researchers from many disciplines in the social sciences and humanities have spent a year in residence at the center as Fellows in the Center for the Scientific Study of Suicide. Their contribution to the spread of suicide prevention has been largely in the academic and scientific realm, but they nonetheless form a significant part of the training function of the LASPC. The overall training program has indeed been one of the major thrusts behind the dynamic movement producing suicide prevention centers across the nation (Heilig, 1970).

General Contributions to Suicidology

The specific contributions of the LASPC discussed above represent the essential means by which the suicide prevention movement was able to get started in the middle of the 1960's. These developments at Los Angeles became the building blocks out of which other communities were able to fashion programs. However, in fairness to the professional staff at the LASPC, it is important to note that there have been other significant results of their labors which, while perhaps less necessary for the spread of service agencies, have been outstanding scientific and professional advancements. Shneidman and Farberow (1965) call attention to these in their report on the LASPC as a demonstration of public health feasibilities. For example, it is largely to the credit of this staff that research into the taboo areas of death and suicide gained a substantial respectability (Shneidman, 1963a,b). Prior to the establishment of this program, there had been very few scientists who were willing to invest their careers in such taboo topics. Clinicians were writing anecdotal reports of their treatment, but genuine research on suicide owes its beginning largely to this pioneering group of behavioral scientists.

With the realization that the taboo against inquiry into suicide and death could be set aside, the immediate and practical applicability of behavioral science in these areas came into focus. Here, the LASPC made another of its special contributions through the development of the psychological autopsy. This procedure of reconstructing the life style of a deceased person was considered initially to be a technique to uncover the intention of the deceased as he approached death. As such, it was useful in providing data which proved essential for the accurate medico-legal certification of mode of death in equivocal cases (Curphey, 1961; Litman, Curphey et al., 1963). As the value of the psychological autopsy spread, other advantages became apparent, and it has become a standard procedure in several larger suicide prevention programs across the country. Recently, the psychological autopsy has been used as a means for gaining early access to survivors for the purpose of providing crisis intervention support in cases of unequivocal suicide. Some suicidologists have expanded the method into a tool to facilitate understanding of the dying process no matter where, when, or how it takes place (Weisman and Kastenbaum, 1968). The contribution to the field of suicidology occasioned by the development of the psychological autopsy at the LASPC can not be overemphasized.

A final aspect of the Los Angeles program is worthy of mention because it has been a forerunner of important later developments. The LASPC staff has, since its inception, demonstrated a thoroughly multidisciplinary approach to clinical service and research. Throughout the organization, one finds a total absence of professional chauvinism and territorial fence-guarding. This norm of the LASPC culture probably contributed most to their ability to accept and promote the nonprofessional volunteer; it certainly was the major factor which made it possible for the volunteers to develop a healthy and positive identity for themselves and their work. Furthermore, it set an example for the rest of the nation, both within professional ranks and with community citizen groups, whose new programs depended upon achieving a similar degree of rapprochement among local professionals. Also, the demonstration of a multidisciplinary attack on suicide from both research and clinical perspectives laid the groundwork for the profession of suicidology, which came into being later in the decade.

THE LAST HALF OF THE DECADE: 1965 TO 1969

Beginning in about 1965, the suicide prevention movement realized its period of most active and unbridled growth. Building upon all that the LASPC had contributed since 1958, professional mental health specialists and lay civic leaders alike began to invest tremendous time and energy in areas related to suicide prevention. The results at the end of the decade were threefold: (1) the development of local community service programs in nearly every state and in all metropolitan areas of the nation; (2) the establishment within the Federal Government of a Center for the Studies of Suicide Prevention; and (3) the formal organization of the profession of Suicidology.

The Development of Local Community Programs for Suicide Prevention

Although there have been several attempts to keep a current inventory of new suicide prevention programs, the fantastic proliferation of agencies has defied all efforts to maintain up-to-date records. The earliest records of the growth of suicide prevention centers are to be found in *VITA*, the official newsletter of the International Association for Suicide Prevention. From various editions of this newsletter, the following information may be gleaned:

Date	VITA Issue	Information Reported
January, 1966	Vol. 2, No. 1	Listed all known centers in U. S.: Total of 18
July, 1966	Vol. 2, No. 2	Listed 11 new centers since last issue (new total: 29)
November, 1966	Vol. 2, No. 3	Listed nine new centers since last issue (new total: 38)
February, 1967	Vol. 3, No. 1	Listed two new centers since last issue (new total: 40)

Another reliable source of data on developing programs came from the Los Angeles center as a supplement to the training manual developed for the volunteers (Farberow, Heilig, and Litman, 1968). This supplement provides the following data:
1. As of January 31, 1968, there were 75 known centers
2. As of December 1, 1968, there were 104 known centers

After the establishment of the Center for Studies of Suicide Prevention at NIMH, the *Bulletin of Suicidology* became the official "Directory of Suicide Prevention Facilities." Two issues of this Directory were published in the *Bulletin*, and the data they provide is partially overlapping with that cited above from the LASPC Training Manual Supplement:
1. Directory as of June, 1967, listed 47 centers
2. Directory as of March, 1969, listed 122 centers

There were no further issues of the Directory prepared at NIMH, but reliable estimates from informed sources placed the number of existing facilities at 145 as of December, 1969. There were 185 centers indexed in the first edition of the *Directory of Suicide Prevention/Crisis Intervention Agencies in the United States*, compiled by the American Association of Suicidology (AAS) in February, 1972. Thus, the rate of growth of suicide prevention services after 1965 was a remarkable social action phenomenon. This growth is more dramatically presented in graphic form in Figure 1.

How this pattern of development will continue during the 1970's is a matter of much speculation. There is little doubt that the rate of growth inevitably must decline, and perhaps it will even reach a plateau by 1973. There is speculation in some quarters that many of the programs which developed hastily and with poorly conceived bases of professional and financial support may find themselves forced to close down. Hence, the graph depicted in Figure 1 actually might show a downward trend if plotted again in 1980. For the present, however, the task is one of understanding and explaining some of the forces which fostered the movement during the years from 1965 through 1969.

One conclusion may be offered at the outset, however. That is that the development of suicide and crisis services was in no way associated with the magnitude of the suicide problem throughout the nation. It may be observed that there was no appreciable fluctuation of the national suicide rate during this period of time. A report from the National Center for Health Statistics (1967) shows that the national suicide rate has been essentially unchanged since 1950, and certainly there was no increase in rate consistent with the growth of prevention programs. Similarly, there is no relationship between the local suicide rate in metropolitan areas and the development of a suicide or crisis intervention agency in the community. Thus, it is evident that the development of these programs was in response to a growing awareness of the problem, together with the availability of

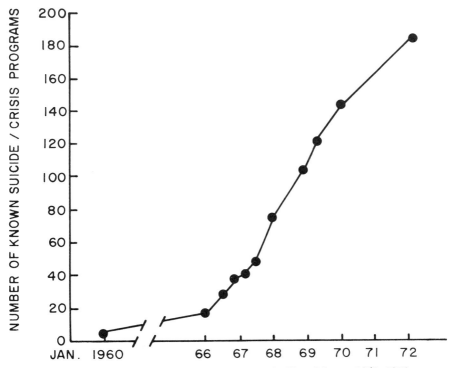

Figure 1. Growth of suicide/crisis programs in the United States, 1960–1972.

a new technology to meet it, and the final awakening of groups of citizens who would undertake the task of initiating social action.

One way to understand this process is to look carefully at the developments in the southeastern section of the country, especially in Florida. In so doing, it must be underscored that this phase of the movement is not being described because it is considered to be unique, or because it had any special influence on the national scene. Rather, the developments in the Southeast are the ones with which this writer is most familiar, through personal experience with the individual agencies and the people who developed them. (These centers are discussed in greater detail in a later chapter.) In many ways, the growth of new centers in the Southeast is very much like that in other regions, and thus can be offered as an example of how new suicide prevention programs came into existence everywhere. For example, new centers have developed in clusters around centers of influence. The greatest geographical concentration of suicide prevention facilities is in the state of California. The 1972 issue of the AAS *Directory* locates 35 of the 185 agencies in California; one-fifth of the total in the nation are located in the vicinity of the LASPC, where the suicide prevention movement began. A second cluster of centers throughout the Southeast all had a common influence in their development. This group of 13 centers spread across the four states of Tennessee, Alabama, Georgia, and Florida. All but two of them were directly influenced in their early planning by the WE CARE suicide prevention center in Orlando, Florida; the means by which that influence was felt around the region is worthy of a more detailed discussion.

As in most places in the country, suicide prevention services developed in the Southeast through the medium of the local Mental Health Association chapters (McGee, 1971). Also, individuals had a great deal to do with the spread of the movement. For example, one layman who has moved into various administrative positions in three states has been primarily responsible for the establishment of programs in Miami, Florida, Greenville, South Carolina, and Montgomery, Alabama. In South Carolina and Alabama he held positions in statewide offices of the Mental Health Association and the Department of Mental Health. He thus was able to stimulate the development of programs across each state. Those in Greenville and Montgomery were the first fruits of his efforts in each state, and they have shown leadership for developing services in the other metropolitan areas.

In the early spring of 1965, the Florida Association for Mental Health, with offices in Orlando, received a letter of inquiry from the Mental Health Association of Tucson, Arizona. The request was for information about the suicide prevention program in Miami, and the Tucson chapter wanted to know how to start such a program in their area. The reference was to FRIENDS, Inc., which had been established in December, 1959. But the Mental Health Association had played no part in that organization, and knew nothing about it to offer in reply. Instead, the Field Director, who coordinated mental health service and educational programming, concluded that what was needed at the time was a model suicide prevention service, located in central Florida, to serve as a stimulus and an example for the rest of the state. She reasoned that if this service could be programmed by the Florida Association staff, they could easily use the resources of the member chapters throughout the state to spread the message. Also, the centralized focus would permit some measure of quality control, while at the same time offering the prestige of the statewide boards of professional advisors and lay directors to legitimize the program.

In principle, what was being considered was a forerunner of a regional association of suicide prevention centers, similar to the Bay Area Association in the San Francisco area (Motto, 1969). An association of centers never materialized in Florida because of a variety of individual and group dynamic factors, mostly having to do with the need for independence, autonomy, and local recognition. But, nonetheless, the Florida Association for Mental Health continued to provide the catalytic and motivational ingredients for the establishment of new services by their local chapters.

The means by which the model program in central Florida came into being to fulfill the plan of the Field Director was quite fortuitous. It happened that simultaneously, and without the knowledge of the State Office, the Orange County Association for Mental Health, also located in Orlando, was spearheading the development of a telephone answering service for suicide prevention. In those days, the Orange County chapter was known for its independent stance in relation to the State Association, and their common interest in a suicide prevention program became known only after the local chapter inquired about funds to support such an unusual project. The story of how the Orange County Association developed WE CARE, Inc., has been told elsewhere (McGee and McGee, 1968), and is repeated briefly in another chapter.

Development of the WE CARE program continued throughout the summer, and the service was inaugurated in October of 1965. Two factors promoted the next developments. One was the television advertising for WE CARE, which was received in other areas of the state; people outside of Orlando became aware of the service. If calls came from other communities, long distance toll charges were encountered by WE CARE, and the Director made an effort to recover some of these costs from the Mental Health Association in the caller's home area. Also, the Florida Association continued to hold its quarterly and annual Board of Directors meetings; and, as lay leaders from various areas of the state came together, the Orange County delegation was receiving more than its share of acclaim for having developed both a valuable personal service and an invaluable source of local publicity for mental health. A type of "bandwagon" phenomenon began to emerge within the state, and it began to be sparked by a (usually) friendly competition which took various forms, from seeing who could get a program started in the shortest period of time to trying to establish the most permanent financial and community support base. Nearly all of this rivalry was healthy, and it served to foster the movement in Florida.

The first community to respond to the implicit challenge issued by Orange County and WE CARE, Inc., was Cocoa Beach, Florida, a recreation and resort area in Brevard County on the doorstep of the John F. Kennedy Space Center. The Brevard County Mental Health Association first expressed interest in late November, 1965, and held preliminary organizational meetings in early December. The WE CARE Director and the Florida Association of Mental Health Field Director were invited to these meetings to stimulate local citizens, who were called in to learn what had been done in Orlando. The Brevard County Suicide Prevention Center began its operation in February of 1966, but it was still some months away from establishing a firm base of operation in the community.

Probably the greatest influence on the rest of the state, and the first opportunity for spreading the movement outside the boundaries of Florida, was a one-day Workshop held by the Florida Association for Mental Health, in conjunction with WE CARE. This meeting was held in Orlando in early April, 1966, and featured Norman Farberow, of the LASPC, and Louis Dublin, retired resident of the Orlando suburb of Winter Park. Participants in the Workshop were the executive directors and representatives of the boards of directors of all the Mental Health Association chapters in the state. The Fulton County (Atlanta), Georgia Mental Health Association also learned of the meeting and sent a 10-member delegation. Mr. Anson Haughton, who was to become the Deputy Chief of a new program to be established at NIMH, also attended, primarily as an observer to learn what influences were at work in the setting up of these programs which his agency was soon to concern itself with.

The program format was simple and straightforward. Dr. Farberow talked about the LASPC and about suicide prevention generally. The Directors of the WE CARE and Brevard County programs talked about recruiting and training volunteers, and about organization and administration, respectively. The Field Director talked about the assistance which was available from the Florida Association for Mental Health. Louis Dublin, in his usually eloquent manner, wrapped up the meeting with a general summary of the day's events and a prediction of hope for the future. It is an historic consequence that at this meeting, attended by the delegation from Atlanta, Dublin, with great emotional impact, reviewed his 33 years of frustration and disappointment over the failure of the public health officials to respond to the need for suicide prevention programs. His message finally struck home, and the Fulton County Board of Commissioners appropriated $100,000 for a suicide prevention service in the County Health Department in August of that same year. It was one of Dublin's sweetest victories, and it gave him great pleasure in the waning years of his life.

Delegates were present from Miami, Tampa, Jacksonville, Vero Beach, St. Petersburg, Gainesville, Sarasota, and 10 other communities in the state. The suicide prevention programs which developed throughout Florida in the next three years were a direct result of interest initially stimulated and information disseminated at this Workshop. The Florida Association for Mental Health followed this Workshop with their own annual meeting and conference at Sarasota three weeks later, and the Florida Psychological Association meeting at Daytona Beach in early May devoted a symposium to the role of psychologists as consultants to the establishment of these community programs. But nothing had the broad and lasting effect of the Orlando Workshop sponsored by the State Mental Health Association.

Outside of Florida, the movement spread in unique ways. A clinical psychology intern from the University of Florida had been a consultant-trainee during the establishment of the WE CARE program. When he finished his training and returned to George Peabody College, he soon found himself encouraging a group of Mental Health Association members to think about such a program in Nashville, Tennessee. He was one of the founders of the Crisis Call Center, and later, he served for two years as the Director of the Suicide and Crisis Intervention Service in Gainesville, Florida. This is how the movement grew in the Southeast during 1965, 1966, and the first half of 1967. In each community where there was new interest developing, the Mental Health Association would hold a meeting or seminar for important civic leaders. In nearly every case, the Director who founded WE CARE in Orlando was invited as a major speaker or workshop group leader. Also, a major influence of these years was provided by the new program in Atlanta, which, through its association with the Department of Psychiatry at Emory University Medical School, had made a major commitment to teaching and training. Conferences on community mental health services were held at the Georgia Mental Health Institute in November, 1966, and again in February, 1968. These two meetings were devoted to suicide prevention centers. By this time, the movement was well along in Florida, but these Atlanta seminars played a great role in stimulating the activity in other parts of the southeastern region.

In addition to the role played by the Mental Health Associations and the established centers, there was a further influence during this period which must not be overlooked. This, too, was a nationwide force, driving the development of suicide and crisis services not just in the Southeast, but throughout the country. This influence was the emerging program for developing comprehensive community mental health centers. Initially proposed by the Joint Commission on Mental Illness and Health and given the full weight of the federal government through President Kennedy's message to the Congress and through the Mental Health Centers Act, Public Law 88-164, passed by Congress in 1963, these community mental health centers became the number one priority of the NIMH. Each mental health center was required by the Congressional act to provide a minimum of five essential services, including an emergency service. An adequate emergency service soon came to be defined as more than an emergency room where psychiatric consultation was accessible; it was deemed complete only when a 24-hour telephone service, walk-in consultation, and home visits were included.

Community mental health centers began receiving funds and starting construction in rapid numbers during 1966, and many of them began delivering services in 1967. Realizing the concurrent growth of two kinds of agencies, each with a goal and a purpose partially overlapping that of the other, the NIMH, through its new Center for Studies of Suicide Prevention, contracted with the Department of Clinical Psychology at the University of Florida to organize a three-day Workshop in September, 1967. The purpose of this meeting was, in part, to bring the local and state level leadership of both movements together and provide the opportunity for them to talk and plan collaboratively for the development of systems to implement their mutual goals. The Proceedings of this Workshop (McGee, 1967b) have been widely distributed by the NIMH and by the Southeastern (Region IV) office of the U.S. Public Health Service. Recent reports indicate that this meeting has had a significant effect in shaping the development of both suicide prevention programs and community mental health centers in various sections of the country.

Later chapters of this book relate more specifically to the relationship between the community mental health center and the suicide prevention service in individual communities. Experiences are still too few and too anecdotal to permit speculation about the ultimate relationships between these agencies which will prove to be most beneficial for delivering community crisis intervention services. In 1966 and 1967, great effort was expended to encourage and persuade suicide prevention programs to include the community mental health center personnel in their organization and development. The goal was to promote and program for the easiest integration of one service with the other. However, at the turn of the decade, this was no longer considered a necessary or even desirable strategy. The Task Force on "Suicide Prevention in the Seventies," convened by the National Institute of Mental Health in January, 1970, deliberated upon the various types of organizational forms a suicide prevention service might take. The community mental health center emergency service was recognized as one of these forms, but by no means was it considered a necessary, or even appropriate, form in all instances. It has even become evident to many suicidologists that some suicide prevention and crisis intervention services have reached the point in their development at which they are relevant community services which should stand side by side with all other helping agencies in a community, including the law enforcement, educational, religious, and health services. To many, crisis and suicide services *need not and should not* be included, either conceptually or administratively, under the rubric of the health or mental health enterprise (McGee et al., 1973). But this stage in the suicide prevention movement is still emerging at the beginning of the 1970's. It comes about partially because of the success of the many service agencies which developed in the last half of the preceding decade. There are other major developments of this period which have been equally as important in the total history of the movement to date.

The Center for Studies of Suicide Prevention, NIMH

The first official announcement of the new thrust which the National Institute of Mental Health was preparing to place behind suicide prevention efforts came in October, 1965, when Dr. Stanley Yolles, NIMH Director, disclosed his plans at a Symposium on Suicide held at George Washington University. Prior to that time, there had been hints and rumors that a new national effort was being formed to take maximum advantage of the developments coming from the Los Angeles center. For example, in 1960, the NIMH, through Dr. Robert Felix, the Director, had asked Louis Dublin to revise his 1933 volume of statistical data on suicide. Before the new book was completed, NIMH convened a two-day conference in February, 1962, for the purpose of learning from Dublin all that he could tell of his recent findings. Then, in 1965, the NIMH began a sweeping reorganization which established Centers within the Institute which would house under one administrative roof all of the activities related to a special problem area. Suicide prevention was to be one of those special areas, according to the Yolles (1967) announcement.

Almost immediately following the George Washington University Symposium, Yolles appointed Edwin Shneidman to the task of making a thorough analysis of the current state of affairs and submitting a recommendation for a comprehensive program of suicide prevention for the NIMH. Shneidman was ideally suited for this assignment, and he undertook it with all of the vision and comprehension at his command. A memorandum outlining a 10-point program was submitted to NIMH on February 1, 1966 (Shneidman, 1967). The search for a Chief of the Center for Studies of Suicide Prevention became the next step, and when all of the formalities of the search were attended to, the obvious choice was the man whose visions the program would strive to implement; Shneidman became Chief of the Center officially in September, 1966. Because this Center played such a dominant role in the developing culture of suicide prevention programming, it is valuable to review Shneidman's 10-point plan in its detail. He organized the 10 points under the three phases which characterize the broad conception of work on the problem of suicide, namely, *prevention, interv*ention, and "*post*-vention." The NIMH Center was programmed in such a way that all of its activities fit into one or the other of these programs, and at the end of 18 months as Chief, Shneidman was able to show the percentage of the Center's resources which had been allocated for each of the 10 areas.

   I. Suicide prevention
      A.   Redefinition and refinement of statistics relating to suicide
      B.   Special programs of education for the "gatekeepers," especially physicians
      C.   Special programs in public education
      D.   Development of a cadre of trained and dedicated professionals
  II. Suicide intervention
      A.   An active program of selective research grants
      B.   Studies of special groups (children, aged, etc.)
      C.   Selection and training of volunteers
 III. Suicide post-vention
      A.   Special programs of follow-up of suicide attempters
      B.   Special follow-up programs for the survivor-victims of suicide
      C.   Program for evaluating the effectiveness of suicide prevention activities

    These 10 areas became the business of the Center for Studies of Suicide Prevention at the NIMH. They clearly had a significant influence on the rate of developing new programs, for the staff at the Center spent much time during 1967 and 1968 organizing regional workshops for public education and providing special programs for "gatekeepers," as well as local professionals. Workshops were held in Buffalo, Kansas City, Chicago, and Athens (Georgia), to name only a few locations. Many people who were planning for new service agencies flocked to these workshops, and the movement spread even further throughout the country.

    Shneidman remained as the Chief of the Center until February, 1969, when he left to take an appointment at Harvard, and he was followed by Dr. Harvey Resnik, who began his suicidology career as a consultant to FRIENDS in Miami. Under Resnik, the Center embarked almost immediately upon a period of planning new goals and emphases. A National Task Force on Suicide in the Seventies was commissioned to make a searching inquiry into six fundamental areas of suicidology and to generate committee reports which would be received by the Center as recommendations for new program directions.

The Task Force met for three days in Phoenix, Arizona, in January of 1970, and deliberated on matters related to: (1) research, (2) education and training, (3) the delivery of services, (4) treatment of suicidal persons, (5) nomenclature and taxonomy, and (6) the broad range of death, dying, and life-threatening behaviors. Over 50 of the most prominent persons in the field were present. It was a grand scheme which might have had a major impact on future developments, but unforeseen events curtailed its importance even before the report of the Task Force was published.

In less than two years, priorities changed within the NIMH, and the Center for Studies of Suicide Prevention failed to demonstrate the validity of its new directions. The support base gradually eroded, and by the time the inevitable fate of the Center was realized, it was too late to prevent its demise. The Center for Studies of Suicide Prevention was dissolved and was converted to a Section on Crisis Intervention, Suicide, and Mental Health Emergencies on July 1, 1972. The NIMH press release dated January 14, 1972, stated that the Institute was taking this action in order to "reflect a more comprehensive crisis intervention program," of which suicide prevention would be a part. Thus, the NIMH, which had played so great a role in the suicide prevention movement, was, like the individual community programs it had fostered, enlarging its scope and focus to encompass the larger concept of crisis intervention. The result was that there was no longer a central focus on suicide prevention research, training, consultation, and programming within the NIMH. But the Center had left its mark on the nation in the form of nearly 200 community programs ready to assume an even larger role in the solution of personal crisis problems.

The Profession of Suicidology

The third major development of the 1965 to 1969 era was the appearance of a new super-specialized profession known as suicidology—the scientific and humane study of self-destruction in man. There were three significant events which enabled the establishment of this professional group, and all three of them came directly out of the Center for Studies of Suicide Prevention under Shneidman's leadership.

The first and perhaps key event was the establishment of a journal to serve as the communication vehicle. The inaugural issue of the *Bulletin of Suicidology* was issued in July, 1967. In the foreword to the first edition, Dr. Yolles indicated that this new journal was intended to signal the inauguration of a new profession. It was, indeed, a necessary first step.

Another important development was the establishment of a professional training program granting Fellowships in suicidology to professional persons who wished to take further postgraduate specialization. Stipends ranged from $9000 to $15,000, depending on experience. The first program of this type was introduced at the Johns Hopkins University through the Department of Psychiatry and Behavioral Sciences. An extensive description of the original curriculum has been prepared and discussed by the directors (Perlin and Schmidt, 1969). The first Fellows began training in September, 1967, under what was to have been a five-year grant. After three years, however, it seemed to be in the best interests of the Johns Hopkins faculty not to apply for renewal of the grant, and the remaining years of support were awarded to the St. Elizabeth's Hospital in Washington, D. C. The Fellowship program was then capable of being administered more directly by the staff of the Center at NIMH. Recent additions to suicidology training have seen two- and 10-week programs organized especially for persons with less than professional preparation. Thus, suicide prevention center personnel are now permitted to take formal training, more extensive than the LASPC three-day Institute, but less than a full year. This has been one of the most forward-looking advancements in the establishment of the new profession.

The third significant development in the formalization of the new profession occurred with the creation of the American Association of Suicidology in March, 1968. The occasion of this development was a Conference on Suicidology, held in Chicago, under the auspices of a grant from NIMH to the University of Chicago. At the conclusion of the Conference, the participants assembled for a business meeting, at which time the new Association was officially formed. Shneidman was elected its first president. The Association continued to grow in numbers and held its first three annual meetings prior to the convention of the American Ortho-psychiatric Association. By holding annual meetings at times which coincided with those of the latter group, the Association was able to attract a larger membership, while at the same time underscoring the multidisciplinary character of its membership. At its 1970 meeting in San Francisco, the AAS formally created its own *Journal of Life-Threatening Behavior*, thereby adding one more support to the profession of suicidology.

In its first few years, the American Association of Suicidology paid little formal attention to the vast numbers of volunteer persons who daily manned the telephones in the suicide prevention service agencies around the country. It permitted volunteers to hold associate membership as nonprofessionals; but in 1972, the Association undertook vast changes in its structure and put an end to its profession-oriented image. The establishment of AAS was a significant development in the growing suicide prevention movement in the late 1960's, but if it continues its present course, it will have an increasing effect on the state of the art in the decade of the seventies.

SUMMARY

The suicide prevention movement in the United States traces its origin to the beginning of 1960. Although there had been a few efforts to establish life-saving services prior to that time, none had achieved a degree of prominence which permitted them to stimulate a national awakening to the need for widespread services. This could happen only after the development of informed leadership which could take the initiative. Such leadership was born in Los Angeles, from two NIMH demonstration grants, beginning in 1958.

From the technology and procedures developed by the LASPC program, the movement began to spread throughout the country. In most sections of the nation, the local units of the Mental Health Association provided the resources and the stimulation. A few key individuals had outstanding influence, among them the professional staff or the lay directors of established centers. Because nearly all new centers utilized the nonprofessional volunteer as the primary crisis intervener on the telephone, a handful of nonprofessional leaders in established centers developed an infectious charisma and were in great demand as speakers when new programs were planned. Thus, while the spread of the suicide prevention movement throughout the country was stimulated and promoted by a handful of early suicidologists, it actually was carried on the backs of a corps of young volunteer women who believed in the power of the trained nonprofessional in the helping relationship.

Simultaneously, the national mental health scene was evolving a new concept of community treatment which, by Congressional law, must include an emergency service. A few communities developed their emergency services so thoroughly that they actually became suicide prevention and crisis intervention services. The majority of mental health centers, however, at least were able to recognize their dependence upon suicide prevention programs, and entered into relationships of active support and cooperation with them.

The total commitment of the NIMH to a national program for suicide prevention led to the creation of the Center for Studies of Suicide Prevention, which, in turn, launched a 10-point program to support research, training, demonstration, and consultation in the area of suicide prevention. This Center established a journal, sponsored workshops and conferences, and eventually gave rise to the profession of suicidology—a cadre of highly trained professionals who began investing their professional careers in the suicide prevention and crisis intervention movement.

All of these developments occurred during the period from 1960 through 1969. It was a time when the number of suicide prevention services increased from four at the beginning of the decade to 145 at its close. No one knows what the future of suicide prevention programs will be. But it can be said with certainty that by the end of 1969, several thousand community-spirited men and women in nearly 200 cities and towns of the United States had taken up the challenge born in Los Angeles and were devoting their personal lives to answering the cry for help. If time and experience should indicate that this venture must pass out of existence, giving way to new and better forms of service, it nevertheless will have been an exciting and magnificent era through which to have passed.

2

A COMMUNITY ORIENTATION FOR CRISIS INTERVENTION PROGRAMS

The era of rapid development of suicide prevention programs was summarized in the preceding chapter. During this exciting period, a countless number of concerned people repeatedly asked the same questions: "How do you start a suicide prevention program?" "How could we get a program started here in our community?" Judging by the great variety of programs now in operation around the country, one is forced to conclude that their consultants must have given widely differing responses to these queries.

It is important at the outset to distinguish between two very different sets of concerns which easily become confused with one another. The first of these is the *process* of organizing a new program, and the second is the *structure* of the final product. Many times, people have asked a consultant, "Tell us what to do to *get a program started*," when it later became evident that they really meant "Tell us *what kind of a program to start*." Unless these two issues are set forth clearly, so that those interested in a new program can keep them in a proper sequence, there is bound to be unnecessary and destructive confusion throughout the course of the endeavor.

It cannot be denied that any individual suicide and crisis service must be programmed according to the characteristics and feasibilities of the community in which it is located. In this sense, no general or universally applicable model is possible. For example, a crisis center existing in an urban area of 350,000 population may find it very effective to institute a program of personal contact with clients who call in on the emergency telephone service. The geographical distances to travel are not so great that such visits during crisis management are impractical. However, in a major metropolitan area, such as Chicago or New York City, the distances to outlying areas included in the telephone system might very well prevent such a service. It has been suggested also that persons living in these large areas are so adapted to the anonymity of the masses of people around them that they would be threatened or annoyed by, or at least tend to avoid, a personal intervention in their lives that is any more intimate than telephone contact. Similarly, it has been suggested that personal contact with crisis clients is unwise in small rural communities because of the high probability that the helper and the caller may find out, to someone's embarrassment, that they are acquainted. Hence, in both the very large and the very small communities, this particular feature of a crisis service may not be appropriate. Whether or not either of these speculations is valid—and there are those who doubt the accuracy of both assertions—the point to be underscored is that each crisis service will have to make certain program decisions which are unique to its own setting and circumstances. Many other examples might be offered to make this same point.

Nevertheless, beginning in 1965, a set of guidelines began to emerge from actual experience which after reflection and considerable discussion became crystallized as *The Community Model for Crisis Intervention Centers*. This model has undergone progressive revision and some refinement, but it has served as the framework for certain ideas for the consideration of those who were undertaking the task of establishing a new suicide prevention or crisis intervention service (McGee, 1965, 1967a, 1968; McGee and McGee, 1968). The remainder of this chapter is a compilation and elaboration of the principles of the community model. As a statement of "how to develop new programs," it is both theoretical and practical. It emerges from both the literature of social science and actual experience with developing suicide and crisis intervention programs.

DEFINITION OF THE COMMUNITY MODEL

The model is not intended to be a "cookbook" formula for suicide prevention and crisis intervention programs. Rather, it is conceptualized as a set of principles and concepts which, if followed, will facilitate the development of new programs. A crisis service which fits the community model has two basic characteristics. First, its organizational history reveals that the program planners had been conscious of and had observed certain recognized community action processes in its development. Secondly, it exhibits certain principles of community mental health programming in its operation. It must be evident that the model does, therefore, presume to answer in a general way the question of both the "process of development" and the "structure of the final product."

As is usually the case, this is an idealized model. There probably is no center anywhere which fulfills all of the conditions. Rather, there is a wide range of variations, some of which approximate the community model quite closely. It is from the apparent success of these latter programs that the model draws its only validity. Its initial formulation grew out of observations of a few centers which, by contrast, had very different orientations.

DEVELOPMENT BY COMMUNITY ACTION PROCESSES

There are a number of excellent discussions of community action processes and dynamics in the social science literature; it is not the purpose of this chapter to present another such analysis. Rather, in the following pages, an attempt is made to apply certain of these principles to the development of suicide and crisis intervention services and to relate them to actual experiences which have occurred in program development. Hopefully, such information will enable directors and managers of existing programs to analyze their own situations and to institute planned change where it is needed or appropriate. Where new programs are still developing, the following discussion is intended to provide guidelines which will facilitate the planning and implementation of an effective and viable community service agency. The primary resources used as a basis for this discussion are Case and Hoffman (1962), Klein (1968), and Sower et al. (1957).

The essential phases, or steps, through which community action must pass are typically listed as: (1) convergence of ideas or interest, (2) initiation of activity, (3) legitimization and sponsorship, (4) development of a plan, (5) development of an organization, (6) implementation, and (7) evaluation. Each of these is discussed below in greater detail.

Convergence of Ideas or Interests

The first step in community action is the focusing of attention on a specific problem by two or more people who are concerned about it. Rarely can one or two people effect adequate action; they must get others interested in the problem to the point where they have at least moral support in their efforts to move ahead. This convergence of interests takes place within the context of some social system, never in a vacuum. The social system may be a group of ministers organized formally into an association, or informally as a mental health consultation group. Some of the people whose interests are converging to initiate action may be outsiders in the system, or they may represent outside interests. For example, the social system may be the board of directors of a mental health association, and one of the members may be a psychiatrist whose attitudes and interests are the result of his position on the staff of a mental health center rather than of his membership in the Mental Health Association social system. The period during which interests are first beginning to converge around the solution of a problem is critical, because this is the time when *commitment* to the action will be gained or lost. Unfortunately, many program developers assume that because the problem needs solving, everyone who has the chance will welcome the opportunity to assist in the solution. If suicide is bad, then suicide prevention is good; and anyone who can will surely support an action to set up a suicide prevention program. Such dependence on untested assumptions early in program planning has led to much needless frustration and inefficiency in planning community programs.

Klein (1968) has identified some of the more common errors which occur during the convergence of interests phase of planning. Among them he includes the problem that those involved may not look far enough for other support, either because they fail to identify other groups who are vitally concerned with the problem, or because they are unable to modify their original objectives to overlap with those of others whose motivations and goals are similar. One of the most frequently occurring patterns in the development of suicide and crisis services has been the assumption that since suicide is a mental health problem, one must have the support of mental health professionals in order to plan a program for it. Two types of errors are often encountered here. The first is in the premise: suicide need *not* be considered a mental health problem exclusively. Certainly the general crises of living are no more mental health problems than they are problems of the educational, religious, law enforcement, and other helping systems. They are all *community* problems, and most communities are larger than their mental health system. The second error is that when one concludes that the mental health professional is the most relevant participant in the planning, there is still a tendency to overlook other interest groups. Experience has shown consistently that where new crisis programs have developed, it has been the medical community, encouraged by the psychiatric fraternity, which offered the greatest *resistance*, while at the same time the law enforcement agencies have been most supportive and helpful.

In short, the interests and ideas of the first group of planners tend frequently to converge with some groups better and more easily than with others, and the greatest convergence is not always where one might assume it will be. Thus, careful attention must be given to the process of rallying interest and securing commitment during this first vital step of community action.

Another common error which can occur during the convergence of interests phase is that the group fails to look into the history of the problem in their community to determine what previous efforts have been made to deal with it, and with what consequences. In one large community, the planning for a new program was well along before it was discovered that there had been a previous program which had tried and failed to get started largely because the organizers neglected to take the local medical community into their confidence. What happened was that for a few months the telephone calls were answered by the county sheriff's office, but the whole effort finally died from lack of publicity. Naturally, when a new action for suicide prevention began, both the medical society and the law enforcement agency had reason to be very cautious in their initial expression of interest. Had the group known of this earlier history, its residue in the minds of these two groups could have been confronted directly and fears could have been expressed, if not eliminated.

Initiation of Activity

The second step in the community action process is that of moving from the initial interest group to start some action. This gives rise to the identification of a special set of actors on the stage known as "initiators." Perhaps one of the most important factors determining the success of an action is related to *who* fills the role of initiator. Of course, it is also necessary that the initiator's ideas and plans be construed as valuable for the community welfare, as defined by the primary decision-makers; but the identity of the initiators is of critical importance. Naturally, ideas and actions will be accepted better from some people in a community than from others. Personal authority and positions of prestige within the relevant social system are important factors. The suspicion that the action is for personal, self-seeking motives, rather than for general social benefit, almost always will result in impotent action. Even though the initiator's motives may be appropriate, a tendency towards defensiveness can be used as an Achilles heel by elements wishing to obstruct the action by leveling the accusation that a "do-gooder" dynamo is at work.

The right to initiate action is not equally distributed throughout a community, nor does the same individual have the privilege of transferring his rights from one social system to another. For example, a university professor with special knowledge relative to the problem and its solution may not be the person who can stimulate action from his neighbors in a suburban area of the community. An "expert" frequently is defined as a consultant who comes from out of town. He may have more influence around the conference table than an equally knowledgeable person from the local scene, but when it comes to actually initiating the action, the outsider is probably the least effective person for this role.

When action actually is started in the community, the first real opposition will be met from those groups who are already involved in activities which they feel fall in the same area as that intended by the new program. Failure to take such already existing groups into the operation is a serious and frequent oversight at this stage of the process. Also, excessive problems arise over the relationship which the initiators may choose to develop with other groups. It may be that after some initial action, the responsibility for the rest of the development should transfer to some other group. Failure to make this transfer because of the personal investment of one or two people can be destructive. On the other hand, programs that were barely begun have been "dumped" upon unwilling and unsuspecting agencies before the latter were ready to assume them appropriately. Sensitivity to the reactions of others and a willingness to confront issues openly is a critical characteristic for successful initiators. One early suicide prevention center was planned and set into operation according to a record-breaking "100-day plan" (McGee, 1968). The interagency conflicts which developed in the community because of too hasty and independent initiation of action cost the program severely in terms of acceptance and sponsorship. While it subsequently has become an active and efficient service, there was unnecessary delay and untold personal bitterness experienced before signs of progress began to appear.

Usually a set of initiators will evolve from among those whose interests converge for solving a problem. These initiators must include those persons who have the social right to initiate action, and the action they initiate must be defined as consistent with the community good. The initiators also must be people with access to others who are in a position to respond to their efforts. A program cannot survive on the basis of the first initiation efforts, although several suicide and crisis services appear to have tried to stop developing at this point; other steps must follow the work of the initiators.

Legitimization and Sponsorship

After a new idea or plan has begun to emerge into some initiated action, the effort cannot continue very long on its own momentum; it soon will run into some form of opposition in the community. In order to be assured of viability, the program must be blessed with legitimization or sanction by certain key persons. In every community, there are some people who can make nearly anything go. For every individual community action program, there are some specific people whose support and endorsement is absolutely necessary. These are the legitimizers, and they must not be overlooked, for their approval is often the key factor which either promotes or prevents general public acceptance of the activity. The legitimizers may be individuals or they may be a group, such as a church, professional society, the Chamber of Commerce, or the City Commissioners.

There are a number of possible pitfalls related to the legitimization phase of an action program. For example, one can put too much emphasis on some legitimizers to the exclusion or neglect of other important ones. One can also make the mistake of confusing legitimizers with experts or consultants in the area concerned with the problem. Legitimizers are people who have the public reputation for doing things that are good for the community. A key member of the Chamber of Commerce may have supported the Dental Society in its campaign for fluoride in the public water system, publicly endorsed the campaign for a new wing on the Children's Hospital, and now may be spearheading the drive for volunteers to begin training for suicide prevention center. His stamp of approval carries influence, but he is not placed in a position of guiding and directing the actual program.

In one suicide prevention center, two psychiatrists were consultants to the program director, but it developed that in the course of their relationship, the psychiatrists were given more and more responsibility for legitimizing the agency's activities. If they did not understand the reason for a specific event, or a request for "permission," they generally behaved so as to prevent it from occurring, thereby avoiding the responsibility that is implied by giving permission. Legitimizers should be people who are able to give sanction on the basis of their public image. Generally, mental health professionals are not such people. They may be helpful in endorsing the program within professional circles, but rarely do they have a public visibility that would facilitate the securing of operating funds, volunteer participation, or special recognition from the local political arena.

Problems always will occur if a group decides that it has sufficient power to override opposition without seeking legitimization in the community. The only thing worse than selecting the wrong legitimizers is failing to select any at all. It may be that the original people whose interests came into convergence may feel that they already have sufficient legitimization. Very rarely will this be the case. For example, a police lieutenant may be a very knowledgeable resource and a most interested participant. His interest, however, will provide neither the public support nor the administrative help which might be secured if he takes his case to the Police Commissioner as a potential legitimizer. Similarly, an emergency room nurse may be one of the most concerned people in the community over the rate of suicide attempts, and as such she may be a fine initiator. But an effective plan for reducing the problem, in the hospital setting, may be effective only if endorsed by the Chairman of the Board of Trustees and the Surgical Chief of Staff. When a mental health agency decides to run a crisis intervention center, it may simply start advertising and taking calls, without bothering to legitimize the new program. It may be a better mental health clinic, but it won't have a truly community service program.

An ounce of prevention may be obtained if the initiator can anticipate in advance where the sources of resistance will occur and take conscious steps in advance to secure legitimization from areas which will neutralize such opposition. It is unfortunately true that the best idea in the world cannot sell itself on its own merits. This point was made dramatically by a bishop who described the resistance coming from some of the clergymen in his diocese over the development of a social action program in the ghetto neighborhood. The program clearly would have benefited one or two of the churches more than others, yet all were contributing to the fund which supported it. With more realism than cynicism, the bishop observed that he would indeed have a very difficult time "even selling Jesus to some of those priests if I weren't constantly being a politician." Since even the best idea cannot stand on its own, careful planning in the legitimization phase may be a sine qua non for a successful program.

Development of a Plan

It is entirely possible that a plan of action may be developed too soon in the course of community action programming. In fact, many groups omit the earlier steps and start with an overall plan for what they want to do. The problem with this strategy is not only that proper care and attention is not given to the initiators and legitimizers, but that when the plan takes on such importance that it is the first priority, it frequently becomes rigidly fixed when it should remain flexible and subject to change.

First, there must have been a convergence of interest around a problem which is to be solved. Some needs must be identified by concerned people, and some ideas must be generated to deal with the problem by the taking of some kind of action. Then, a set of initiators must be identified, and they must begin to take some action, and some legitimizers must be approached for their stamp of approval on the idea of taking some kind of action against the community problem. Now is the time, after all this early groundwork is complete, for serious thinking about a *specific plan* to implement the solution.

The plan for developing a suicide prevention program in the community usually starts off with the effort to develop a plan for operating the program once it is established. For example, how long should the volunteers work on the telephone? What should they be trained to do? Should they be permitted to have personal contact with clients? Should they give out their own names? There are a thousand such detailed questions which get thrown into the system when it comes time to plan a new program. Actually, at this phase, all such questions are premature and wasteful. The planning group is not ready to think of such details because they are not yet to the point at which they even know what questions to ask. It may be important to note that the asking of such questions—and, to a very limited extent, even the answering of them in a tentative manner—serves to reduce some of the tension and anxiety that is building up in the group.

In community action, there is excessive ambiguity as an occupational hazard; those who have a low tolerance for ambiguity would do well to be aware of their tendency to create premature structure. A wise consultant, however, will skillfully avoid letting himself be pulled into giving information of this sort at a time when the group should be devoting its attention to more important matters. He will, hopefully, find other ways to observe the group's anxiety and to deal with it appropriately.

The plan to be developed at this point is one which sets timetables for accomplishing certain sequential subgoals along the way, identifies and organizes the individual committees which will be needed, schedules key events, plans publicity, and generally sets up the structure of the remaining planning activities. Developing such plans has been called the "planning for planning" phase of program development.

Development of an Organization

By the time a group has reached the point at which a plan for social action has been developed, they are already working pretty hard together. They undoubtedly have knocked heads with one another on a few occasions, and a flare of tempers is, by now, not uncommon. A work group must be more than a collection of people. Somewhere along the line, it must go through the ordeal of developing its own organization. Usually, the people whose interest in a suicide prevention program has led them to this point are the same ones who will be taking an active role on the staff of the new agency once it is established. Consequently, it may very likely be the case that the organizational development necessary for the execution of that plan which gets the program started will also serve to organize the group which will operate it and keep it going later.

The almost universal observation about action groups is that unless they consciously seek organizational development assistance, they tend to begin their work at the end and then work backwards through the necessary steps of getting organized. Essentially, organizational development strategy assumes that there is a series of decisions which *every member* of the work group must make. When any member fails to make a decision in its proper place in the sequence, he must eventually "back up" until he has made the missed decision, and then he can go forward with his share of the group's work once again. A member may miss making a decision because he is preoccupied with decision-making from an earlier stage, or because the group activity is poorly planned, and hence there is no opportunity provided for any member to make the necessary decisions. Obviously, when someone is finding it necessary to revert to a former decision point, he is unable to devote his full attention or capacity to the task, and the group process is encumbered to that extent. A group which attempts to ignore organizational development stages will create for itself a situation wherein nearly all of its members are engaged in doing their own decision-making, rather than participating as members of a whole system; complete organizational chaos can result, with the possible consequence that the program under development may be lost.

The series of individual decisions which each member must make may be identified as follows.

1. *In-Out.* "Am I a member of this group, or not?" "Do I *want* to be a member of this group?" "Do they (the other members, or specific individuals) want me as a member of the group? Do they perceive me as belonging here?" It is important to note that this decision cannot be made for a while; it may take two or three meetings of the group before everyone can make the stay in-get out decision. Obviously, those who decide on their own that they are not members or don't want to be must be permitted to withdraw easily. A surprising number of groups carry a lot of "dead wood" because either the system or a persuasive person does not permit the exit of people who do fail, for whatever reason, to make the first decision that enables them to contribute to the organization. At more than one meeting called to plan a suicide prevention center, people came because their supervisor or agency director told them to "go and find out what's going on." Frequently, the initiators identify a key legitimizer group—the medical society, or the ministerial association—and ask the president to send a representative. Such a tactic is good from the standpoint of spreading the idea to other groups who may have a vested interest, but for that particular representative and his participation in the new program, it can be very painful and frustrating. A person may be "in" the group he represents, but that does not assure that he will choose to be "in" the group he is attending. Such membership should not be assumed unless there is time and opportunity for every member to indicate and act upon the outcome of his own in-out decision.

2. *Control.* Each member of the group must make a conscious decision concerning how much control he wants to have in the group and how much he wants to allow each other member to have, and he must have a clear idea as to how much control each other member is willing to let him have. These decisions require a great deal of group interaction before there are enough data "on the table" for members to make their decisions. It is particularly important to note here that it is an informal control that is at stake. There may be an obvious "chairman," who is probably the initiator or legitimizer who called the meeting in the first place. Control in this sense is not the legal right to call and adjourn meetings and make assignments of duties. Rather, this control *is the permission to influence the ideas and thoughts of another person.*

Each member must decide how much he is going to let each other member influence his thinking. Frequently, this decision of control is made hastily and capriciously, and one must "back up" until better decisions are made. It frequently happens that previous experiences between members or their stereotypes determine the decisions about control issues. Mental health professionals who are prone to chauvinistic fence-guarding will decide automatically that they had better resist being influenced by one another until they are sure they can influence in return; it is always unacceptable if a member of one discipline appears to know more than a member from a different discipline.

One of the most devastating tactics is to try to force the group into premature decision-making while it is working on the control decisions. At the first meeting of the action group which finally launched a suicide prevention program in one major city, the chairman attempted to force the group into electing officers who could carry on the mechanics of calling meetings and taking minutes. It was utterly impossible for the group to do so, since most of them did not even know that they were going to be "in" the group when it met the second time. It was a needlessly frustrating and discouraging experience for the chairman and for some of the legitimizers who were there. They could have been spared that grief by not even having such a formal agenda. Until a group is really ready to go to work on its task, it is as important to provide the temporary formal leadership and secretary as it is to find a room in which to meet.

3. *Resource Identification.* After each member has determined how much he is willing to relinquish control, and to whom, he must then begin a search for the resources in the group. He must also learn what role he can play and which of his resources the group wants him to exhibit. Before this can happen, each member must be permitted to reveal his own resources; most members are willing to reveal their "expertise" in early organizational meetings. It is therefore very important that an opportunity be deliberately programmed into the organizational process for each member to tell who he is, what he knows, and how much experience he has had, etc. Most of the other members will not be listening at this point, but neither can he listen to them until he has had his chance. Many groups have great

difficulty getting started because some few people have not been permitted to do an adequate job of revealing their resources and learning which ones are valued by the group.

It is an interesting paradox that when a consultant comes in to meet with a group in the early stages, he usually is billed as an expert who has resources to which the group needs to be exposed. However, if he allows himself to be flattered into playing the all-knowing role at an early meeting when there is little organization accomplished, he will find himself in a rather embarrassing dilemma. He may believe that he is only providing needed information and that he is perceived as a resource by the group. It comes as a shock to discover—after it is too late—that he is embroiled in an argument with someone who hasn't even decided how much influence or control they want to let him have. Other members may interrupt his remarks to respond to his adversary, thereby indicating that as far as they are concerned, he isn't even "in" the group.

Consequently, the only way out of such impossible situations is to recognize that a work group organizing itself to carry out a community action program must take time to work on *itself* before it can work on its task. At this stage of development, a consultant in group process or organizational dynamics is far more valuable than an expert in suicide prevention or crisis intervention.

4. *Goals.* After the group has made some decisions about itself as an organization, it is ready to begin working on the task. The first task-step is to set goals for the organization. This is the time to state the broad purposes of the agency that they are going to create. If it is a suicide prevention program, they may decide upon whether or not the goal is really *pre*vention or *inter*vention. They may need to decide whether the purpose is to serve only suicidal people or to provide a general crisis intervention service. Now that some substantive content must be entered into the decision-making, it is time for the group to use its own resources and to bring in expert specialists *of whom they are now ready to ask appropriate questions.*

5–7. *Policies, Procedures, Final Product.* These three final task-oriented stages may be identified and discussed as one. They require more and more specifically content-oriented planning and more specialized consultation. However, they must proceed in order from the most general to the most specific. Now, it can be seen how much work a group has omitted if it begins its first meeting by raising questions about specific procedures to be followed by a suicide prevention center (final product), which may not be the answer to the community problem in the first place. The natural tendency of groups to start at the bottom and work backwards on this list can be observed easily. A little conscious attention to organizational development tactics will save a lot of time in the long run, and it will produce an organization with a greater potential for serving the broad community need for which it is being created.

Implementation

The implementation phase of community action is by far the most exciting and rewarding if the previous stages have been attended to appropriately. This is the time when the program goes into operation—the end point of the long period of planning. It is the emergence of the final product of the organization developed in the preceding phase. For a suicide and crisis service, this is a very hectic phase, when the director worries about whether or not the personnel have had enough of the right kind of training. The workers worry over whether or not anyone will call, or what will happen if there are too many calls and there are not enough people on duty to cover. If the planning and organizational development has preceded this phase, there will be well-enunciated goals, specific policies to cover most situations, and carefully worded procedure statements to accomplish each of the purposes of the agency. All that is needed now is time and experience, and most important of all, the willingness to follow and observe the final principle of community action.

Evaluation

The task is not over once the program has been put into operation. If it is going to be a valuable community service, it must be continually evaluated as to its progress toward its goals. Its procedures must be tested and retested to determine whether or not they are serving their purpose. Action-oriented, evaluative research, as a necessary ingredient for a community type of service, is discussed later in this chapter.

It must be recognized that evaluation is not merely a final step of the development process for community action programs. In fact, evaluation must proceed simultaneously with the entire action from the earliest convergence of interest to the final implementation. At each step in the process, it is important to stop and examine what has been accomplished. For example, are the initiators the best available? Can they start the action? Do they possess the social right to initiate action within the social system under consideration? Case and Hoffman (1962) have graphically illustrated this aspect of the evaluation principle in their discussion of community action procedures. They created a special symbol in the form of an arrow with a circular shaft which "goes in a circle and then takes off again" to represent the pause which should come between each two steps. This symbol is inserted in their discussion at the point at which one action step leads to another. This pause provides time for evaluation, decision, planning, and then more action. After completing each step, one must evaluate what has happened thus far. Then it is possible to make a decision about the goal during the next step of the process, and then a plan can be developed for reaching this new goal. Then it is time to move into action on the next step. Hence, the evaluation of everything that has happened thus far is a part of the total process of developing, as well as operating, a community agency or service program.

The preceding sections have gone into much detail about the process of how to start a community-oriented suicide prevention or crisis intervention agency. The need for following such established principles has been observed in several of the programs which have been studied over the past five years. There are some notable examples of centers which completely failed to observe such procedures in their organization, and they found themselves serving only a very small element of their community, and for the most part doing even that rather badly. They never achieved the status of being a formal agency, hence they could never realize the goal of being the answer to a community problem. For some services, this is not a criticism, for it was never their desire or intent to become a community agency. If a group wants to develop a project with very limited scope, these principles are unnecessary. But if it wishes to become or to put forth the image of a serious, dedicated agency for the service of all the people, it cannot go about its process of development in a haphazard manner. A community crisis center, then, must set about to develop itself by following well-established and validated processes for planned community action.

COMMUNITY MENTAL HEALTH
PRINCIPLES IN THE DESIGN OF CENTERS

In earlier formulations of the Community Model for suicide and crisis services (McGee, 1965, 1967a, 1968; McGee and McGee, 1968), the emphasis was placed on certain principles or concepts of mental health programming which were emerging and becoming crystallized during the last half of the 1960's. At that time, these concepts formed what may be thought of as "the new look" in the delivery of mental health services, and they seemed appropriate for designing suicide prevention services. With increasing experience gained from a variety of individual centers, it now has become questionable whether or not suicide prevention and crisis intervention programs are necessarily *mental health* agencies, although some of their work clearly may be considered a mental health-related activity. Nevertheless, the modern concepts of delivering services which had been introduced gradually into community psychology and community psychiatry since the publication of the Joint Commission Report (1961) are major innovations, and they are still valid when applied to, or used as criteria for, any type of service agency—mental health, law enforcement, or whatever.

Each of these principles is discussed in the remainder of this chapter. They are, briefly: (1) utilization of nonprofessional personnel, (2) utilization of professional people as consultants, (3) an emphasis on prevention rather than treatment, (4) avoidance of a pathology model, (5) membership in a network of agencies, and (6) commitment to evaluation research.

Utilization of Nonprofessional Personnel

It was noted in the last chapter that the utilization of the volunteer was the single most important innovation which permitted the spread of the suicide prevention center movement beginning in 1965. The volunteer crisis therapist should become an ubiquitous element in suicide and crisis centers in this country before 1975. At one time, the volunteer was considered the answer to a critical manpower shortage—there were not enough mental health professionals to staff suicide and crisis programs, so the solution was to fill the void with the volunteer. In the course of the past five years, the nonprofessionals have proven to be so valuable in these programs that many people believe they are even more effective than the professionals. Volunteers are no longer the stopgap measure used to eliminate a shortage or deficiency; they are the primary resource, valuable in their own right.

There is still a serious lack of basic empirical research data on the volunteer crisis worker. There are no valid criteria for on-the-job performance, for screening and selection, or for results of training courses. There are no universal job descriptions, and thus there is still a lot unknown about just how far the nonprofessional person can move in the crisis management relationship. Such questions are currently under investigation at the Center for Crisis Intervention Research at the University of Florida.

Both in terms of the a priori rationale and the actual experiences generated to date with volunteers, it is very difficult to understand why some suicide and crisis services have not incorporated this feature of the Community Model. It is laudable that certain medical and professional schools operate crisis centers for their professional training purposes. It is appropriate that the physicians, clinical psychologists, clergymen, and policemen learn crisis intervention principles to apply in their professional practice. Professionals in training also deserve the opportunity to experience working relationships with volunteers in order to better learn the consultation role. But in the real world outside the university setting, it is the nonprofessional volunteer in the community agencies who is handling the role. The volunteer crisis worker with access to professional consultation is an absolute essential for community crisis centers..

Utilization of Professional People as Consultants

Most mental health specialists long ago realized that they are not the only ones who can make decisions skillfully and implement action programs in a therapeutic setting. Whereas, in the 1950-vintage child guidance clinic, "disturbed" children were separated from the classroom in which they were disturbing their peers and were taken across town to the therapist's specially equipped play therapy room for expert treatment, in 1970, the same child was being treated by the teacher right in the classroom setting with minimal disruption to the instructional program. A consultant in behavior modification set up the program, and the teacher managed the implementation of the child's treatment in the setting in which the behavior occurred. This is just one more example of the gradual decline of the professional specialist as the primary care-giver in community systems and agencies. Of course, the professional may still practice clinical functions in the solitude of his private office, but this is hardly a community agency or service.

It is important to note that it is just as necessary to have professionals serve as consultants in crisis centers as it is to have them give up the treatment role to volunteer nonprofessionals. There are only a few crisis programs which make no use of consultation. Interestingly, those centers which use professional personnel as the primary crisis worker are the most likely ones to avoid outside consultation.

There are several styles of consultation, and it is important that a center select its consultants just as carefully as it does its volunteers. Experience has shown that there tend to be three kinds of consultants to community crisis programs. They may be generally conceptualized as follows: (1) consultants who reduce anxiety, extend support, and encourage independence; (2) consultants who are critical, cautious, conservative, and supervisory; and (3) consultants who are indifferent, disinterested, perfunctory, and apathetic. Some consultants do an outstanding job of promoting a program throughout the entire community, but especially within the established professional market places. In one program, for example, a psychiatrist wrote personal letters to all of the mental health professionals practicing in the area and urged their cooperation with the new crisis center, even to the point of donating two or three hours of professional time to help screen the volunteer applicants. In other programs, the professionals who serve in advisory capacities devote a great deal of time to training of volunteer recruits. In such cases, one is immediately impressed with the fact that the professional people are there to serve the crisis program. They hold themselves in an ancillary position, and their supportive behavior earns them the title of "para-volunteer specialists." Some special considerations relating to consultants for crisis centers are discussed in greater detail in a later chapter.

Emphasis on Prevention

With the development of concepts underlying community mental health programs, there has been a distinct turn away from what has been known as the "Medical Model" toward the "Public Health Model" of program operation. The medical model is primarily one of treatment after a disease condition has occurred. Mental health clinics and state hospitals serve the treatment function, or what is considered "secondary prevention" in the public health model. Agencies following the latter concepts focus on programs of primary prevention, which seek to eliminate a condition before it can reach the clinical pathology stage. Thus, mental health programming beginning in the 1960's began to adopt the philosophy that rather than concentrating all of the limited professional energies on treating mentally ill people, it was more appropriate to devote a large share of attention to eliminating those conditions in homes, schools, businesses, and communities, which were inimical to the development of positive mental health.

Similarly, many suicide and crisis intervention services have adopted a purpose or goal which directs them to focus not only on the immediate suicidal threat, but on the deficient coping style and problem-solving strategy which allowed a client to become so desperate in the first place. The crisis center should be prepared to deal effectively with all types of crisis problems, in whatever area of life they occur, and not just those cases in which suicide is a currently contemplated alternative for the solution to a problem. If individuals can be helped prior to the time when they are pushed to the point of self-destructive thoughts, they may never need to reach the point of life-threatening behavior.

It is in this sense that a crisis intervention center assumes unequivocally the philosophy of primary prevention, which is crucial to the public health model for community services. By providing help at the earlier stage in the development of a problem, the center will prevent a large number of more serious cases from developing. In these instances, not only actual suicide, but the more severe psychiatric casualties, such as schizophrenia, may be prevented.

It has been observed that there is probably no suicide prevention center in the country which goes as far as it might in the prevention of self-destruction. Whereas many programs do engage in actual crisis intervention which may have some individual prevention properties, no center has designed an active program to seek out the high-risk populations and intervene directly in their social lives at the level of daily living. There is nothing yet in the field of suicidology equivalent to the chest X-ray for diagnosing early signs of subclinical suicide; nor is there any program of immunization which sets up a psychological barrier to the onset of self-destruction. This would be genuine prevention, but it remains a wide open field for both research and social action programs. However, the time is coming, maybe during the 1970's, when any service which uses the term "suicide prevention" in its official name will be forced to recognize its shortcoming and avoid the misleading terminology unless true prevention efforts are instituted.

Avoidance of a Pathology Model

It follows from the transition from a medical to a public health frame of reference that much of what a crisis center must handle is not appropriately called sickness. There is a lingering myth in the folklore of suicidology that suicide is a "crazy" or "insane" act (Pokorny, 1968). To many people, especially law enforcement officers, judges, physicians, and nurses, it is natural to think that a suicidal person is psychiatrically sick. Deeper reflection reveals the error of this myth, especially when it is recognized that nonpsychiatric personnel have become the main point of entry through which society has mobilized a treatment program. Also, it is rare to find formal training in suicidology in the professional curricula of psychiatric residency and clinical psychology internship programs.

The most realistic and appropriate conceptualization of suicide is that it is a tentatively considered, only occasionally acted upon, solution to a problem which an individual contemplates during a period of crisis when his usual methods of coping are nonfunctional. Worries, fears, and doubts relating to vocation, marriage, child-rearing, and physical health may be severe, seemingly insolvable, but they are not signs of sicknesses. As long as the problems are real, the psychological stress that they create is a normal human reaction, not a neurosis or other psychiatric condition. Prolonged inability to solve problems, leading to more and more unresolved issues, eventually can lead to psychiatric illness, as discussed in the paragraphs above. But it is of critical importance to the community model of suicide and crisis services that the psychopathology concept be eliminated from the underlying rationale for the development of programs and procedures.

This is the only approach which is consistent with the utilization of non-professional personnel as the primary care-givers, and with the utilization of attorneys, policemen, ministers, and other professionals in addition to mental health experts as consultants.

Membership in a Network of Agencies

It was once characteristic of mental health clinics that they observed such careful control over the "confidentiality" of their patient's problems that they were forced to refrain from any exchange of information with ministers, schools, employers, and even family members. Naturally, this placed the patient in an agency setting which was like an island in the community. Such lack of inter-agency communication is declining steadily in the mental health field, to the point where there are some community mental health centers operating as a consortium of independent agencies "not all under one roof" but giving optimum care to the public. It is inconceivable that a suicide and crisis intervention program can function without being a part of a total community network of interrelating, independent service programs. It still may be possible for mental health or school agencies to be largely uninvolved with other services, but it is completely unthinkable that a crisis service can hope to function in that way. To be sure, there are some crisis centers which appear to be trying to do so, but the evidence is clear that it cannot happen for very long. There are several programs which have tried it and are no longer operating. Whether or not their failure is a direct result of their inability to link up with the other agencies can be only speculative; it is hard to believe it was not contributory. However, it is unequivocally true that because of the lack of interagency participation, the closing of these few suicide services was a fortunate event for the clients they might have tried to serve alone.

There are a number of ways of trying to insure that such community participation is accomplished. One method which has served well in many places is the development of a community advisory board. Such a board may become a formal board of directors for the first few years of the life of a new agency. At least such a body should be convened as a steering committee from the community agencies for the initial study and planning for a new crisis service. Agencies which have already been established without such broad representation should develop a multidisciplinary committee of consultants and advisors whose knowledge about and appreciation of the crisis service program can be increased to the point where their own agency can find ways of using the crisis service staff in working with mutual clients. A few crisis services have developed the practice of participating in case conferences held on a regularly scheduled basis in other agencies in their network. Such exchange procedures have been very helpful in patient management, but the other essential consequence is that the crisis service has a "place at the table" with all of the other helping agencies which exist in the community.

There are now a number of communities in which established suicide prevention and crisis intervention services are in the position of assisting the development of the comprehensive community mental health center. This leads to some interesting and sometimes difficult decisions about the role of the crisis service in relation to the emergency service which the community mental health center must establish. Certainly, the crisis service must be in some definite and direct relationship to this new program as a part of the community net. There is a tendency in some places for the suicide and crisis service to cease to exist as such and to be incorporated wholly into the new mental health center. This may be a feasible plan in some communities, but it is not necessarily the best universal approach. It is certainly not required that this occur in order to establish collaborative and cooperative relationships with the mental health center. This issue has been discussed elsewhere in greater detail than is relevant here (McGee, 1967a; McGee et al., 1973).

Commitment to Evaluation Research

It was pointed out in an earlier section of this chapter that the evaluation process must proceed simultaneously with the separate steps of the social action which establishes a new community program. It is equally important that the program, once established, continue through action research methods to evaluate its effectiveness. Action research, initially developed in anthropology, has become increasingly important as a tool for the community-oriented professional. It is a procedure which formerly was taboo in psychology and other basic social sciences, primarily because the investigator deliberately designs his research so as to influence the outcome. Action research implements a value system, which, of course, the basic laboratory scientist would be very remiss for doing.

Every community agency must define its purposes and its goals in terms as specific and operational as possible. Further, it must keep records to determine the extent to which these goals are being met. It must be prepared to change its procedures so as to bring the program more in line with the need being met, or in order to eliminate procedures which apparently are not working effectively. This is the purpose and the contribution of evaluation research in an agency. Unfortunately, such research does not have a long history in mental health programs. Rarely does a private mental health specialist in his own office ever conduct research on the accuracy of his diagnoses or the effectiveness of his treatment programs. A few mental health clinics and hospitals have performed these studies, but mainly in the form of recording readmission rates for statewide statistical computations. A suicide and crisis service, on the other hand, must keep daily check of how each of its personnel is doing. Their performance should be evaluated periodically for the level of their technical competence to handle the calls, which require careful assessment, sometimes quick action, and warm and genuine understanding of the people and the problems involved. It is true that there are very few adequate tools available for making some of the evaluations required in a suicide and crisis intervention service, but this should not discourage all centers from making some efforts to develop local methods. Those centers which have the personnel and the facilities should take an active research interest in developing some of the basic concepts and methods which will make the evaluation problem more manageable for all centers to handle.

SUMMARY

The foregoing paragraphs have outlined the principles of community action and some of the modern concepts of mental health agencies which combine to form the community model for suicide and crisis intervention services. It should be obvious that the output of any agency is based in part upon that combination of factors which precede and influence its development. For example, the assumptions which are held by the people who initiate an action and by those legitimizers who are in a position to promote it are very powerful determinants of the direction in which the program develops. If the program planners believe in certain important new developments in the mental health field, and these are included in the planning, a particular type of service must result. Such an agency automatically will develop a cadre of volunteer nonprofessional personnel; it will reserve, but definitely utilize, the professional as a consultant; it will seek to prevent a condition from developing with as much energy as it treats the cases already stricken; it will focus attention on the normal stress reactions of people experiencing normal crises in the life cycle; and it will try to find out how well it is performing its service. These things will be built in, because of the underlying attitudes and the motives for initiating the program.

Any program which includes these principles in its development and in its operation is, by definition, a community suicide and crisis service; it will be a community approach to its target problem. Otherwise, a service is only masquerading under the banner of the community model. It can be *located in* a community; it may even be *supported by* community funds; it may *serve all* members of a community; it might even have been *established by* citizen action. But if it adheres to philosophies and procedures of rendering service which were characteristic of the 1940 era, it will still be but another proliferation of the outmoded establishment.

3
THE HISTORICAL DEVELOPMENT OF 10 PROGRAMS

The first suicide prevention program in the southeastern United States was FRIENDS, organized in Miami, Florida, in 1959. At the time the present study was begun in 1967, there were a total of 10 centers in Florida, Georgia, Tennessee, and North Carolina. In January of 1971, the number had grown to 19, including new programs in Alabama and South Carolina. It would be nearly impossible to keep pace with this development during the course of one research program; therefore, only 10 centers have been selected for intensive investigation in the chapters which follow. These 10 centers which constitute the study sample represent a variety of program models and serve a broad cross-section of communities in the Southeast. It is doubtful whether any suicide prevention or crisis intervention program in the country today is so unique that it cannot find itself represented in the descriptions of at least one of these 10 centers.

Each of the centers in the study was asked to provide data on its own history and development. Of particular interest were data indicating the manner in which the service was initiated in the community and changes which had occurred during the growth and evolution of the program. Accordingly, one of the two purposes of this chapter is that of reporting these important historical data for the value they have in permitting new programs to learn from the experiences of established ones. Secondly, this chapter identifies and describes the individual agencies in the study sample. Historical events are reported candidly as they occurred. Some aspects of the study findings that are reported in later chapters encourage comparisons to be made between programs, and, in such cases, the data may be reported anonymously.

It must be recognized that no brief review can do justice to all of the many important details and events which contribute to the impression a program makes upon an outsider. Nevertheless, an effort is made to describe each of the 10 centers in terms of the model for program development discussed in the last chapter. The intent is to present the events which had occurred in the organization of the program as it was at the time the study was made in the years 1967 through 1969.

SUICIDE PREVENTION IN MIAMI, FLORIDA

In the history of suicide prevention in the United States, few programs have been more prominent than the FRIENDS of Miami. Perhaps FRIENDS has been second only to the Los Angeles Center because, while they were separated by a continent in geographical distance, they were also "worlds apart" in other ways as well. It was not the Los Angeles program, but Chad Varah and the Samaritans of England, which influenced and stimulated the development of FRIENDS.

The initiator of the FRIENDS organization was a young newspaper reporter on the staff of the *Miami Herald*. Like many program initiators, he had experienced a close brush with suicide during college days when his roommate took his own life. Feeling somewhat responsible, as do all those who survive a victim of suicide, he vowed to find a way to prevent such untimely deaths. When word began to circulate about the befriending functions of the Samaritans, this seemed to be the answer. Hence, he used the power of the press to awaken the community to the problem and to a potential solution for it. As a result, in the fall of 1959, a handful of people met to organize a corporation. Of the initial group of 47 interested persons, 26 remained after several more meetings. They elected officers and began to develop a training manual. They were given free advertising in the newspaper, and the facilities of a telephone answering service were donated. They went into operation in December of 1959.

The initiator became the first president of the group. He made contact with the department of psychiatry at Jackson Memorial Hospital to learn whether or not any professional help would be available. Reactions of the psychiatrists were mixed; only the senior resident showed any serious interest. His mentors on the faculty were indifferent; his peers were disinterested. Nevertheless, he joined the group and worked with them until he finished his residency and moved to another city to practice psychiatry. Within a few months, the initiator from the newspaper also moved to another city. He had wanted to abandon the program, but there was strong opposition to closing down, so the management of the group was turned over to a close friend.

FRIENDS never established collaborative relationships with the helping resources in the Miami area. After the departures of the one psychiatrist who had been their sole professional supporter and the initiator who had served continuously as president, the group was completely on its own. They made minimum efforts to seek recognition and acceptance from established community social, health, and law enforcement agencies. It is unclear whether the FRIENDS who remained in charge would have valued such relations, but were refused admission to the network of helping services, or whether they never sought affiliation with professional care-givers. The initial intention of the newspaperman was to create a group of "everyday people." When the time came that legitimizers were needed, the program philosophy and precedent prevented their involvement.

After two years of existence, the valiant group had reached its peak and began a long, slow demise. The telephone answering service began charging a modest fee, and there was a need to raise money for the telephone bill. The bill frequently went unpaid for two or three months, and just before the service was terminated, an unexpected donor would come forth with $35 or $40, and FRIENDS was once again in business. During these months of financial stress, in-group fighting for control of the organization began to take its toll. FRIENDS was operating in a very large community, including two major cities, each with its own ethnic and socioeconomic culture. Representatives from both cultures were members of FRIENDS; each group wanted to claim the organization as its own. For four years, the dominant culture characterized by the white Anglo-Saxon Protestant establishment ruled the program. Problems mounted, and interpersonal relationships steadily worsened.

In 1964, FRIENDS applied to the Mental Health Association (MHA) for help. They proposed that the MHA should agree to support the service financially and that they would accept direction and consultation from the association's professional advisory board, if this were required by the Association. However, the professional members of the MHA wanted nothing to do with FRIENDS and refused to negotiate.

A year later, however, the Association Executive Director, who had personally supported the FRIENDS' proposal, resubmitted the idea to a new group of professional advisors; this time it was accepted on a trial basis.

Early in 1966, the Mental Health Association appointed an ad hoc committee of its Board of Directors, charging it with the responsibility of reorganizing FRIENDS. By this time, WE CARE, Inc., had been established in Orlando according to the community model discussed in the previous chapter. Through the auspices of the Florida Association for Mental Health, the WE CARE program had been publicized among the member MHA chapters throughout the state. Consequently, the initiator of WE CARE was invited to Miami for consultation on the reorganization of FRIENDS. Again there was a cultural clash, for most of the program principles underlying WE CARE were acceptable to the MHA professionals but were totally alien and unacceptable to the FRIENDS members. The keeping of case records and the collection of statistical or research data, especially information concerning individual workers and their performance, were not part of the FRIENDS program. These trappings had the image of professionalism and academia, and were not immediately identifiable as aids to the better serving of clients. Another struggle developed, this time between the MHA Crisis Intervention Committee chairman, who was herself a professional person, and the president of FRIENDS. The FRIENDS withdrew from the organization and went on their own again. They elected to give up the security of financial support rather than compromise their own position by accepting standards imposed upon them by the "professionalism" of the MHA.

The departure of FRIENDS left a void in the association; it had a functioning committee with inspired leadership, but no project on which to dissipate its generated energy. The solution was obvious: establish its own suicide prevention service. A battle cry of "We'll show them!" became the rallying point of the new organization named LIFELINE, which opened nearly a year later, in January of 1967. FRIENDS went their own way for the time being. Spurred by renewed faith in their own program and challenged by the new LIFELINE, FRIENDS managed to secure two donations of $500 each from the Lions Club to sustain them over the next few years. However, new problems plagued the group. It was discovered that the answering service was not answering the calls which came in at night. Consequently, the president had the FRIENDS number installed in her own home and monitored all the calls. While the rate of calls tripled what it had been, this was an extreme burden for one person to handle. When a new answering service was employed, it was still necessary for one person to take all calls every night between 1:00 and 5:00 a.m. Such personnel schedules reflect the serious problems FRIENDS continued to have in keeping active members on the job.

Meanwhile, LIFELINE became an active and apparently viable project of the Mental Health Association. The ad hoc committee became a standing committee of the Board. The Executive Director of the MHA arranged for them to have a small suite of offices in the building owned by the association. He also arranged with the President of the National Council of Jewish Women for members of that group to serve as telephone volunteers during the daytime hours. This was the first instance known in which crisis workers came into a center by virtue of being members of some other organization. The problem which was later to strike at the heart of the LIFELINE program started here. Basically, it was an issue of responsibility without authority, coupled with the unilateral exercise of authority without communication with the people involved. The arrangement with the National Council of Jewish Women for daytime volunteers was made without the knowledge of the Crisis Intervention Committee chairman, whose responsibility it was to recruit and train workers. She came into the office one day and found these new volunteers on the job; then she learned of the agreement. Naturally, the conflict which developed was one of which leadership to acknowledge. The National Council president had appointed her own committee chairman, and the members saw their own associate as the "coordinator." When a volunteer wished to remain at home rather than come to the office to take calls, the organization chairman would grant permission. Gradually, the office was used less and less. One day, the MHA committee chairman came in and found that, without her knowledge, the office had been taken away and the program had been moved to a small room across the hall. With such administrative actions taking place, factions and loyalties developed within the organization which soon resulted in rendering the program ineffective and which nearly destroyed it.

LIFELINE experienced a major disruption in its leadership in November, 1968, after which it continued to operate with only a small corps of workers. By continued determination on the part of the MHA Board, it was saved from ceasing operation until the spring of 1969, when the current form of crisis intervention service in Miami began to take form. LIFELINE operated as an MHA project for approximately 30 months. During this time, it was subjected to the administration of three different MHA executive directors. It was often the pawn in the political in-fighting which accompanied each turnover of executive leadership. The LIFE-LINE experience was one of the most significant elements in the observations about the management of suicide prevention services by mental health associations which led to the development of some guidelines on this subject (McGee, 1971a).

Thus, for all of its problems, LIFELINE did contribute some important data to the field of suicidology. Further, throughout its organization and working history, LIFELINE was another example of the community model in action. It had a specialized advisory board, whose members represented other helping services. (This group had little responsibility other than to train volunteers, and it had no administrative authority.) It did utilize professionals as consultants, and it kept some records which could be used for partial program evaluation. LIFELINE kept in close touch with some of the other community agencies. It might have survived had it been able to develop its own centralized authority, rather than remain as "the tail wagging the dog" of the MHA.

At the beginning of 1969, a new executive director was recruited from the West Coast to take up the reins of the MHA. He brought with him some prior experience and some personnel whose responsibility it was going to be to reestablish LIFELINE and to attempt once again to integrate the FRIENDS into the Mental Health Association crisis intervention program. Within a few months, a new series of discussions began with FRIENDS, and new recruiting activities were undertaken to secure a corps of volunteers. From the earliest planning, the new director determined that "there will be a new crisis intervention service in Miami. It will not be called FRIENDS, and it may not be called LIFELINE." By summer of 1969, this prediction had come true, and the "Personal Crisis Service" was inaugurated. FRIENDS dropped out of existence after nearly 10 years of faithful and dedicated service, its own program structure and organization being the means of its self-destruction. FRIENDS members joined the Personal Crisis Service program, together with the remnants of LIFELINE and a large group of new workers not previously affiliated with either tradition.

After two and one-half years, the new Personal Crisis Service is continuing to develop and to provide new directions of service. It is, in the opinion of its directors, fulfilling its goals and its mission in the Miami area with very satisfying success. Part of the reason for this success has been the determination of the present coordinators to avoid all reference to the conflicts of the past which sorely afflicted both the FRIENDS and the LIFELINE programs. Personal Crisis Service is a new program which is building its image on new concepts and procedures which were a part of neither parent organization. For example, the new program is seen as a "telephone psychiatric emergency service" which is to be integrated with the total system of mental health services in order to provide a continuum of psychiatric care from crisis to aftercare. Despite the fact that many suicidologists and crisis interventionists fail to see a necessary relationship between psychiatric illness and personal crisis, or even suicide, the directors of the Personal Crisis Service are confident that theirs is the best system for delivering helping services to people in the Miami area. The eventual outcome of the program in relation to all other mental health and social services will be another valuable lesson arising out of the Miami experience.

There are many lessons to be learned from the lengthy history of suicide and crisis intervention in Miami. Organizational problems were plentiful in both FRIENDS and LIFELINE. Neither of them ever established themselves as an independent *agency*. FRIENDS never had an office of its own; LIFELINE had one for a while, but never became anything more than an MHA project. The Personal Crisis Service apparently is committed to remaining in that same role with the MHA, but has developed a broader mission for itself in the community. Generally, if a program is to become an entity in its own right and be able to stand side by side with the rest of the helping community, an office and an independent identity are necessary bases from which to function. Perhaps a goal or a purpose for existing can also provide a source of solidarity; if so, the Personal Crisis Service may continue to be the appropriate method for delivering crisis services in the Miami community.

PINELLAS COUNTY EMERGENCY MENTAL HEALTH SERVICE

The Emergency Mental Health Service in St. Petersburg and Clearwater, Florida, has been unique among the suicide prevention and crisis intervention services in the Southeast. The development of the program began in 1961, and resulted in the inauguration of services in October, 1962. To understand the dynamics of the organization of the St. Petersburg program, it is necessary to review some of the social background of the community.

Pinellas County is one of the smaller Florida counties, by number of square miles. Yet it has one of the largest populations, and hence the greatest population density of any area of the state. The median age of the population was 45 years in 1960, the highest median age of any metropolitan center in the state. Therefore, it is evident that the county is a major retirement center. The majority of the population reside in St. Petersburg, but a second concentration of retirees live in Clearwater. Nearly all public agencies have two branch offices, one to serve each of these communities. As may be expected for an older, largely retired population, the sociopolitical philosophy of the area is strongly conservative and Republican. On the other hand, the community also has a very progressive, liberal newspaper which is widely circulated throughout the state and which keeps a constructive balance of political influence alive within Pinellas County.

Thus it was that in 1961, the newly elected Democratic sheriff went to the Board of County Commissioners with a request for additional funds to remodel and update a portion of the County Jail for the incarceration of mental patients awaiting commitment to the state hospitals. Jailing of mental patients had been a practice in most Florida counties for years, since there were few facilities in local hospitals for nonpaying patients. One viewpoint held that the sheriff was seeking to provide for the patients in a better, more humanitarian manner by cleaning up a section of the jail. The opposing view held that such a program would formalize the jailing of mental patients and tend to institutionalize a practice which many people had been disdainfully tolerating.

The Clearwater Mental Health Association decided that this was the time to take some action to force a change in the practices. Hence, they contacted the assistant director of the County Health Department and learned about a program he had previously established in Hagerstown, Maryland (Cameron, 1961, 1962). Exactly the same drama had been enacted in Maryland just two years earlier, and the solution there was to develop an emergency telephone service which would enable citizens to call for help with mentally ill relatives at any hour of the day or night. Each call would result in a team of professional personnel—usually a physician and a nurse—from the county health department going to the patient's home immediately. Once there, they could provide medication if necessary, counsel the family regarding management of the patient's behavior, and assist with admission to a nursing home or a private hospital where this management was possible. It seemed reasonable to the Mental Health Association that this same type of program could be developed in Pinellas County. The health officer agreed, and they set to work.

The first step was to convince the Board of County Commissioners that the sheriff's proposal should be carried even further. To do this, it was necessary to substitute another plan. The Maryland program was just right, and the initiator of it was now living in the local community; he was also a county employee. Finally, because no program can be established in a community on its own merits, but by the skillful application of political expertise, it was necessary to appeal to the partisan elements in the county court house. Fortunately, there was a slim Democratic majority on the County Commission. When the jailing of mental patients versus an emergency home visiting program was put into a political context of Republicans versus Democrats, and when it was strongly supported by the liberal newspaper editorial staff, the Democrats won out. The County Commissioners authorized funds for the Emergency Mental Health Service in the County Health Department.

The Pinellas County program was never intended to be a suicide prevention service. Only because on a few occasions they were called to a home in which a depressed patient was threatening suicide did the staff begin to list the service in the classified section of the telephone directory under the category of Suicide Prevention. Also, the Pinellas program was operating during those months of 1965 and 1966 when other Florida communities were developing emergency telephone services primarily for suicide prevention. The current zeitgeist was adopted somewhat by the Pinellas County program, although its staff never lost their original purpose of protecting the psychiatrically disturbed citizens from incarceration and from state hospital commitment when better services were available in the local community.

The results of the Emergency Mental Health Service program after just one year were published in a variety of places (Ballard, 1963; Cameron, 1965, 1967; Cameron and Walters, 1965). During the first year of the program, the small staff handled 1215 cases. The most outstanding result was the "virtual elimination of jail detention" for psychiatric patients. In the period from January 1, 1961, through June 30, 1962, the sheriff's office reported that 82 patients had been confined from 15 to 30 days, for a total of 1273 prison days. By contrast, during the first six months of the operation of the new emergency service, no patients were incarcerated. Similarly, the commitment of new patients to the state hospitals was greatly reduced. Finally, a third result of the program was the unequivocal conclusion that the home visit at the site of the crisis was absolutely essential for a complete evaluation of the patient's condition and an assessment of the natural family resources available to him.

The Pinellas County Emergency Service has never accepted a volunteer worker into their program. Initially staffed with public health nurses, the service has been under the direction of a certified social worker since 1963. Other professional workers have joined the staff, which has continued as a small group. At some times, there have been as few as two people running the entire program. Always, at least one person works out of the Clearwater office. During the period of this study, the program had four employees plus a secretary. Two of the staff were psychology majors, one having nearly completed an M.A. degree. One was a psychiatric nurse, and the other a social worker. In order to provide coverage for the county, these four people work a schedule which calls for two of them to be on duty 24 hours a day for seven days at a time. These week-long shifts occur twice each month for each person. The unusually long hours make recruiting new manpower a difficult task, but the agency has never been inclined to move toward volunteers to lighten the load. The reason given is that the program is sponsored by a county agency, and there has been no money problem which would necessitate using unpaid people.

Through the years from 1962 to 1967, the Emergency Service grew in reputation throughout the community and the state of Florida. Without ever intending to, the Service became recognized and listed by the Center for Studies of Suicide Prevention at NIMH as one of the operating suicide prevention agencies in the Southeast. The greatest single criterion of its success outside of the service rendered to its own county is the role played by the Pinellas County program in the establishment of the Emergency Mental Health Service in Atlanta, Georgia. The Florida Association for Mental Health held a workshop in Orlando in April, 1966, designed to acquaint local community leaders, particularly in mental health association chapters, with the WE CARE program in Orlando and the Suicide Prevention Center in Brevard County (see Chapter 1). The Metropolitan Atlanta Mental Health Association heard about the meeting and sent a group of seven people to Orlando. The contingent included personnel from the Georgia State Division of Mental Health, the Mental Health Association, and a newspaper reporter from the *Atlanta Constitution*. After the workshop, they spent three days in St. Petersburg learning about the Emergency Mental Health Service. The group was so impressed, and the consequent series of newspaper articles was so laudatory, that within two months a second visit was made to Pinellas County. The second group included members of the Fulton County Board of County Commissioners, who wanted to learn from the Pinellas County Commissioners how they operated such a program on so little money. Cameron (1967) estimates that it costs only $15,000 per 100,000 population per year to staff a program like that developed in Pinellas County. As a result of their visit to St. Petersburg, the Fulton County Commissioners returned to Atlanta and voted the appropriation of funds for the Atlanta center. It should have been a proud day for the Pinellas County staff, and they were surely appropriately aware of this significant validation of their program. However, at that time, they too were in the midst of a transition.

In the summer of 1966, the Pinellas County Commission appointed a committee of lay and professional people to study the feasibility of a comprehensive community mental health center in the county. The county had been well cared for by very substantial private and independent agencies which were well supported by donations from wealthy retirees in the area. Private enterprise, rather than public tax-supported institutions, had a strong following in this conservative community. These private agencies could see that they would benefit very little from joining a consortium of helping agencies "not all under one roof," as the mental health center legislation prescribed. Thus, resistance to the comprehensive community program was great. The committee had to accomplish something, and there was one problem which the Emergency Mental Health Center had faced without satisfactory solution. Being a unit of the County Health Department, the Emergency Service was sanctioned in its operation so long as it served primarily indigent persons. However, if it sought to provide help for the "paying patients," even when services were requested by or for these persons, there was frequently repercussion from the private medical establishment. Some system was needed whereby the domain of the Emergency Service could be legitimately broadened. Traditionally, supervision and/or management by a physician will serve this end, and in the area of mental health services, success is facilitated when that physician is a psychiatrist, rather than a county health officer.

Consequently, the committee, which was having a hard time building interest in the community mental health program, hit upon the idea of transferring the Emergency Mental Health Service from the Health Department to the Adult Mental Health Clinic. This transfer was completed in November, 1966, after a series of negotiations in which both agencies seemed more apathetic than self-seeking with regard to the future of the emergency service. It was easy to reach an agreement; no one seemed to care too much. It is unclear how much the four-man staff of the service participated in these negotiations. They went ahead and performed their service while the decisions about their fate were being made. Subsequently, the Emergency Service has found itself established as one of three major divisions of the Adult Mental Health Clinic, the other two being Social Services and Psychological Services. They are legitimately part of a solid agency structure, well established in the community. The staff is providing emergency care which is both consistent with the original design, developed in 1961, and in keeping with the modern community mental health service, which includes early intervention in acute personal crises.

There are several principles of program development demonstrated by the Pinellas County Emergency Mental Health Service. First, one must see clearly in this case how the fate and fortune of a community agency is dependent upon the social and political climate of the area in which it is located. To attempt to develop such a program without an awareness of the extra-program forces and influences which potentially bear upon its operation is to invite frustration and possibly failure. Secondly, this agency demonstrates that a program can be effective if it is created to meet a specific need in the community it serves, and it may survive if it continues steadfastly in its efforts to meet that problem. Many crisis programs have not been so oriented toward the solution of a specific problem. It has been pointed out earlier that some seem to have been developed more to meet the needs of the program organizers than of the community; this surely was not the case with the Pinellas County program. Finally, the history of this service reveals how an agency must organize and structure itself according to the individual features and characteristics of the community it serves. The structure of the Pinellas County service might have been less appropriate in Jacksonville or Miami; there are probably few places in the nation where county health departments would take up the challenge to provide this type of service. Yet, as any program develops and faces new problems, and as the community needs and conditions change, a viable program must be prepared to adapt its activities and its base of operation accordingly.

THE SUICIDE PREVENTION SERVICE IN CHATTANOOGA, TENNESSEE

The Suicide Prevention Service in Chattanooga is another example of a program originally conceived to meet a specific need in the local community. The need in this case was for a program to offer some assistance to those people who make suicide attempts and are subsequently treated and released in the hospital emergency rooms. The program has never developed a service capable of meeting that problem, but it was initially proposed with that goal in mind. In October of 1963, the Mental Health Association, under the auspices of its Education Committee, sponsored an in-service training program for all law enforcement officers in the Chattanooga and Hamilton County area. Even highway patrolmen were included, along with constables and officers from small municipality police units in the area.

The seminar was built around the film *The Cry for Help*, because it specifically portrays the role of the police officer in the handling of suicide attempts.

Unknown to the people who were conducting the seminar, the MHA publicity chairman had informed all of the local press of the meeting, and a number of newspaper and radio reports of the meeting appeared in the community. These reports cited much of the content of the film, attributing it instead to various professional persons on the panel which followed the presentation of the film. Therefore, the community was told in several newspaper articles that "a suicide attempt is a cry for help when previous attempts to communicate fail;" that "most people don't realize how hard it is to kill themselves by cutting their wrists;" and that "few people who take pills know how many to take the first time." In essence, the community was told that suicide attempts might be the answer to some personal problems, and that attempting suicide with wrist cuts and overdoses was a relatively safe way to get across the point that one is experiencing personal stress.

Following this seminar, and the publicity that attended it, there was a marked increase in the number of suicide attempts treated in the three hospitals in the immediate metropolitan area. Most were treated and released without any specific plans for follow-up of the case. Two of the three hospitals had clergymen serving as chaplains who received reports of all such cases daily. These two chaplains happened to be members of a mental health consultation group for ministers which had been meeting weekly at the State Psychiatric Hospital in town. The number of suicide attempts and what might be done about them became a topic of conversation at these meetings for several weeks. Finally, after the usual increase in suicidal behavior over the Christmas holiday season, the group decided to take some kind of action. A special interest group was formed, and the chief psychologist at the hospital, who had planned and officiated at the police seminar in the fall, agreed to write a tentative proposal for a program design (McGee, 1965).

The interest group, armed with a specific proposal and some professional backing, began the search for local legitimizers. The two people contacted were the hospital administrator of the large, general, partially tax-supported hospital, and the county health officer. Specific decisions at this point ruled out going to local mental health authorities because the psychiatric professionals in the community were perceived as being highly conservative and largely unimpressed with any of the innovative community mental health notions which were beginning to come into focus. However, with this start, it was possible to reach other necessary groups. The health officer agreed to take the proposal to the County Medical Society, the chaplains would promote it with the ministerial association, and the hospital administrator would support the program with local businessmen and other community agencies with whose boards of directors he had influence. Finally, armed with the backing of these key legitimizers, the interest group approached the Metropolitan Council for Community Services. They asked this group to organize the development of the program by sponsoring the meetings which would have to be held to negotiate roles and formalize plans of action. The Council agreed to assume the role of catalyst without taking an advocate position either for or against the development of a suicide prevention program.

Very early in the planning, correspondence was initiated with the Mental Health Services program director in the regional office of the U. S. Public Health Service. Valuable advice was obtained from this source, including a suggestion which cast the die for the developing agency. The suggestion was that rather than establish a new agency, the group might seek to formalize a program which would maximize the utilization of the agencies already existing in the community. This sounded like a noble idea, and one which should certainly both please and appease any elements in the community which might wish to see the group's interest frustrated. However, before the program became firmly established several years later, this strategy was destined to become a double bind which prevented the program from reaching its potential fulfillment in the community.

The regional office had another suggestion to make to the interest group. That was that the consultation of Harold Hildreth from the NIMH office might be available if the group would contact him. Hildreth had been associated with the development of the Los Angeles Suicide Prevention Center and was an acknowledged authority within the NIMH.

While awaiting word from Hildreth, the interest group proceeded to collect some data on the incidence of suicide and suicide attempts in the area. They discovered, among other things, that there was an average of 44 suicide attempts per month in the county, and that 27 of these 44 were not known to any of the helping services in the area, either before or as a result of the suicide attempt. With the data from the survey, and the tentative proposal for an action program, which by this time had been approved by the medical and ministerial groups, the Metropolitan Council called its first meeting of community agencies in November, 1964. This meeting was being held nearly 14 months after the law enforcement seminar, and nearly a year after the special interest group decided to take some definitive action. As a result of reviewing the slow, painstaking steps of development of the Chattanooga center, one member coined the motto of the group: "Above all, let's make haste slowly."

At the November meeting of community service representatives, the director of the Metropolitan Council explained his agency's role. The interest group presented its data and its plan, and they informed the group that consultation from Dr. Hildreth would be available the following month.

Following Hildreth's visit, in which the group received enthusiastic support and encouragement for their intentions and their organized manner of implementing the program, a committee was formed to investigate various possibilities for locating the nucleus of the program in existing agencies. They were also to investigate the Training Institute held semiannually at the Los Angeles Center and to determine the feasibility of sending representatives. The committee reported a number of failures to locate support from an appropriate agency, although they did send a psychiatrist, the two hospital chaplains, and a sociologist from the University to Los Angeles in April, 1965.

By July, 1965, it was evident that there was not going to be a community agency which would commit any of its resources to coordinating the suicide prevention service, nor would any agency provide physical space from which to operate. Consequently, remembering the suggestion that it might be unwise to establish a new agency to do what existing ones would not do, the group undertook a "feasibility study." This timid expression of determination to proceed with their goals characterized the life of the Chattanooga Suicide Prevention Service. Once committed to a feasibility study for a one-year period, the group was faced with certain realities. A new telephone directory was to be published in the fall, and the service should be listed. However, with the summer vacation already at hand, it would be impossible to recruit and train volunteers to man the telephones by the time the new listing was published. Consequently, they elected to list the service in the new directory, but not to publicize it elsewhere until the first training class was completed. When the new directory came out, a core group of five ministers, two psychiatrists, and two M.A.-level psychologists prepared themselves to answer the telephone if it should ring. An answering service was employed, and duty shifts were taken by the volunteers on duty at home.

Essentially, this program was only a "night watch." It operated from 5:00 p.m. until 9:00 a.m., and on Saturdays, Sundays, and holidays. There was a specific assumption that existing agencies would handle all suicide cases during the regular clinic and business hours of the week days. The program began this way on September 17, 1965. A training program was slated to begin in November, with 21 volunteers to be recruited from existing agencies. Following the Christmas season, a series of publicity releases announced the program to the community on January 3, 1966. By this time, there had been a two-year span between initial action and tangible evidence of an action program to solve the problem identified by the interest group.

There were two factors which account primarily for the long delay in program development in Chattanooga. One was the frequent loss of key leadership. A number of the original people moved away from the city, leaving the group to find replacements. Secondly, there was no commitment on the part of the community power structure for the program. The individuals and agencies which could have helped greatly were at best indifferent, and at worst, passively destructive of the efforts being made. Knowing the sensitive issues involved among the agencies and professionals, the Metropolitan Council continued to play only a catalytic role, whereas, had the idea been more popular, it could have been a successful advocate and accomplished the task in less than half the time finally consumed. Only the undaunted determination of the ministerial group made possible the establishment of the program under the "feasibility study" strategy in September, 1965.

At the end of the first year, the plan called for the study to be evaluated. The evaluation was to determine whether or not it was appropriate to establish a permanent suicide prevention service in the community. An alternative action had been written into the study plan: the feasibility study could be continued longer if desired. Consequently, it was extended. Later it was extended again. The original plan called for incorporating the core group for legal protection of the volunteers. Two years later, this still had not been accomplished. In January, 1969, after three years of service to the Chattanooga community, Suicide Prevention Service was still a "feasibility study" being run as a project of the Mental Health Association out of the MHA office. One member of the MHA Board of Directors was a more-or-less permanent chairman of the Suicide Prevention Committee. Although he was one of the clergymen originally interested in the program six years earlier, he had become involved increasingly in other community programs which were designed to meet the needs of people in trouble. For example, a CONTACT group had been established in the community through a project of the Methodist churches. CONTACT workers saw themselves as providing general crisis intervention services; they urged that Suicide Prevention Service confine its activity only to suicide and that it avoid becoming a general crisis intervention service. This violated the goals of the Executive Director of the Mental Health Association, who was aware of the trend in other suicide programs around the Southeast to become general crisis services.

By the end of 1969, the Suicide Prevention Service was definitely on the way to either final termination or drastic renovation of its program. The "feasibility study" had been an unqualified failure. Because of a low frequency of calls, the volunteers were losing interest, and since the CONTACT group was receiving a reported 1500 calls per month, the Mental Health Association was willing to let them take over the suicide service. They seemed to be ready to do it. However, the Mental Health Association announced it would terminate its support of the service December 31, 1969. In January, 1970, the program was taken over by the Psychiatric Clinic, which was beginning to foresee the possibility of the program's becoming a part of the emergency service which was required for the comprehensive community mental health center which might be developed in the area eventually. A new program of recruiting and training volunteers began, and the possibility of a suicide prevention telephone service was once more given new hope. However, this was not an adequate antidote. The program continued to function during 1970 without any serious efforts to develop it further. Finally, on June 30, 1971, the telephone number was discontinued, and it was all over.

In looking back through the long and nearly futile history of developing a viable community crisis service in the Chattanooga area, one must wonder what could have kept the program so impotent after it had such a potentially good start. Part of the explanation has been focused on the lack of consistent leadership and the lack of commitment on the part of the existing agencies. Had the Chattanooga group had the benefit of a home in the Health Department or the

Psychiatric Clinic, and had they been willing to use paid professional personnel, as the Pinellas County, Florida, Emergency Mental Health Service had done, they might have had a chance. However, Chattanooga is a community with an outstanding concentration of private medical and professional interests. It is a highly conservative community, dominated by a small but entrenched power structure. A suicide prevention service, operated by trained volunteers, following the community programming principles discussed in Chapter 2, was far too removed from the cultural context which was to be found in Chattanooga in 1965. The small group which had this vision lacked the political and professional clout to push it through.

The primary opposition came from the Psychiatric Clinic, which eventually found itself ready to take over the program and save it from total elimination. One of the psychiatrists who had been involved with the planning since 1965 stated that his role in the Suicide Prevention Service was to offer consultation and to "see that the interests of the Psychiatric Clinic were properly represented." The best demonstration of how well he performed his role was the decision to make the "feasibility study" program only a night watch. To operate around the clock, especially during the time the Clinic was open, would be an open admission that the Psychiatric Clinic needed some supplemental program to deal with suicide in the community. The major motive throughout the Chattanooga program has been to avoid casting a doubt upon or becoming a threat to the professional personnel in the Clinic. They successfully maintained its impotence when it might have begun to fulfill its mission. One must wonder if the time will ever come when the interests of the Clinic can be served by a strong, active, and involved group of crisis intervention volunteers in the community. The need of the Chattanooga community for crisis intervention service and for professional psychiatric care are both being well satisfied, but the small group of enthusiastic optimists who tried for seven years to bring the two together under the Suicide Prevention Service finally were forced to give up in defeat. It is a valuable lesson for those who insist that crisis services must be a part of local mental health systems.

WE CARE, INC., IN ORLANDO, FLORIDA

The story of the development of the Orlando crisis intervention center has been told elsewhere (McGee, 1971b; McGee and McGee, 1968), but will be repeated here for the sake of maintaining the continuity of this chapter. In many respects, WE CARE was the original demonstration of the community model of crisis centers. Many of the elements first attempted in that program served as the basis for procedures built into the research and service program described in the final chapters of this book. Further, during the years of greatest program development, nearly all of the crisis services in the Southeast, and others from as far away as Albuquerque, New Mexico, received their early stimulation and general direction from the WE CARE model.

The origin of the suicide prevention program in Orlando has been credited to a Mental Health Association volunteer who made weekly visits to the psychiatric unit of a private hospital in the area. On one such routine visit, she met and talked at length with a patient who had made severe knife wounds in her abdomen in a suicide attempt. The patient related that she had told her husband and relatives of her depression and hopelessness. However, no one seemed to pay any attention until she took more extreme action. "They acted as if they didn't even care." Recognizing the loneliness of the woman's plight, and believing that some other volunteers like herself might be found who would be the caring resources for such people, the worker decided to investigate a program for suicide prevention. She became the initiator of WE CARE, and started the planning process sometime around February, 1965. The first few months were spent in reading all the books which were available at the time: *Clues to Suicide* (Shneidman and Farberow, 1957), *The Cry for Help* (Farberow and Shneidman, 1961), *Suicide and the Soul* (Hillman, 1964), and probably most important of all for the WE CARE program, *Suicide: A Sociological and Statistical Study* (Dublin, 1963).

After becoming prepared for the undertaking with some background in the classical literature of suicidology, the initiator then began to look for some legitimization in the community. She was still an interest group of one person; it remained an almost single-handed effort for several months. Legitimization was sought first from the county Mental Health Association; the Board of Directors was asked if they would endorse and underwrite the minimal costs which were expected. They expressed interest and agreed to look into the project with the initiator. Someone on the Board had two suggestions to make. First, the author of *Suicide: A Sociological and Statistical Study*, Louis Dublin, had retired from the insurance company and had taken up residence in Winter Park, a city adjoining Orlando. Perhaps a personal visit with Dublin would enable an evaluation of the feasibility and practicality of a suicide prevention program. Secondly, since Orlando happened to be the home of the Florida Association for Mental Health, the local chapter might be well advised to consult with the state office concerning resources to support such a unique program. (The activity of the Clearwater Mental Health Association in establishing the Pinellas County Emergency Mental Health Service three years earlier was unknown to the Orlando chapter.) Contact was made with the state association in May, 1965.

The first encounter with the state office was a major setback for the initiator of the local program. She was told to drop everything and not to move any further until consultation could be arranged with a psychologist at the University who had already been involved in discussions with them concerning a suicide prevention service in central Florida. This psychologist had earlier written the tentative program proposal for the Chattanooga ministers to submit to the health officer and hospital administrator. Upon moving to Florida and becoming involved in community psychology programs, he had been asked to serve as program chairman for the annual meeting and conference of the State Mental Health

Association. The meeting was in April, and a number of discussions had been held with the state staff during the fall and winter. On one of these occasions, the Education Chairman produced a letter from the Mental Health Association in Phoenix, Arizona. They had heard about the suicide prevention group called FRIENDS operating in Miami, and wanted information from the Mental Health Association about the service. There was no information to be given, since the office had had no contact with the group. They only knew that their MHA chapter in Miami was not completely happy with the organization and had recently refused to support it financially. These simple facts led inevitably to a "brainstorming" session in which the idea was proposed that a demonstration center in the central Florida area, under the sponsorship and perhaps the management of the state office, would provide a means for answering such letters as the one received from Phoenix. Also, it seemed that the way things were going in the delivery of mental health services, such a program probably would have a lot of potential for setting a new pattern. The psychologist had a program design and confidence in its workability; the state association staff had the motive. Then along came the local chapter with an initiator already at work and ready to start a suicide prevention program.

The big question, of course, was whether or not these separate elements could get together and agree on the type of program to develop. Questions of leadership, control, procedures, and most of all, financial support, began to occupy much of the planning energy. By June, the initiator had been given the green light by the state association and a guarded acceptance by the county MHA chapter, the leadership of which did not yet trust the psychologist-consultant. Early in June, a community advisory board was recruited and convened in its first meeting. Their support was enthusiastic, led primarily by the law enforcement, ministerial, and hospital administrator representatives. A key legitimizer who emerged at this meeting was to become the most ardent supporter of the program throughout its development and life to date. He was a pathologist and the county medical examiner. More importantly, he was the only medical person in the area to realize fully the potential of the program without ever being personally threatened by it. Many times in future months he saved the program from destruction by the poor communication and suspicion which characterized the relationships between the psychologist from out of town and the local professional advisors.

With the backing of the advisory board of local agency representatives and professionals, the program initiator began the task of recruiting volunteers for a training class to begin in the fall. With a telephone answering service donated by a local hospital, trained volunteers ready to work in their homes, and a night watch comprised of volunteer clergy from the ministerial association, WE CARE was ready to inaugurate service in October, 1965.

In November, the initiator, who had become the program coordinator, made the trip to Los Angeles for the semiannual Training Institute. When she returned, a new in-service training program was initiated, and the volunteers met in the sheriff's auditorium every other week for a discussion of their experiences and problems. In 1966, the consulting psychologist persuaded the coordinator to capitalize upon the opportunity to observe carefully the effects of training and the influence of the program on the statistics of suicidal behavior in the county. A research grant from the Florida Council for Training and Research in Mental Health in the amount of $5000 supported these investigations during 1966. Regular consultation and in-service training lectures by the visiting psychologist helped to solidify the volunteer group and tended to ease some of the tensions, at least temporarily, with the advisory board.

During 1966, the NIMH established the Center for Studies of Suicide Prevention, and an appropriation of research grant funds needed to be utilized. The Center began to invite research grant applications; even demonstration projects were acceptable in those early days. WE CARE was beginning to feel the pinch of not having an office or a full-time paid coordinator. In the late summer, the initiator moved to another city and left the program in the hands of one of the volunteers. Transitions always bring turmoil, and this one was particularly disruptive because of the loss of so many volunteers who had developed a personal loyalty to a person rather than to a program. Many of the stalwarts in the program somehow found themselves too busy to continue. Something had to be done quickly to save the program. It could not maintain its status quo; it must either leap ahead or fall backward, maybe to the point of closing down. Almost simultaneously, the NIMH center invited a research grant from the consulting psychologist, whose interest in suicidology was becoming recognized. A second fortuitous congruence of circumstances had played a role in the WE CARE developmental history.

Consultations were held with the medical examiner and the law enforcement agencies. Perhaps the original goal of the Chattanooga program—follow-up and intervention with suicide attempters—could be the basis of a research grant that would not only provide some operating expense money for a paid coordinator and an office, but really put WE CARE on the map. With national recognition, surely the community would come forth with continuing support. A research plan was developed, revised, submitted to the Advisory Board in a formal session called for that purpose, and approved. The grant application was submitted to NIMH in December, 1966, found acceptable, and awarded in the spring of 1967.

Then began a long series of painful negotiations between the professional consultants, Advisory Board, the coordinator, and the psychologist, who was now no longer a consultant, but a "principal investigator" with a big stake in the outcome of the program. The professional advisors were two psychiatrists, the medical examiner, and a local psychologist in private practice. The latter two were to be paid modest consulting fees from the grant budget. The two psychiatrists were asked to be the primary advocates and sponsors of the experimental service program with the medical community and the hospital emergency rooms. All of a sudden, the psychiatrists behaved as if they were caught off guard. They appeared to know nothing of the program. No one had remembered that neither one had been present months earlier, when the Advisory Board had approved the grant application. They had been sent copies of it with a request for their recommendations and suggestions, but no feedback was ever obtained. Now, with the grant money in hand and a program ready to implement, active opposition was encountered. The resulting events taught several important lessons about the roles of professional consultants in community crisis programs (McGee, 1971b). Some of these are discussed in Chapter 6, relating to manpower in suicide and crisis intervention services.

Eventually, the program was implemented; but before it was, the design was so compromised and the energy and morale of the WE CARE staff was so depleted that it was barely successful as a service program and was a near disaster as a research project. For the next 27 months, WE CARE was able to support itself and become established as a visible and valued part of the community. As the grant neared expiration, a local effort began to find continuing financial support.

The coordinator began with a visit to the editor of one of the local newspapers. He had previously been very supportive of the WE CARE program, using the newspaper as a means of continually favorable publicity. Now, when faced with the request for an appeal to the community for $15,000 for the next year, he responded by placing a call to the director of the local United Appeal Agency. The United Appeal had a surplus in its emergency fund that year, and the editor was aware of these monies, since he was a member of the funding agency's Board of Directors. After being reminded that the newspaper contributed heavily to the annual United Appeal drive and being assured that it was to the advantage of the agency to make an emergency appropriation to WE CARE, the director granted the request. WE CARE is now a United Appeal agency.

Other steps in the development of the program as a permanent community agency have occurred along the way. Close relationships have persisted with the law enforcement agencies since the beginning. In-service training in crisis intervention, especially the handling of suicide cases, has been provided regularly to police trainees. In recognition of this program, the coordinator has been made an official instructor in the police training school in the area. Finally, in recognition of the indispensable role WE CARE had built for itself through the multiplicity of services it was performing, the county health department established a position of Health Educator, and thus provided permanent employment for the WE CARE coordinator. After five years, the program is now supported by the United Appeal and the Orange County Health Department, as well as by private donations. It appears to be permanently established in the community. Although early efforts to join forces with the comprehensive community mental health center were rejected, an active cooperation between the two agencies has developed slowly. A staff psychologist at the mental health center has become a valuable local advisor in initiating a Teen Hotline sponsored by WE CARE. This new program has been vastly more successful than the suicide attempt follow-up demonstration, which leads to some interesting speculations about the dynamics of the whole WE CARE development.

What contributed to the WE CARE success which was not present in Chattanooga? How could one program become established in less than 10 months, and the other require more than two years? It must be evident that there were many differences, most of them subtle and unobtrusive. However, the one basic distinction is that WE CARE had an initiator who was not to be frustrated in her efforts to establish the program. Her drive, determination, and enthusiasm were not only a powerful mover of people, they were contagious and spread among the key advisors and volunteers. In Chattanooga, this drive was diffused through several people, all of them involved in their own business or professional roles. The driving force of the initiator must be a focused, concentrated source of consistently applied power. When the first coordinator left town, it was several months before the WE CARE group found another to apply the same steady pressure to the community and to the system.

Furthermore, WE CARE has always perceived itself as an independent agency within the network of helping services of the Orlando community. By its own self-image, it has caused the other services to perceive it as a member of the social welfare system. It was an incorporated entity, never content to remain a project of the Mental Health Association. When it finally developed its own security and maturity, it was able to shed the restraints of professional advisors whose behaviors might have served to stunt the growth of the program. All of these characteristics distinguish WE CARE from other suicide prevention and crisis intervention services studied in this project.

There was one other distinguishing feature of the Orlando program development which probably accounts more than any other for the success of WE CARE. That was the already referred-to availability of Louis Dublin as advisor and stimulator. He had been constantly convinced of the vast superiority of the nonprofessional volunteer as a suicide prevention worker, as evidenced by the outstanding regard in which he held Chad Varah and the Samaritans. WE CARE was the embodiment of ideals and hopes he had held since he published *To Be Or Not To Be* (Dublin and Bunzel, 1933). He gave continual encouragement and candid advice; and, by his expectations for the program, he issued a challenge for excellence which one would dare not fail to achieve. Whatever else may be its achievements in the area of service to the local community, WE CARE always will be regarded by some as a living memorial to Louis Dublin.

THE SUICIDE PREVENTION CENTER OF BREVARD COUNTY, FLORIDA

One of the most stormy developmental histories of any suicide prevention program was that experienced by the initiators of the Brevard County service. Yet, despite the ordeal they encountered, their efforts have been among the most successful and have brought about more valuable benefits to the community than most of the other centers studied in the project.

The Brevard County program has been partially described elsewhere (McGee, 1968), and it remains famous for the abortive "100-day plan" which was developed to guide its entry into the community. The beginning of interest in suicide prevention in Brevard County appeared right after the opening of WE CARE in Orlando. Brevard County is immediately east of Orange County and includes a narrow strip of Atlantic coastline approximately 30 miles wide and over 75 miles long. At its center is the John F. Kennedy Space Center, together with the space-related military and industrial support facilities. The County had a population of 23,000 in 1950, which grew to 250,000 by 1965. It was the fastest growing community in the United States for a number of years. The County currently includes 12 municipalities. Although most had been chartered prior to 1950, their population grew almost overnight to accommodate the influx of people on the space industry payrolls. These people are widely diverse in social background, but generally represent above-average educational and technical competence. They brought not only their skills but their human problems to an area which had never developed a spectrum of social service agencies. Previously, Brevard County had been a citrus, cattle, and sport fishing area; it did not even have a county welfare office in 1950.

The agencies which had developed in the community did not have a high degree of vested interest in their own independence. Such competition and protection of territory found in other cities was unnecessary, inasmuch as there was an overload of work for everyone. Actually, everything which existed in Brevard County at the time that the suicide prevention center was being planned was there as a result of recent change. Social action and social change were the order of the day in this area, but the expectation was for orderly, planned, integrated, and collaborative action. It was into this context that the planning of the suicide prevention center burst like an exploding Roman candle, blazed momentarily, and then nearly fizzled out before it was followed by the even bigger fireball which it helped to ignite.

Because of their proximity to Orlando, Brevard County television viewers began to see public service messages about the availability of help from WE CARE in October, 1965. Many of them responded and called Orlando for help. Working out of their own homes, the WE CARE volunteers were finding themselves placing long distance calls, frequently running into lengthy calls and high toll costs, to the Brevard County callers. Finally, WE CARE asked the Brevard County Mental Health Association to reimburse them for the costs of this service to their citizens.

Consequently, the Brevard County MHA became one of the first groups to entertain thoughts which said, in effect, "If they can do it, we can too!" The president of the Mental Health Association had just finished organizing and directing the campaign which built a public library for the community, and he knew that there was very little Brevard County citizens could not do if they wanted to. Consequently, he called a meeting of some local Mental Health Association members and invited the coordinator of WE CARE to present her program to his group. The only professional person at the first meeting was a psychologist from the Guidance Clinic who just happened to be working late in the office next door. He was invited to sit in as a courtesy, but the last-minute nature of the invitation was later identified by one of his associates as a reflection of the attitude of the initiator.

Some statistics concerning suicide deaths and attempts in the county were presented to the group. They definitely revealed a need for a prevention program. These statistics were questioned later, and neither their source nor their reliability was ever verified. This meeting was held in early December, 1965. It resulted in a favorable response to the WE CARE type of program. A decision was made, presumably by those attending the meeting, that the Mental Health Association should ask the United Fund for money to support a suicide prevention center. Immediately the request was made, and a response was received which said, in effect, that the United Fund would have to receive a report and recommendation from the Community Services Council before any funds could be made available for the new agency. However, until that time, the United Fund director expressed his belief that such a program might be a worthwhile service in Brevard County, and he offered to provide whatever organizational assistance might be helpful in establishing such a service. He requested a meeting with the MHA president to discuss the procedural steps that would be necessary for establishing the program, but no such meeting was ever held. Instead, the initiator elected to go ahead largely on his own.

Within two weeks, he had recruited three prominent business people to serve as legitimizers and incorporated them into a Board of Trustees. He drew up the suicide prevention center organizational plan, wrote its charter, contacted the Los Angeles center for its literature package, arranged to rent a suite of offices on Cocoa Beach, had stationery printed, contracted with an accounting firm for services, opened a bank account, contacted a local psychologist in private practice about part-time employment as center director at a salary of $8000, and formulated the 100-day plan which was to have the center operating and offering service to the public by March 15, 1966. That was 100 days from the date of the first meeting in December. When all of this was done, a second meeting was held on December 20, 1965.

Because of the involvement of WE CARE in the early planning of the Brevard County program, the latter group became aware of the availability of consultation from the psychology department at the University. Such assistance was sought, but was not followed consistently. Efforts at inserting a community-wide advisory board and a slower, more deliberate organizational timetable were not heeded. It remained for the local power structure to apply the brakes and to assure that orderly planning and appropriate board leadership were introduced.

However, the United Fund stuck by its commitment not to provide any funds until the Community Services Council made a study of the program plan and offered its recommendation. On February 7, the Council was officially requested to make the study and recommendation to United Fund. Anticipating the eventual approval of the program, the suicide prevention group went ahead with its plan. The psychologist director was hired, volunteers were recruited, a training program was set for March 1, and an answering service was employed to handle the calls. This activity created a vast amount of ill will in the minds of the Community Services Council. Not only did they object to the program's proceeding without their endorsement, but they opposed its moving with such haste and without the broadly representative Board of Directors and professional advisors. The Council study committee began to drag its feet. Among other strategies, it began to raise the question of whether or not the suicide prevention service should be an independent agency or a part of an existing service, such as the Guidance Clinic. This question began to suggest a need to look at the entire mental health services program in the county. The Guidance Clinic was primarily a children's service; an adult mental health outpatient clinic was sorely needed. Funds should be provided for it. An inpatient service in a local hospital was badly needed; funds should be set aside for that, too. The Comprehensive Community Mental Health Centers act would provide for all of these things. There were already people who were thinking about a comprehensive community mental health center for the area. But such planning takes many, many months, and in the meantime, something had to be done with the suicide prevention center.

The program began operating on March 15, 1966, right on schedule according to the 100-day plan. By the end of March, the Mental Health Association had spent all of the Special Project money it had allocated to the program. It asked the United Fund to supply a special appropriation, not to the suicide center, because the Council report was not in yet, but to the Mental Health Association, so that it could continue to operate the suicide program. This grant was approved, and enough money was provided to support the program until the end of May.

On May 18, 1966, the Community Services Council submitted its report to the United Fund. It specifically recommended the development of all of the basic services of a comprehensive community mental health center, including suicide prevention and crisis intervention services. It recommended that the Guidance Clinic assume the operation of the suicide prevention center which was to be the beginning of mental health services to adults. The Guidance Clinic agreed to this proposal, providing that the United Fund would pay for the costs of the suicide prevention center, including $10,000 for the salary of a psychologist who would spend part of his time directing it. All of these agreements were reached, and at the end of June, 1966, when the suicide prevention program was evicted from its quarters for nonpayment of rent, the Clinic was ready to receive it as an official part of the agency structure. Early in 1967, a Community Mental Health Council was formed to seek comprehensive mental health center funds, which were subsequently awarded. When the total mental health program was developed, the

Brevard County Suicide Prevention Center was no longer an incorporated entity; but its services were still being rendered to the public through trained nonprofessional volunteers according to the original goal.

This was a program which had been dropped into the community and left to be managed. No group wanted to be responsible for letting it die out, yet none could support it, because of the manner in which it had been developed. It was a two-headed monster that had to be preserved, yet it could not be allowed to continue in the manner that the initiator was insisting upon. Through the wisdom of the United Fund and the Community Services Council, and the spirit of cooperation which characterized their working toward the attainment of mutual goals, the Brevard County mental health program was given its opportunity to develop. It may have been the greatest service that the suicide prevention center has rendered to its community. When it was all over, and the history was reviewed, the original initiator proudly claimed that the total mental health program was his primary goal all along, and that the 100-day plan for suicide prevention was, in fact, only a vehicle for forcing the community into planning for and implementing the larger mental health services system. There are still those who are of a different opinion about the value of his role and overall contribution.

The measure of a program's success is not how smoothly it becomes established, but what it can grow into as it matures. The Brevard County suicide prevention service has become a full-scale crisis intervention program which enjoys the cooperative support of many agencies in the community. The result has been a continually improving system for responding to people in crises. As only one example, it might be mentioned that the Mental Health Center expanded its program to initiate the first Teen Hotline in the State. Other communities have followed Brevard County's lead in this new movement.

The best evaluation of this history and development has been made by the editor of the Brevard County edition of the *Orlando Sentinel*, writing in an editorial published Wednesday, June 1, 1966:

Suicide Group Part of Plan

Brevard's on again-off again suicide prevention plan has apparently found the high road to fulfillment following a study of the county's mental health needs by the Community Services Council (CSC).

Enthusiastic advocates of the suicide prevention service ran into difficulties some months ago when they 'took the bit in their teeth' and failed to follow procedures recommended and required by the United Fund. Charges and counter-charges flew for a while until supporters of the suicide prevention center understood that observance of proper procedures is especially important in organizations which draw their support from voluntary contributions. . . .

The editorial goes on to praise suicide prevention efforts wherever they exist, and especially to endorse the new program to be developed within the mental health service framework in Brevard County. The important point which the editorial writer has signaled for every program developer in any community is that there is a right way and a wrong way to engage in a social action. No matter how valid and necessary the task may be, it will not be acceptable in the community unless some force is applied to insure the "proper atmosphere," which must include orderly future planning for all necessary, continuous resources.

THE SUICIDE PREVENTION CENTER
IN HALIFAX COUNTY, NORTH CAROLINA

The initiator of the Halifax County program may have been several people simultaneously. There was definitely a joint effort by many individuals, representing primarily three separate organizations, but generally it was the County Health Director who is given the credit for having been the prime catalyst who led the constructive channeling of diverse energies. It was in the spring of 1966 when the interest began in Halifax County, and the program initiated its operation in the summer of 1967.

Not infrequently, a precipitating factor in the initiation of social action is a single event which touches the lives of many people simultaneously. The suicide of a prominent citizen who had practiced medicine in the community for a number of years provided such an event. Almost immediately, reactions were mobilized by the County Medical Society, the Mental Health Association, and by a group of clergy representing the local ministerial association. Among their concerns was the fact that their small, primarily rural, predominantly black, and agricultural population had a suicide rate which was somewhat higher than the national average. Of even greater concern was the fact that most of these deaths were occurring in a single small community, whose rate of suicide was about 70 per 100,000; this was over six times the national average. Finally, there were those in the community who already knew the potential benefits to be derived for small communities from the comprehensive community mental health center legislation. A suicide prevention program was considered a good place to begin planning for the eventual development of a full-scale mental health service. It had already been predicted that " . . . a Suicide Prevention Center offers one channel through which to launch a new (mental health) program on its way" (McGee, 1965). Halifax County was to become one of the first communities to put this assertion to the test.

The county had a special advantage which aided the development of their suicide prevention efforts. Since 1959, the county had been the focus of community mental health consultation from a group of community psychologists from Duke University. These consultants visited the county weekly for consultations with the health officer, public health nurses, school administrators and teachers, clergy, and physicians. The method of consultation to community agencies advocated by Caplan (1970) was the key ingredient, but further modifications and elaborations for work with groups soon developed (Altrocchi, Spielberger, and Eisdorfer, 1965). One of the goals was the enrichment of local communities and their leadership to the point where they could identify local problems, organize and implement social action to meet the needs, and evaluate the results. With the consultants from Duke providing the helping context within which change could occur, the idea for a suicide prevention center began to spread.

At this point, with both community leaders and consultants interested in the project, it became feasible to begin planning a service for the county. A first step was taken by the Health Director when he organized an Advisory Council to investigate the issues. This Council was carefully chosen. It included a prominent state senator and attorney, the head of the rescue squad, the president of the Mental Health Association, the county sheriff, the county auditor, the Health Director, a public health nurse, an official from the telephone company, and the two psychologists from the Duke consultation team. The Council was chaired by a local minister. It had representation from most of the groups that either dealt with the suicide problem already or would be involved when the prevention program was established.

Once the Advisory Council was formed, the decision was made that more information was needed concerning the methods and procedures for suicide prevention on the telephone. Consequently, one of the consultants was selected to visit the Los Angeles Suicide Prevention Center and to attend the semiannual Training Institute. He returned with the extensive packet of manuscripts and reprints developed by the LASPC staff for training nonprofessional volunteer telephone workers, and the work of establishing a new program in the community was ready to begin in earnest.

Halifax County was one of the suicide prevention programs which began their recruiting efforts according to the *nomination* method. A total of 56 people were identified by the Advisory Council, Health Department staff, and consultants as those who should be expected to be "good at this kind of work." The nominees were contacted by the Health Department nurse, who was to be the program coordinator, and if they were at all interested, they were scheduled for an interview with one of the consultants, and arrangements were made to administer a Minnesota Multiphasic Personality Inventory. As a result of this screening, only two people were rejected, and 54 began training. During the training program, 33 trainees chose to leave the program because of a lack of commitment, and at the end of training, one more applicant had demonstrated lack of suitability and was eliminated. Thus, 20 people began to answer the telephone when the program opened.

One of the unique features of the Halifax County service which was discovered during this project is the tenacity with which these 20 volunteers continued to serve their program, despite the paucity of calls. It has been reported that after eight months of operation, the service had received "eleven calls from seven people, excluding three crank calls" (Altrocchi and Batton, 1968). A later report indicated that the tally rose to "twelve calls from eight people in the first nine months of service" (Altrocchi and Gutman, 1968). When the service had been in operation for 13 months, there had been approximately 18 calls from 12 people, and these calls had been taken by 11 of the volunteers. Still, all 20 workers continually took their duty shifts, went regularly to scheduled in-service training meetings with the consultant and coordinator, and showed the highest degree of internal morale. After four years, there were still six of the original 20 volunteers serving the program.

This is exactly contrary to what Farberow (1966) had reported for the volunteers at the Los Angeles Center. He had found that they became restless and discouraged when there was not enough work to do, and frequently would leave the program if stimulation were not provided by the professional staff. Altrocchi and Batton (1968) explained their unusual results on the basis that volunteers were permitted to work in their own homes, and hence were not inconvenienced by the great infrequency of calls. In fact, the workers reported being greatly relieved at the end of each shift when there had been no call. One might wonder if the positive reinforcement from the anxiety reduction was sufficiently strong to maintain the scheduling and waiting-by-the-phone behavior over such an extended period of time. In fact, there were other rewards reported, primarily the covert feeling of being available to meet an important social need and thereby performing a valuable act of community service. There was an additional factor which the coordinator believes to be the major contribution to the overall success of the Halifax County service. She would have the credit go to Dr. John Altrocchi, one of the consultants from Duke University. "It was really because of his perseverance, charm, and inspiration that the program succeeded."

After two years of maintaining the operation, there were those who began to believe that more active publicity and a broader general crisis intervention image for the service would stimulate greater response from the public. The program began to move in these directions.

In 1968, the Comprehensive Community Mental Health Center was established in Halifax County. This was a significant accomplishment in itself for a county of under 70,000 population, but it was the result of the same concerted community planning which had earlier resulted in the development of the suicide prevention center. When the larger mental health program was funded, the suicide service immediately became an integral part of the emergency service component. In addition, there is an emergency walk-in service in the outpatient unit, and there is the typical emergency room of the hospital. The suicide prevention center telephone service was moved to the mental health center during its office hours, and the secretaries who answer the regular business phone take the crisis calls. They have completed the suicide counselor training course, and are regular members of the suicide center group.

As has been the case with many suicide prevention programs, it also happened in Halifax County that when the program became affiliated with the mental health center, it lost its own independent advisory council. The work of the counselors is being supervised now by the professional staff of the mental health center. In Halifax, there have appeared to be no problems in this relationship, as each group maintains a healthy respect for the other. The Suicide Prevention Service is essentially a telephone answering service operating during nights and weekends, and it serves to funnel clients into the mental health program.

In the final analysis, the local citizens and their professional consultants succeeded in developing a complete mental health program for their rural community. They faced the usual delays and frustrations of local funding, state and national approvals, and recruiting of professional staff for the larger community mental health center. As a community, they were able to move ahead with the establishment of an emergency service provided by trained nonprofessionals on the local scene. In this way, Halifax County succeeded in demonstrating that a suicide prevention and crisis intervention service can be a source of support and stimulation for the establishment of a new mental health program.

ATLANTA'S EMERGENCY MENTAL HEALTH SERVICE

In the development of suicide prevention centers, 1966 was a very busy year across the country, as well as in the Southeast. The third program to begin taking shape during this year was the unique example of program planning and community support which appeared in the Metropolitan Atlanta area. The first official steps toward this new service were taken in February, 1966, and the actual program implementation was completed by August of the same year. It was an unequivocal demonstration of the potency of a united political and professional clout and of the magnitude of a service which can be established when the right people can be influenced appropriately. In Atlanta, all of these elements were present, along with an adequate financial resource. It is the second example in this project of a center which grew out of an established institutional structure and which hence did not have the problem of finding a home once it became recognized as a needed entity within the community.

As in other communities throughout the Southeast, the local Mental Health Association played a leading role in the initiation of the Atlanta program, and the key person who spearheaded the committee activities and provided the administrative and technical support was a member of the MHA staff. In February, 1966, he wrote a Proposed Operating Plan for the center and submitted it to the MHA Special Committee on Emergency Services and Suicide Prevention. This committee had been formed because of the growing awareness of the limited emergency facilities in the Fulton County health system, especially for psychiatric emergencies. In December, 1965, Grady Memorial Hospital had expanded its psychiatric inpatient service, and there were plans to open an outpatient mental health service in July, 1966. But nothing was being programmed for emergency services, beyond the existing rotation of one first-year psychiatric resident in the Grady emergency room. The Mental Health Association was determined to see that adequate planning was done in this vital area as well. To implement their desires, the Association formed the Special Committee to study the problem, and one of the first activities was a review of the local suicide rates. It was discovered that the Atlanta area had recorded a rate of 12.6 suicides per 100,000 population during 1963. Concluding that this was nearly 25% in excess of the national rate in 1960, the Committee asked the Association staff to draft a proposal which would outline a prevention service.

This proposal described three separate functions of a total program: (1) hospital emergency and inpatient care, (2) telephone answering service 24 hours daily, and (3) a volunteer counselor team. It spelled out specific plans for locating the services and for apportioning the costs between Fulton and DeKalb Counties, which would receive the primary service benefits. Consistent with the planning strategies of the mid-1960's, the proposal also provided for educational and consultation services by a psychologist and for research activities under the direction of a social scientist. The total operating cost of the program was projected to be $60,000.

Armed with a concrete proposal, the MHA then went to its Professional Advisory Committee and to a variety of citizens' groups to build support for its ideas. Finally, the Advisory Committee appointed a task force to carry the planning into final stages. This task force consisted of the MHA staff worker, two psychiatrists, public health officers of the two counties, a newspaper reporter, and interested citizens. It was this task force which visited Florida in April, 1966, spending one day at the Orlando Workshop and making an additional visit to the Pinellas County Emergency Mental Health Service in St. Petersburg. Upon returning home, the task force presented its findings to the Fulton County Commissioners, who within a span of only three weeks allotted $50,000 for the new program.

In the meantime, there had been a great deal of energy generated within the key community systems. The Metropolitan Atlanta Citizens Health Committee appointed by the County and City governmental units pushed for the suicide prevention program. The Public Health Departments of Fulton and DeKalb Counties actively supported it. A series of six newspaper articles entitled "Suicide: Unanswered SOS" appeared in the *Atlanta Constitution* following the Florida visit of the task force. All sources of influence were marshalled and turned toward the accomplishment of the social action goal in a thoroughly organized manner. There was never any indication that the motivating force behind the Atlanta program was the satisfaction of some personal need of the initiator; it was a community effort.

In July of 1966, a psychiatrist was employed part-time as the first director of the center. He spent several days visiting the Los Angeles center and the Pinellas County, Florida service. He then began recruiting and training the telephone counselors. The original proposal written in February was modified only slightly, and the early idea of employing nonprofessional staff on a full-time basis, with two part-time shifts to cover the weekends, was adopted. The Atlanta program began operating in August, 1966, with six paid counselors and the part-time director. Within a month, the DeKalb County Commission also appropriated its share of the operating costs, and a firm financial structure was assured for the service. The development has been continuously in the direction of positive growth throughout its operation.

There have been a number of additions to the service program over the years. The first notable one occurred within a few months—the changing of the name. Originally called the Fulton-DeKalb Suicide Prevention Center, the program soon became known as the Emergency Mental Health Service. This was done primarily to reflect the broad nature of its operational concepts and its services. However, there were also those who saw in the name change an identification of the Atlanta program with its Pinellas County model. In any event, the change to a name which reflected a broad type of emergency intervention service was one of the many ways in which the Atlanta program has exercised leadership.

In December, 1966, a major step was taken with the employment of a psychiatric nurse, whose role became one of coordinating home visits by professional personnel. Usually, these visiting teams were nurses, but psychology interns in training at the Georgia Mental Health Institute also were included. This initial program soon proved successful, and in September, 1967, it was supplemented by a full-time staff of psychiatric and public health nurses as the home visit team. The same team began to contact each person who was treated in the Grady Emergency Room following a suicide attempt. Thus, the Atlanta program after only one year began to pioneer the use of an outreach service to augment its telephone answering service. Unfortunately, Atlanta has received less acclaim for this innovation than it might deserve, and this may well be because of the use of professional rather than nonprofessional personnel. At least it was a major step in a new direction of service which is only very recently being developed in a few centers.

The Atlanta program also began making use of volunteer nonprofessionals during 1968, although they never relinquished the pattern of employed counselors as the primary telephone crisis workers.

One of the unique features of the Atlanta program has been the educational activities it has sponsored. Through the collaboration of Emory University and the Georgia Mental Health Institute, a series of seminars were held in 1967 and 1968. These activities laid the basis for a Regional Training Program on the Organization of Suicide Prevention Services which attracted participants from across the country as well as from the southeastern region. This project was sponsored by an NIMH grant from the Center for Studies of Suicide Prevention during 1968 and 1969.

Soon after its organization, the Atlanta center implemented another of the far-sighted proposals of the initial MHA plan when it employed a sociologist as full-time research director. As a result, the program has produced a refinement of the Los Angeles method of assessing lethality through a factor analysis of data obtained over several hundred callers. Also, by comparing the characteristics of its own caller population with those of nine other centers in large metropolitan areas, the Atlanta program has contributed important demographic information about the type of people who utilize the services of suicide and crisis intervention programs (Whittemore, 1970).

In many ways, the Fulton-DeKalb Emergency Mental Health Service has attempted to become a southeastern replica of the Los Angeles center. Although research productivity has not been its major asset, and some have questioned the extent of its innovations in the delivery of service, the Atlanta program has been a continual example of outstanding community support and involvement among participating agencies. Moreover, it was the first major program to begin with a recognition that suicide was a public health problem which should be faced and attacked by a public health program. It was the first of a very few delayed responses to Dublin's appeal (1965) to the American Public Health Association. Despite the fact that its full-time research sociologist, its professional home visit team, and its substantial budget from governmental funds have made it atypical of most community programs and out of the reach of nearly every other city in the region, the Atlanta program has been a leader in community programming of crisis intervention services in the Southeast. By its existence in so large a metropolitan area, it is a demonstration of the reality that community crisis services are both necessary and feasible. It symbolizes the success which can accrue from organized cooperation among service agencies, professional specialists, and governmental officials.

NASHVILLE CRISIS CALL CENTER

Whereas the Fulton-DeKalb Emergency Mental Health Service was the first suicide prevention center to change its name to reflect the scope of services requested from such agencies, it was the Nashville, Tennessee program that first adopted the concept of *crisis intervention*. This latter notion has come to be the most widely accepted generic label for what was once considered the role of a suicide prevention center. This is only one of the ways in which the Crisis Call Center has been the leader of programs in medium-sized cities of the Southeast. Other innovations are discussed in the course of this review.

Unlike most of the centers in the Southeast, the Crisis Call Center developers went about their business in a formal and carefully organized manner. Minutes were recorded and stored from nearly every meeting in which a decision was made or even a small group of people convened for deliberation. Therefore, the history of the early development of the program can be retold with greater detail and accuracy than is usually the case. It should be mentioned that this feature of the Nashville program is at least partially the result of the influence of Anson

Haughton, who was at the time the Deputy Chief of the Center for Studies of Suicide Prevention at NIMH. Haughton was an active influence in the development of many centers during the middle and late 1960's, and his influence was present in the Nashville program more than in any of the other southeastern communities. It was always a special urging that Haughton brought to each new center when he directed them to "keep a careful diary of each event during the planning process." Few programs have heeded this simple advice as the Crisis Call Center did; but all future program planners would do well to follow the example.

Again, as so frequently was the case, the initial interest for a suicide prevention program grew out of the local Mental Health Association. In Nashville, suicide prevention was born, and nearly died, as a result of the Mental Health Association involvement; wise initial planning and contiguous circumstances prevented an untimely demise of a potentially outstanding program.

Several lines of influence impinged upon the Nashville scene in the fall of 1966. There was a general awareness that the Chattanooga suicide prevention program was operating out of the Mental Health Association under a "feasibility study" plan. Also, there had been communications with the Metropolitan Atlanta Mental Health Association, which had allowed the Nashville chapter to follow the course of planning activity for the Atlanta program the previous summer. It was the Executive Director of the Mental Health Association who became the initiator in Nashville. She called together a few persons who she believed would be especially interested and could, if they decided to do so, organize a proper planning effort. Included in this initial interest group were a prominent minister, a police detective, an attorney, and a community-oriented psychiatrist. The minister was asked to be chairman of the planning committee, and he agreed to do so if a community-wide seminar were held before a final decision was made to go ahead.

An announcement was received that the Atlanta program was planning its first Annual Symposium in November, 1966. The program, entitled "Suicide Prevention: A Community Response to a Personal Crisis," appeared to be exactly "what the doctor ordered" for the new interest developing in Nashville, so the attorney in the interest group made plans to attend. At this seminar, he became the first one in the local area to directly encounter some of the leaders in the field, such as Shneidman from Los Angeles, Edwards from Atlanta, Cameron from Pinellas County, Florida, and Jean Pennington from Orlando's WE CARE. He also learned that there was a psychologist in Nashville, associated with George Peabody College, who had been actively involved in the early development of the WE CARE program while he was serving his clinical internship in Florida. The attorney returned to his group a week later armed with much information and with the emotional fervor which the Atlanta group had freely generated in the participants. This event tipped the scales in favor of a final commitment from the Nashville planners, and an enlarged Suicide Prevention Committee was formed as a subcommittee of the MHA Community Service Committee. Its first meeting was held later in November.

At that initial meeting, a decision was made to poll the professional groups of psychiatrists, psychologists, social workers, clergymen, and law enforcement officers to learn of their potential interest and support for a suicide prevention program. Reports of contacts with these groups were to constitute the agenda at the next meeting.

At the second meeting of the group early in December, the psychologist from Peabody was present and brought an associate who had earned a national reputation in community mental health planning. This began an association which proved to be a major advantage for the Crisis Call Center throughout its existence, because of the quality of consultation and broad perspective which it has added to the program. Also present were professional personnel representing the medical and psychiatric interests at the two medical schools in the Nashville community, as well as some prominent private practitioners. The degree of support and active endorsement which the Nashville program has enjoyed from its local professional community has been without parallel in any other center studied, and it may be largely attributable to the fact that these persons allowed themselves to be included in the very earliest of the planning activities.

At the second planning meeting, the police detective not only brought the pledge of support from the Police Department, but he supplied the group with a statistical review of suicide cases from the police files which was so complete that the committee decided a further survey was not needed. As a final action, the chairman directed the Peabody College psychologists to formulate a set of guidelines to be followed in starting the program, and left the date of the next meeting to be determined when these guidelines were completed.

At the third meeting, which was held in January, 1967, a plan was presented which identified separate issues to be resolved and offered suggestions as to individual persons who should assume responsibility for them. These issues were selection, research, training, advisory board membership, publicity and public relations, and finance. Each was to be a subcommittee of the larger Suicide Prevention Committee, under the overall direction of the minister who was the original chairman. From that time on "The Committee" became the governing body, at least in name, of the Crisis Call Center.

The plan also called for the community-wide seminar to be held as a kick-off to public planning. This same strategy was to be followed later in Jacksonville and Tampa, but the idea originated in Nashville. The purposes of this one-day seminar were threefold: First, to provide information about suicide as a response to a personal crisis; secondly, to consider methods of dealing with crisis situations; and finally, to consider the alternatives for the community in developing a suicide prevention program. Plans were begun, and this seminar was held in mid-March of 1967. The topics considered at the seminar are important because they reflect the kinds of concerns which went into the groundwork of the Crisis Call Center. Discussion groups focused attention on three areas: "Professional Consultation and Research in Suicide Prevention," "Community-Wide Planning and Administration in Suicide Prevention," and "Inter-Agency Communications and Cooperation in Suicide Prevention." Finally, as a wrap-up, the entire group of specially invited community representatives addressed themselves to "An Emerging Design of a Suicide Prevention Program for Nashville." The planning committee had agreed not to proceed with the program unless the seminar participants encouraged them to do so. The community leaders in attendance expressed themselves overwhelmingly in favor of the project, so the die was cast.

Thus, the Committee met again and began to address such issues as the necessity for a coordinator of the service, the location of an office, the roles of advisory board members and professional consultants, and the methods by which the service would function. For example, one critical decision was that the program would be developed under the auspices of the Mental Health Association, but that the Association would not continue to operate it as a permanent activity. Further, while the new center needed an office from which to operate, this should not be the Mental Health Association office, and the coordinator should not be the Mental Health Association director. A tentative date for beginning the service was set for January 1, 1968, still eight months away, in order to allow time for continued steady planning.

By September, a prospective coordinator had been identified and recruited, and she was commissioned by the Committee to represent the Nashville group at a workshop in Gainesville, Florida, on the Planning of Emergency Services for Comprehensive Community Mental Health Centers (McGee, 1967). Although Nashville already enjoyed a wide range of mental health and other agency resources, there was still talk of a new comprehensive community mental health program, and as a result of stimulation from this Florida workshop, the Suicide Prevention Committee renewed its vow to become a partner in the total community effort. In October, an opportunity arose which appeared to lead in that direction, but which in actuality served to seduce the Committee away from one of its previously determined directions. The search for office space led to a proposal, encouraged largely by the United Givers Fund, which was to provide money for the coordinator's salary through the Mental Health Association, that the new suicide prevention service should share a large suite of offices with other agencies. Included in the group were the Council on Alcoholism, the Planned Parenthood Association, and the Mental Health Association. The reason given was economy in purchasing of supplies as well as consolidation of rent and secretarial support facilities needed by each of the UGF agencies. The rationale seemed valid, and the plan was adopted. Although it gave the suicide prevention group a home base from which to launch its program, the arrangement prevented the detachment from the Mental Health Association which had been originally planned. It should be recognized that very often—and this was a prime example of the fact—it is necessary for a developing agency to make compromises in its program ideals in order to placate funding sources whose sophistication is in monetary matters rather than in areas of design and organization of service delivery systems.

Whether or not it is wiser in the long run to hold out for the implementation of carefully considered program designs at the risk of losing possible funding, or to capitulate to the wishes of budget brokers, is a decision which must be faced by nearly every program. FRIENDS faced the decision in Miami, and chose to preserve their integrity despite great financial hardship. The Committee in Nashville was more practical, but the cost was also great in the long run.

In the meantime, planning continued throughout the fall and early winter of 1967 and 1968. A program was drawn up for training volunteers, involving the identification of professional persons in the community who would serve as Trainers. Characteristic of the thoroughness of the group was the decision that professional people might not be sufficiently trained themselves in suicide and crisis intervention theory and practice. Hence, a plan was developed to train the Trainers which included a second visit by Anson Haughton from NIMH to meet with the Trainers in early December.

The system for the selection of volunteer applicants developed by the Committee has been copied in several other centers in the Southeast. Essentially, it involved subjecting applicants to a series of steps, including an interview with a screener who was a professional practitioner in the community. Many applicants dropped out during the process. Those who remained were the ones whose motivation and determination to work in the program were both more sincere and more appropriate. Of sixteen professional practitioners in the community who were contacted, only one refused to contribute unremunerated time to screening applicants for the center.

As a final stage in developmental program planning, the Committee secured its own position by forming a Community Advisory Board. This was in part the result of continued urging by the psychologist who had seen the value of such a group in the Orlando program. However, unlike the WE CARE Advisory Board, the one developed in Nashville served truly an advisory rather than a governing function. In January, the Advisory Board was convened for the first time and was informed about the progress of the planning over the past year. Members of this body represented every conceivable social, mental health, governmental, religious, and health agency or institution in the community. Over 30 persons were included. They met only once or twice a year thereafter; but as a group, their suggestions and opinions were sought, and their aid was solicited in helping the program get started when it was launched.

This strategy has some very interesting implications. By the time the Advisory Board was convened, the Nashville suicide program was already certain to become a reality. These key community leaders were brought together to be advised and informed, and to be invited to help in whatever way they might. Since most of them had attended the community seminar, they felt they had been participants in the original idea. This distinction between the Nashville Advisory Board and that of other agencies is a notable one, and it may be a key factor in the success of the Crisis Call Center.

The final name for the program was not decided until almost the last detail had been worked out. The concept of suicide prevention had prevailed thus far, but as time drew near for inaugurating the service, a discussion was held about the broader image for the service, and the new name won out. Cards and other advertisements have continually identified the Crisis Call Center as Nashville's Suicide Prevention Service; thus both concepts are preserved.

The service began operating on March 17, 1968. It was just one year to the day after the community-wide seminar had been held to study the problem. It was also just three days before the establishment of the American Association of Suicidology, which took place in Chicago at the First Annual Conference on Suicidology. The Crisis Call Center was two to three years behind some centers in getting started; but at its inception, it was still in the midst of the evolution of suicide and crisis intervention activities, and it was still in plenty of time to have a powerful influence on other centers still to be developed.

The original coordinator served the Crisis Call Center for nine months after it began operating. There were reports of frequent conflicts between the Center coordinator and the Mental Health Association staff, seemingly over lack of consistent agreement as to the locus of ultimate authority. Some saw it as residing in the Committee. Others felt that the Committee was nothing more than an instrument of the Mental Health Association Board, to be administered by the Association staff. A second coordinator came into the program in November of 1968 and lasted only six months. A third coordinator stuck it out nearly a year before the Committee and nearly everyone involved realized that the close proximity between the Center and the Association must come to an end if the program was to survive. It was a second example of the difficulty which can develop when a parent organization perceives a suicide or crisis center as a "project" to be managed by procedures and concepts which are satisfactory for voluntary associations but not for service agencies. Of course, each change in leadership left the volunteers with divided loyalties and disrupted morale.

As the program matured in its service activities, the professional assistance from psychologists in the local universities and medical schools became increasingly clear in the form of data collection and analysis. The Crisis Call Center has been one of the few centers, probably the only one, with a completely volunteer staff to maintain current statistical records of its caseload. This is an added luxury, available only because of an attitude towards utilizing the interests and professional skills of local university personnel. Such help has been abundantly available in Nashville, as in other places; but the Nashville program has capitalized upon it like few others.

During 1969, after the program was in its second year, plans began to form for the comprehensive community mental health center at Meharry Medical School. This naturally re-aroused the earlier interest in the center, becoming an integral part of the total mental health program. Meharry was to have the first comprehensive center in the Nashville area, but plans were for it to be followed by others. Once more, the influence of Anson Haughton began to emerge with the idea that the Crisis Call Center might serve as a central telephone answering service for all of the emergency services in the several mental health center service areas. Haughton (1967) had proposed that idea at the Gainesville workshop two years earlier. As time went on, various delays occurred in the construction and staffing of the Meharry center, but by midyear in 1970, the Crisis Call Center had removed itself from the budget and the control of the Mental Health Association. Currently housed in the new center at the medical school, the crisis service has become a central arm of the community mental health emergency service. Already, it is apparent that a new set of decisions and relationships will be negotiated as other community mental health programs are developed.

Members of the original Committee still serve a valuable leadership role, but official governing responsibility lies with the department of psychiatry at Meharry College of Medicine and its affiliate, Hubbard Hospital. The director of the community mental health center and the chief of the emergency service have been added to the list of "people in authority." The coordinator of the Center, who is paid by Meharry, still "directs" the service program. Just how all of these "chiefs" will work together to wage war on suicide and crises in Nashville, and what effect their relationships will have on the volunteer "Indians," remain to be seen. Like other dynamic centers, the development of the Crisis Call Center is still going on. Its future, no less than its past, will have much to teach the field of suicidology.

THE SUICIDE PREVENTION SERVICE IN KNOXVILLE, TENNESSEE

The primary influence on the initiation of the Suicide Prevention Service in Knoxville came through the avenue of the clergy and hospital chaplains who were aware of the involvement of some colleagues in the Chattanooga "feasibility study." A chaplain at East Tennessee Baptist Hospital must have been acquainted personally with the two chaplains who occupied key roles in the Chattanooga program, for he presented the idea and a proposal for a similar program at a meeting of the Knoxville Academy of Religion and Mental Health. This was in the spring of 1967, after the Chattanooga program had been in operation for only a few months.

One of the clergymen from Chattanooga was invited to Knoxville to address an open meeting of representatives from the law enforcement agencies, mental health association, the Knoxville Mental Health Clinic, Eastern State Hospital, and the United Fund. The result of that meeting was the formation of a Special Committee which included, among others, the chaplain and the psychiatrist who served as director of the Mental Health Clinic. A series of three organizational meetings was held by this committee over the next few weeks, and the discussions focused almost entirely on specific procedural issues. What type of telephone system would be used? What kind of volunteers should be recruited? Who would handle the scheduling of volunteers?

It is apparent that the Knoxville group felt they needed no further legitimization within their community than that which was included on their Committee. Issues of how to arouse community support were not considered relevant, at least in relation to the technical details of running the service. The reasons for this unusual program planning lie in the nature of the service that was to be developed.

Very early in the decision-making, the director of the clinic emerged as the unchallenged director of the Suicide Prevention Service. Without apparently any consideration of other alternatives, the program began to develop as a new service to be administered as part of the program of the already established Mental Health Clinic. This agency already enjoyed community support and endorsement. It was one of the many such centers established through the assistance of the Tennessee Department of Mental Health in the 1950's. It had been serving the mental health needs of Knox County residents long before there was any thought of comprehensive community mental health care sponsored by the federal government. The clinic enjoyed endorsement and active support from the medical and mental health professional community, especially a strong group of private psychologists who were influential in east Tennessee. Unlike the Chattanooga clinic in the early 1960's, the Knoxville agency had welcomed and encouraged affiliation and involvement of other professional groups, such as the ministers and teachers. Hence, the clinic staff had no need to develop support from these quarters. In short, whatever the clinic wanted to do under the psychiatrist's direction had immediate and automatic sanction within the important sectors of the community.

As the organization began to take shape, the chaplain was designated certain responsibilities for the program which included keeping a list of suicide deaths in the area, compiling a scrapbook of news releases, and making out the monthly duty rosters of the volunteers. Later, the Executive Director of the Mental Health Association was added to the Committee and gradually began to take over the duties of the chaplain, who found himself too busy with other community commitments to maintain his involvement.

By July of 1967, a date for beginning operation had been set. Final arrangements were made with the telephone company and the police department regarding cooperation in the management of suicide attempts and other highly lethal calls. The chaplain and the clinic director attended the Gainesville Workshop on Emergency Services in September, and the program began its official operation on October 1.

Knoxville's Suicide Prevention Service has been unique in the Southeast from the standpoint of its manpower. It utilized volunteers as telephone crisis workers from its inception until December, 1970. However, for the first 18 months, these volunteers were all *professional* people from the community. Initially, the volunteer group included one psychiatrist, nine clinical psychologists, 12 social workers, and seven ministers. Many, although not all, of the volunteers were also members of the Mental Health Clinic staff, and they took calls on an "availability" basis during the weekday hours when the clinic was open. The telephone, which was answered by the clinic secretaries during office hours, was switched to an answering service during the evening. Since it was the professional practitioner who was the volunteer, Knoxville faced a unique difficulty which other programs did not encounter. This was that the period of time between the closing of the office at five o'clock and the time when the professional volunteer arrived home from his office was not covered by any available crisis worker. Gradually, accommodations had to be made, and the move toward the nonprofessional volunteer was considered an alternative quite early. By May, 1969, the evidence was clear that the professionals had lost interest in the program. As they began dropping out, nonprofessional trainees were added. As more nonprofessionals became available, the professionals dropped out at a faster rate, and plans were made to have the "after-hours" telephone service covered by nonprofessional volunteers completely by January, 1970.

However, by the time that target date had arrived, an entirely different plan had been adopted. In the early months of 1969, the Mental Health Clinic began to expand its service to encompass the full comprehensive community mental health center program. This meant a large increase in professional staff, with the introduction of new services and innovative concepts. By the end of 1970, the suicide prevention phone number had been discontinued, and the mental health center went on a 24-hour, seven-days-a-week operation, with professional crisis teams handling all incoming telephone calls. The Suicide Prevention Service ceased to exist as such. The nonprofessional volunteers moved into the Mental Health Center and became members of the crisis intervention teams. Each team was headed by a psychiatrist and included a social worker and a volunteer. In January, 1971, the Center had organized two Community Intervention Teams which began to go out into the community for follow-up of individual cases. They visited patients who had been treated in hospital emergency rooms for suicide attempts, patients referred to the Mental Health Center who did not follow through on the referral, and serious-sounding calls which came in on the telephone line. In some instances, these teams have gone out and brought in patients immediately as the result of a highly disturbing call to the center. The interesting aspect of this program, and one which is unique for the centers studied, is that these Community Intervention Teams are completely staffed by volunteer nonprofessional persons who have become an important element of the Mental Health Center staffing pattern. At first, only two teams were formed, each one on duty during a different day of the week. However, the success of the venture has prompted the director to develop additional teams to provide full-time coverage.

The Knoxville Suicide Prevention Service began as a telephone answering service in a manner which appeared initially to be neither inspired nor inspiring. Its professional volunteers lost interest, as was to be expected, and it survived a gradual transition to the nonprofessional. Simultaneously, the program experienced an extensive modification within its parent agency as the Mental Health

Clinic took on a vastly expanded role in the community. When the evolution of the larger program was complete, the remains of the initial crisis center organization had disappeared; even its telephone number, which was its single independent identity, was lost, but the role and the service it might have potentially fulfilled had been integrated into the total system of mental health care. No center studied during this project has provided the kind of service which the volunteer non-professionals on the community intervention teams are providing in Knoxville. Other centers have not survived the integration into the mental health system, but in other cases, their former roles were even more restricted, rather than expanded to full fruition.

No one could argue effectively that the present system for community crisis intervention service in Knoxville came about because of, or as a result of, the prior existence of the Suicide Prevention Service. Most observers would give credit to the psychiatrist-director of the Mental Health Clinic, who envisioned and developed the system over the years. But neither can it be denied that, as director of the suicide service, he had at his disposal a set of service concepts and a viable vehicle with which to demonstrate the validity of his plans as he was developing them into a larger framework.

The Knoxville program for suicide and crisis intervention was neither developed nor operated as the result of organized community action. Rather, the outcome of the past four years was the result of fortuitous circumstances which brought together the right combination of professional specialists with an emerging idea and sufficient local sanctions to develop a unique service. Whether or not the process could be duplicated in any other community is a moot question, but the final product is a goal which deserves careful study and which may be highly attractive to some planners of emergency service programs.

CHARACTERISTICS OF 10 CRISIS INTERVENTION PROGRAMS: 1967-1970

4
PHYSICAL SETTINGS AND FACILITIES

Whatever may be the organizational pattern or professional sanctions under which a suicide or crisis service is programmed to operate, it is an undeniable fact that the quality of its service program is limited by the physical facilities at its disposal. In the rush to establish new services, many program initiators thought only about the issues of recruiting and training volunteers and of securing professional support. Among the important matters not attended to adequately are the office facilities and the telephone answering system. It is evident that most suicide prevention services were conceived of literally as telephone answering programs, and nothing more. As long as the telephones were answered, it was concluded that the goal of the program was being accomplished.

This chapter presents an analysis of the office and telephone facilities which were established by the 10 centers in this study. It should be remembered that these centers were among the earliest pioneers in the community crisis intervention movement. As they grew, some changed their systems and enhanced their base of operations; or they failed to survive and are no longer in operation. However, their meager beginnings are important to record and analyze so that new programs, yet to be organized, do not run aground on some of the same hidden dangers of partial nonexistence.

SUICIDE PREVENTION PROGRAM OFFICES

Although most suicide prevention agencies called themselves "centers," this concept was actually quite misleading in the majority of cases. It is most likely that the concept of "suicide prevention center" was adopted in a rather indiscriminate manner from the name of the original Los Angeles program, which was an agency and a center in every sense of the word. The very minimum that is implied by the term "center" is that the program has an office, or an identifiable base from which its operations are directed. Actually, this was rarely the case.

Type of Office Facility

At the time the 10 programs actually were studied, all but two of them had established offices of some kind. Neither FRIENDS nor the Halifax County programs ever had space to call their own. In Orlando, WE CARE had no office for the first 15 months of its operation, but moved into its own quarters with the aid of the demonstration research grant from NIMH. Operating a suicide prevention or crisis intervention service without any office at all presents a number of distinct problems.

It is immediately evident that, without an office, the program is required to use a telephone answering service full-time, and the volunteers are required to be on duty at their homes. This means that they must keep their private telephones free from personal use during the duty shift, but there are other disadvantages of this method which are discussed later. The primary complication with having volunteers operate out of their homes is that there is no central record or filing system for clinical case material. Thus, a worker cannot refer to records of previous contact with a caller in order to know what action plans or intervention styles have been effective in the past. The workers become vulnerable to the caller who repeatedly contacts different people, giving each a different story, but generating anxiety and tensions within the system while, at the same time, remaining completely inaccessible to the help which a program might offer.

If records are kept of the calls, they must be mailed to some designated location, usually the home of the coordinator, and stored there until someone else assumes responsibility. By the time they are moved a number of times and new filing methods have been imposed, it becomes almost impossible to collect systematic information about the service as a whole, much less about individual clients. FRIENDS resolved this problem by denying the value of records in the first place. They strongly disapproved of keeping records for research purposes and kept a minimum of information about the service. The activity of their program may have been recorded in a manner somewhat like a daily telephone call log, but nothing resembling case files was ever kept. In Orlando, the volunteers began by filling out a face sheet for each client and placing it in a file folder. These folders subsequently were handed or mailed to the coordinator, who filed them alphabetically in a cardboard box in her bedroom. The only way that case material was available to the workers during a call was in the case of identifiable, "chronic" callers. When it became evident that the service was receiving repeated calls from one person, the coordinator would write a brief description of the case, along with the suggested method of handling it, and mail these to each of the volunteers. Presumably, they had these case descriptions available during their phone shifts. A similar method was used in Halifax County, except that the volunteers mailed the face sheets to the coordinator, who filed them in her office in the public health department.

Naturally, there were many cases which became lost. Often, volunteers forgot to fill out the forms or to mail them in for several days. By that time, other calls had been received, but the volunteers did not have the original material about a client to use when taking the later calls. There were some volunteers in Orlando who refused ever to file a report; consequently, the program had no record whatever of its service to the community when these people were on duty. Such a deficiency in organization is not only a sign of limited cohesiveness, it is also a dangerous practice which allows incompetent and inept workers to interact with clients with no method of holding them accountable for their clinical behavior.

Six of the 10 services did not have an office, but did have space given to them by another agency. Two of these were located in Mental Health Association offices, and the remaining four were housed in professional mental health clinics. Each type of "living-in" arrangement presented its own difficulties. The two services which occupied space in mental health associations were in Nashville and Chattanooga, Tennessee. They both were sponsored by these associations. The Chattanooga program had a desk and a file cabinet, but the Nashville Crisis Call Center had two large rooms for its own use. There was always a great difference between these two service programs. The Chattanooga service never became a viable part of its community. Its telephones were never answered in the office space it occupied, and its management was always vaguely defined. It finally failed to attract sufficient interest among its prime supporters to justify remaining in operation. In Nashville, on the other hand, the program survived the death grip which the MHA had on its operation and was able to move out into other space. Eventually, it moved into the Community Mental Health Center that was established within the Meharry Medical College complex.

In Miami, LIFELINE also had its original space provided in the Mental Health Association office. One Monday morning, after the program had been in operation over a year, the director went into the office and found that over the weekend her suicide prevention program had been moved across the hall. She never was able to get any explanation for this move, but it obviously was necessary for the needs of the MHA organization. The offices across the hall were occupied by a psychiatrist with a private clinic practice. He had two or three other persons working with him, and the result was a small mental health center organization supported in part by the Mental Health Association. The LIFELINE program found itself sitting at a small desk in these crowded clinic quarters.

The obvious complication of "living-in" with a parent sponsoring organization is that the program never has a chance to grow into a maturity of its own. This is somewhat true of services living within the mental health center structure, too, but the effect is much less pronounced than with the associations. A Mental Health Association is not—and by national policy should not be—a treatment agency. Yet the crisis center takes on a commitment to the public for personal services, and the demands placed upon the operation are foreign to the Association. Furthermore, the crisis service must operate 24 hours a day, seven days a week. It is open for business more than three times as much as the Association office. A suicide or crisis service soon becomes like "the tail wagging the dog" when it is housed in an MHA facility (McGee, 1971a).

The suicide services in Knoxville, Tennessee and in Brevard County and St. Petersburg, Florida, were organized by and housed in mental health centers. In such settings, the suicide and crisis service was considered to be a program of the professional clinic. Thus, its program was highly constricted by the boundaries drawn between volunteer telephone service and professional patient care. During the early months of the suicide prevention center movement, the total comprehensive crisis intervention service had not been conceptualized; suicide prevention telephone answering was the order of the day. Such limited activities could be added to a mental health clinic without difficulty, but as soon as the telephone service wanted to grow into more of a comprehensive service to people in trouble, problems began to appear. For example, the services which were housed in mental health operations found that they were referring the largest proportion of their clients to the professional treatment services of the clinic. People who wanted to be seen or who needed immediate personal support from another helper could receive face-to-face counseling only from the mental health clinic staff, rather than from the crisis workers. The telephone service, then, served to funnel clients into the mental health system; this was probably appropriate for some of them, but clearly not necessary or appropriate for most.

There were two services which stand out from the others in that they acquired their own private, separate office space. They either paid rent to a landlord or were given a lease agreement by the public agency. They had total control over their own space. They determined who worked there, and, most of all, they determined what was done there. These two services were the Emergency Mental Health Service in Atlanta and WE CARE in Orlando. They became recognized in their communities as *agencies* in the network of community helping systems. This was possible because they held this concept of themselves at their inception, and this concept was the chief factor which enabled them to set the occupancy of their own office as a necessary condition to their operation.

Utilization of the Office Space

Of the eight services which had some type of office space, only two of them used the space for personal interviewing of walk-in clients. Both WE CARE and the Nashville Crisis Call Center occasionally had walk-in clients, although neither advertised or encouraged the use of such service. The Atlanta Emergency Mental Health Service used public health nurses to make home visits to clients, but never had callers come into the office for personal counseling or crisis work. Seven of the services answered the telephone in their office space, but only in Atlanta was the telephone answered there around the clock. The others maintained what were essentially business offices, which closed evenings and weekends.

Four of the centers used their office space for training new volunteers, but only two of them, in Atlanta and Nashville, conducted all of their training there. In Orlando and Brevard County, the services did most of the training elsewhere. All eight of the programs had some contacts for using other community space for meetings of volunteers and training seminars. In Halifax County, the group met in a public room maintained by a local bank; Knoxville and Chattanooga services used various churches for their meetings; WE CARE regularly held bimonthly training meetings in the auditorium of the County Sheriff's office in the Court House, and FRIENDS used facilities of the Miami Police Department.

In planning a community crisis service, the director or initiator must be aware of the psychological advantage of having a place that the program can call its own. The center staff or board of directors must be able to determine how the space will be utilized, how much space is necessary, how it should be decorated and functionally equipped, and when the space is to be in operation. But most of all, having an office space for its own operation tells the crisis workers: "We *exist!* We are an entity that has a place in this community. We are more than a name, more than an ideal. more than a program on paper." The lack of a physical setting which enables the community at large to be continually aware of the reality of the agency will cast a program into the realm of "partial nonexistence." The greatest danger to a program in such a condition is the absence of external validating behaviors on the part of the community. Without the nourishment which comes from other community agencies' and care-givers' frequently acknowledging the existence of the service, it will be very vulnerable to apathy, indifference, and disillusionment within its own ranks.

There are very few crisis services which have been organized since 1970 which have not had their own independent office facilities. Many of them have been in new community mental health center buildings, but at least they have a place of their own. To be a community agency, the service must have an identifiable locus of operation. The days of the simple telephone answering service have gone by the wayside, lost in the early history of a new development. The programs that have survived those early days have grown into mature crisis intervention agencies; they have set the precedents for service systems, and new programs have come into existence without having to begin at the primitive level which once characterized the field.

TELEPHONE ANSWERING SYSTEMS
IN SUICIDE PREVENTION PROGRAMS

Just as with office space, the telephone procedures have received a minimum of attention in the planning of suicide and crisis services. This finding was most surprising, since there is no denying that the telephone should be the backbone of the system. Of course, costs can be great if elaborate equipment is installed, and for small-budget programs this has been a prohibitive factor. However, some programs actually are spending more money for an inferior system than they would need to spend for a considerably better one.

Number of Telephone Lines

It was very surprising to discover that only two of the 10 centers had considered the need for a business line in addition to their emergency line. Perhaps it was because the program had no concept of carrying on any other type of conversations beyond the immediate emergency response to people in trouble. However, volunteers must be contacted or must call the service regarding their duty shifts. Calls must be placed to other agencies to determine if clients have kept transfer agreements, and, in an emergency, calls must be placed to rescue units in cases of suicide attempts. Program planners seem to have thought only of incoming calls and have not provided for the outgoing traffic. Some of the centers which were located in other agencies were able to make use of the telephone service installed in the host agency. Thus, they actually had some access to telephones, but the business lines were not listed in the Directory as being associated with the suicide service. Consequently, when people needed to call the service about a client, or to request information, they had only the emergency line to use. Keeping emergency lines tied up for such purposes severely reduces the ability of the program to fulfill its mission in the community.

Furthermore, only five of the 10 centers had installed additional rotary lines on their emergency number. The rotary is a simple mechanism which merely connects two or more lines so that when the primary advertised number is busy, another one automatically rings. One may also wonder at the fact that four of the five services which had rotaries also had their volunteers taking calls at home during all or part of the 24-hour period. Consequently, the rotary was only partially effective. The second number could be answered by the operator at the answering service, but there was nothing she could do with the call until the volunteer at home reported that she was free.

A final deficiency which must be mentioned involves the lack of additional equipment to permit emergency calls during the time that the original incoming call is still on the line. Obviously, it is totally impractical to think of such an arrangement when volunteers are working out of their homes, and when they do, it is even more rare that they are located in the same room. Yet, even in the offices, only the WE CARE center had thought to install an unlisted number on a separate instrument at the crisis worker's desk. This permits the volunteer to keep the caller on the line *without putting him on "hold"* while emergency rescue units are dispatched. There are other important advantages of such a facility. Volunteers who have a difficult case can use the other line to call a consultant and ask for quick suggestions as to how they might handle the caller. This makes the worker much more secure. Sometimes a caller will not identify himself, yet the worker believes he knows who it is. Using the other line while still talking to the caller, one can determine if the suspected person's phone number is busy. While this is by no means conclusive evidence, it does help to establish more certainty about the caller's identity. On several occasions, volunteers have used this method to determine an accurate identification and the location of a client during a call. It is also possible to use an automatic dial telephone for this unlisted line. Various types are available which are activated by preprogrammed tape or plastic cards.

Both save the volunteer time and require a minimum amount of his attention in order to get the desired help without hanging up on the caller.

Finally, a word should be added about the "hold" button on telephones in crisis centers. *Playboy Magazine* once defined a "born loser" as "a person who calls the suicide prevention center and gets put on hold." This is a totally unacceptable practice; there simply is no rationale which justifies it. It is often very difficult to keep a person on the line under any condition. But when the worker must cut him off, for any reason at all, and he must sit there listening to a dead line, not knowing what is going on behind the blank silence, any caller will be tempted to hang up. When a second emergency line beings to ring, the worker must answer the other line. In this case, he needs an extra-long cord on the receiver to enable him to walk across the room to the other desk, where he can answer another telephone instrument. As he goes, he apologizes to the first caller, explaining that he must answer the other line but will be back in a minute. The first caller can already hear the other phone ringing, and he can hear as the worker does what he says he is going to do. There is immediate credibility; the caller is certain he is being treated without deceit. While he is on "hold" he does not know. There are also times when the worker may need to call for help from someone else, such as the tracing operator, or a staff consultant, and does not want the caller to hear this conversation. In such cases, the volunteer can place a hand securely over the mouthpiece, rather than use the holding circuit. The auditory cues of an open line are still present, and the caller has the feeling of being in contact. In fact, the worker can still hear him, and may learn some very helpful information from what the caller may say to someone at his end of the line which he would not have said directly over the phone. This is often a useful way to determine if the call is a prank which is being used to "entertain" people at the point of origin.

In a brief summary, a fully adequate telephone system includes separate business lines, rotary connections on the emergency lines, a separate telephone instrument for each of the emergency lines, and an automatic dial telephone on an unlisted number available for emergency outgoing calls. Only two of the 10 centers studied approached this level of preparedness, and even one of them reverted to using volunteers at home after hours.

Commercial Answering Services

Of the programs studied, only the one in Atlanta covered its telephone around the clock in its own office. The others either had no office or kept it open only part of the time. They needed a commercial answering service to do their initial work for them. In Halifax County, a commerical service was not available, but the telephones were answered in the Roanoke Rapids Police station by the desk officer on duty. In Orlando, WE CARE's telephone initially was placed in the nursing station of the psychiatric unit in a general hospital. This was a community service gesture of the hospital administrator, who was a member of the WE CARE Board of Directors. However, the nurses were not so involved in the new program. It was a great source of stress to them, and their own nursing responsibilities with patients naturally took priority over the ringing of WE CARE's telephone. Among the several humorous anecdotes associated with the WE CARE service, one related to the telephone service stands out. It occurred in the early morning hours when a prominent physician called the service to report on the condition of a suicide attempter he had treated in the emergency room earlier that night. Had he not been a retired miliary physician and a surgeon, with the personality of both professions, the incident might have gone unnoticed. However, he was known throughout the medical community, particularly in this hospital, for his human relations skills, which were other than well polished. On this particular occasion, he thought he was calling the crisis worker at home, and when the line was finally answered after many rings, he apologized for waking up the worker in the middle of the night. The duty nurse, however, knowing she was not asleep on duty and resenting the accusation, could only interpret this doctor's remark as hostile sarcasm. She proceeded to tell him just what she thought about the suicide prevention program, and threw in a few comments to describe her feelings for the doctor as well. The hospital administrator gave the WE CARE director 12 hours to find another system for answering the telephones, and a commercial answering service was chosen.

In Orlando, and perhaps in Halifax County, a commercial answering service would perhaps be an improvement over the other method, but in nearly every case, such services have more disadvantages than advantages. In the first place, they nearly always cost money. Only in Nashville has the telephone answering been provided as a free, donated service. Others have paid from $18 to $32 per month for the service. In Knoxville, the operators reduced their charge to $10 as a community service, but very quickly, when they got into operation, raised the rate to $25. Each of the programs was asked to designate some of the advantages it realized from the use of its answering service. These ranged from the mere fact that they were "available" to the belief that the operators were very skilled at establishing the first link with the distressed caller. Some said that the service was inexpensive or that it was donated. Nearly all who used an answering service pointed out that the service was also one which served medical personnel in the community. In Miami, LIFELINE used the same telephone service which served the coordinator's law practice and her husband's medical practice. In Knoxville, the answering service was a specialized one which served all of the psychiatrists and psychologists in private practice in the area. In each of these instances, it was claimed by the suicide prevention service that its answering service was especially qualified *because of* its other medical or psychological clients. In retrospect, this has to be the classic example of a universal "sweet lemons" rationalization. None of the crisis centers would agree to the contention that its service was anything like a medical or psychiatric practice in nature. Why the answering service should be especially experienced in taking stress calls from psychiatrists' patients remains a mystery. Every commercial telephone answering service, even those which serve plumbers and building inspectors, is in business because all of its clients need to receive calls for help at any hour. To the people making those calls, they are of emergency proportion, and there is some psychological stress present. In short, answering services must be capable of dealing with people under stress, and the issues are those of efficiency, clarity of communication, and courtesy—not therapeutic competence. Obviously, it was no advantage in Knoxville for the answering service to specialize in taking calls from patients of mental health professionals; it did not prevent the operators from being so stressed that they had to more than double their fee once the calls started coming.

At the same time, each center was able to point out some distinct disadvantages of its answering service. These were primarily in terms of the reactions of the operators when they received crank calls or apparently serious calls for which they could not get a number or name to pass on to the worker. It is necessary for the coordinator to keep constantly at work "mending fences" with the answering service personnel. If one has ever experienced stress in a crisis center, he probably has been a witness to the coordinator's anxiety over the threat of losing the answering service. When a 24-hours-a-day availability has been advertised to the public, this threatened loss is a highly untenable position for the crisis service to be in. The use of a commercial service takes a lot of necessary control out of the hands of the program director; it is far better not to risk that situation in the first place. In fact, one can argue that there is an ethical issue involved in advertising a service and then providing something less than the public is led to expect. It is highly risky and may be a moral question for a center director to delegate to anyone not under his direct control the responsibility for assuring that his commitment to the public is being met (McGee, Richard, and Bercun, 1972).

A further complication with the answering service is the need to break the connection with the caller. It can be as much as an hour, or even more, before the call can be relayed to the worker. In Miami, FRIENDS discovered that they were getting less than half of their calls because the operator was screening them and deciding not to send many of them through. There is no way of knowing what effect this may have had on the callers, but it is certain that it did not help FRIENDS' image in the community. However, some answering services will "patch" a call right through to the worker if it sounds like an emergency. The problem with this is that it is a violation of the FCC regulations, and the answering service places itself in jeopardy for doing so. Also, when the call is patched through the switchboard, there is no disconnect signal to the operator. Thus, the operator must either keep cutting in on the line—a distraction to the caller—or leave the worker's phone tied up for unknown periods of time when the call is finished. On several occasions, workers in Orlando have found it necessary to run next door and use a neighbor's phone to call the answering service and ask them to disconnect so that an outgoing call could be made to aid the client.

Telephone answering services are among the first items to be ruled out when adequate funds are available to run the program as the coordinator would like. Each of the 10 centers was asked to consider the ideal telephone system it would install, assuming it had unlimited funds. Only five of them responded to this question, but four indicated that they would eliminate the answering service and have their own workers answer the telephone directly in the office around the clock. Ironically, it is not the matter of finances which prevents this arrangement. Rather, it is the willingness to require that volunteers come into the office to take their shifts. For some persons, this represents a "hardship." Some people want to volunteer time and service only if it is no inconvenience to them to do so. In some cases, the crisis center is located in a part of town which middle-class white housewives feel that they should avoid, even during the daytime, but especially at night. Unfortunately, once a program has started operation in one manner, it is very difficult to change. Therefore, initiators of new programs must give very careful thought to planning the telephone system and must start from the beginning with the best that can be designed. Generally, experienced crisis center directors agree that around-the-clock coverage in the office, without an answering service, is the only efficient system.

Tape Recording of Calls

The potential use of taping equipment is another issue which should be planned in advance of setting up the service. There are a number of complicated issues which arise in connection with taping calls, mostly revolving around the legality and ethics of making tapes. These issues can be resolved very easily, and have been by those centers which have studied them. Nearly all of the programs studied had approached the issue; only two of them made tapes. The others concluded that it was too expensive to purchase the equipment and rationalized their not doing so on the grounds that it was "probably illegal" or that their professional advisors felt that it was "unethical." Neither of these excuses is valid. The two centers in Atlanta and Orlando which made tapes found them extremely useful for worker training, as well as for emergency identification when necessary. Both of these programs included more and better taping equipment in their plans for an ideal telephone system. A detailed discussion of the legality and ethics of taping is included in Chapter 16, under the section describing this very important method for collecting research data in a community crisis service.

Directory Listing of Suicide Prevention Services

A discussion of the telephone service would not be complete without a brief discussion of directory listings. Once more, it was surprising to learn how little attention had been given to this simple strategy.

For example, in Halifax County, the local telephone service covered six small, rural communities, all of which were listed in the same local directory. However, the suicide prevention service was indexed in regular small-case type in the white pages of only the one community which the telephone was answered. After the program had been in operation for several months, it occurred to the coordinator that it should also be listed in the sections for the other five communities. Every center should have its listing in the classified section of the directory as well. However, only six of the 10 centers were listed in the yellow pages. The telephone company index system includes several standard categories which could be used. The major one is the "Suicide Prevention" category. However, it is also possible to list a center under the "Clinics" category, or under "Mental Health Consultants." Imaginative thought by the director will permit the identification of several listings for the center, one of which will certainly catch the eye of some potential caller who needs the service and cannot remember its exact name. For example, a program entitled "Suicide and Crisis Intervention Service" should be listed not only in the yellow pages under "Suicide Prevention," but also in the white pages under both "Suicide" and "Crisis." Such listings do not cost very much. There is usually a free white page listing for every telephone line, which should provide at least three free listings for any well-designed telephone system. Yellow page listings need not be expensive display ads, and unless special designs are used, they will not cost very much. Complete directory listings for a crisis service will cost only 10 percent (or less) of the monthly charge for a commercial answering service.

At the time that this study was made, the Bell Telephone Company systems had a policy which forbade placing the suicide prevention service under the emergency listings on the inside of the front cover of directories. This policy subsequently has been revised, and the emergency listing will be made if the initiator requests it. It is necessary only to satisfy the telephone officials that the service will, in fact, be manned with an answering person on duty 24 hours a day, seven days a week, and that the service will continue to be provided throughout the life of the directory. This is usually for one year. Every crisis service should be able to satisfy these requirements, at least by the time it has been in operation for a few months.

Survey of Telephone Answering Systems

Partly as a result of the finding of this study, a larger survey was made of 19 suicide and crisis services in the Southeast. All of the 10 centers, plus nine others which had recently come into existence, were surveyed as to the type of telephone answering system they had developed. A full report of this study is available elsewhere (McGee, Richard, and Bercun, 1972), but a few of the major findings and conclusions are relevant here.

Four calls were placed to each of the 19 centers. They were distributed in time in such a way that they permitted observation of the various systems (1) during weekday office hours, (2) during early evening hours, (3) during middle-of-the-night hours, and (4) during the weekend. To allow for these observations, the calls were placed on consecutive days as follows:

1. Period I: Between 3:00 and 5:00 p.m., Friday
2. Period II: Between 7:00 and 9:00 p.m., Friday
3. Period III: Between 1:00 and 3:00 a.m., Saturday
4. Period IV: Between 10:00 a.m. and 12:00 noon, Saturday

As a result of the study, eight different telephone systems were identified during the 76 calls. They are identified as follows:
1. The call is answered directly by the crisis worker on duty.
2. The call is answered by an operator or receptionist in the office, who then switches the call to the crisis worker on duty.
3. The call is answered by a commercial answering service, which then places the call through the switchboard to the worker on duty at home.
4. The call is answered by a commercial answering service, which takes the caller's name and number and notifies the worker, who returns the call.
5. The call is answered by personnel in another agency, who take the caller's name and number and notify the worker, who returns the call.
6. The phone is answered by personnel in another agency, who give the caller the name and number of the worker on duty and instruct him to re-dial the call.
7. A mechanical recording device informs the caller of another number he can dial to reach a crisis worker on duty.
8. There is no answer at all after several attempts (including a request for assistance from the long distance operator).

It was evident from these data that most centers use more than one of the several systems. In fact, only five of the 19 centers used the same procedure during all of the four periods. Five centers employed as many as three different systems during the four periods, while the remaining nine centers had two different systems in operation.

It was observed that where the service had its volunteers on duty to answer the phone directly, the time taken to reach a crisis worker was less than 20 seconds over a total of 27 different calls. Where the answering service patches directly to the worker, the time can increase to as much as three minutes. However, if the answering party must contact the worker and have the call returned, it can take as long as 49 minutes. The average time to complete 23 calls was just under 15 minutes under such procedures. Further, when some other agency answered the call, it was not even completed two out of three times. Failure to reach a worker occurred once out of 19 calls which were taken by commercial answering services.

These findings clearly show that the only certain method of delivering around-the-clock emergency telephone crisis intervention services is to provide a trained worker on duty full-time at the point where the calls are received. This is by far the most efficient procedure and the one which yields the greatest personal satisfaction to the staff of the crisis center. It is the only system which maximizes control over the program in the hands of the people who are responsible to the community for delivering what they promise in their publicity.

There is one hopeful note in these data. Five of the centers contacted began operations during 1970. Of the 20 calls placed to these new centers, 16 were answered directly by the crisis worker on duty. Perhaps it may be concluded that because these newest programs have instituted this type of system, we may expect more and more agencies to move in this direction in the future.

The authors concluded that the type of telephone answering system employed reflects the interest and motivation of a crisis center for performing a quality job in the community. The telephone system also reveals the level of development of the service itself. The growth and development of individual community suicide and crisis services may be charted by the history of their autonomy and control over the answering of the initial call. Some suicide and crisis services are in danger of unknowingly providing inferior and dangerously low-quality service because they fail to maintain maximum control over their own telephone answering system 24 hours a day.

SUMMARY AND IMPLICATIONS

Throughout this chapter, the existing physical settings and telephone systems have been discussed and criticized. However, a brief review is appropriate for the benefit of program directors and initiators who are still in a position to plan for comprehensive crisis intervention services.

The office space and telephone systems of early suicide prevention centers were woefully inadequately planned. It was apparent that the goal of the program was to get a group of people and then to list a telephone number which could be answered by someone, someplace; it did not seem to matter who or where. Severe complications arose in the operation of these services. Only two of them had their own offices, and both have grown into substantial community service agencies. Of the others, four have ceased to exist altogether. None would say that having an office preserves a community service all by itself. What is apparent, however, is that those services which think of themselves as important, vital, community agencies will have an office and independent telephone control as one of the several expressions of that self-concept. If an agency is going to develop a permanent role in its community, it cannot do so without behaving as if it deserves to be recognized. The type of office space and telephone system which is planned is a good indication of the amount of determination a center has for fulfilling its mission.

Actually, it is difficult to imagine how some of the programs have survived as long as they have. Undoubtedly, they would not have made it without the community mental health center to provide them an office and telephone coverage. Those which have survived their meager beginnings have established valuable precedents for new programs. It would be highly unwise at this point in time for new programs to attempt to start their services by operating out of homes or without adequate telephone coverage. Such programs have little to offer the community, and the community can now expect much better crisis service.

5

CLINICAL SERVICE PROGRAMS AND PRACTICES

What does a crisis intervention service do? What kind of help does it offer its callers? Does it provide a really necessary program in the community? Does it do anything unique which is not already being done by existing services? These and related questions have been asked frequently of the volunteers and the directors who have manned the telephones in suicide and crisis intervention agencies. They are relevant questions. Yet, the answers are often disappointing. Each of the 10 centers surveyed in this study was asked a series of questions for the purpose of determining its attitudes and its approaches to providing personal helping services. This chapter presents a review of the clinical service programs of these 10 suicide centers during the period from 1966 to 1969. It may be remembered that most of these programs were new—some of them just getting started—at that time. However, for some of them, the earliest practices are still in effect at present.

TELEPHONE COUNSELING

The telephone systems of the 10 centers were discussed in the last chapter. It was found that all 10 of the centers did provide a 24-hour telephone service, even though only one of them was in complete control of its service around the clock. All of the programs did operate, and advertise, a telephone number which people could call for help with problems. They all had crisis workers on duty somewhere to either answer the phone or take a relayed message and call the client back. In short, every program was at least a telephone answering service. But beyond that one similarity, there were great differences in them. Some of these more important differences are discussed in this chapter.

All of the centers seemed to expect the workers to identify the caller and to record his name, address, and telephone number. Eight of the programs had developed a printed form on which such information was recorded, and these were filed in various ways, supposedly for future use. However, only two of the programs seemed to make any real effort to see that these forms were completed in every case. One service reported that probably 80 percent of its files had only a name and telephone number of a caller; there were no notes or description of what had happened during the call.

Eight of the 10 centers indicated that they required their workers to make an assessment of lethality. Presumably all of the programs tried to determine if the caller was suicidal, or if his call was of a less serious crisis nature. However, only four of them had any type of lethality scale or questionnaire to aid in collecting this important information. The Los Angeles Lethality Scale, or a modification of it, was used by three of these centers, but the Nashville Crisis Call Center had developed its own method for evaluating lethality.

REFERRAL AND TRANSFER TO OTHER AGENCIES

Nine of the crisis programs indicated that a primary goal of the service was to refer a caller to some other service in the community when he needed help. All of these agencies had prepared a directory of local services for their workers to use, but the directories which were used by workers at home were generally less complete than those maintained in the offices. The programs differed greatly in the extent to which they facilitated the caller's getting to the other services. For example, only four of the 10 were inclined to call the referral source and make an appointment for the client. Only three of them were willing to provide the transportation if it was necessary to assist a client in making his contact with the other helping service. Five of the programs would give out individual names of doctors or therapists that the caller might contact if he wished, but five programs had been advised that the practice violated some kind of professional ethic. Although they would not often make the appointments for the clients, five of the centers would call ahead to the other agency and inform them that the caller might contact them for help. Four of these programs would then forward a copy of their information to that agency if the caller became a client there.

After an initial call, most of the crisis programs felt that it was up to the client to indicate if he wanted any more contact. Once a referral was made, that was the end of the concern on the part of the crisis center. Only three of them would contact the other agency to see if appointments had been kept. These same three would call the client back and try to find out why he had failed to follow through if he had not accepted the referral. Yet only two of the 10 agencies would make it a routine practice to recontact the caller automatically several weeks after contact to determine how he was doing, and express continued interest in his crisis resolution.

WE CARE was one of the agencies which made these routine follow-up calls. They reported finding that the clients were very grateful for the continued interest of the center. Even as much as a year after first contact, the volunteer was still welcomed when she called to inquire as to the client's present adjustment. These reports clearly invalidate the suspicions and rationalizations that follow-up procedures are "violations of the caller's rights to privacy" or that one should "let sleeping dogs lie." Such admonitions usually come from professional persons who have never tried to follow patients and who really don't have any personal experience on which to base their warnings. However, sanctions against follow-up of crisis clients is only one of the ways in which professional practitioners stifled the growth of clinical service in the early suicide prevention programs.

FACE-TO-FACE CONTACT

The greatest deficit in early crisis service programming was in the restriction placed against most of the centers that forbade them to undertake direct client contact as a vehicle for delivering personal service. The current method for providing such services via the CARE Team is thoroughly discussed in Chapter 15. However, among the 10 centers studied, only five ever had any contact with callers. One program, the Emergency Service in St. Petersburg, made personal contact one of its strongest points. The director realized that such service was the only way to get to know a community and the problems its citizens were facing. The staff routinely met callers anywhere and anytime, and they saw between 60 and 70 percent of their callers personally. Three of the programs actively discouraged face-to-face contact, but did permit workers to see clients under "controlled" conditions. These conditions were usually that someone else also had to be present and that the contact had to occur in a public place, such as a hospital lobby or a restaurant. Going to a person's home or motel room was strictly out of the question; yet this too was done on rare occasions by a few workers who were more concerned about the client than about the anxieties of their director. Probably none of the workers was ever in any danger as a result of the visit, and most likely none ever used grossly poor judgment in the approach.

The interesting finding concerning face-to-face contact was that in those centers where it did occur, it was a violation of the rules; yet the workers who tried it found that this was really the satisfying way to be certain that they were helping as much as possible. They continued to see clients more and more. It became open policy in WE CARE after a few months, but volunteers never have been required to hold interviews if they didn't wish to. The reasons given by some centers for not having face-to-face contact suggest that they either have a very different kind of worker, or else they never tried it. One center director reported that her volunteers would refuse to see people; they would quit if that became part of the program. There is a very strong suspicion that this was a cover-up for the director's own anxiety, or a protection against violating the restrictions of the program sponsors. Other services attributed their lack of personal contact to the fact that their workers were not professionals, and that only psychiatrists should see people face-to-face. Those programs which were affiliated in any way with mental health clinics were actively prevented from seeing clients on the grounds that they should be seen only by the clinic staff.

SERVICE TO SUICIDE ATTEMPTERS

Only three of the suicide programs had routine procedures for follow-up with suicide attempters. Atlanta and St. Petersburg Emergency Mental Health programs were established in professional agencies. They received reports from the hospitals or the police and contacted the patients. WE CARE was the only program which used volunteer workers to perform this service, and there were a number of difficulties between the service and its professional advisors when this effort was established. Nevertheless, these three agencies used their knowledge and insights as suicidology experts to deal with this most important population at risk. Any service which has suicide prevention in its name or in its self-image has no excuse for failing to make itself available to the people who need it the most, *even though these people do not call for help directly.* A suicide attempt may be seen as a cry for help to the community at large. Only the suicide prevention workers are fully capable of understanding suicidal ambivalence, the cry for help dynamic, and the need for immediate crisis resolution via communication with significant others. Yet in seven of the 10 centers, this potentially unique service was undeveloped and unavailable to the community which needed it.

POST-VENTION WITH SURVIVORS OF SUICIDE VICTIMS

Only three of the programs had ever contacted a survivor of a suicide victim to offer crisis intervention in this most difficult of all bereavement situations. These programs only occasionally made such interventions, but had done so with the families of former clients. None reported any plans to make such counseling a permanent part of its service, however. Failure to enter into such practice might be attributed largely to the "state of the art" at the time this study was being carried out. This would be clearly true if it were not for the lack of face-to-face contact with callers and with suicide attempters in most of the centers. However, it is evident that most of the programs were oriented to the telephone, and that additional service beyond talking on the telephone to people who called the center was not part of the system. It is now possible to look back and see that programs must evolve slowly until experiences are gained and shared with other centers. By 1970, however, there was no reason whatever for any new program's not providing a full range of suicide prevention or crisis intervention services. Immediate rescue in cases of suicide attempt is the least service which a program must be able to offer if it thinks of itself as a suicide prevention service. Although rescue of attempters is really only *intervention* rather than *prevention,* there is a high probability that actual prevention is accomplished by active, efficient, and knowledgeable service to suicide attempters and survivors.

SERVICES TO HYPOTHETICAL CASES

In order to learn how each center reacted to fairly conventional cases, three hypothetical situations were described to each center coordinator, and he was asked how his volunteers *should* respond in such a case. A few examples of the responses will suggest the variance which was found.

Case 1

A call is received from a man who reports just having cut his wrists. It is 2:00 a.m.

Responses:

"Get a friend or the police to take him to the hospital."

"Find out where he is, and if anyone is with him. Talk them into taking him to the hospital. If not, call the police to take him. Contact the emergency room at the hospital once he is on the way."

"Tell the caller to be on the lookout for someone to help him."

"They should go to the man, and take him to the hospital. If he refuses to go, call the police."

"Call the police and make arrangements to meet the man and the policeman at the emergency room."

Case 2

A call is received from a middle-aged woman who says she cannot sleep and is very concerned over a fear that she may have cancer. She thinks at times that she may commit suicide. It is 4:30 a.m.

Responses:

"She needs someone to listen to her. Encourage her to see her physician, or make an appointment at the County Medical clinic. Next day, follow-up to see that she made an appointment."

"Go see her."

"Spend an hour or two on the phone with her till she is feeling better."

"Try to find out what is really bothering her. Play it by ear."

"A continuous follow-up of this type caller is important. It is especially important to see if they kept their appointment and to encourage continued treatment."

Case 3

A call is received from an elderly man who states that he is a burden to his family and wants to explain why he must kill himself. He intends to carry out his plan in two days. It is 2:30 p.m.

Responses:

"Ask what method he plans to use for his suicide. Contact the relatives as soon as the call is finished."

"Call back early in the evening and see how he is feeling then. Notify relatives."

"Encourage man that life is worthwhile."

"Try to determine how open he is to the suggestion of seeking professional help. Contact relatives."

"Depend primarily on significant others. Suggest activities for retired people."

"If he is over 70 take him to a nursing home."

These brief excerpts from the action plans which were developed for the three hypothetical cases show that most of the programs studied do not think of themselves as suicide prevention services at all. In fact, one of the groups which had the words "suicide prevention" in its name actually denied that it was a suicide prevention service when filling out the clinical portion of the study questionnaire. In the "comments" section, the director indicated that his group was really a telephone service, not a suicide prevention center.

It is, unfortunately, very clear that at least seven of these 10 services were little more than telephone answering programs. Their style was to hide behind the telephone. They seemed not to think in terms of getting out where the people were and really attempting to help them with a serious application of suicide prevention or crisis intervention principles. Only the agencies in St. Petersburg, Atlanta, and Orlando seemed to take their mission seriously, but each of them had something less than a full range of services to offer clients. The findings of this section of the study suggest that a really comprehensive crisis service did not exist in the Southeast prior to 1969. Recently established programs have, however, developed policies which encourage walk-in clients, face-to-face crisis counseling by volunteers, mobile teams of crisis workers going out into the community, aggressive follow-up of all suicide attempts, and immediate crisis counseling for families of suicide victims. When programs are no longer afraid to put people in contact with people, then crisis intervention services will have reached a maturity and a validity with which they can begin to really make a difference in the lives of their community. It cannot be done just on the telephone; as Louis Dublin emphasized in 1968, " . . . one must put content into the contact." It must be done with active case management, including frequent follow-up contacts during the active phase of the crisis, face-to-face contact at the scene of the problem, and aggressive delivery of service to high-risk populations such as attempters and survivors.

By the limited scope of their clinical service programs and practices, the crisis centers of the 1960's have revealed shortcomings and deficiencies which are now enabling the crisis centers of the 1970's to become vital, necessary, and unique services to people.

Growth of new services and the development of new technologies proceed slowly, and become evident only as one generation improves upon the deficiencies of previous ones. One cannot fault Henry Ford because his Model T was less of an automobile than the modern luxury car; yet one would be justified in his disappointment if Ford were to offer the Model T for sale in 1970.

6
MANPOWER IN CRISIS CENTERS

Each of the 10 centers in the study was asked to describe the people associated with its program in terms of their positions and roles in all phases of the service activity. Only seven programs responded to this part of the study; reports were not received from Chattanooga, St. Petersburg, or LIFELINE in Miami. However, enough is known about each of those agencies to enable some appropriate comments to be made about them as well. The primary questions asked about personnel in each center revolved around the issues of professional involvement, utilization of nonprofessional volunteers, and recruitment and training of all personnel. Some interesting findings emerged in response to these questions, especially as they pertain to the professional personnel. It is interesting to note that the centers in operation during 1966, 1967, and 1968 had different views and attitudes toward their manpower than has been evident since 1970. These differences reflect a change toward less fear and apprehension between the professionals and the volunteers. In the early years of suicide prevention, the courtship was an often stormy one, characterized more by tension than by open, mutual respect. Those centers which survived this period of revolution in manpower trends have created a valuable legacy for the helping professions—one in which the nonprofessional has the right to expect that professionals will either lead, follow, or get out of the way so that the job can be done. It was not always that way, as the following data indicate.

A GENERAL OVERVIEW OF MANPOWER

There are various ways to classify telephone crisis workers. They can be professionals or nonprofessionals; they can be volunteers or salaried. There can be all combinations of these two dimensions, and, in fact, all combinations were found among the 10 centers studied, as shown in Table 1.

By far the most common practice found was the use of nonprofessional volunteer persons, usually housewives and businessmen, as telephone workers. This was the pattern found in Orlando, Brevard County, FRIENDS, and LIFE-LINE in Miami, Nashville, and Halifax County. All of them had professional

Table 1 Type of crisis worker manpower used by the 10 programs

	Nonprofessional	Professional
Volunteers	Orlando Nashville Brevard County Halifax County Miami—FRIENDS Miami—LIFELINE	Knoxville Chattanooga
Salaried	Atlanta	St. Petersburg

persons in the mental health disciplines offering consultation, training, and various other services, but the crisis work was performed by the volunteers. In Chattanooga, the volunteers were all recruited from a special group of persons, largely ministers and agency representatives already engaged in some type of professional helping service. In Knoxville, volunteers were also used on the telephone, but they were all highly trained mental health professionals, or professionals in some health-related field. Only two programs utilized salaried personnel on the telephone. In Atlanta, the workers were nonprofessionals, but they were employed for 40-hour-per-week shifts. In St. Petersburg, the personnel were all professional mental health workers, employed for the specific purpose of operating the emergency service. Two of these models have tended to be unique and have not been copied elsewhere by later centers. Atlanta still has the only program in which nonprofessionals are paid regular salaries for crisis work on the telephone. Knoxville's method did not last long even in that center, as the professionals grew very tired of taking voluntary duty shifts; it was not long before nonprofessional volunteers were recruited, as in the majority of centers. There continue to be a few programs which employ professional persons only, but they are still a distinct minority of the crisis intervention center movement.

PROFESSIONAL PERSONNEL IN SUICIDE AND CRISIS PROGRAMS

It is true that every one of the 10 programs studied had some professional mental health workers involved in some way. The degree of "professionalism" varied greatly from FRIENDS, which had only nominal contact, to Knoxville, where the workers all were professionals. Most of the programs listed between four and six professionals from the community who served in consultative capacity, either directly to the program coordinator or indirectly through the Board of Advisors. Only three of the centers had any professionals answering the telephone, and in all the rest, they were consultants. It is of interest to note that those programs which used professionals on the telephone reported no outside consultants available to offer objective advice about clients or program policy. Consultation seems to be something professionals do not feel they need for themselves, but reserve only for the nonprofessional workers.

The Nashville Crisis Call Center has always been an especially interesting program from the standpoint of its professional support. That center reported nearly 50 professionals involved in some way with its activity. They were all volunteering their time to aid and assist the volunteer workers. Many of them were consultants, available to be called by the worker should the need arise during the management of a case. In addition, there were 10 or 15 who regularly participated in the training of new volunteer classes. Another group served as advisors to the Board of Directors, and finally, a group served as screeners and held no-cost interviews with each person who applied to become a volunteer. Naturally, several of the professionals fulfilled more than one of these functions, but the total number of different people was far greater than at any other center. Nashville's program has been a hallmark of cooperation between the professional community and the crisis center. The professionals have been unusually free from defensiveness or hostility toward the volunteers. They have played the role of para-volunteer specialists, a role which should be emulated in every community if crisis programs are to be maximally effective. Nashville has been one of the foremost contributors to the successful demonstration that volunteers function very adequately with access to professional consultation.

The recruitment of professional personnel for the programs has been largely by personal contact. One or two professional supporters tend to serve as legitimizers with the rest of the professional community, and by their own role modeling, they attract others into the system. It is of interest that only FRIENDS had no program at all for attracting professionals; a few came along every now and then who volunteered to help out and who were permitted to join until they proved a disappointment. It follows naturally that FRIENDS is the only group that had any experience with separating its professional personnel when they were found to be undesirable to the program. The answering service was instructed merely to not put any more calls through to them, and the crisis workers were instructed not to call them for assistance. Other programs had severe difficulties with their local advisors. Orlando's WE CARE probably had the most difficult time with two local psychiatrists, but they were unable to find any way to eliminate them other than to wait passively for their term of office on the Board to expire according to the by-laws and then replace them. Most programs prior to 1968 felt themselves totally impotent to function without the presence of local professional practitioners, yet, for the most part, they were equally unable to relate freely to them.

The practice of "doctor worshipping" is best seen in terms of the attitudes of centers toward training experiences for their professionals prior to their serving as consultants. Three of the centers had no training for their professionals at all; they were expected to already know everything about suicide and crisis intervention.

Two programs ran special training seminars for their consultants. These were directed by professionals who had deliberately studied the suicidology literature and who had visited other programs prior to taking on the task. Nashville's Crisis Call Center held an extensive training program for all of its professionals, and then, once the training course had been tried out, they used the same program on the first class of volunteers. In Halifax County, the program arranged to send one of its founders and consultants to Los Angeles for the semiannual Training Institute held at the Los Angeles Suicide Prevention Center. Two programs gave their professionals some handout reading material, but this was merely as a courtesy, and there was no urging or expectation that they would read it. In short, the training of professional persons for their role in suicide prevention programs was extremely limited and ineffective. It may well be that most of the problems which centers experienced with their professional personnel could be traced directly to this gross oversight in program planning.

Each of the centers was asked to identify some of the characteristics of its professionals which made them especially helpful and valuable to the program. Similarly, the centers were also asked to describe those characteristics of professionals which made them undesirable and unacceptable to the volunteer workers. As might be expected, the majority of responses indicated that the best and most effective of the professionals were those "who demonstrated an acceptance of the volunteer as a capable person," and who did not "appear threatened or defensive about letting volunteer workers assume major responsibility for delivering crisis services." Another praised characteristic was "personal involvement and commitment to the program." Those professionals who were apathetic, perfunctory, or condescending in their attitudes toward the program were quite unpopular. Professionals who are "willing to learn" and especially those "willing to learn from the volunteer" were named as especially desirable by two centers, and those who "do not try too hard to run everything" were valued especially in two others.

The professional persons who were least helpful and who were described as actually destructive to the program were those who "failed to appreciate the significance of the suicide or crisis situation." Some continuously labeled suicide threats as mere manipulations or suicide attempts as simple gestures. They made the volunteers feel "put down" for feeling concerned about the callers. Furthermore, some professionals made themselves unpopular by denying the importance of a crisis, indicating that in their opinion it was something so mild that a volunteer could handle it. They gave the impression that only "real illness" was worth worrying about. A most unpopular tendency of professionals in all centers was the occasional tendency to place too tight restrictions and constraints on the workers. In some centers, workers were forbidden to make return calls to a client to follow up on his progress with the action plan or transfer recommendation. In other centers, professionals seemed to use the center to foster their own professional practice, sometimes blatantly requiring volunteers to refer callers to them. Those who were rigidly cast in their doctor role and who found it difficult to relate as fellow human beings to the nonprofessionals were cited as quite disruptive to the volunteer morale.

There are three kinds of consultants, and it matters greatly which kind is recruited for a program. First, there is the consultant who strives to relieve anxiety, to extend support, and to encourage independence. Secondly, there is the consultant whose stance is critical, cautious, conservative, and supervisory. Finally, there is the consultant who is indifferent, disinterested, perfunctory, and largely apathetic.

The findings of this portion of the study suggest certain conclusions about the stance which crisis centers should take toward the professional consultant in those programs in which the services are provided primarily by volunteer nonprofessionals.

1. *Consultants must be evaluated and selected just as carefully and with just as much deliberation as are the nonprofessional volunteers.* A consultant should not be selected because he will be a "rubber stamp" and render indifferent, passive acceptance to whatever the program director proposes. Rather, a professional should be recruited as a consultant because his attitudes toward community services are forward-looking and progressive. He must respond to curiosity and challenge and be secure in the knowledge that when the volunteers assume clinical responsibility, the foundations of his own professional calling are not under attack. He must not feel threatened by the demonstration that somebody who is not a professional can do a job with people as well as—maybe even better than—he can do it. There are many psychiatrists, psychologists, and social workers in this country who have the qualifications to be good consultants. These potential consultants are not always visible; they are not always to be found in the private offices of the medical shopping centers in suburbia; they are not always available without fee, but they can be found. The point is that they must be deliberately sought and not just brought into the program because they are the first ones to say, "Yes, I've got a few hours with nothing better to do." No one would accept a volunteer on this basis, and exceptions should not be made for consultants.

2. *Consultants must be given the same training opportunities and exposed to the same training material as that provided for the nonprofessional volunteers.* One of the worst spots that a professional person can be placed in occurs when it is assumed that either he already knows something which he does not know, or he thinks he knows it all and does not want to learn anything more. When a new consultant comes into a program, he needs to know the norms of the culture. If the norms are derived from Litman's paper on telephone techniques (1963), or Farberow's paper on therapy in the suicidal crisis (1967), or Shneidman's taxonomy of self-destruction (1963), the consultant needs to be acquainted with these. It should not be assumed that any professional is familiar with all the professional literature. No one would hesitate to let the volunteers know that there are some things they must learn before they start to work in a suicide prevention program; the same courtesy is due to professional consultants.

3. Consultants must be given a realistic role, appropriate to their skills and consistent with the responsibilities which they can reasonably expect to fulfill. A consultant should be asked to be a helper in the problem-solving process. He should be asked to help carry out the solutions to a problem. He should not become identified as the problem himself if he does not come up with a solution immediately. He should not be asked to assume responsibility or liability for aspects of the program not directly related to his consultation. He should not be given the job of making administrative decisions unless he is actively involved as a duly elected decision-maker in the organization structure. (The role of administrator is different than the role of consultant, inasmuch as consultants usually come from outside the system.) A consultant to a system does not have the responsibility for an individual; responsibility resides with the system, in this case with the crisis intervention center. A consultant is not a supervisor; supervision is a process of responsibility and advice-giving which is organized vertically within a work group. Ordinarily, supervision of psychology students should be by the psychologists; supervision of volunteers should be only by older, more experienced volunteers.

One looks to the consultants for help in getting to the heart of problems and for the suggestion of alternatives through which to find a solution. Centers insist that their volunteers learn their limitations and not get in over their heads; they owe the consultants the same protection. Another important function of the consultant in addition to advice-giving is giving general support to the program. Support comes primarily from offering comfort and anxiety release for the volunteers on the front line; and support also means public commendation of the value of the program within the larger community.

VOLUNTEER NONPROFESSIONALS IN SUICIDE AND CRISIS CENTERS

Five of the seven programs which responded to this portion of the study, and one which did not respond, utilized the nonprofessional exclusively as the crisis worker on the telephone. The centers were asked to describe their methods for recruiting, screening, training, and evaluating their volunteer personnel. Once more, it should be remembered that these programs were all in existence prior to 1967; consequently, they were among the first to develop very new techniques for using volunteers in suicide prevention centers.

Four of the five centers did their recruiting primarily by public announcements in the local news media. They employed radio and television spot announcements, newspaper feature articles, and talks before local civic clubs as their major recruiting methods. At the same time, all five of the programs relied somewhat on their professional advisors for recruiting. In the "nomination" process of finding workers, local ministers, physicians, mental health specialists, and the Mental Health Association are asked to suggest names of persons who would be well qualified for crisis work on the telephone. Once the names are secured, the program director contacts each nominee and attempts to obtain his agreement. This is sometimes a difficult task, and not infrequently, by the time the last volunteers are signed up, the first ones contacted have lost their interest because of the long delay in the start of training. The nomination procedure is grossly inefficient, although it does appear to result in some high-quality workers' being nominated and eventually selected for service.

One of the programs used a special technique for obtaining workers—the group membership method. In this method, a local women's club is approached and asked to take on the task of providing the crisis center manpower for the coming year. The club supplies a coordinator for recruitment and selection, and there can be an unnecessary ambiguity about who is "in charge" of the volunteer program. When a conflict of interests occurred in the one center studied, membership in the club took precedence over being a crisis service volunteer. It is easy for hard feelings and low morale to result from such a situation. The group membership method results in bringing large numbers of volunteer applicants, but has great disadvantages which make it unsuitable for use.

Nearly all of the crisis centers used more than one means of screening their applicants. Most of them gave some type of psychological test, and usually it was the Minnesota Multiphasic Personality Inventory (MMPI). The use of the MMPI can be traced originally to the Los Angeles center, and it appears to have been transposed uncritically to most of the early centers. FRIENDS made use of only one interview for selecting its new members, whereas some programs required two or even three different interviews for new applicants. All but one of the programs considered their training program to be a functional part of selection and would use a trainee's performance during the classes as a means of collecting additional information prior to making final acceptance decisions. There is no indication what criteria the centers were using or what they looked for in their screening interviews. It was reported that a very few people were screened out because of markedly deviant MMPI profiles, but no evidence has yet been presented to show that any particular profile is associated with either especially good or especially incompetent persons. The facts are simply that in 1967, *there were no criteria.* No one knew what traits or behaviors characterized a "good" volunteer crisis worker. The entire screening process was a "seat of the pants" operation. It is, in some ways, astounding that the early centers were able to attract the good workers that they did, and the fact that they selected people who could do the work is testimony to the devotion and dedication of the program leaders to make the new kind of service work effectively.

Characteristics of Unacceptable Volunteers

Although no one really knew what kind of volunteers they wanted or how to identify them, nearly every center director knew on some a priori basis what kinds of people were undesirable. The most frequently cited reason for separating a volunteer from the program was a violation of confidence of a client. A gossip universally was eliminated. Other centers would rid themselves of workers who were not committed and involved in the program or who put their own needs and wishes ahead of those of the center. Those who revealed that they could not be trained to perform specific functions or to hold locally valued attitudes about people in crisis were unacceptable. Three centers cited "too much involvement" with clients or "doing too much" for callers as an undesirable trait. It is interesting that these three programs were those which were strongly influenced by professional advisors. It is obvious that the professional consultants were ill-informed about the nature of crisis and crisis intervention and were erroneously applying the criteria for professional psychotherapy to the work of volunteers in crisis intervention. One center emphasized that an undesirable volunteer was one who would not follow the directions of the professionals.

Although the undesirable characteristics were well-defined, there were no well-developed methods for eliminating volunteers once they started to work and proved themselves unsatisfactory. This was a major problem for all of the center directors. The easiest way out of a difficult situation was to just not schedule the person for any more duty shifts. The tendency was to avoid a confrontation with the worker about his inadequacies. Two of the programs would try to find some type of work for the volunteer to do in the center other than work on the telephone, but it was evident that there was little regard for the needs and feelings of the worker who was unsuitable for duty. This is clearly an issue to which program directors should pay careful attention in current programs.

Attitude Toward Management of Volunteers

How does one approach a volunteer in terms of his commitment to the program? Since he is, in fact, not being paid, should he not be treated with kid gloves, coddled, and allowed pretty much to have his way? Or is it appropriate to set firm limits and expectations on volunteers? Four of the centers were explicit in their belief that a volunteer crisis worker should be dealt with as if he were an employee from whom the program had the right to demand and expect a certain level and extent of service. Only two centers preferred to treat their people as if they were entitled to make their own decisions about when and how they should perform their voluntary role. One director said she expected her volunteers to show "commitment without any question" to the program. Another director said that he expected a lot from the workers, and that if they were going to get anything out of the work they would have to give a lot. In general, observations of the centers which have used volunteers have led to the conclusion that those programs which demand high levels of commitment and expect unflinching performance from their people are the ones with fewest morale problems and the most satisfactory programs. Such an attitude conveys the notion that the center means business in every aspect of its operation. It is not a hobby or a part-time activity to be discarded when people are through playing the game. Rather, the crisis center that makes heavy demands upon its workers for performance and loyalty also tends to take its mission with clients seriously.

Training of Volunteer Crisis Workers

There are still many questions which are unanswered about the training of crisis intervention personnel. In 1967, the programs were doing an admirable job if they did any training at all. The first thing which the early programs thought of was that it was necessary to get a psychiatrist to lecture on the symptoms of emotional disorder. Many centers included a lecture on personality types, diagnostic categories of mental illness, and neurotic defense mechanisms. This was a standard elementary course in psychopathology, and it was felt that it was absolutely necessary for crisis intervention personnel. Hardly any center uses such material at the present time.

Five of the programs made extensive use of films during their training. In those days, there were only two or three films, *The Cry for Help* being the most popular. Other training techniques included role playing, listening to tapes of calls previously taken in the center or borrowed from other programs, and assigning readings in the few books which were available in the field. The papers distributed from the Los Angeles Suicide Prevention Center constituted most of the reading. Nearly all programs used a format which involved lectures from professional people, followed by a general group discussion. One center even developed multiple-choice quizzes to give the workers as a measure of how well they had learned their material, but these were discontinued when it was discovered that the test scores bore no relationship to the workers' performance on the job.

Six of the seven programs indicated that they had learned that the best approach to training was to give a general orientation and then to start the trainees to work on the telephones observing and in an apprenticeship role with more experienced volunteers. They followed this with regular and systematic in-service training. There was only one center which required its people to have all of their training before they went to work. Actually, this is one of the most significant findings of the earlier crisis programs. They would never have started their programs if they had decided to wait until the techniques were already developed. They went ahead, learned by doing, and have established procedures which new centers can use with a high degree of confidence. The training by orientation, followed by in-service training once or twice a month, is a procedure which nearly all centers adopt sooner or later. It should be recognized as a solid contribution from the early pioneer programs.

There is no denying that suicide and crisis intervention centers of the present era owe much to the programs which attempted to chart new courses during the latter part of the 1960's. The greatest debt is owed because of the unequivocal demonstration of the feasibility and desirability of the volunteer nonprofessional manpower pool. Other contributions came from the early experiences of programs with their professional personnel. Many hard battles were fought, many tempers flared, and feelings were hurt because the programs were feeling their way in the dark as volunteers tried timidly to court and win the affection of the professionals. One hospital administrator in a major city put it simply: "These people have come here asking us if we'll get out on the floor and dance with them. We don't dance with strangers!'" Such statements, repeated hundreds of times in different ways, resulted in frustrations and hard knocks before the techniques of getting along with professionalized interests could be passed on to the current generation of crisis intervention systems. The result, however, has been worth the struggle, and as a result of the brave programs which pioneered unknown man- power issues, both volunteers and professionals now have a role in community crisis programs. No longer are there manpower shortages in the field of helping services. Only professional mental health practitioners are still in short supply. The real professional crisis worker has emerged in the form of the volunteer, whose availability has only begun to be tapped and whose devotion and dedica- tion to the needs of fellow human beings are not constrained by time-honored roles and artificial status distinctions. The manpower issues in crisis intervention programs are now the easiest problems to solve when a new program is organized.

7
RECORD KEEPING AND STATISTICS IN CRISIS PROGRAMS

Some directors of crisis intervention centers find it difficult to overemphasize the importance of record keeping in their programs. On the other hand, there are others for whom record keeping has been a very neglected and low-priority practice. Both types of programs appeared in this study. Each of the 10 programs was asked to complete a questionnaire designed to elicit a description of its record-keeping system, the uses to which it was put, and the statistical compilation of data which the program made of its service activity. The responses ranged from none at all to very complete descriptions and elaborate documents containing tables of data on the services being rendered. An analysis of the responses made to this portion of the study yields the conclusion that the records and statistics a center keeps may be used as another reflection of the concept that the center holds of itself, of its service program, and of its mission in the community.

Some of the centers submitted documents which were formal annual reports prepared for the Board of Directors. These documents clearly indicated that the program considered itself to be an agency within the community, and that it wanted to be both recognized and held accountable by the community for the quantity of service it was producing. Other centers submitted sets of tables which were periodically compiled for the purpose of informing the workers and other interested parties as to what the program had accomplished during the past few months. There were at least five programs which had prepared no data at all on their operations, and three of these could not even get together sufficient data out of their own files to fill out the questionnaire for this study. (They agreed to permit one of the investigators to visit their center and compile whatever was considered desirable by tallying entries out of individual case files.)

Record keeping, like the telephone answering system, seems on the surface to be such an important aspect of program operation that the wide variance in the extent of planning for it would never have been suspected had this study not been undertaken. Since it does emerge as an often neglected area, it may be necessary to indicate some of the basic reasons for keeping records and compiling statistical summaries.

The first, and most obvious, reason for keeping records is to provide a consistent clinical service to individual clients who contact the center for help. Unless a program sees itself as successfully managing every problem presented during the first telephone call, it must expect that clients will contact the center on subsequent occasions. There must be a continuity to the service each client receives; otherwise, each new worker must start all over at the beginning on each call. This information must be systematically recorded in the client's file. Printed forms specifically calling for essential factual data and narrative summaries of the problem and the interaction with the client should be included. One of the first indications that a center properly values and uses clinical records in its service may be obtained from learning whether or not the workers answer the calls in the office, where there is access to filing systems, or whether they try to work out of their homes, with no case records available.

The second reason for keeping records is to learn what operational demands the program must meet. What are the busiest days, times of day, months of the year? Is it possible to plan for the times when two or more workers must be available to meet the expected caseload? A center which has never asked such questions or which has never tried to answer them systematically is revealing a minimum of planning for its operation. Is the program receiving more calls at any given time than one month or six months earlier? Such information can reveal whether or not a service is still growing into a viable community service or whether it is losing its image as a source of personal help.

A third reason for record keeping is to find out about the characteristics of callers that a center is attracting. Is the program reaching the high-risk population relative to suicide and suicide attempts in the community? Are the clients predominantly of one subpopulation of the community, so that the workers should be recruited who can understand and help this population? Are some populations not represented at all, and if so, why not?

Records kept in the crisis center should have broad community interest and value. Certainly, in an area of scientific investigation which is still growing to the extent that is true of suicidology, accurate and complete research data must be available from many sources. Not only will newspaper articles about the service stimulate its utilization, but authentic and scholarly reporting of suicide will aid in removing the taboo which is still associated with the behavior. The suicide and crisis service has an obligation to facilitate such a movement. Finally, other agencies and helpers also have a responsibility to clients and may be better able to assist them if there is a sharing of information with the crisis center.

The greatest benefit to the center itself from complete and accurate record keeping would derive from presenting regular data concerning the service effectiveness to the local United Way campaign, the local city and county governments, and all other organizations which might be possible funding sources. Any appeal for public money must be supported by statistical evidence that the program is doing something. If this self-seeking purpose were the only reason to keep records, it is still amazing that five of the centers studied could produce no data on their programs. Perhaps it is not an unrelated fact that three of these five programs are now no longer in operation, and the other two have been absorbed into other agencies which manage their records for them.

This chapter discusses both the record keeping practices and the statistics compiled in the 10 programs surveyed. The distinction between record keeping and statistics should be made clear. Records are considered the "raw data" from which summaries can be developed to describe the program. Statistics considered in this chapter are those descriptive summaries which are compiled from the records. It is very possible that records may be kept systematically but that no statistics are ever compiled. This may be because there is no one in the program to do it or because no one in the center knows what summary tables are relevant. More likely, however, the lack of statistical presentations is the result of insufficient planning of the recording system, so that the information cannot be retrieved with any degree of facility.

RECORD KEEPING IN SUICIDE PREVENTION CENTERS

Only two of the 10 centers failed to respond to this portion of the study; neither LIFELINE nor FRIENDS gave any information about their records. It is known, however, that both programs considered record keeping as a very low-priority activity and one which was barely emphasized by the program coordinators. One of the difficulties FRIENDS had in making its merger with the Mental Health Association in Dade County was over the issue of records. They had never kept records, and they explicitly resented the implication that "research interests" might take precedence over their service to clients. LIFELINE, on the other hand, did keep records, but they were very careless about them. Partly as a result of this study, and as a favor to the director for participating in it, the investigator agreed to take all of the program's records and compile what data could be gleaned from them. After one year's existence, a total of 138 record forms had been filed in the office. However, the answering service had logged approximately 600 calls transferred to the workers. Consequently, only very rough estimates could be projected of the service from a small sample of cases.

The participating programs were asked to indicate what types of records they routinely kept. Their responses are tallied in Table 1. It is evident that only Orlando and Nashville centers kept all five types of data. Halifax County and Atlanta centers kept four types of data regularly. It is not coincidental that all four of these programs had been influenced heavily by psychologists or sociologists during their early planning and development. Those programs which had the benefit of social science technology were led to plan carefully for the task of record keeping and did an adequate job of it.

Only three of the centers described the details of their record keeping systems; very little is known about the others. Obviously, they all had some type

Table 1 Types of records which were regularly kept by each of the suicide prevention programs

Center	Clinical records on clients	Records on operation of the program	Suicide behavior in local area	Records to be used solely for research	Records on individual crisis workers
Nashville	X	X	X	X	X
Knoxville	X				
Atlanta	X	X	X	X	
Chattanooga	X		X		
Orlando	X	X	X	X	X
St. Petersburg	X	X			
Halifax	X	X	X	X	
Brevard County	X	X			X

of client file, with at least a face sheet and maybe a narrative summary of the case. Most programs keep a telephone log, also. This log should be used to record every incoming call. It should contain notations as to whether the call is a new case, a repeater, or a continuing case under current management. It should also indicate the type of problem presented by the client, the name of the volunteer who took the call, the length of time spent, and of course, the date and time of the call. Nearly all necessary data about the operation of a crisis center can be taken from a well-planned and properly used telephone log. Some centers also use the same log for recording outgoing calls to clients for case management activities. Fully adequate incoming and outgoing telephone logs can be used to yield a complete picture of the activity within a crisis intervention center.

All of the centers indicated that their records were available to all personnel in the program, with only two exceptions. These included the restriction of records concerning the workers to the professional staff, and the restriction of client records to those volunteers who had successfully finished training and definitely were going to work on the telephone. There seems to be no secrecy about the records as far as the workers are concerned. It might be added here that occasionally a center finds itself in the position of having workers volunteer for training and duty who have themselves been prior clients. In such cases, the staff usually removes their files from the system and maintains them separately. Many centers have the experience of providing emergency help to one of their own workers during an acute crisis. In such cases, usually the case is treated as an "informal favor" rendered to a friend, and no case file is even made. Such cases are not even counted as crisis center business.

Sharing Records with Persons outside the Center

Eight of the 10 centers submitted an indication of how their records might be used by others outside of their agency. A series of 15 hypothetical situations was presented, and the center was asked if its records would be released in each situation. The center was given three options for responding to each item:

1. The records definitely would be released;
2. The records might be released, but clearance would be necessary;
3. The records definitely would not be released.

Table 2 reproduces these 15 items and indicates how the programs responded to them. It is evident in this table that there is high agreement on some of the issues,

Table 2 Number of crisis intervention centers which would or would not release their records in 15 different situations

Condition of request for records	Attitude toward sharing records		
	Definitely would give (1)	Would not give unless cleared (2)	Definitely would not give (3)
1. A physician asks for information about one of his patients who called you	7	1	0
2. A college student wants to write a term paper about types of people who call your center	2	3	3
3. A neighbor knows one of your callers and wants to know how to help him	0	6	2
4. A graduate student in sociology wants to study the demography of your cases for his Ph.D. dissertation	3	5	0
5. A local physician wants to look at your case records to see how many of his patients have ever called you	0	6	2

Table 2 continued on next page.

Table 2 continued.

Condition of request for records	Attitude toward sharing records		
	Definitely would give (1)	Would not give unless cleared (2)	Definitely would not give (3)
6. A local psychiatrist wants to study the personality character-istics of all your volunteers	1	7	0
7. The newspaper wants to write a feature story about specific cases (unnamed) and how you have helped them	0	5	3
8. An insurance company representa-tive wants to check your records for information prior to writing policies for customers	0	1	7
9. An insurance company executive wants to study your files in order to learn about suicide statistics in the area	1	4	3
10. The United Fund board wants to study your records to learn what you do before deciding to grant you support	2	5	1
11. One of your volunteers wants to learn as much as possible about all the volunteers before making a talk to a civic club on what kinds of people you like to recruit	4	4	0
12. A social scientist from a distant university wants to study how your volunteers handle cases	4	4	0
13. An investigator from another suicide center wants to search your records to compare your program with others	4	4	0

continued.

Table 2 continued.

Condition of request for records	Attitude toward sharing records		
	Definitely would give (1)	Would not give unless cleared (2)	Definitely would not give (3)
14. A minister wants to check your records in order to learn which people in the community need a church affiliation	0	3	5
15. The dean at a local college wants to send someone in to determine how many and which students need help	0	6	2

but no clearly consistent attitude toward others. For example, the attitudes toward giving information about clients to physicians is clearly positive, whereas the attitude of giving information to an insurance agent is equally clear and negative. The tendency to give information to a student writing a term paper is highly variable among the centers. It was observed immediately that the centers differed greatly from one another on the number of times they selected the "definitely would give" and "definitely would not give" options. Table 3 was produced to enable a more careful study of this difference. This table shows how many times each center elected each of the three options. Naturally, the more times a center reports it definitely would give information, together with the fewer times it reported it definitely would not give information, the more the center sees itself as cooperating freely with other people and agencies in the community. Thus, a "Cooperation ratio" can be computed for each of the centers by dividing the number of responses to option number 1 by the number of responses to option number 3. The cooperation ratio is shown in Table 3.

The data in the column for option number 2 in Table 3 may be some indication of how much freedom and autonomy a center director has in making decisions for the program. Those centers in which option number 2 was elected frequently require that someone in authority give clearance to release information. One center which chose this option for 12 out of the 15 items appended a note saying that the medical director would have to approve any release of information. It may be suspected that some information would not be released unless permission were granted by the client, but there were only a few items which related to individual client information.

A further analysis of the data in Table 2 reveals that the 15 items can be grouped into four categories. When the responses of the eight crisis centers were

Table 3 Individual center attitudes toward sharing records with other persons or agencies

Center	Number of items checked			
	Would give (1)	Must be cleared (2)	Would not give (3)	Cooperation ratio*
Orlando	7	6	2	3.50
St. Petersburg	2	12	1	2.00
Brevard County	5	7	3	1.67
Halifax County	5	5	5	1.00
Nashville	2	10	3	0.67
Knoxville	3	7	5	0.60
Chattanooga	3	5	7	0.43
Atlanta	1	11	3	0.33

*Cooperation Ratio = $\dfrac{\text{option (1)}}{\text{option (3)}}$

tallied and observed with reference to these categories, it was possible to see the operation of specific attitudes reflected in the use of center records. These data may be observed in Table 4. It is interesting to note that only one of the programs responded "definitely would give" information to two of the three items related to sharing information for purposes related to general community interests. The two centers which responded "definitely no" in two of the three community items had certain characteristics in common. Both were highly dominated by the local mental health system, and neither service was well integrated into its community; neither center is still operating.

The other very interesting observation in Table 4 relates to the tendency to give or to withhold information requested by individuals about clients or about the general caseload. It is a revealing fact that seven of the eight programs unhesitatingly would give information to a physician about an individual client. However, they would not give information to an insurance agent. What is more surprising is that five of the eight definitely would not give information to a minister. Two programs would not provide any help to a dean of students, a concerned neighbor, or a physician who wanted to learn something about his patients generally. It is a clear demonstration of the "doctor worshipping" phenomenon to note that nearly all the centers appear to feel that information given to a physician would be used ethically, legitimately, and for a purpose which

Table 4 Individual center attitudes toward giving out specific types of information from their records

Release of information	St. Petersburg	Nashville	Knoxville	Brevard County	Chattanooga	Atlanta	Orlando	Halifax County
Relative to community interests								
United Fund	+*		−				+	
Newspaper		−			−	−		
Insurance rates			−			−	+	−
About crisis workers								
To psychiatrist							+	
To civic group	+	+				+	+	
For research purposes								
Student's paper		−	+	+	−		−	+
Study how cases handled				+	+		+	+
Compare programs				+	+		+	+
Ph.D. dissertation				+				
Personal/professional interest in clients								
Neighbor			−	−				
Minister			−	−	−	−		−
Dean of students				−				−
Physician (1)	+	+	+	+	+		+	+
Physician (2)				−		−		
Insurance agent	−	−	−	−	−		−	−

* +, definitely would give; −, definitely would not give; no entry indicates need for clearance.

would be helpful to clients, whereas information given to neighbors, deans, insurance agents, and ministers would be harmful and perhaps illegitimately used against the client's welfare. There is an assumption that the interests of an insurance agent in a community are less valuable or honorable than those of a physician. If patient data must be guarded for confidentiality and privacy—as it certainly must—then the same ethic should apply equally to all who might ask for the information. It might be interesting to determine how many of the centers which would give information unhesitatingly to a physician might receive patient information from the doctor if they were to ask him for it! If a center truly thinks of itself as a member of the helping community, it will find a way to share data equally with all persons who may serve the community or the clients and will find ways to provide this assistance within a context of client privacy and confidentiality.

Efficiency of the Record Systems

Records which contain information that cannot be retrieved when needed are barely better than having no records at all. Each of the programs was asked to indicate how accessible certain facts were in its record systems. The centers were asked to indicate whether each of 26 different types of information:

1. was always available at fingertip;
2. could be obtained easily in the office;
3. could be obtained with difficulty;
4. probably could not be obtained at all.

Table 5 reproduces these 26 items and shows the number of times each of the four options was selected by the eight centers responding.

Table 5 Number of crisis intervention centers whose information is accessible in four levels of availability

	The information			
Question to be answered	Available at fingertip always (1)	Can be obtained easily in office (2)	Can be obtained but with difficulty (3)	Probably could not be obtained (4)
1. Has Mary Smith ever called before?	2	6		
2. What was done for her; outcome?		7	1	
3. A patient called 6 months ago; how is he now?		3	1	4
4. How many people who call are being seen by psychiatrists?			5	3
5. What was suicide rate in area the five years before the program started?	1	3	3	1
6. In which area of town do most of the callers live?	1	2	5	
7. Which day of week is busiest?		4	4	
8. What percentage of suicide deaths are due to specific methods of injury?	1	2	4	1

continued.

Table 5 continued.

Question to be answered	The information			
	Available at fingertip always (1)	Can be obtained easily in office (2)	Can be obtained but with difficulty (3)	Probably could not be obtained (4)
9. How many meetings has Mr. X (volunteer) attended? How many missed?		3	4	1
10. Is Mrs. Y. (volunteer) a reliable worker?	1	4	2	1
11. Which volunteer has the best success with cases?	1	1	5	1
12. How many calls come into the program each day?		8		
13. What percentage of calls involve marital crises?		5	2	1
14. Do people who repeat get more serious on later calls?		7	1	
15. How many volunteers do you have with a college degree?	1	4	3	
16. What is the average age of the female volunteers?		4	4	
17. Has John Smith made a suicide attempt?	1	3	1	3
18. Has the number of serious suicide calls decreased in last six months?		4	3	1
19. A famous personality commits suicide. What effect does this have on suicidal behavior in your community?	1	1	3	3

Table 5 continued on next page.

Table 5 continued.

	The information			
Question to be answered	Available at fingertip always (1)	Can be obtained easily in office (2)	Can be obtained but with difficulty (3)	Probably could not be obtained (4)
20. What percentage of callers do you refer to "X" community agency?		4	3	1
21. How many calls have you had so far this year?	1	7		
22. Is this more or less than last year?	1	7		
23. Is the suicide death rate higher or lower than this time in previous years?	1	5	2	
24. What is average number of *new* cases each week?		6		1
25. What percentage of callers are referred to psychiatrists for treatment?		4	4	
26. What percent of callers have followed your referral recommendations?		1	4	3

Once more, the individual centers differed greatly in the number of times they selected the four response options to describe the accessibility of their data. These differences may be observed directly in Table 6. Here, it may be seen that some programs can retrieve information very easily, whereas others seem not to have many answers to important questions available to them. By combining these data, it is possible to compute a "record efficiency index" for each center. This index was computed by adding two times the number of responses to option number 1 to the number of responses to option number 2. This sum was then divided by the sum of responses to option number 3 plus two times the number of responses to option number 4. The centers are listed in Table 6 in the order of their record efficiency index.

This information merely indicates whether or not a center tends to value records and if they have established a system for storing and retrieving them when

Table 6 Relative availability of 26 items of information in the records of each center

| Center | Number of items checked | | | | Record efficiency index* |
	Always available (1)	Easily computed (2)	Difficult to compute (3)	Could not be obtained (4)	
Halifax	9	9	5	3	2.45
Brevard County	0	19	6	1	2.38
Nashville	0	18	7	1	2.00
Atlanta	1	14	10	1	1.33
St. Petersburg	1	14	9	2	1.23
Orlando	0	15	8	3	1.07
Knoxville	1	12	8	5	0.50
Chattanooga	1	4	12	9	0.20

*Record efficiency index $= \dfrac{2(1) + (2)}{(3) + 2(4)}$

necessary. It is also possible to determine what kind of records the centers tend to value most by looking carefully at their individual responses to the 26 items in Table 5. These items can be grouped into six categories, as shown in Table 7. Each center then was given a score for its responses to the items in each category. The score was determined by assigning weights and plus or minus values to the responses to each option as follows:

response to option number 1 = +2
response to option number 2 = +1
response to option number 3 = −1
response to option number 4 = −2

Then the algebraic sum of these response values was obtained for each center for the items in each data category. These scores ranged from high-positive to low-negative values. However, since it was not important to compare the individual centers a second time, the scores for each center were ranked in order to show which of the six data categories was most valued. A value of six was assigned to the category having the highest score in each center's column. These ranks are seen in Table 7.

It is reasonable to conclude that the ease with which a center can retrieve

Table 7 Ranking of categories of information according to availability in each center

Categories of records	Halifax County	Brevard County	Nashville	Atlanta	St. Petersburg	Orlando	Knoxville	Chattanooga
Individual callers (items 1; 2; 3; 17)*	2.5	2	5	5.5	5	3.5	3	5
Characteristics of callers in general (items 6; 13; 14; 18)	2.5	4	2	3	3	5	5.5	3.5
Extent of call traffic (items 7; 12; 21; 22; 24)	5	5.5	6 ·	5.5	6	6	5.5	6
Local suicide (items 5; 8; 19; 23)	6	1	3	2	2	3.5	3	3.5
Success in referral of callers (items 4; 20; 25; 26)	1	3	4	1	1	1	3	1
Crisis workers (items 9; 10; 11; 15; 16)	4	5.5	1	4	4	2	1	2

*See Table 5 for description of item.

information from its files reflects the potential value which that information has for the agency. Those which are interested in certain kinds of data will have arranged to extract it from their files. If they have made little or no provision for obtaining it, the reason is probably that they have little or no interest in such information. Table 7 reveals that all of the centers place a high premium on data reflecting the amount of traffic through their telephone system. Likewise, there is a fairly consistent disinterest in knowing how successful they are in making effective referrals of clients to other agencies. Only one of the centers seems to value information on the suicidal behavior in its local area; similarly, only one is relatively interested in having accessible information about its crisis workers.

STATISTICAL COMPILATION OF DATA IN CRISIS INTERVENTION CENTERS

Each of the programs was asked to provide some descriptive data on its caseloads. The centers were asked to submit some information to show the characteristics of their clients and of their program operation. Only five centers had any such data available. These programs sent copies of reports, statistical summaries, and other documents which provided the requested information. It is not relevant for purposes of this chapter to reproduce the data provided by these centers. What is important is a listing of the tables, charts, and other statistical statements which a center is able to make about itself upon request. Table 8 is a listing of these tables and other data. For each center, the information is listed as either a table (T), a chart or a figure (C), or a narrative statement (N).

Table 8 reveals that four of the five programs have compiled data relative to suicidal behavior in their immediate service area. These data varied considerably in

Table 8 Descriptive statistics compiled by each suicide prevention program in annual reports or periodic summaries of the service

Center	Form	Data compiled in statistical form
Atlanta	T*	Suicides in Fulton County: race and sex distribution
	T	Suicides in Fulton County: age distribution
	T	Suicides in Fulton County: marital status distribution
	T	Percentage of suicidal and nonsuicidal persons with mental illness
	T	New calls to the center by month
	T	New calls to the center by day of the week
	T	Hourly distribution of new calls by sex of caller
	T	Age distribution of new callers and local population
	T	Marital status of new callers and local population by sex
	T	Resources to which callers were referred
	T	Suicidal history of new callers
	T	Suicidal involvement at time of call
	N	Alcohol consumption at time of call
	N	Employment at time of call
	N	History of psychiatric treatment of new callers
	T	County of residence of new callers
	N	Characteristics of initial contacts
Knoxville	N	Mean age of suicides in Knox County
	T	Suicides in Knox County by sex and race
	T	Suicides in Knox County by time of day
	T	Marital status of suicides in Knox County
	T	Age and sex of suicides in Knox County
	T	Location of suicides in Knox County by sex
	T	Method of injury of suicides in Knox County by sex
	C	Frequency of suicides in Knox County on each day of week by sex
	C	Frequency of suicides in Knox County each month by sex
	C	Frequency of suicides in Knox County for each a.m. hour by sex
	C	Frequency of suicides in Knox County for each p.m. hour by sex

Table 8 continued on next page.

Table 8 continued.

Center	Form	Data compiled in statistical form
Orlando	T	Number of callers by race and sex, 1968
	T	Number of callers by age groups, 1968
	T	Number of callers by marital status, 1968
	T	Number of callers by day of week and hour of day
	T	Types of calls by month
	N	Number of individual callers and calls per individual client
	T	Number of identified and unidentified callers
	T	Suicide attempts by sex and race
	T	Suicide attempts by age groups
	T	Suicide attempts by marital status
	T	Methods employed in suicide attempts
	T	Suicide attempts by day of week
	T	Suicide deaths by sex and race in Orange County
	T	Suicide deaths by age groups in Orange County
	T	Suicide deaths by marital status in Orange County
	T	Suicide deaths by method of injury in Orange County
	T	Suicide deaths by age and sex in Orange County
Nashville	T	Types of calls by month
	N	Residence of callers
	N	Number of cases initiated by client, friends, other agencies
	N	Suicide history of callers
	N	Number of clients identified and not identified
	N	Previous counseling or treatment of callers
	N	Outcome of calls in terms of successful referrals or deaths
	T	Number of callers reporting specific types of problems
	T	Distribution of callers by sex and race
	T	Distribution of callers by age groups
	T	Distribution of calls by day of week
	T	Distribution of calls during periods of the day
	T	Number of new cases presenting specific situations
	T	Number of new cases in which crisis worker took specific actions
	T	Method of injury in suicide attempts, metropolitan Nashville
	T	Suicide attempts by race and sex, metropolitan Nashville
	T	Suicide attempts by age groups, metropolitan Nashville
	T	Methods of injury in suicide deaths, 5 years in metropolitan Nashville
	T	Suicide deaths by race and sex for 5 years, metropolitan Nashville
	T	Suicide deaths by age groups for 5 years, metropolitan Nashville
	T	Suicide deaths by month, for 5 years, metropolitan Nashville
	C	Methods of suicide attempts and deaths in Nashville
	C	Suicide deaths and attempts by age groups in Nashville
	C	Callers to Crisis Call Center by type of problem

continued.

Table 8 continued.

Center	Form	Data compiled in statistical form
	C	Callers to Crisis Call Center by age groups
	T	Number of callers by sex
	T	Number of callers by age groups
Miami	T	Number of callers by marital status
(LIFELINE)	T	Number of callers by employment status
	T	Prior suicidal behavior of callers
	T	Number of new cases and repeaters
	T	Frequency of specific actions by crisis workers
	T	Other resources called in to aid caller
	T	Mobilization plan developed for caller
	T	Outcome of crisis intervention contact
	T	Number of calls by month
	T	Number of calls by day of week
	T	Number of calls by time of day

*T, table; C, chart or figure; N, narrative statement.

form. One center reported numbers of actual deaths for the six years prior to opening the service. It did not report population data or compute suicide rates in the customary manner. Only one center reproduced any actual rate data for its area. Likewise, four of the five programs produced several tables reflecting the extent of telephone traffic at different times, on different days, and during the 12 months. A study of Table 8 may give a center director a good indication of the kind of statistical information compiled by a small sample of centers. Perhaps some of these tables and charts are not totally necessary, but the majority of them would be very beneficial to have on hand to influence local funding sources, to orient volunteers as to the task of the program in the community, or to assure a board of directors that the program is a worthwhile activity.

In summary, it should be reemphasized that record keeping and statistical compilation of data is an absolutely essential aspect of a community crisis intervention program. It is a sine qua non for any service which considers itself an agency in the network of helping services in the community. Further, there are a number of distinct advantages even for a program that is content to be just a telephone service. The attention and serious interest which a program director gives to the record system reflects as much about the center and its program as do the quality and efficiency of its telephone answering system. Both are a measure of the maturity and development of the program, and both reflect its capacity to fulfill its mission to people needing crisis intervention services.

8
PUBLIC RELATIONS AND COMMUNITY INVOLVEMENT OF CRISIS INTERVENTION PROGRAMS

When the Nashville Crisis Call Center moved into the Community Mental Health Center at Meharry Medical Center, the psychiatrist-director of the new mental health program made a very explicit statement about the new relationship. She said, "Crisis Call Center is now a part of our mental health program, but it does not belong to Meharry. Crisis Call Center belongs to the Nashville community, and it will continue to belong to the community." The Nashville program was planned as a community crisis center and has continually been one example of the community model of crisis centers described in Chapter 2. One of the essential characteristics of the community model is the requirement that a program function as a cooperative unit within the total network of helping services in the community. Some of the 10 centers studied in this project fulfill that requirement and some clearly do not.

A crisis intervention system must belong to the entire community. The nature of its work, together with the fact that there are no eligibility requirements for receiving service, demand that it be able to respond with equal potency and credibility to problems brought by every segment of the population. There are no fees; thus, the well-to-do and the disadvantaged receive equally active treatment. Crisis knows no racial or ethnic boundaries and favors no special age group. It occurs as frequently among the conservative establishment as among the liberal counter-culture. The inebriated housewife whose husband has locked her out of the $50,000 home in the suburbs, the radical student "tripping" on LSD, and the illiterate migrant farm laborer drifting through town all need a bed for the night and perhaps some emotional support to encounter the decisions which may come with sunrise the next day. A motel might take one of them; the Salvation Army surely would not take more than one. Another might find a bed in a hospital emergency room. One, or perhaps two, might be able to spend the night in jail. One might call the crisis center directly; two might be referred by the police. Perhaps friends would call about two of the clients, and one might be sent by the ticket agent at the Greyhound Bus station. In all three cases, it is very likely that the crisis intervention center would be asked to locate immediate shelter, provide transportation, and plan follow-up action. The crisis center must be able to "walk on all sides of the street" at the same time.

It is obvious from the simple example cited above that the crisis center is unlike any other helping system in the community, in that its client population lacks the restricted range which characterizes other populations. Obviously, some agencies serve only the disadvantaged. Some serve only the affluent or the elderly. Some serve primarily the middle class, educated, psychologically oriented suburban dwellers. Agencies with service programs designed for or adapted through years of relationship with specific subgroups of the population must maintain a certain level of involvement with the total community, but a crisis intervention service must have quite a different degree of involvement. It must develop and maintain a public image that is markedly different from those of other agencies. There are two primary considerations in assessing the community involvement of crisis intervention systems. These are: (1) the advertising and publicity practices that the center employs, and (2) the degree of involvement it has with other helping services in the area. The remainder of this chapter is devoted to a discussion of these two issues as they were observed in the study sample.

ADVERTISING AND PUBLICITY

How many helping agencies in the community actively advertise their ability to the public? How many personal services strive to maintain maximum visibility to the public? How many need to? One of the major distinctions between crisis intervention services and the mental health system is in the degree of active advertising each pursues. It must be carried out by the former, and it is considered unethical by the latter.

Most suicide prevention and crisis intervention systems have made extensive use of free public service spot announcements on local radio and television stations. Nearly all programs have been the subject of newspaper articles. The initial opening of each center nearly always was carried in news articles. Its continued operation and service program was monitored periodically in feature articles on the women's page or in family sections of Sunday editions. Some centers have been especially creative in their advertising schemes. For instance, in Orlando, the director arranged with a local technical training school to use the printing of advertising cards for city buses as a training experience for the printing shop trainees. The crisis center paid $9 for materials, and cards advertising WE

Table 1 Number of centers using specific methods to make the public aware of the service

Advertising method	Number of centers using	Votes for most effect-ive method	Votes for least effect-ive method
Radio/television spot announcements	6	2	
Newspaper ads	2	2	
News/feature articles	10	5	1
Radio/television programs	5		2
Billboards; bus card ads	2		
Posters in public buildings	1		
Speakers Bureau	4		1
Mailing to groups	4		1
Arrangements with:			
police	7		
hospitals	6		
motels	3		
taxi drivers	2		
Yellow pages phone book	8		1
Brochures, pamphlets, business cards	6		

CARE, Inc., were carried as a public service in all of the buses in all parts of the city.

Each of the programs was asked to indicate which advertising methods it had used and to report the ones which it felt were most and least effective. The results of this inquiry are shown in Table 1.

It is evident from the table that newspaper articles are the most popular in terms of both their universal use and their effectiveness. Nearly all the programs have made arrangements also with local police to refer or bring in clients who are suicidal. Several have similar arrangements with the hospitals, and two have thought of the taxi driver as another significant gatekeeper for lonely, distressed people. The classified section of the telephone directory is another frequently used method of advertising. At the time this study was made, it was not acceptable to the Bell Telephone system to list the suicide prevention programs on the inside front cover of the directory with other emergency numbers. However, beginning in 1971, that policy relaxed in the Southeast, and any program which is covered 24 hours a day and which shows promise of being in operation throughout the life of the directory can qualify for an emergency listing on the inside front cover.

Each of the centers was also asked about the frequency of its advertising on the radio and television stations and in the newspaper. They reported usually five or six articles in the paper per year. The range was from three articles in four months to 30 in two and one-half years. None of the programs had established special arrangements with individual newspaper reporters. They were not on anyone's "beat" for regular reporting or feature writing. Table 2 shows the frequency of advertising in the mass media for the nine centers which provided information. It is of interest that two of them do not make any public announcements regularly in the newspapers or on radio and television. It should be noted that newspaper advertising is not the same as news or feature reporting. Table 2 reflects only actual advertisements in the classified section, usually under the "Personal" heading.

Table 2 Frequency with which individual centers are advertised in mass media

Center	Frequency of advertising in media			Frequency of new copy
	Radio spots (all stations)	Television spots (all stations)	Newspaper ads	
LIFELINE			1/day	Not changed
Nashville	15–20/day			3 weeks
St. Petersburg	Make no public announcements			
Knoxville	4/day	1/week		2 months
Atlanta	Information not reported			
Orlando	2/day	2/week		4–6 weeks
Brevard County	Sporadic	Sporadic		Not changed
Chattanooga	3/week			4 weeks
FRIENDS			1/day	Not changed
Halifax County	Make no public announcements			

It is possible to make some inference about how seriously a center takes its advertising efforts from the frequency with which its copy is changed. A few centers make an arrangement for a particular ad, and it is left unchanged. Others regularly and routinely vary their copy. Obviously, fresh copy attracts more attention and may reach new populations, but it requires effort and the concentration of attention on the advertising program. For some centers, extensive public awareness is not worth either the money or the effort, or perhaps both. In one program, which was part of the community mental health system, it was a violation of its professionalized self-concept to actively solicit the attention of the public.

Naturally, it should be of interest to those centers which do advertise in various media to know which of their methods are most successful in actually attracting clients, or whether their notices are differentially reaching specific populations of citizens. Surprisingly, however, none of the centers required that the telephone crisis workers attempt to ascertain how each caller had heard about the program. Three of them replied that they encouraged their people to ask for that information, but there was no place on the record forms for it to be entered. Often, they felt it inappropriate to ask such a question, or the telephone workers felt uncomfortable asking it. Although three centers encouraged the collection of such information, only one made even occasional efforts to collate the data from its files. Obviously, there was very little attention paid to this seemingly important piece of data about the public image of the crisis center. Six of the programs could make no estimates of the percentage of clients who heard about the service from the various sources. Among the other four, newspaper articles were credited with bringing in between 10 and 40 percent of the clients. Radio and television spot announcements were credited with bringing in between 30 and 40 percent of the clients. Police agencies were named by two centers as sending 10 percent, and a third agency received 10 percent of its callers as a result of public speeches made to church and civic groups. In Halifax County, local ministers referred approximately 25 percent of the cases. Two centers estimated that 25 and 40 percent of the callers, respectively, came from informal referral or word-of-mouth information shared among citizens of the community, rather than as a direct result of any formal advertising. It should be emphasized that these statements are only very rough approximations and are not based upon any substantial data collected by any of the four agencies. It may be that the most accurate statements are those from the six centers which reported that they had no idea how their callers heard about the service.

In a further effort to assess how much public awareness there was about each of the crisis centers, they were asked to estimate how often other people seem to be already aware of the existence of the program when they are contacted about clients. Once more, six of the centers could make no reply to this question. The responses of the other four are shown in Table 3. The columns representing the frequency with which relatives and friends of the client are aware of the service

Table 3 Estimates of awareness of the community that the crisis center existed

Center*	Percentage of times people knew of the center when they were contacted regarding a crisis center caller				
	Caller's relatives	Caller's friends	Caller's physician	Caller's minister	Other agencies
Halifax County	100	75	100	100	90
Orlando	75	50	90	95	90
Knoxville	20	10	20	75	90
Nashville	50	10	90	25	90

*Only four centers responded.

probably reflect the extent of effective advertising among the general public. It is not surprising that groups of physicians, ministers, and other helping agencies knew about the service through selective announcements which could not be considered public advertising. This explains the typically high percentage of occasions that physicians and other agencies are aware of the crisis service when they are contacted by the service in behalf of a caller.

One response to this question should receive specific mention. It came from a mental health center affiliated program which replied that its service policy was based upon "one-to-one patient care" practices, and thus they would not contact anyone else in regard to their clients. Such a practice is typical of, and appropriate to, the mental health clinic of the 1950 era, but has no relevant or appropriate place in the suicide prevention or crisis intervention systems which have developed under the community mental health influence of the 1960's. One needs only to be aware of the practices of crisis intervention therapy outlined by Farberow (1967) to know that the utilization of significant other persons is basic good practice in crisis work. When the time arrives that crisis intervention systems are evaluated and certified, and when concepts of appropriate practice are standardized in crisis intervention, a system which seeks to handle a case totally on its own, without including friends, relatives, other professional and agency resources, might find itself censored for malpractice. That day is coming, probably during the 1970's, and such findings as this may hasten its arrival.

Each of the programs was asked to relate any specific reactions to its advertising which might be useful to other programs. Three centers responded to this request, and all three noted that there was an observable increase in the rate of calls received immediately following an article or series of articles in the newspaper. This observation corresponds with those made in the early 1960's by the Los Angeles center. Apparently, the advantage of printed material in papers and magazines is that it can be left lying around and referred to later as needed. On the other hand, radio and television announcements are likely to be 10- or 20-second spots which are practically over by the time they secure the listener's attention. It follows, then, that the best advertising program may be a regular arrangement with the local newspaper to print a feature on a different aspect of the service periodically. There was no center in this study group that ran regular educational columns on suicide, suicide prevention, crisis management, or related topics. Such columns appear regularly on topics such as safety, general health, and managing personal finances. Community education through regular newspaper features has yet to be developed by the suicide and crisis intervention services.

One center reported a unique response to its advertising. This came from the university area of the city in the form of a marked increase in prank calls following each advertising message. These calls ranged among hoax suicide threats, nuisance pseudo-requests for information, and obscene calls. Efforts were made to *prevent* any advertising about the service from reaching into the fraternity house and dormitory populations. It would have been quite interesting to know what types of messages were included in this publicity. It is clearly evident that the university population did not feel the message was seriously directed at them. They not only were not identified with the effort being made in the community; they were uniquely hostile to it. This experience is totally unlike that of other centers in university communities. In many places, the students actively and eagerly try to become volunteers in the crisis programs. It may well have been that this center and its worker population also perceived and fostered a large social distance between itself and its university population. It clearly behaved so as to increase rather than decrease its distance from the psychological life of the students. But then, this particular center was only minimally involved in any segment of the community outside itself. The reaction it aroused from local students was probably only one manifestation of its being functionally on the periphery of the community.

It may be recalled that Tables 1 and 2 report that two centers used classified advertising as their primary announcement in the public media. There is no evidence as to how effective such advertising may be, although both of the programs using it indicated the belief that it was their most effective method. One might wonder who reads the "Personal" column in the newspaper except, perhaps, for idle curiosity or humor. Obviously, the ads placed there are intended to attract a certain segment of the population. For example, one edition of the classified ads was submitted by one of the services as an example of its advertising copy. That section on that particular day contained the following ads:

1 for the Suicide Prevention Center
2 advertising to pay immediate cash to blood donors
3 advertising to purchase trading stamps

2 announcing that marriages can be performed quickly
1 announcing a dating service
1 advertising availability of Ho-Ho the clown for birthday parties
1 announcing a home for the aged
1 advertising a Psychic Spiritual Advisor and reader
1 seeking members to join a large new nudist club.

There may be some value to determining what image a center's ad casts in the total community. Doubtless, there are people who need such a service and who would not know about it except by the classified newspaper ad. However, if such is the only, or the primary, advertising a center has, it is very possible that its reception in other sections of the community may be influenced by the general nature of the other services advertised in a similar manner. Parts of the community might draw the wrong conclusion about the sophistication and the quality of the service through such associations. These ads should be offset by another type of message for the larger community. They should be eliminated altogether if the other advertisers are announcing the availability of a service with which the crisis service does not want to be associated.

Advertising a crisis intervention service is not a simple matter. It cannot be entered into without serious, dedicated effort to create just the right public image for each of the populations which the center may be serving. It may be a full-time job to coordinate public advertising effectively. It is not only the means to announce the availability of the service to the public, it is also the means by which large segments of the community draw conclusions about the quality and the sophistication of the services being offered.

INVOLVEMENT WITH OTHER COMMUNITY AGENCIES

In the questionnaire which each of the centers was asked to complete, a list of 23 community agencies was presented, along with the request that the crisis center indicate briefly the frequency and the quality of relationships it enjoyed with each. Only eight of the 10 programs completed this section of the self-study, and much variance was noted in their responses. Since these responses are not quantitative and are not suitable for combining into broad categories, they will be presented in the same manner that they were rendered by the individual centers. It is possible to see which crisis centers relate to their local sister agencies and also to learn which of the other community resources are related to the crisis intervention type of service.

Local Police Department

Nashville—Participate in the training of police officers. Police notify the center of suicidal clients and refer people to center. Police readily respond to any request for help from center.

Knoxville—Relations are good. Police refer clients; will give center information regarding suicide cases if center asks for it.

Chattanooga—Police respond when called by center. Center assists in training police officers. Contact between police and center regarding individual people is rare.

Orlando—Police send routine reports of all suicide attempts to center and sometimes refer people who threaten suicide. Center assists in training of police officers. Chief of Police is on Board of Directors. Relationships are excellent.

Brevard County—There are 15 police departments in county. Amount and quality of relationship varies with the individual department. Center uses police as a last resort.

Halifax County—The relations are good. Police answer the emergency telephone in the police station. They were not initially whole-heartedly accepting, but relations are much improved.

Atlanta—Crisis workers call police to investigate callers who may have attempted suicide. Sometimes use police for transportation to emergency room. Police send reports of suicide attempts to center and infrequently call for information about citizens.

St. Petersburg—Excellent cooperation between center and police. They are called to take suicide cases to emergency room. Police send about one-third of their cases to emergency service.

County Sheriff's Department

Nashville—Metropolitan government is in Davidson County; therefore, there is only one police agency.

Knoxville—Rarely have contact.

Chattanooga—Participate in training of deputies, but contact is rare.

Orlando—Use sheriff's office for center training meetings. Very good relationships. Assist in training deputies. Sheriff reports all suicide attempts to center. Has representative on Board of Directors.

Brevard County—No official policy between center and sheriff. Sheriff will call ambulance for center, but never will contact the center.

Halifax County—Sheriff is on Advisory Board; more cooperative than police.

Atlanta—Same relations as with city police. Referrals and frequent contact both ways. Good relationships.

St. Petersburg—Call sheriff every one or two months. Most people in area live in city. Same kind and amount of relationship as with police.

Other Law Enforcement Agency

Nashville—No relationship.

Knoxville—Infrequent relationship with university police.

Chattanooga—No relationship.

Orlando—No relationship.

Brevard County—No relationship. Might contact Highway Patrol sometimes.
Halifax County—No relationship.
Atlanta—No relationship.
St. Petersburg—No relationship.

Fire Department
Nashville—Never a reason for contact.
Knoxville—No relationship.
Chattanooga—No relationship.
Orlando—Participate in training of firemen. They call center for help with suicide threats or attempts.
Brevard County—No relationship.
Halifax County—No relationship.
Atlanta—No relationship.
St. Petersburg—Very little contact. They may call center twice a year; center never calls them.

Ambulance Service
Nashville—Ambulance service never calls center; center calls them to take clients to emergency room, and center pays the fee.
Knoxville—No relationship.
Chattanooga—No contact.
Orlando—They call center when dealing with suicidal people. Relationships good.
Brevard County—Center has used ambulance service rarely.
Halifax County—No relationship.
Atlanta—Very infrequent use of hospital ambulance services.
St. Petersburg—Police call ambulance for emergency service clients. Ambulance service sends center the bills, but they are not being paid. Relationships are confused, and things have not come to a head.

Other Rescue Services
Nashville—None in the area.
Knoxville—No relationship.
Chattanooga—Mutually satisfactory relationship. Center does not call rescue service, but two of volunteers are leaders in the other rescue program.
Orlando—None in the area.
Brevard County—None in the area.
Halifax County—Very enthusiastic regarding center; both call each other for help.
Atlanta—No relationship.
St. Petersburg—None in the area.

Local Hospitals
Nashville—Six hospitals in area. Two have psychiatrists in the emergency room. Very good relationships with four; no contact with two.

Knoxville—Five hospitals in area. Major relationship is with State Hospital. University Hospital interns have asked center to help with alcoholic patients, but they do not seem to understand that this is only a telephone service. The other three have no contact or relationship with center.

Chattanooga—Four hospitals, but there are relationships with only two.

Orlando—Six hospitals. Center has good reception in emergency room of four; no acceptance in two. Hospital administrator of one has been very important in development of center. General relationships range from fair to excellent.

Brevard County—Four hospitals in area. One takes psychiatric patients, another is closing its psychiatric unit. There is no relationship with other two.

Halifax County—Good relationships with one, but no relationship with other. Emergency room refers attempters to center. Two nurses are volunteers in center.

Atlanta—Primary contact with City-County Hospital. Center makes direct referrals to emergency room and outpatient clinic. Center receives suicide attempt reports from emergency room and requests to follow up patients seen in emergency room.

St. Petersburg—Four in area; all private. Two have psychiatric units, but center clients taken primarily to one. Emergency room sends center the bills for indigent patients, but they are sent back unpaid. Relationship is unclear.

Mental Health Clinics, Counseling Centers

Nashville—Poor relationships because mental health center won't take emergency referrals; it takes two weeks to be seen.

Knoxville—Center is part of mental health center. Director runs both programs; staff serve as crisis center volunteers.

Chattanooga—Very tense relationship. Clinic provides regular consultation to center. Clinic takes all calls during day time, but will not give center the information regarding clients. They are glad to accept referrals of clients who call in at night.

Orlando—Accept referrals from center. Seem to respect center's evaluation of clients and are helpful in admitting callers to hospital units. Two clinics in city; both are cooperative.

Brevard County—Center is part of mental health center. No others in the area.

Halifax County—Center is in process of becoming part of the mental health center. Crisis center came first, assisted in getting mental health program started.

Atlanta—Seven in area. Reciprocal referrals with all of them. Good relationships.

St. Petersburg—Center is part of the only mental health center in the area.

Family Service Agency

Nashville—Excellent relationships.

Knoxville—Staff of family service agency are volunteers in the center. Center refers to family services but no reciprocal referrals from them.

Chattanooga—Center refers occasionally to them, but gets no information back.

Orlando—None in the area.

Brevard County—Excellent relationships. The two programs are tied together in the community mental health system.

Halifax County—None in the area.

Atlanta—Reciprocal referrals. Good relationships.

St. Petersburg—Family service is mainly an adoption agency. Center refers about 1 percent of its clients to them. They refer all their psychiatric patients to mental health center.

Welfare Agencies

Nashville—Two agencies in area. Good relationships with both.

Knoxville—No relationships.

Chattanooga—No contact. Center has very few indigent cases.

Orlando—Members of departments on Board of Directors. Contact regarding clients is very good.

Brevard County—Infrequent contact. Center rarely uses them for clients.

Halifax County—No relationships.

Atlanta—No relationships.

St. Petersburg—Little contact because of turnover of personnel in welfare agency. They sometimes send elderly people to center, but they are really not a service agency.

Salvation Army

Nashville—Good relationships related to clients.

Knoxville—No relationships.

Chattanooga—No contact. Salvation Army does not want clients with mental problems.

Orlando—Very cooperative relationships regarding individual clients.

Brevard County—Relationship is excellent. Salvation Army has small staff. They call center freely when necessary and always try to help with center's clients.

Halifax County—None in the area.

Atlanta—Reciprocal referrals.

St. Petersburg—Salvation Army calls center to unload its mentally ill. They do not want mental cases from the center.

Alcoholics Anonymous

Nashville—AA will not handle people who are intoxicated. Center sends only clients who are already AA members.

Knoxville—No relationship.

Chattanooga—Rare contact. Not many clients referred to them.

Orlando—Very cooperative in helping clients and in sharing information.

Brevard County—Good cooperation between AA and center. AA representatives

will go to a caller when contacted by center, and they refer their members to the center.
Halifax County—No relationship.
Atlanta—Reciprocal referrals.
St. Petersburg—Tried to train AA people regarding psychiatric cases. AA does not use the emergency service.

Other Alcohol Programs

Nashville—Detoxification Center at Central State Hospital. Relationships good. Alcohol Information Service. Very good relationships.
Knoxville—Good relations with Detox Center at Eastern State Hospital.
Chattanooga—Good relationships with Alcoholic Council. Three volunteers are leaders in the Council. Refer all clients there.
Orlando—Alcoholic Rehabilitation Clinic very helpful in accepting referrals and sharing information.
Brevard County—Mental Health Clinic has its own alcohol program.
Halifax County—None in the area.
Atlanta—Reciprocal referrals to Emory University Alcohol Rehabilitation project.
St. Petersburg—Rehabilitation clinic in Tampa, but it has no relationship to the center.

University Services

Nashville—Vanderbilt and Peabody. Very good relationships. Other colleges indicate that they can take care of their own when they have problems.
Knoxville—No relationship.
Chattanooga—No relationship.
Orlando—Good contacts. Assist in training of dorm personnel regarding student suicide and personal crises.
Brevard County—No relationships.
Halifax County—None in the area.
Atlanta—Formal referral arrangements with Atlanta University campus. Informal arrangements with all other campuses.
St. Petersburg—No relationships.

Taxi Companies

Nashville—Three companies. All cooperate completely in transporting clients for center.
Knoxville—One company offered its service, but center has never used it.
Chattanooga—No relationship.
Orlando—One company picks up and transports clients for center at no cost; they are very helpful.
Brevard County—No relationship.

Halifax County—No relationship.
Atlanta—No relationship.
St. Petersburg—No relationship.

Local Churches

Nashville—Frequent contact. Most ministers very helpful whenever called.
Knoxville—No relationships.
Chattanooga—Five ministers work as volunteers in center. Center refers to specific ministers who are clinically trained. General relationships with churches are good.
Orlando—Routinely contact the minister of callers. Twelve ministers are volunteers in center. Good relationships. Churches help to recruit volunteers.
Brevard County—Churches help to recruit volunteers. No other relationships.
Halifax County—Cooperative relationships with ministers. Many referrals from churches.
Atlanta—Reciprocal referrals with Georgia Association of Pastoral Care and many local ministers.
St. Petersburg—No relationships with any churches; the clergy rotates too frequently.

Civic Clubs

Nashville—Frequent contact to provide speakers for meetings. Two groups have contributed money, and one regularly supports center.
Knoxville—Respond to requests for speakers.
Chattanooga—Respond to request for speakers.
Orlando—Provide speakers when requested.
Brevard County—Provide speakers two or three times per month. Recruit volunteers through civic clubs. Community education through speaking to club meetings.
Halifax County—No relationships.
Atlanta—Have provided speakers for over 50 meetings. Encourage referrals and participation of club members.
St. Petersburg—Very rare contact with these groups.

Telephone Company

Nashville—Moderately helpful. Provide display materials.
Knoxville—No relationship other than commercial answering service.
Chattanooga—No relationship other than commercial answering service.
Orlando—Chief operator was one of first center volunteers. Operators assist by tracing calls and providing other very helpful assistance as needed.
Brevard County—Operators have called center with suicidal callers and also help in emergencies.
Halifax County—No relationships.

Atlanta—Refers emergency callers, attempts to locate suicide callers. Very helpful to center.

St. Petersburg—Operators call emergency service and then block the caller's line until center returns the call. Telephone company more cooperative with the police than with the center; center sometimes calls police to get information from the telephone company.

Mental Health Association

Nashville—Extremely difficult relationships as long as center a part of mental health association. MHA started the center and would have destroyed it had the center not moved out.

Knoxville—Executive Director is coordinator of center. Share offices in a new building. MHA started center. Relationships still good.

Chattanooga—MHA is sponsoring agency. Center coordinator is free from control by executive director. MHA Board has the final control over the center.

Orlando—MHA initially supported center. Now it is independent, but rents office space in MHA building. Very cooperative relationships.

Brevard County—MHA started center, but all ties have been cut as far as administrative matters concerned. MHA sometimes donates money to center for special needs.

Halifax County—No relationships.

Atlanta—Very active with the center. Refer workers and cases. Help to distribute educational material.

St. Petersburg—MHA competed with emergency service for a number of years. Executive Director ran a one-person emergency counseling program; when she left, MHA stopped doing emergency service.

Local Psychiatrists

Nashville—Excellent relationships with individual psychiatrists who serve on Advisory Board. Mutual respect, healthy independence between center and psychiatrists.

Knoxville—No special relationships with any outside clinic.

Chattanooga—None are hostile to center. Most will accept referrals from the center.

Orlando—Two local psychiatrists on Board of Directors. Relationships generally good, cooperative. Better than in the past.

Brevard County—Relationships satisfactory because the center is part of the mental health program.

Halifax County—None in the area.

Atlanta—Reciprocal referrals from most psychiatrists in the city.

St. Petersburg—Cooperative relationships with seven of the 10 local psychiatrists. Some will call emergency service for home visits or will instruct their patients to call the center for help if they are going to be out of town for the weekend.

Local Medical Society

Nashville—No contact.
Knoxville—No relationship.
Chattanooga—Medical Society has called center about individual clients. Relationships good.
Orlando—Presented training film for society meeting. Contact is infrequent.
Brevard County—No relationships.
Halifax County—No relationships.
Atlanta—Little contact.
St. Petersburg—Very little contact.

Public Health Department

Nashville—No contact.
Knoxville—No relationships.
Chattanooga—Public Health nurses may make contacts with center callers. Relationships are good.
Orlando—Very good relationships. Health Director is on Board of Directors. Center director's salary is paid from Health Department budget under classification of "Health Educator." Help train public health nurses for work with disturbed patients.
Brevard County—Works closely with Day Care program of the mental health center, where most of the crisis callers are treated.
Halifax County—Very good relationships. Coordinator of center is one of the Health Department nurses. Nurses all are cooperative with crisis center cases.
Atlanta—Center is part of the Health Department. Frequent and cooperative help from nurses. Help to train nurses.
St. Petersburg—Originally, center was part of Health Department before it moved to mental health center. Nurses still call emergency service more than center calls them regarding clients.

County Coroner, Medical Examiner

Nashville—No relationship.
Knoxville—No relationship.
Chattanooga—No relationship.
Orlando—Medical Examiner on the Board of Directors; one of the most active supporters since beginning of the program. Regularly supplies information regarding local suicide cases.
Brevard County—No relationship.
Halifax County—No relationship.
Atlanta—Supplies center with suicide data regularly.
St. Petersburg—No relationship.

Other Local Agencies with Whom There is an Active Relationship

Nashville—Consumer Credit Counseling Center; Nashville Housing Authority; local school system; Big Brothers; Sisters of the Poor. All have excellent relationships with the center.
Knoxville—None.
Chattanooga—Vocational Rehabilitation; Travelers Aid.
Orlando—Vocational Rehabilitation.
Brevard County—Junior College; Ministerial Association.
Halifax County—None.
Atlanta—Travelers Aid.
St. Petersburg—Child Guidance Clinic; Juvenile Welfare Agency; Catholic Charities; Juvenile Court; Jewish Community Center; Vocational Rehabilitation. All agencies have reciprocal referrals with the emergency service.

It is obvious in the foregoing list of agency relationships that certain patterns emerge. Clearly, some crisis agencies have many more relationships than others; some have almost unique relationships, for example, with the fire department or with taxi companies. It is evident that a few centers have fairly well isolated themselves, whereas others have made inroads into a wide variety of other helping services. These data are summarized in Table 4, in which the number of clearly positive relationships and vague and infrequent relationships and number of agencies with which there are no relationships are tabulated for each center.

A simple index of community involvement can be computed by adding together the number of agencies with which each center reports clearly positive relationships. This value derives from adding the data in columns 1 and 5 in Table 4. Further, the number of agencies which exist in the area, but with which the center has not developed relationships, as indicated in column 3, is subtracted. This yields a rough measure of the extent to which an agency has taken advantage of the other community resources and has seen its role as a collaborative one with them collectively. The crisis centers are listed in Table 4 in descending order of their community involvement index.

It is very clear that some crisis centers were functioning in their communities as simple telephone answering services and were not seen by other agencies as a source of help for clients. One-way referrals suggest a lack of mutual confidence and respect; where an agency will accept referrals but not send them or exchange information regarding clients, it is clear that that agency has no high regard for the crisis center as a viable and meaningful helping element in the community. That is entirely the crisis center's responsibility. It must be the center's responsibility to establish a service program of sufficient breadth and scope to enable it to meet the needs of the other community agencies. It is also the crisis center's responsibility to describe and operate its program in such a manner that the other agencies cannot remain uncertain as to what services it is capable of performing. If other

Table 4 Interactions with other community agencies reported by the individual crisis centers

	Degree of relationship between the center and 23 specific agencies				Other agencies listed by the center (5)	Community involvement index* (6)
	Number of agencies with good, positive relationships (1)	Number of agencies with vague, infrequent relationships (2)	Number of agencies with no relationships (3)	None in the area (4)		
Orlando	19	1	2	1	1	18
Atlanta	16	3	4	0	1	13
Nashville	13	3	6	1	5	12
Brevard County	12	4	6	1	2	8
St. Petersburg	4	11	7	1	6	3
Chattanooga	7	7	9	0	2	0
Halifax County	7	0	11	5	0	-4
Knoxville	5	5	13	0	0	-8

*Community involvement index = (1) + (5) − (3)

agencies do not know what it does, the crisis center must be held accountable for keeping its program obscure.

No suicide prevention or crisis intervention center has ever been established in any community solely for the purpose of meeting needs identified by the existing community agencies. Crisis centers grow up in a community initially to meet the needs of the program developers; there are private agendas to be satisfied in every case. In many of these cases, the private agenda of the initiator has not been in conflict with the larger community interests; in most, they have been quite congruent. However, no suicide or crisis service has had a completely easy and uneventful birth into the family of community agencies. There are always resistances, cautious and tenuous relationships, and sometimes outright avoidances by some existing agencies. The programs which have overcome these initial attitudes have done so with continuous effort and determination to become an integral part of the total helping system. Those which either felt they were omnipotent and needed no affiliations or which did not want to expend the effort to establish a high quality of public relations have continued almost as uninvolved with the local community as they were prior to their inception. It is not surprising that all of the centers which seemed disinterested in interacting with their community either have gone out of existence or have gained their involvement with the community by being taken under the wing of another larger agency. The one remaining independent crisis intervention center in this study group is the one which had the greatest community involvement index. It continues to be one of the model programs for community crisis centers (McGee and McGee, 1968).

9
AN EVALUATION OF CRISIS INTERVENTION PROGRAMS

The preceding chapters have discussed the information provided by the 10 centers studied concerning their telephone and office facilities, clinical services, manpower, record keeping, statistical presentations, and level of involvement with the community. It is very evident that the centers varied markedly in these areas. There have been wide differences in all of the areas studied; furthermore, when the 10 centers were arranged in an ordinal scale from highest to lowest on the individual indices, a fairly consistent pattern appeared in the data. The purpose of this chapter is to combine the various indices of center operation and to develop an overall evaluation of the 10 centers studied.

The evaluation of suicide and crisis intervention programs has been a relatively undeveloped area until the early 1970's. In the beginning of the suicide prevention and crisis intervention movement, there was the feeling that it was too early to attempt to set standards or to develop models for service delivery. However, as more and more centers emerged, and as many of them clearly were deficient in the services they were providing, the need for universally applied standards became clear. The Bay Area Association of Suicide Prevention Centers was the first group to recognize this need formally. Like the CONTACT programs associated with Teleministry, Inc., and the Samaritans in England, the Bay Area group set standards which member centers must meet to qualify for affiliation in the Association. Motto (1969) and Ross and Motto (1971) have provided detailed discussions of both the rationale and the specific criteria used in the evaluation of the member centers in the Bay Area Association. A similar format may be adopted by the American Association of Suicidology during the 1970's. Evaluation of crisis services is an absolute must for future developments in the delivery of crisis services.

One of the problems, however, is the development of criteria to use in comparing one center with another and determining minimum levels of acceptable service operation. Lester (1970) has presented a series of four brief papers in which he discusses several measures to be applied for the evaluation of a suicide prevention center. He includes the following variables:

1. Counselor ratings of caller improvement as a result of the call
2. Success in referring callers to the center for face-to-face interviews
3. Success in referring clients to other agencies
4. Knowledge of the existence of the service among high-risk groups
5. Number of completed suicides who had called the center
6. Length of time required to get a counselor on the telephone
7. Adequacy of record form completion
8. Counselor effectiveness in providing therapeutic conditions
9. Cost of the services rendered per call.

All of these measures may be applied within any one center to provide a continual accounting of the program activities. However, since the data call for highly specialized record-keeping systems, it is doubtful that more than a handful of programs keep records which would permit them to be compared with one another on such dimensions.

There is still an extensive amount of research and planning necessary for the development of universal criteria with which to evaluate and compare centers. The methods used in this chapter are not offered as a simple solution to the problem. However, they are considered a definite step in this direction.

COMPARISON OF THE 10 CENTERS IN THE SOUTHEAST

It should be noted in the beginning of this comparison that the process of evaluating a service agency is basically an assessment procedure which rates an activity at a given point in time. It is not intended as a prediction of any kind; no valid statements or conclusions can be made regarding the probability that a center with a particular rating will save more lives, intervene more effectively, or perform any particular function at any specific level of performance. Assessments merely report the condition of a program at the present, in terms of specified criteria. The criteria themselves may be questioned. Assessments serve only to implement a value system; the rating reflects the degree to which the underlying value system is present. There are many value systems which might be used in any evaluation procedure. Acceptance of the results of an evaluation is largely a function of the degree to which the underlying value system is accepted.

In this evaluation, two separate and largely independent ratings are presented. The first one stems directly from the community model for crisis intervention services presented in Chapter 2. The second evaluation is taken from the material provided by the 10 centers on four dimensions of program operation. Each of the dimensions has its own value system, and the assessment is based upon the degree to which it is met. These separate dimensions are then combined for an overall estimate of each center's ranking among the total group of 10. Thus, the final ranking is a sum of ranks on four dimensions, each of which was developed independently from the responses to questionnaire items. Perhaps it may be argued that the writing of the questionnaire itself—the decision to include specific items—reflects an underlying value system which prejudices the outcome. To the extent that this is true, the two evaluations in this chapter naturally are correlated, each being a different manifestation of the author's orientation toward the delivery of suicide and crisis services. On the other hand, the rationale for each evaluation may be set forth clearly, and the data will speak for themselves.

Evaluation of the 10 Centers on the Community Model

In Chapter 2, six aspects of the community model were presented. Briefly, these criteria include the following:
1. Utilization of nonprofessional crisis workers
2. Utilization of professional persons as consultants rather than as direct service personnel
3. Emphasis on prevention
4. Avoidance of the pathology, or "sickness" concept
5. Membership in the total network of helping services
6. Commitment to program evaluation research.

It is possible to examine all of the 10 centers for the extent to which they reveal each of these principles in their operation.

Utilization of nonprofessionals. This fact can be determined directly from the data on manpower, presented in Chapter 6. Only seven of the 10 programs met this criterion.

Utilization of professional persons as consultants. It was determined that those agencies which used professional personnel as crisis workers tended not to have outside consultants assist them. Those agencies which did have professional persons on their staff generally gave these persons administrative roles, rather than consultation roles. Consequently, this criterion reflects whether or not the agency had professional persons who were called in from outside the system to provide genuine consultation to the system. Only five of the centers met this criterion.

Emphasis on prevention. This is a difficult item to judge, since no program has attempted a public relations or community education project specifically aimed at preventing suicide in high-risk groups. Therefore an indirect measure is necessary. It is taken from the data on the clinical service practices of each center, presented in Chapter 5. Specifically, the criterion relates to the center's having a policy of responding to suicide attempt cases or to the needs of survivors of suicide deaths. These two groups of people are among the most important for receiving skillful crisis intervention service. It is known that suicide attempters often repeat their self-injuries and self-poisonings, and that these subsequent acts are more lethal than earlier ones. Primary *prevention* is probably accomplished best by intervention after attempts and deaths. The centers which reported a history of such interventions score positively on this criterion.

Avoidance of the pathology concept. This was another criterion which required indirect assessment. The data were taken from several sources. Attitudes of the center were evident in the comments that agencies made about their relations with other resources in the community involvement section reported in Chapter 8. For example, some centers described their relationships with the Salvation Army and with Alcoholics Anonymous with statements such as: "They are not helpful because they don't want referrals of mentally ill people." "They send their psychiatric cases to our clinic." Such statements indicate that the center sees its clients as mentally ill or psychiatric cases in the typically medical mental health model of conceptualizing disorder. Other data are evident in the referral patterns of the centers. Those which send most of their cases into the mental health center with which they are affiliated are clearly indicating a bias that their clients need psychiatric service. An extreme form of this attitude is seen easily in the case of a center which developed its service in such a way that the psychiatric clinic staff answered the telephone during the daytime. All callers became patients in the case files of the clinic. When the crisis service "went on duty" at night, they likewise were expected to send their callers to the clinic the next day. Only five of the 10 centers maintained such a degree of independence from the mental health system that they were able to relate freely and frequently to many nonmedical agencies in the community.

Membership in a network of agencies. The criterion for this measure naturally is taken from Chapter 8 as well. The community involvement index reported in Table 4 of Chapter 8 is the best measure of this variable. It reflects the number of agencies with which a center has positive associations among the total that are available in its community. The criterion for this aspect of the community model is that the center merely "breaks even." That is, it should have positive relationships with at least as many agencies in the area as the number with which it has not established any relationship. Thus, for a center to qualify, the sum of positive relationships less the number of no-relationships should be at least zero, or higher. Only eight of the centers provided data in this area, and of these, only six met the criterion.

Commitment to evaluation research. This measure was taken from the information provided by the programs in the section relating to record keeping discussed in Chapter 7. The data presented in Table 1 of Chapter 7 show the number of centers which record information relative to the operation of their program. Such data present the basic ingredient for evaluation research. Again, only eight programs provided responses to this section of the study, and only six qualified on this criterion. The others either kept no records at all or the records that they reported keeping did not include information on program operations.

The evaluation of the 10 centers on the characteristics of the community model is summarized in Table 1. The centers are listed across the columns of the table in the order of their total scores. Scores were derived by counting the number of community characteristics manifested by the center. These scores ranged from zero to six. When these scores are arranged in rank order, three groups emerge which are labeled as "high," "medium," and "low" on the community dimension.

Evaluation of the 10 Centers on the Data Collected for This Study

The data for this second evaluation procedure are taken from Chapters 4, 5, 7, and 8. Each of the four variables is discussed in order to clarify how the measure was derived for the overall evaluation.

Office and telephone facilities. It was indicated in Chapter 4 that a service must have its own office if it expects to become a functional part of the community in which it is attempting to operate. Similarly, it must have maximum control over its own telephone operation, since that is the primary service it is advertising to the public. The centers varied widely on these two individual

Table 1 Evaluation of the 10 crisis services according to the characteristics of the community model

Characteristics	Orlando	Nashville	Atlanta	Brevard County	St. Petersburg	Halifax County	LIFELINE	FRIENDS	Chattanooga	Knoxville
Use of nonprofessional workers	X	X	X	X		X	X	X		
Use of outside professionals as consultants	X	X				X	X		X	
Emphasis on prevention	X	X	X		X					
Avoidance of pathology concept	X	X	X				X	X		
Membership in a network of agencies	X	X	X	X	X					
Evaluation research	X	X	X	X	X	X				
Number of community characteristics	6		5	3	3	3	3	2	1	0
Rank	9.5	9.5	8	5.5	5.5	5.5	5.5	3	2	1
Evaluation on community model		High				Medium			Low	

dimensions, and when they were combined, the variance was naturally greater. Two four-unit dimensions were created, and ranks were assigned to the centers as a result of their position on each. The sum of their two rankings was used as an indication of their relative standing with regard to office and telephone facilities. It should be noted that these two scales may not be equal interval scales, and thus only ordinal ranks have been assigned:

Office facilities:

1. Have own office. Rank 9.5: Atlanta, Orlando
2. Have own space in shared office. Rank 7: Nashville, St. Petersburg, LIFELINE
3. Use common space in shared office. Rank 4: Chattanooga, Knoxville, Brevard County
4. Have no office space. Rank 1.5: Halifax County, FRIENDS

Telephone facilities:

1. Answer 24 hours a day in office. Rank 10: Atlanta
2. Answer part of day in office. Rank 7: Orlando, Brevard County, St. Petersburg, Knoxville, Nashville

Table 2 Evaluation of office and telephone facilities developed by the 10 programs

Center	Sum of positions on two evaluative dimensions	Rank
Atlanta	19.5	10
Orlando	16.5	9
Nashville	14	7.5
St. Petersburg	14	7.5
Brevard County	11	5.5
Knoxville	11	5.5
LIFELINE	10.5	4
Chattanooga	5.5	3
FRIENDS	5.0	2
Halifax County	3	1

3. Use a commercial answering service 24 hours a day. Rank 3.5: FRIENDS, LIFELINE

4. Telephone answered by staff in another agency. Rank 1.5: Chattanooga, Halifax County

The preceding list yields an overall evaluation of the office and telephone facilities of the 10 centers. These data are shown in Table 2.

Clinical service activities. One of the characteristics which differentiates crisis intervention programs, especially those which emphasize suicide prevention services, is the level of activity within the center on behalf of clients. Each of the centers in this study was asked to describe the clinical activities in which it engages for its clients. These data are shown in Table 3.

The number of affirmative responses in each column was entered as that center's index of clinical activity. It may be seen that these scores ranged from 13 to only 1. These sums also may be ranked in order to reflect each center's relative position among the others in terms of its clinical services. It should be noted that this accounting does not weigh the different activities for whatever differential value they might have. Clearly, some activities may be judged as being more important than others; but, without some logical basis for assigning weights, they are treated as equal activities in this measure. It is evident that some centers *do more* for their clients than others.

Record keeping. Chapter 7 includes several aspects of record keeping as practiced by the individual programs. These separate indices have been combined in Table 4. The variables included in this table are: (1) the number of types of information recorded (from Table 1 in Chapter 7); (2) the cooperation ratio computed for each center (from Table 3, Chapter 7); (3) the record efficiency index (from data in Table 6, Chapter 7). Thus, Table 4 sums up the ranks of each program on the separate measures and yields an additional rank ordering of the combined record-keeping practices of each center.

Community involvement. This criterion is used in both of the evaluation procedures discussed in this chapter, and, once more, it is taken from the community involvement index presented in Table 4 of Chapter 8. Previously, in assessing the 10 programs according to the principles of the community model, this index was used to divide the centers into two discrete groups. However, in this assessment, the total ordinal scale is employed, and the rank assigned to each of the centers is taken to reflect its relative position among the 10 programs.

All of the data relative to these four primary dimensions are combined in Table 5. The 10 centers are shown in their rank order on each of the measures and in a final ordering based upon the combination of the four sets of ranks.

The column on the far right of Table 5 is the ranking of the 10 centers in the overall evaluation based upon data they report on their own operation. It may be recalled that two of the programs failed to make any reports of their community activities and record-keeping practices. These centers, therefore, had zero scores

Table 3 Clinical service activities of the 10 centers

Activity	Orlando	Nashville	Atlanta	Brevard County	St. Petersburg	Knoxville	Halifax County	FRIENDS	Chattanooga	LIFELINE
24-Hour telephone service	X	X	X	X	X	X	X	X	X	X
Attempt to assess lethality	X	X	X	X	X	X	X	X	X	
Use standard lethality interview	X	X	X					X		
Make appointment for client in other agency		X	X	X	X	X	X			
Provide transportation for clients	X		X							
Give names of individual physicians, therapists		X		X	X					
Contact other agency to notify them of client	X	X	X	X		X				
Send copy of report to other agency	X									

Contact agency to see if appointment kept	X	X									
Contact client to learn why appointment not kept	X	X									
Routine follow-up to determine client condition	X	X	X	X							
Face-to-face contact with clients	X	X			X	X	X				
Contact suicide attempters	X		X		X						
Contact survivors of suicide deaths	X		X								
Walk-in crisis counseling	X	X		X	X						
Total number of activities	13	12	11	8	6	6.5	6	4	4	4	2	1
Rank	10	9	8	6.5	6.5	4	4	4	2	1		

Table 4 Overall evaluation of record-keeping practices by the centers

	Rank on three aspects of record system			Sum of ranks	Rank in overall evaluation of record system
	Number of types of records*	Cooperation ratio†	Record-keeping efficiency‡		
Orlando	7.5	8	3	18.5	9.5
Halifax	5.5	5	8	18.5	9.5
Nashville	7.5	4	6	17.5	8
Brevard	4	6	7	17.0	8
St. Petersburg	2.5	7	4	13.5	6
Atlanta	5.5	1	5	11.5	5
Knoxville	1	3	2	6.0	4
Chattanooga	2.5	2	1	5.5	3
FRIENDS §					1.5
LIFELINE §					1.5

*Chapter 7, Table 1
†See Chapter 7, Table 3
‡See Chapter 7, Table 6
§Provided no report

on these two dimensions. They were given a tied score in the accounting in Table 5 in order to have a relative measure for all 10 of the programs studied. It may be argued that had these programs submitted a report, their position might have been somewhat higher. However, enough is known about those two programs to satisfy the investigator that the lack of data does not misrepresent their actual practices in these two areas.

Comparison of the Two Evaluation Methods

It should be apparent that the two evaluation procedures yield very similar results. This fact is evident in the direct comparison of the two methods shown in Table 6.

A few comments are appropriate to document further the findings in Table 6. In the first place, there is an identical ranking of the top three programs by both of the evaluation methods. These three crisis intervention programs have certain

Table 5 Evaluation of 10 centers on the variables included in this project

| Center | Center ranking on each individual measure | | | | Sum of ranks | Relative position of each center in overall evaluation |
	Office and telephone facilities	Clinical service activities	Record keeping	Community involve-ment		
Orlando	9	10	9.5	10	38.5	10
Nashville	7.5	9	8	8	32.5	9
Atlanta	10	8	5	9	32.0	8
St. Petersburg	7.5	6.5	6	6	26.0	6.5
Brevard County	5.5	6.5	7	7	26.0	6.5
Halifax County	1	4	9.5	4	18.5	4.5
Knoxville	5.5	4	4	5	18.5	4.5
Chattanooga	3	2	3	3	11.0	3
FRIENDS	2	4	1.5	1.5	9.0	2
LIFELINE	4	1	1.5	1.5	8.0	1

Table 6 Comparison of the two methods for evaluating the 10 centers in this study

Center	Ranking of individual centers in each method of evaluation	
	Community model characteristics	Data reported by the centers in this study
Orlando	9.5	10
Nashville	9.5	9
Atlanta	8	8
St. Petersburg	5.5	6.5
Brevard County	5.5	6.5
Halifax County	5.5	4.5
LIFELINE	5.5	1
FRIENDS	3	2
Chattanooga	2	3
Knoxville	1	4.5

things in common. They are all independent service agencies. Two of them are funded through other agencies in the community, but the crisis service is not a functional part of the larger agency, other than for budgetary purposes. All three of these programs are integrated completely into the total community service system. They each have administrative boards or personnel unaffiliated with the funding source. They all see themselves as permanent agencies on their own and not merely as units of other services.

This is not true for the other programs. Those occupying the mid-range positions on the rankings also have in common the fact that they are highly integrated into the mental health system of the community. They were operating as units of the existing mental health system in their area.

Finally, there is a further observation from these two sets of evaluative rankings. The lowest three ranks in both sets are assigned to a group of four centers, two of which are among the lowest three on both sets. These four programs also have something in common: *none of them was still operating two years after the study was completed.* They all failed to survive as suicide prevention or crisis intervention services in their communities. This fact is offered as external validity for the methods of evaluation used in this chapter. It is also empirical evidence for the theoretical validity of the community model for crisis services. Those centers which are highest on this variable are well-functioning, comprehensive community crisis services. Those centers which followed these simple principles of community service programming are continuing to make a vital and viable contribution. Those which did not are no longer in existence.

There may be those who do not accept the value orientation underlying the methods of assessment in this chapter. They will agree wholeheartedly that their center should be low in the rankings because it did not, or does not, try to be the kind of center which follows that value system. These critics have their own value system for the operation of their programs. Their position will be one further demonstration of the point, made frequently throughout this book, that conventional mental health-oriented agencies and the crisis intervention agencies do not share a common service orientation and philosophy. This study was conducted with 10 programs which, in 1967, considered themselves suicide prevention or crisis intervention services. This was true of all of the centers except the Emergency Mental Health Service in St. Petersburg. This program never did think of itself as a suicide prevention program. It never has seen itself as a crisis intervention center. It was included in this study primarily because it was considered a relevant program by the Center for Studies of Suicide Prevention at NIMH, because of its role in creating the Atlanta program, because it was asserting leadership in face-to-face intervention at the scene of a crisis, and because it was listed in the local telephone directory under the heading of "Suicide Prevention."

However, the St. Petersburg program is still functioning and making a valuable contribution to its community, whatever its philosophical or professional orientation. Four other programs which failed to survive did think of themselves as suicide prevention services and advertised themselves as such. However, they fell victim to program planners who could not conceive of comprehensive crisis services extending beyond the answering of a telephone. One might wonder whether the passing of these programs was in fact more of a benefit to the community than was the original development of the service.

10
GUIDELINES FOR THE ESTABLISHMENT OF CRISIS INTERVENTION PROGRAMS

It is possible to formulate some general conclusions from the history and the operation of the 10 centers which have been reviewed in the preceding chapters. These conclusions are intended to serve as guidelines for the consideration of program developers whose work may be just beginning. They are discussed under seven topic headings, most of which were touched upon, if only slightly, in the individual center histories. This chapter is intended to highlight problem areas which every existing center has already encountered and which new programs may expect to face along the way. Guidelines are included which attempt to focus attention on the critical issues in each of the seven areas. These areas may be considered the "problems of living" which an agency must be prepared to meet in its process of maturation toward ultimate establishment in the community.

THE MOTIVATION OF THE INITIATOR

A question which is most frequently asked, but seldom adequately answered, is, "Why should a suicide prevention or crisis intervention service be set up in this community?" "Who wants to establish the program?" "Whose needs will the program satisfy?" It is possible to identify at least three distinct motives for the establishment of the 10 centers studied in this project. Additional motives are sometimes evident and are mentioned also.

One motive of the initiator has been that of establishing a new program to meet a *personal problem* as presented by a specific, identifiable patient. Several initiators have had personal contact with a person who was suicidal, or knew a family where there had been a suicide, and decided that there must be hundreds of similarly distressed persons in the community who also need help. The roots of the program grew from this single experience. One difficulty with this approach is that it tends to take on the character of a "do-gooder" effort and frequently can lack the broad base of enthusiasm which is necessary to move the planning through an interest group to a set of legitimizers. Also, the initiator's enthusiasm may wane after a few frustrations, and the effort may continue with a half-hearted thrust which, at best, avoids the embarrassment of abandoning the program.

A second motive which has been apparent is that of establishing a program to meet a broadly perceived *public problem.* In this approach, the problem is recognized through statistical or agency reports which reveal the need on a nomothetic, rather than an idiographic, basis. This initial motive generally has the advantage of coming from an established organization or agency, such as the public health department, police department, or mental health center. The planning program may lack the personal dynamism of a public-spirited organizer, but it makes up for this deficiency in its stability and capacity to overcome organized opposition.

A third motive for establishing these programs has been to establish a component of a large-scale community mental health program. The developers of comprehensive centers have been alert to the requirements which must be met for federal construction and staffing grants, and they are eager to find every shred of evidence of having at least partially met these requirements when they submit the applications for funds. It has been observed several times that local communities can establish a suicide prevention or crisis intervention service much more quickly and easily and with considerably less financial cost than they can develop the comprehensive community mental health program. Therefore, the mental health planners have either developed the suicide prevention center first or supported its development by a local interest group while the major program was being prepared. In either case, the initial interest included a long-range plan for the suicide prevention program eventually to become the emergency service of the comprehensive program.

There are some additional motives which are generally inferred from the lack of any systematic purpose or goal. In some centers, there has been a "bandwagon" approach: "Other communities have done it, so if they can, why shouldn't we?" Some programs appear to have been started with little more than the initiator's desire not to be left behind when friends and associates in other cities were getting favorable publicity for their efforts. This motive has been at least partially present in several of the services which developed primarily out of mental health associations. Similarly, one occasionally detects a tendency for a program to get its start from the need to find "this year's project." One community, not included in the 10 studied in this project, tried but never succeeded in getting a program going from a motive which was so devious as to predetermine failure. The interest group happened to be angry at the two or three psychiatrists practicing in the community, and felt that it could show them up by establishing a volunteer-operated service such as a suicide prevention center. Of course, this motive was partially unconscious, but it was not difficult for the consultant to uncover during the early planning sessions.

The important point in considering the motive of the initiator is to remember that motives are not always clearly understood, either by the initiator or by the interest group. It is absolutely essential for successful program development to make the motives as explicit and as unambiguous as possible. It is the task of a program consultant to see that a group undertakes the task of defining its purpose. When a group does not have a consultant in the early stages, it is the duty and responsibility of the initiator to make his motives and goals absolutely public. Making motives public naturally tends to whitewash them so as to provide the respectability which would gain support. When that task becomes too difficult, and if it results in too much ambiguity for the interest group and legitimizers to understand, then it is symptomatic of a program plan which probably should be discarded. Undoubtedly, some programs would not have started, and many people would have been saved much trouble and personal hurt, if some of the initiators' motives had been understood better in the beginning.

Finally, it may be observed that most of the centers studied appeared to have been developed to meet the needs of the people who were developing them. Only in one of the communities studied did the key people inquire as to how many persons and agencies actually wanted such a service. When it is determined that the program meets a general need experienced by broad groups of people and agencies, then the motive of the initiator becomes less of a factor in the ultimate success of the service.

Guideline I

A. The initiator(s) of a crisis intervention service must determine the extent to which there is a need for the service in the community.

B. The specific individuals and agencies who perceive a need for the crisis service must be identified, and documentation of the need as they perceive it must be elicited.

Guideline II

The initiator(s) of the crisis intervention service should remain vigilant to the tendency for personal needs and motives to interfere with effective and comprehensive planning for a community service.

LENGTH OF TIME DEVOTED TO PLANNING

It is impossible as well as unwise to attempt any definite guidelines on time periods. Among the centers studied here, the planning ranged from the 100-day plan developed for Brevard County, Florida, to the 24 months required to initiate the "feasibility study" in Chattanooga. The apparent success of a program in a community is definitely unrelated to the length of time spent on its planning. It is almost platitudinous to state that what matters most is not *how much* time is spent, but *how* the time is spent. For example, the time taken to plan the Atlanta program can be measured in terms of weeks, but the people who were involved and the extent of their support made the difference. Similarly, it took over a year to launch the program in Nashville, but again, the degree of involvement from significant elements in the community was far greater in the long run than most centers were able to develop.

The important part of planning and evaluating an organizational development plan is not the amount time that is taken, but rather the allotment of enough time to touch base with all of the proper people and procedures along the way. If these people and procedures are to be left out of the process, then the time element is unimportant anyway.

Guideline III

The early planning for a new agency proceeds most efficiently when it is managed by the focused energy of one or two key persons, rather than diffused throughout a committee of persons with marginal involvement in the program.

Guideline IV

Planning must be a continuous, dynamic process which is not completed once an agency is established, but which continues indefinitely throughout the life of a service.

Guideline V

The initiator and other key persons must adopt an attitude which permits and even encourages controlled growth and/or change of original ideas, goals, procedures, and structures as the program develops.

POLITICAL ASPECTS OF PROGRAM PLANNING

Several of the 10 centers studied demonstrate the fact that no idea, no matter how good or valuable it may be, will sell itself in the community. One must always make maximum use of the political expertise of legitimizers. This is obviously true where government support is required in the form of space or financial assistance. But even in the broadest sense of "good public relations skills," one must be a successful politician to get any new program started. The best example of success at this phase of the development process is the Atlanta center. The manner by which both the need for a program and the right supporting data to document its value were presented to the governmental units was a masterful job of utilizing political skill successfully.

Similarly, the task of winning support and appreciation of the professional community is a type of jungle in which political skill must be artfully applied. It is generally found that professional personnel, especially mental health professionals in private practice, are still highly threatened by suicide and crisis intervention services which utilize trained nonprofessional volunteers as crisis workers. Their reaction to hearing that a program is being planned may range all the way from passive indifference to very active opposition. Either tack can present very big hurdles for a program to overcome. Some agencies have found that even asking reluctant professionals to serve on advisory boards does not soften their opposition. In fact, one suicide program in this study found that one of its so-called "consultants" was very willing to accept center funds to finance a vacation with his wife while he attended the International Association for Suicide Prevention meeting in Los Angeles as the center's representative. Once there, however, he visited his professional colleagues rather than attending the meetings, and he returned home loaded with reasons why suicide prevention programs should not be encouraged. He thereafter spent much energy trying to prevent the program from developing into anything more than a telephone answering service.

The greatest problem that crisis intervention centers have had with the professional in the community has come from giving him too much authority and control over the program. Especially where the center is an independent organization with a professional consultant or advisory board, it is important to keep roles and duties well defined. When a center forces the professional, who is associated with it only through his own good will, to be the responsible decision-maker or the parent-figure who must give his permission, the relationship is likely to turn sour. For one thing, giving permission implies assuming responsibility, and responsibility without authority is sterile. Therefore, there is a double message involved which easily turns into conflict.

The Crisis Call Center in Nashville is the outstanding example of a program which worked out very smooth relationships with its professional helpers from the community. It should be noted once more, however, that with but one or two exceptions these professionals were all from the local university or medical school settings. Their institutional affiliation gave them and the program that they served a general sanction within the private professional community.

The history of FRIENDS demonstrates that the absence of professional supporters can be fatal for a once-viable program, and the Chattanooga story shows that too much involvement with professional advisors can be equally harmful if the support is of the wrong kind. The skillful and practical application of human relations politics is an absolute must for suicide and crisis program initiators and directors.

Guideline VI

The initiator(s) and director(s) of a community crisis intervention service must acquaint themselves with the social-political climate of their local professional and governmental systems and must consciously evaluate the degree of congruence between their goals for the service and these elements of the community power structure.

Guideline VII

A. A crisis service initiator and/or director must engage professional consultants in a collaborative effort to define the roles and expectations which determine the professional's relationship to the program and the individual crisis workers.

B. Care should be exercised that the extent of power and control that a professional person is given does not exceed that which is appropriate for: (1) his position in the formal structure of the service; (2) his knowledge and experience in the field of crisis intervention; (3) his personal commitment to the goals of the program; and (4) his willingness to assume professional and personal responsibility for the outcome of procedures and policies affecting client care.

RELATIONSHIPS WITH OTHER AGENCIES

Not only the number and quality of professional relationships which a program develops, but the extent of its involvement with other agencies and helping services are of great importance in its maturation. Several of the centers studied made their contacts with other agencies early in the planning and established their relationships through the vehicle of a Community Advisory Board. This board is nearly always composed of representatives from all of the major helping services in the community.

The primary advantage of such a Board is that when the new service begins operation, it definitely is going to make an impact on the other agencies. This will require some knowledge of their procedures for making referrals, and the new service also will need to be on good negotiating terms for defining the scope of its own service. Moreover, a suicide prevention and crisis intervention service always will encounter problems which cannot be solved readily in a community. It will discover the gaps which exist in services, and simultaneously, it will discover where specific agencies are not fulfilling their own missions. Such disclosures require close and cooperative relationships, so that communications can be most effective in closing the service gaps and meeting the existing needs. The Advisory Board representing the other services can facilitate the solution of all of these problems.

The manner in which an Advisory Board is used varies considerably among the centers studied. In Orlando, the Board was called upon to sanction everything the initiator wanted to do. In Nashville, it was used to inform the community agencies what the Crisis Call Center was going to do. In another program, it was used as a power source to stand behind the program director and to give support in the conflicts which frequently occurred with the management role of the Mental Health Association.

It is of special importance to define carefully the reason for forming an Advisory Board and then to be certain that it is used accordingly. If the Board is for the primary purpose of *establishing* effective relationships with the other agencies in the community, its job may be over once the program is established. The task of *maintaining* these effective agency relationships is an almost daily one which must be performed regularly within the context of service to clients. This is best done directly by the program coordinator with each agency on an individual basis, rather than as part of a group.

The centers studied varied greatly in the extent to which they attempted to develop agency relationships. FRIENDS seemed to want little or no contact with other groups, and the Knoxville program did not appear to need any in order to do its job. Programs like WE CARE could not have functioned without a wide range of effective interactions with other services. In Atlanta, and possibly in St. Petersburg, the agency relationships were built into the center, since they were part of the long-established county health departments. There is a danger in assuming that any program can operate completely on its own. If a suicide prevention or crisis intervention service operates from a philosophy that suicidal people or people in crisis are automatically psychiatric patients, then it may appropriately serve as a funnel to direct all clients into the mental health program. Under such conditions, the program will need few relationships elsewhere. On the other hand, it will likewise have a very limited potential for serving its clients and will not develop into a general community crisis service.

Strangely, most communities have found that the agencies which were most supportive and most eager to see the development of a suicide prevention service were the police and sheriff departments. These are the agencies which have long been involved with suicide cases and which receive many types of personal crisis calls in the regular performance of their duties. They welcome help from persons who are appropriately skilled, and they rarely get much help from professional mental health agencies. They never are threatened by nonprofessionals, as some agencies tend to be. In a larger sense, a fully operative suicide prevention and crisis intervention service needs two things much more than it needs physicians, psychologists, and psychiatrists. These are efficient communication and rapid transportation, neither of which has ever been characteristic of the mental health field. Both of them are to be found with the police. When both characteristics are combined with the authority of the local law enforcement agencies, then this combination is an unequaled asset to the crisis service. Any program would add considerably to its role in the community by developing the closest possible relationships with the police departments in its area.

Guideline VIII

The initiator of a community crisis intervention service must develop some mechanism for establishing and maintaining effective and collaborative communication with all of the helping resources in the community.

Guideline IX

A. A crisis center initiator must realize that the entry of a new service into the network of helping services necessarily will have an effect upon the operation of the existing agencies.

B. The quality of interagency cooperation experienced by a crisis intervention center will be determined by the extent to which the existing agencies are included in the planning of the crisis center's role in the community.

Guideline X

A. A crisis intervention service initiator or director should avoid the stereotype that only health or mental health-related agencies and personnel are essential collaborators in suicide prevention or crisis intervention activities.

B. It never should be overlooked that representatives from the field of law enforcement have been especially cooperative and may be uniquely equipped to facilitate the operation of a crisis intervention service in the community.

INTERNAL STRIFE WITHIN THE AGENCY

One of the essential features of any crisis center initiator or director must be an ability to function as a conflict resolution expert. It is frequently very difficult to resolve a conflict if one is embroiled in it as a principal. Rarely were the centers studied free of internal strife, but it was obviously more pronounced in some than in others.

As a general rule, tensions were much more evident in those programs which continued to be tied to the mental health association after their program began operating (McGee, 1971a).

It clearly behooves an agency director not to be naive about how difficult it is for people to work together in a crisis service. For one thing, the nature of the task is such that a high level of tension is continually maintained about the clients and about one's own ability in the program. Each volunteer needs to know how well he handled that last case and whether or not it is going to work out. His discomfort at not knowing how he is perceived is easily projected onto the director for not providing that feedback. When the worker is a volunteer and feels that his time is not sufficiently rewarded, he has an even greater reason to project angry feelings. If a director sees a volunteer only once a week, and each elects to say nothing to one another about conflicts, hoping they will go away, a potentially unhealthy suppression of feelings is nurtured. The only way to escape such a morass of human relations is to hold, and to expect involvement in, regular meetings of all the staff for the purpose of open communication and feedback around work problems. A director who is not himself a skillful encounter group leader would do well to be certain that there is a consultant available who does have such skills and to make regular use of his abilities.

One of the biggest sources of internal strife encountered in this study was that caused by turnover of key personnel. This was a primary reason why the Chattanooga program was so long in developing and why it developed no more than a perfunctory role in the community. Orlando's WE CARE and the Nashville Crisis Call Center are other examples where the frequency of changes in coordinators was a major source of stress for the workers. In both of the latter programs, it has been some coordinator other than the original initiator who has been able to move the service towards permanent stability in the community. It may be observed from several of the programs that the prime initiator may not be the best person to continue to operate the service once it is actually started. It should be built into the planning of the program that a coordinator or director be selected early to work with the initiator in getting the final phases of the center ready to become operational. Then the initiator may be retired, and the director, who has been selected partially for potential longevity, should take complete control. Failure to follow such procedures has resulted in painful and damaging internal strife and tensions for the centers and for the people who are trying to serve clients in crisis.

Finally, strife and turmoil are inevitable whenever there is ambiguity beyond what people are able to tolerate. When the nature of the work is itself ambiguous as to quality or outcome, it behooves a center director to maintain the maximum degree of structure and clarity in the organization. This especially means that the goals and purposes of the organization are well understood. Particularly, it means that the lines of authority are clear and structured. It means that there must be openness in interpersonal relations and clarity of expectation with regard to duty and performance. This is a tall order for any director, but constant attention to worker morale will result in reduced inner tension in the long run.

Guideline XI

The role of the initiator of a community crisis program is not the same as the role of program director once it becomes operational.

Guideline XII

The director(s) of a crisis service should be carefully selected with attention to potential longevity, so that turnover of key personnel can be kept to a minimum.

Guideline XIII

It is of utmost importance in operating a crisis service to recognize and structure the satisfaction of the needs of the individual crisis workers; this is especially critical if the workers are volunteers.

PROBLEMS OF FUNDING

How to adequately support a community suicide prevention or crisis intervention program has been one of the most difficult and unsolved problems to be confronted across the country. None of the centers has solved the problem completely. Even those few programs which are financed by budgets of more than $100,000 per year have not found ideal circumstances. For example, the Buffalo, New York Suicide Prevention and Crisis Service has been very generously supported by the Erie County Division of Mental Health. Along with the support comes an authority and control over program planning which for a time turned the crisis service into a conventional mental health outpatient clinic. Whereas the director would prefer to establish the mobile care teams and active outreach services, he was told that such services are perceived as belonging within another agency. It was several months before he could develop them, even though it could be done for much less money than he was forced to spend for professional persons who were keeping full calendars of long-term therapy cases. It must be remembered that the funding of services frequently presents a demand for the program director to compromise his goals in order not to sacrifice the entire program.

There are few agencies which have been able to secure their total funding from governmental sources. Atlanta and St. Petersburg have the only two centers in this study in such a funding category. Both claim that money has not been a problem in their operation.

Those centers which have moved under the auspices of the comprehensive community mental health centers have been able to secure a permanent place in the community, but they seldom have been given a budget comparable to their importance in the overall program. Usually, the salary of a coordinator has been provided, along with office space and telephones, but budgets and program sanctions for mobile crisis teams or other aspects of a complete program are not usually available.

The United Fund has not been a satisfactory source of support for most crisis centers, generally because it does not have sufficient money to give to operate a program completely. Usually, the United Fund policy prohibits other fund raising by a member agency, and crisis services cannot sustain themselves on what one agency can provide. Donations from the public usually supply minimum operating expense, but only after the program has been operating for a while, and these cannot be counted on for raising a budget.

The ideal program plan includes a sharing of costs among city and county governments, the United Fund, and the mental health center. All of these agencies benefit from the presence of the crisis service, and all should participate. However, there is a tendency for city and county officials to see the program as a functional part of a mental health clinic. There is no instance in the Southeast of a government funding a crisis service through the law enforcement agency, or directly via contracts with its Board of Directors. The area of funding crisis services is one in which almost no imagination and creative thought has been exercised. It is a virgin territory in which some innovative program will eventually make some outstanding contribution to the profession of suicidology; but for the present, there is little that can be offered to new program initiators other than an encouragement to be persistent in the face of frustration and defeat and a fervent wish for Godspeed in a nearly impossible task. WE CARE operated on $300 during its first year, gradually built up strength to apply for a research grant which provided $20,000 per year, and then went on United Fund and County Health Department budgets as a permanent agency. There is hope for determined agencies to survive as independent organizations, although it is much easier to be absorbed into some other service if the compromises are not too great.

Very few of the programs studied had arranged their eventual funding in the early stages of planning. The Brevard County 100-day plan made the tacit assumption that United Fund would pick up the tab. That assumption eventually proved correct, but only after a great delay. In most of the centers, other than those connected with county health departments, the agency was established with little concern for money. Money becomes a problem only when the program wants to grow beyond a telephone service, or when the need for a permanent coordinator becomes apparent. If the majority of crisis intervention services had waited until funding were assured, most of them would never have come into existence. However, this is not to say that planning groups should not take funding problems into account in the early stages. Strangely, none of the centers which had advisory boards had remembered to include sources of financial strength on the board. Psychiatrists and psychologists make very poor fund raisers. Policemen and ministers rarely have the necessary political clout. It has been a consistent oversight, which future planners should carefully correct, that bankers, industrialists, and prominent business leaders have not been considered as necessary as the professional care-givers.

Guideline XIV

A. Potential methods for permanent funding of community crisis services should be included in the earliest planning for a new program.

B Representatives from the banking, industrial, and business community should be included as key persons on an Advisory Board or Board of Directors.

Guideline XV

A program director must recognize that it will be necessary to surrender the program to the control of external forces if public money is sought from local governments or voluntary contribution agencies; it may be necessary to compromise the goals of the program in order to establish a substantial funding base.

STATUS OF THE SERVICE AS AN AGENCY IN THE COMMUNITY

Of the original 10 centers which have been studied in this project, only six remain in operation. Two of them disappeared, then reemerged when another service took their place in the community. That service has remained as a project of the local mental health association. Of the other eight, two were developed initially in the county health department, and both became the emergency service of the total community mental health program. In five of the remaining six centers, the program merged with or was started within a mental health clinic or center and has lost its individual identity in the community. Some of these have even lost their own telephone number, and their crisis workers have been replaced by mental health center secretaries during part of the 24-hour day. Only one center remains as an independent agency. WE CARE has continued its development into a separate agency in the community. There have been other programs initiated in recent months which are not included in this study and which have also achieved and maintained their status as separate agencies, but of those in existence in 1967, that is a rare feat. Perhaps it is a phenomenon of the early vintage services that they grew into subunits of other agencies rather than developing on their own. Perhaps this was the result of direct program planning which was successfully completed. It may be that the merger was for practical and expedient reasons brought on by financial problems. There are those who believe that a measure of successful development is reached when services are expanded in an existing agency rather than when a new agency is created.

In any event, merger with an existing service or with a concurrently develop- ing service is one option which program planners may choose to exercise. There is no reason why crisis services should not merge with mental health programs; likewise, there is no reason inherent in the service why they should. Crisis services must relate just as effectively with law enforcement, vocational, welfare, educa- tional, health, and legal services as with the mental health clinic. There is no reason why they should be mental health-affiliated any more than the ambulance service should be a mental health agency because it sometimes transports a psychotic patient to the psychiatric service. It is possible for a suicide prevention and crisis intervention service to establish and maintain an independent emergency service organization, under its own directorate body, and still relate effectively to all helping persons and agencies. Like the area of financing, the formation of crisis services into community agencies is a potentially fruitful area for exploratory creativity. A program planner who dares to be innovative may find a deeply satisfying experience at the end of the planning process.

Guideline XVI

The needs and resources of the local community must determine whether it is in the best interests of the community to establish a new agency for the delivery of crisis intervention services.

Guideline XVII

If a crisis intervention center is to become a functional part of the community's total network of helping agencies, it must establish itself as an identifiable service entity with a unique domain of responsibility in a manner similar to that of any other individual agency.

PUTTING IT ALL TOGETHER INTO A NEW SERVICE MODEL

11
THE SUICIDE AND CRISIS INTERVENTION SERVICE OF GAINESVILLE, FLORIDA

"Why is there a suicide prevention or crisis intervention center in this city? What is the reason for developing a program here?"

These are questions which every initiator of a new crisis service must be prepared to answer. One will not proceed very far in the development of a new program without someone's posing such seemingly obvious questions. If they are not asked by the community, the questions should be raised by the initiator himself. What motives or purposes lie behind his development of his program?

Such questions can be answered for the Suicide and Crisis Intervention Service (SCIS), which was developed in Gainesville, Florida, in the fall of 1969. Perhaps, for a small town like Gainesville, the questions are even more relevant and more pressing than is usually the case in a larger city. In any event, any new program may be expected to emerge more or less for the purpose of meeting the needs of the initiator; only when these needs are not in conflict with those of the larger community can the program demonstrate its own worth and attract the support which will keep it viable. The ultimate value of a program will not be apparent in the beginning, and it cannot be "sold" to the community on the basis of its promise for the future. Therefore, it must be initiated under one set of purposes and supports and then be slowly transferred to the community if it merits perpetuation once the initial purposes have been met. This principle has been followed and clearly demonstrated by the SCIS in Gainesville.

RATIONALE OF THE PROGRAM

The basic purpose behind the development of the Gainesville center was that of building a system to demonstrate the community model for a helping service.

After studying the other 10 programs in the Southeast, which have been described in the first two sections of this book, it was a natural next step to combine the observations and reported experiences from these programs into a conglomerate which took maximum advantage of their histories. All of the best features could be included, and the pitfalls and errors could be avoided.

Furthermore, such a program could serve as a locus for developing and demonstrating new procedures and methods for delivering crisis intervention services. Since other programs naturally were less able to alter their established systems and experiment with new procedures, it was necessary to build a totally new agency if radical departures from conventional methods were to be developed. The Gainesville SCIS was initiated within the context of a determination to expand the limits of the current technology for suicide prevention and crisis intervention delivery.

Finally, the third important agenda behind the development of the Gainesville program was basic research on the lay volunteer as an element in the delivery system. It has been well documented throughout the earlier sections of this book that the volunteer had already become the central feature of suicide prevention centers; the volunteer was the one development which permitted the movement to spread across the country. By 1969, over 80 percent of the centers existing at that time used the volunteer as the key person on the telephone. However, there were no systematic data on how to recruit, select, train, or evaluate the performance of volunteers in crisis centers. This deficiency had to be overcome through basic research. Thus, the need for a functioning crisis center to serve as a living laboratory for the study of volunteer workers was the third part of the rationale for the Gainesville center.

These motives were admittedly those of the initiator, but they were not hidden agenda items; they were made explicit to the community and to the original steering committee. The motives were not those of the community, nor were they shared by it, but they were not in conflict with it. At the same time, they served to give the community a program which, experience has shown, was badly needed, and which it is not willing to give up after little more than two years.

THE GREAT EXPERIMENT

The operation of the SCIS has been like a series of experiments. These have not been formal scientific experiments with control or comparison groups and careful definition of the variables. Instead, they have been a series of attempts to try some new things with the rather unscientific faith—even stubborn determination— that they would work. New procedures and new ideas or attitudes constituted the experiments. The attitudes have not always been popular ones, and they often represent unique deviations from the opinions which are held by many of the leading authorities in suicidology; their uniqueness is part of the reason that they must be subjected to experimental inquiry. Some of the more important "experiments" in the SCIS should be discussed if a clear picture of the program is to emerge.

A New Type of Agency

The SCIS would have offered nothing to its own community, nor to the suicidology profession, if it had been just another telephone answering service. Enough had been learned from the 10 centers studied in the Southeast to know that a telephone answering service is largely an impotent and minimally effective service program. Therefore, a new concept of crisis centers was to be developed—one which emphasized extensive face-to-face contact with people in crisis, not only in the office but at the scene of the problem.

Full Utilization of Volunteers

Unlike most of the other centers which had been started in this country, the SCIS began with an unlimited level of faith and confidence in the capacity of the trained volunteer. Rather than viewing the volunteer as a person who "would probably not do too much harm if he were carefully supervised," the SCIS attitude was that the volunteer was the answer to a monumental manpower crisis in community mental health programming. The volunteer had never been fully utilized; the limits of his ability to render helpful service to humanity had never been appropriately tested. His capacity for personal involvement and dedication to a professional service was unstimulated; his potential to become a professional crisis worker was unknown. All of this had to be demonstrated, and it was the goal of the SCIS to push to the very limits of the capacity and potential ability of the volunteers by developing a program design in which only the most able and most devoted could stand to participate. Those who survived the test have proven the boundless worth of trained volunteers in crisis intervention centers.

Philosophy of Crisis Services

It should be obvious that the underlying philosophy of a program will determine its actual service procedures. Any program which adopted the same philosophy would develop a set of clinical services very similar to those of the SCIS. Thus, it is not the actual practices which are important so much as the underlying concepts about crisis service delivery. The policy of the SCIS is a very simple one: *"The policy of this center is merely to respond to every request to participate in the solution of any human problem whenever and wherever it occurs."* It is impossible to imagine a problem which falls outside the scope of appropriate involvement by the crisis center. The saying that "The buck stops here!" was never more true than when applied to the crisis center service policy.

It should be noted that the center policy does not say that the crisis service will solve every problem, but merely that it will not turn away from participating in the solution of any problem. There are no eligibility requirements. The solution to problems must include participation from the client, if this is possible, and often requires the participation of other agencies and specialists. The crisis center is best conceptualized as an ombudsman in behalf of people with any type of problem. The crisis center may go to court with a client and explain to the judge that it is working to secure employment for the person, and that if he can get a job to pay off his bad checks this would contribute more to his total rehabilitation than spending 30 days in jail. A two-week delay in sentencing could give both the client and the crisis center a chance to act; if that fails, the law prescribes the justice and he may go to jail. In other cases, the crisis center may aid in reestablishing communication between a juvenile runaway and his parents. The need for food, clothing, and shelter can be just as much of an emergency to a family as the need for impartial mediating intervention in an angry family dispute. Both types of human problem receive equal attention with suicide threats and attempts when they are brought to the crisis center by a client or by another community agency.

Attitudes Toward People in Crisis

Probably nowhere in the operation of the SCIS is there a more "experimental" aspect than in the testing of new attitudes about people in crisis. There has been a continuous, conscious avoidance of those stereotyped ways of thinking about people which abound in the clinical professions related to the delivery of conventional mental health services. These new attitudes have also had a large role in shaping the directions of the service program. They may be summarized as follows:

1. People in crisis are not sick. Crisis intervention is not necessarily a medical service, nor even a health-related service.
2. People in crisis are not mentally ill. Crisis intervention is not necessarily a mental health service.
3. People in crisis need immediate, active, aggressive intervention.
4. People in crisis are the responsibility of the local community. Crisis intervention service is as much a rightful expectation of every citizen as the availability of public education, public health, police and fire protection, and public utilities.

Crisis Intervention as a Health Service

It is true that some clients need medical care immediately, and for them, no other service is adequate. Some clients need housing, clothing, food, and employment. It is hardly reasonable to expect a medical unit to provide for such needs. A crisis intervention system which is ancillary to the medical or health enterprise and a unit of it will be unable to meet many of the human needs which are present in the community. Of all the agencies and helping services in the community, the medical establishment is the most formalized, institutionalized, and regimented. Such a structure serves medicine and its practitioners well, but it is hardly capable of meeting all of the needs of the community citizens, especially when they do not require health care.

Consequently, the SCIS attempts, wherever possible, to involve clients with their own family physicians or with agencies which offer special clinical services. It is not the role of the crisis center to approach people in crisis in the role of a health advocate, seeking to promote a specific type of service system.

Crisis Intervention as a Mental Health Service

Those agencies in the 10-center study which were affiliated with, or functionally a part of, the community mental health center had a single characteristic in common. They all functioned as a large net designed to catch people in crisis and funnel them into the mental health system. The same comments made above about the medical enterprise are applicable here, for most of the mental health programs are influenced if not dominated by the strategies of the medical model. As a rule, the mental health system is a passive one. There may be walk-in service, with no waiting lists for intake, but rarely is the mental health system functional 24 hours a day. If it does provide around-the-clock coverage, it is more inclined to function for the benefit of an acute schizophrenic reaction than for a jobless transient with no money. Once the system accepts him for treatment, the mental health client is expected to have his problems once a week, for an hour, by appointment. The service teaches him to talk about the problem abstractly, but rarely is this discussion rendered in the setting in which both the client and the helper can experience the problem almost as it is happening.

The mental health system has a long way to go before it can accommodate itself—if in fact it even should—to the needs of the person facing a general acute crisis. The professionalism and social distance which separate the mental health practitioner from most of the community make it highly unlikely that the ombudsman role of the crisis intervener could be implemented from a mental health setting. The typical policy statement of a mental health setting is essentially: "We're here to help clients who want our help, but if they don't want to cooperate (i.e., play by our rules) *that's their problem!*" This policy works effectively in preventing manipulating neurotics from developing pathological dependency. It is inappropriate for ambivalent suicidal cases or for the immobilized, crisis-ridden client.

Need for Active, Aggressive Intervention

People in a crisis need immediate response. They generally feel helpless and impotent in the face of their problems. When they call out for help and learn that they can get no help until the next day, or until Monday morning, they feel even more helpless and powerless. On the other hand, when they call the crisis center and perhaps get a mobile CARE Team (see Chapter 14) activated in their behalf, they immediately become people with the ability to make something happen.

They feel some hope because they have been able to evoke a response. They have been able to move a system into action. The aggressive activity of the crisis worker, unlike the passive, reflective stance of other systems, gives a feeling of support and courage to get through the crisis.

Most community agencies find they are able to function most effectively with stable, well-regimented procedures. It enables them to be fair to all and prevents unequal distribution of the agencies' resources. This is probably the best reason why crisis intervention services have not developed within many existing agency structures. Other systems do not adapt to an unsuitable role, and should not be forced to accept one.

The need to provide an immediate response, both by telephone and through personal contact, has led the Gainesville crisis center into a very close involvement with the law enforcement agencies. It has been the reason behind the development of a mobile radio system for the CARE Team. It has been the reason behind a policy that the crisis center will respond automatically to every request for help from a law officer. The police or deputy sheriff are usually the first ones contacted and the first ones on the scene in personal problems involving a citizen and his community or social environment. When the police call the center, they are asking for immediate and active intervention, similar to that which they provide, but with a different focus.

Crisis Intervention as a Community Service

The Gainesville crisis intervention service operates from a belief that the community needs its fire department, hospital, churches, mental health clinic, schools, welfare office, police and court system, physicians, utilities, and a crisis intervention service. More and more, communities are realizing that there are human service responsibilities to be met by public agencies. Police departments are establishing community service divisions which actively seek to identify and relieve the sources of stress in high-crime neighborhoods. Other neighborhoods are establishing community action centers with programs of adult basic education and home economics training. Some such centers are even organizing for the delivery of free health service to area residents by operating medical clinics two nights a week in ghetto churches.

The crisis intervention service seeks to serve all citizens, regardless of the type of problem that they present. It seeks to do so on an immediate, no-fee basis at any time of the day or night. Why should not the crisis center be supported by the local government? It is the government's responsibility to care for the well-being of its citizens. It provides welfare for the poor, health care for the sick, redress for the victimized, and protection for the property holders. Why not help for everyone, and for all types of personal crises?

It has been the goal of the Gainesville program to develop a response system which would serve the widest possible range of human problems, without doing so under the auspices of any specific helping system, but collaboratively with them all. It has been the goal of the program to show the feasibility of a new type of community service, not by describing it theoretically and abstractly, but by demonstrating it in action for all to experience.

A Demonstration of Applied Community Psychology

The final aspect of the SCIS which describes its experimental nature is related to the practice of community psychology as a new form of professional psychology. Clinical psychology has had its role models and its professional service systems over the years. They have largely been tied to medicine and psychiatry in medical settings; some have been associated with the educational system. Professional psychology has long been in search of its own home wherein it could serve clients who require only psychological or behavioral understanding and alteration. There has been increasing doubt among community psychologists that the modern community mental health center would be such a place. Many have seen these programs as "old wine in new bottles." Community psychology was quick to eschew the label of "community mental health" for its activities. Although the distinction between community psychology and community mental health never has been a clear one, most community psychologists have insisted that there is a difference, and the latter term has been considered equivalent to clinical psychology in the community rather than to community psychology. However, there is an increasing identification of crisis theory and crisis intervention procedures with community psychology (Kalis, 1970). The Gainesville SCIS grew out of a desire to provide a place for psychology students and interns to experience a new form of helping service to the community. It has been an experiment in developing a new service system which allows professional psychologists to function as care-givers and as consultants to volunteer care-givers.

HISTORY AND DEVELOPMENT OF THE SCIS PROGRAM

In order to support the basic research program on volunteer crisis workers, it was necessary to apply for and receive an NIMH research grant. This application was made through the Center for Studies of Suicide Prevention in the spring of 1969 and was awarded in the fall of the same year. Obviously, the research program depended totally upon the availability of a functioning crisis center to serve as the laboratory, and thus the first step in the implementation of the research program was the development of the crisis center. However, the research grant was awarded to the Department of Clinical Psychology of the University of Florida, and the SCIS was not intended to be a University of Florida agency. To resolve this apparent difficulty, a system was established which has not been well understood by many people in the Gainesville community. Actually, not one agency, but two sister agencies were created. One was the Center for Crisis Intervention Research, which is described in greater detail in a later chapter. The other was the Suicide and Crisis Intervention Service, Inc., a private, nonprofit corporation chartered in

Gainesville under the laws of the state of Florida. For the first two years, this SCIS corporation had no assets and no source of income. Therefore, the Center for Crisis Intervention Research, which was a research unit under the Department of Clinical Psychology at the University, loaned personnel, space, and facilities for the SCIS to carry out its service to the community. It was understood with the granting agency of NIMH that the costs of providing crisis services would be withdrawn gradually from the research budget, so that at the end of three years, the SCIS would be totally on its own, financially. It had a guaranteed life of two years, but during that time it had to prove its worth to the community sufficiently so that if the community felt it was worth preserving, it would provide the means from local sources.

The First Corporation

In order to establish the corporation, the initiator invited a group of local citizens and agency representatives to a series of meetings in the County Health Department. The local chapter of the Mental Health Association was the sponsoring agency; throughout the early development, the Mental Health Association, not the University, was given the public credit for establishing the service. In the first few meetings, the idea of a suicide prevention and crisis intervention program was presented and described, together with the fact that such a program was feasible for the local area with the temporary help of the research program. To further generate interest and involvement, three center directors were invited to visit Gainesville and present their own crisis intervention programs to the local leaders. These guest consultants came from WE CARE in Orlando, the Crisis Call Center in Nashville, Tennessee, and the Suicide Prevention Center in Jacksonville, Florida. After hearing these directors describe crisis intervention services from real experience, the group voted to form a steering committee to implement the service and to incorporate itself into a Board of Directors.

Thus, the Suicide and Crisis Intervention Service, Inc., was established and began to provide crisis services to the community in December, 1969. Its Board of Directors operated the program for two and one-half years. However, this Board had been carefully selected to include primarily legitimizers who would provide the easiest entry for the new service into the community of helping agencies. The members were primarily professionals in health-related disciplines; they were not business people and they were not fund raisers. When the SCIS began to lose its support from the research program at the end of the second year, it immediately needed a new type of structure and sources of support. Consequently, the program underwent a drastic revision at the administrative level.

The Case of the "Shattered Syllogism"

It was just as true in Gainesville as in all other programs that when public support was requested, the program had to pay for it by giving up its own freedom and autonomy. People who put money into a system are immediately in a position to become the decision-makers for the system. In Gainesville, the cost of public money was the requirement that the center surrender to an error in logic. There had been another service program established in Gainesville just prior to the SCIS. This was a drug abuse treatment and education program called the "Corner Drug Store." It had some funds from the state and from the University, but it also was seeking local support from the United Way and the city and country governments. Because drug abuse problems and suicide are both considered *mental health problems* by laymen, the County Commissioners sought advice from the director of the County Mental Health Services. Without a moment's hesitation, he recalled that in his former city, two such programs had been combined into one because they provided the same services. Local businessmen who support the United Way and who sit on its Board of Directors also reasoned that the Corner Drug Store and the SCIS were identical agencies and that they should be combined and work together rather than separately.

No amount of reasoning would appease the community leaders after their minds were made up. The directors of the SCIS and the Corner Drug Store concurred that merger of the two service programs was absolutely impossible because of the great disparity in their nature and program designs. They also agreed that the value of merger was obvious from the business and fiscal management points of view. Therefore, the directors set about to accomplish the merger as easily and as quickly as possible. In doing so, they consciously agreed to let the logical error stand and to let experience reveal the foolishness of the conclusion. The fallacious argument went this way: the SCIS uses volunteers for its manpower; so does the Corner Drug Store. The SCIS operates a 24-hour telephone service for people to call; so does the Corner Drug Store. The SCIS has a CARE Team which will go to people who need immediate help; so does the Corner Drug Store. Suicide is a specific type of problem; so is drug abuse. Therefore, because of these four similarities, the two programs are identical, competing services which do the same things in the community. This argument is like saying that the fire department and the sewer system are identical agencies because they both send water through pipes. But since the minds of the community leaders were made up, there was no purpose in trying to dissuade those who might support both programs if their will were done. Because the SCIS routinely referred all drug cases to the Corner Drug Store, which in turn referred suicide and non-drug-related crises to the SCIS, there was already a history of good collaborative relationships between the two agencies.

The Community Crisis Corner, Inc.

The two Boards of Directors elected negotiating representatives to meet and to iron out the details of the merger. Eventually, the Corner Drug Store dissolved its corporation, and the SCIS Board amended its charter to change its name and broaden its purpose to include the drug treatment program. Thus was born the

Community Crisis Corner, Inc. The name was not chosen so as to combine the two agency names, but because that was the only name which the secretary of state could assign; other names requested were already chartered within the state.

The result has been the merger of two Boards of Directors, plus the addition of new members who had not previously served on either. This has resulted in a much stronger Board of Directors than either service previously enjoyed. The members are prominent citizens of the Gainesville business and social community. They are people who enjoy the respect of widely diverse segments of the population and who can attract funds from sources which naturally demand wise and efficient business management. The Community Crisis Corner, Inc., is like a holding company which manages the business affairs, finances, personnel matters, and fund raising of its two distinct service divisions. The Corner Drug Store and the SCIS still exist as service programs under their own individual names. The general public has already learned to trust and respect these names. Yet, neither is a corporation any longer, and both are dependent upon a common management system.

The development of the new corporation came about for the wrong reasons, but it was a definite advantage for the two services. Merger at the management level is clearly more economical and efficient. Fund raising will be greatly improved and simplified. However, the two service systems are so vastly different from one another that they probably never can be combined either physically or under the same clinical director. The SCIS program utilizes tape recorders, television cameras, two-way mobile radios, and an intimate relationship with law enforcement officers. Such equipment and liaisons would be inimical to the operation of the Corner Drug Store. The SCIS must serve all segments of the community, whereas the Corner Drug Store serves largely the drug users in the youth culture. The social distance between some "straight" and some counter-culture elements of the society are such that they could not easily mix in the same waiting room without one or the other service losing some credibility with its clients.

Because the argument which brought about the merger of the two programs was fallacious, and because neither of the program directors was consulted before the decision was made about their fate, it would have been easy enough to have resisted and stubbornly refused to accept the external pressures for the programs to merge. To have taken this stance, however, would have been destructive to both services. It is necessary to recognize that growth and development must go in very unusual directions which program initiators never can foresee fully when the community takes over the program. Actually, it is a token of commendation to both programs that the community leaders felt so positively about the services that they proposed such a radical procedure. Had either of the programs been less effective or seen as less desirable for the community, they could have been ignored easily and disposed of by the elected leadership.

Emergency Mental Health Service in a 10-County Region

The third major step in the historical development of the SCIS involves its relationship with the North Central Florida Community Mental Health Center. Gainesville had been trying to establish a community mental health center since 1964. There had been a number of abortive starts on construction grants and finally on a staffing grant. However, with the employment of a psychiatrist-director and the appointment of a 15-member District Board, the mental health center finally began to become a reality in 1972. The only problem with the plan was that the service area established by the state guidelines combined Alachua County and nine other very sparsely populated rural counties, comprising a total of 6105 square miles and 250,000 population. Among these counties were three which had no medical or health facilities at all. The area spread from the Gulf of Mexico to the Georgia border, a distance of 140 miles from one end to the other. The community mental health center must have an emergency program among its five essential services. Thus, a formal, contractural agreement was established between the District Board of the North Central Florida Community Mental Health Center and the Community Crisis Corner, Inc., whereby the SCIS Division of the Corporation would provide the 10-county emergency service. A proposal was written and agreed to by the Director of the SCIS and the Director of the Mental Health Center whereby the SCIS would establish two branch offices in outlying cities in the service area. There would be 10 CARE Team bases, approximately one for each of the counties, and the telephone network which would keep all of the offices tied together for consultation and case management activities. Thus, before the SCIS was three years old, the service program which it had developed for its own community of 104,000 was to be expanded into an area seven times the size with more than twice the population. Problems of providing crisis intervention services in widely scattered and thinly populated rural areas are unknown in cities. The presence of multiple family party lines discourages many from using the telephone to request help for personal problems. Travel distances between small towns make the CARE Team function come complex. But the basic philosophy and concepts of providing crisis intervention services are unchanged, and the same program format will be provided equally throughout all 10 counties.

This brief historical account takes the SCIS through its first two and one-half years. It relates briefly the details of its original founding, its growth and its loss of funds by original arrangement with the funding agency, and its merger with another community agency into a combined business management system. Finally, the SCIS entered into a major service contract with the formal mental health center throughout a 10-county service area. In all of these associations with the Center for Crisis Intervention Research, the Community Crisis Corner, Inc., and the North Central Florida Community Mental Health Center, the SCIS has continued to function as an individual agency within the total system of community agencies, interrelated with all of them, but identifiable as a distinct and separate service entity of its own. It has its role to perform in and for the community; it has negotiated various agreements and compromises whereby that role not only can be fulfilled, but nurtured and developed to its fullest possible extent.

SOME RESULTS OF THE EXPERIMENT

Whether or not the SCIS has been an effective program in the Gainesville community is not an easy question to answer. Outcome criteria are very difficult to collect in an agency in which part of nearly every action plan includes involvement with one or more other agencies. How can the success of one system be measured when that effect is the result of work by other people and agencies not directly associated with it? One way of assessing the effect of the program is to look at the extent of its acceptance in the community. Is it being utilized? Do people know of its existence? Is it operating at the level which might reasonably be expected of it? These and related questions can be answered from data which have been systematically recorded on telephone logs and case data sheets and coded for computer processing.

Before the data on the program activity can be meaningful, a brief description of the community in which it is located is in order. Gainesville is the county seat of Alachua County and the home of the University of Florida. Its population numbered 64,000 within the city limits and 104,000 within the total county area in 1970. This population base includes approximately 22,000 students at the University.

The toll-free telephone system covers the entire county. The population is approximately 30 percent black. Aside from the University, the main industry in the area is real estate development and construction, with some agriculture. However, the major Florida industries of tourism, space engineering, and citrus are not major factors in the economy. The social-political climate of the community is mixed, but because of the influence of the University campus, the voting record within the city is largely liberal and Democratic.

The community has a full range of helping services, both state and county supported and private. All of the usual services are present, except for Travelers Aid. There are five psychiatrists and six psychologists in private practice in the community, as well as the University Medical Center and the Veterans Administration Hospital.

Into this setting, the SCIS began to operate on December 15, 1969. Within just a few months, it was evident that the program was going to meet a need in the community which other services were not providing. The caseload was immediately surprisingly active, as the data in Table 1 indicate.

This listing of activity for the first three months of the service shows that the program was starting an average of approximately 60 new cases per month. Data

Table 1 Crisis center activity during its first three months of service

New cases opened	191
Total calls from (or about) clients	1367
Total nuisance calls	47
Outgoing calls to clients	667
Outgoing calls to agencies about clients	310
Outgoing calls to others about clients	294
CARE Team contacts in the community	173
CARE Team contacts in the office	132
Total of all incoming calls	2189
Total of all outgoing calls	1318

presented later show that this figure doubled after the first year. There is no doubt that the SCIS started off at a high level of activity and has maintained a steady growth in terms of its utilization. Table 1 shows a total of 2189 incoming calls of all types during these first three months. This figure may be compared with 2119 calls received during the entire 12 months of 1969 by WE CARE in Orlando. This was the fourth year of WE CARE's operation in an area of more than 400,000 population. The difference may be explained by two factors. First, the program practices at SCIS encourage frequent calls by clients while their cases are open and currently active. WE CARE reported 2.6 calls per case, whereas the SCIS recorded nearly four calls per case. Secondly, the SCIS program was opening many more cases than WE CARE. By the end of the first six months, the SCIS had recorded 496 new cases, exceeding the 460 individual cases opened by WE CARE in 1968. This difference is due largely to the level of advertising activity in Gainesville. The local radio stations were very cooperative in publicizing the program, and although there were no commercial television stations in the immediate area, the community was saturated with awareness of the SCIS program. In April, 1970, a survey was made of the community by a student in the journalism department at the University. He discovered that 80 percent of a random sample of telephone subscribers listed in the local directory knew of the existence of the SCIS. Although only 62 percent indicated they might call the program for themselves, 85 percent indicated that they would call the SCIS in behalf of a friend or relative who was experiencing depression and/or suicidal ideas. Thus, there is good reason to believe that the community learned of the SCIS relatively quickly and began to respond to the availability of the service at a rate twice that of the Orlando area's response to WE CARE, despite the latter's four-times-larger population and four years more experience with the program. The SCIS was well known in its area, in comparison with one of the outstanding programs in the Southeast.

Several indices are available to reflect the steady growth of the SCIS caseload over its first 24 months. Table 2 shows the number of new cases opened for each month of the first two years. These data include both telephone cases and suicide attempt cases which were referred to the center by the local law enforcement agencies. However, they do not include the one-name or John/Jane Doe cases. The SCIS does not consider these as actual cases, since without identification of the client there is insufficient information to use in formulating an action plan and helping the client carry it through to completion. The unidentified cases represent only about 15 percent of the total telephone traffic.

Table 3 compares the total number of calls logged through the system during the first six months of 1970 and 1971. There is an obvious increase during the second year. The increase in outgoing calls reflects a steady increase in the case management potential of the program. A later chapter defines the "four-phase process of crisis intervention" which the SCIS has developed and explains the activity of the phase II or management aspect of the process.

Table 4 indicates the number of new cases, continuing current cases, and reopened former cases during the first six months of the second year of the

Table 2 Number of new cases opened each month during first two years

1970		1971	
Month	Number	Month	Number
January	47	January	83
February	82	February	127
March	62	March	90
April	106	April	66
May	86	May	86
June	113	June	72
July	109	July	61
August	105	August	67
September	95	September	70
October	101	October	87
November	103	November	84
December	92	December	58

Table 3 Telephone activity for first six months of 1970 and 1971

	Incoming		Outgoing		Total	
	Jan.–July 1970	Jan.–July 1971	Jan.–July 1970	Jan.–July 1971	Jan.–July 1970	Jan.–July 1971
No. of calls	3748	4263	2308	3242	6056	7505
Average per month	624.7	710.5	384.7	540.3	1009.3	1250.8
Average per day	20.0	23.7	12.8	18.0	32.8	41.7
Percentage of increase 1970–1971	13.7		40.7		23.9	

program. It should be noted that only a small (2.4 percent) portion of the caseload is due to previous clients' becoming reactivated. This is despite the routine follow-up procedure (phase IV) which the SCIS has initiated. Closed cases are recontacted automatically after six to eight weeks to see how they are getting along. This table also shows the monthly and daily average of new cases and current cases logged. Both of these figures are minimum estimates, since it is possible, especially with the current case callers, for phone calls to escape being logged.

Table 5 presents a demographic description of the cases which were handled and closed during the first 12 months of the program's operation. The total number of individual cases was approximately 1300. In addition to these data in Table 5, a more detailed narrative description of the SCIS caseload is possible from the cross-tabulations computed for these first 1300 cases.

The caller was generally the person who was himself in crisis or a person who

Table 4 Status of cases represented in telephone activity, Jan. 1, 1971–June 30, 1971

	New Case	Current Case	Former Case
Number of calls	754	5291	150
Percentage	12.2	85.4	2.4
Average per month	125.7	881.8	25.0
Average per day	4.2	29.4	0.83

Table 5 Characteristics of crisis center clients during first year of service (N = approximately 1300)

Characteristic	Percent of caseload
Sex	
Male	36.5
Female	63.5
Race	
White	84.7
Black	15.3
Age	
Under 18	16.1
18–20	19.0
21–25	25.8
26–30	9.9
31–40	10.9
41–50	11.1
51–60	4.9
Over 60	2.3
Employment	
Student	35.6
Employed	29.6
Housewife	9.6
Retired	1.5
Disabled	0.7
Unemployed	21.9
Unknown	1.1
Residence	
University of Fla. campus	8.6
Gainesville	59.5
County outside Gainesville	23.9
Other Fla. county	7.0
Other state	1.0

was related in a significant way to the distressed and disturbed person. Only 8 percent of these clients had previously contacted the service and were seeking help from the SCIS for the second or third time. Sixty-three percent of all clients were female, and 37 percent were male. Out of 700 cases in which race was indicated, 14 percent were black and 84 percent were white.

Clients varied in age from six to 83 years. There were more clients 21 years old than any other year of age. The years of age with the second and third highest number of clients were 19 and 18, respectively. The number of clients for each year of age drops off quickly below 18, but tapers off gradually over 21, so that clients in their late 20's, 30's, 40's, and even older were numerous. Of 1042 clients for whom age was identified, only 9.1 percent were 50 years of age or older.

Fifty-eight percent of all cases were initiated by the clients themselves. The remaining 42 percent were initiated by a variety of significant other persons, such as friend (14.5%), city police department (4.8%), county sheriff's department (4.3%), relative other than spouse, parent or child (2.5%), spouse (2.2%), parent (2.1%), neighbor (1.9%), community agencies other than law enforcement, hospital, or mental health (1.6%), and campus housing resident assistant or resident counselor (1.0%).

Almost half of all clients (49.5%) were single. Twenty-five percent were married for the first time. The remainder were either married for other than the first time, widowed, or divorced. Seventy-one percent of all cases reported no children in the home.

The employment status of clients was recorded. Twenty-two percent of all clients were unemployed. Only 30 percent were employed. The remaining employment categories were student (32.3%), housewife (9.6%), employed student (3.3%), retired (1.5%), and disabled (0.7%). The SCIS thus can anticipate having two-thirds of its client population made up of students and unemployed persons and 10 percent made up of housewives.

Fifty-eight percent of the 793 cases in which therapy situation at the time of the initial call was obtained reported no psychotherapy in the past or present. The remainder either were in therapy or had been in therapy or counseling at a variety of campus and community agencies.

Since fewer than 15 percent of all case openings were assessed formally for lethality, the relative percentages of low, medium, and high lethality cannot be applied to all cases closed during this time period. The summary figures for these cases were low, 49.1%, medium, 34.0%, and high, 16.1%. When lethality is not assessed or recorded, it may be assumed that it is not a suicide case, and lethality is rated low. For these 373 cases that were assessed, the highest percentage of low lethality occurred on Saturdays (53.2%), the highest percentage of medium lethality occurred on Thursdays (41.8%), and the highest percentage of high lethality occurred on Monday and Sunday (20%).

Eleven percent of all cases were activated either during or immediately following a suicide attempt. Of the remaining clients, 16 percent threatened suicide while talking to the volunteer telephone worker or the CARE Team. Although 72 percent of all clients neither threatened nor attempted suicide at the time of the initial contact, many of these clients gave evidence of depression and suicidal ideation. Twice as many clients threatened suicide upon contact during the second activation than during the first activation.

For those clients for whom the nature of the crisis was identified (1107 of 1233 cases), for both sexes combined, the six largest problem areas were marriage (10.5%), finance (9.2%), parent-child relationships (7.2%), problem pregnancy (6.9%), physical-medical problems (6%), and personal inadequacy (5.4%). The primary nature of the crisis varied with sex. For males only, the six largest problem areas were finance (9.4%), drugs (7%), physical-medical problems (6.3%), marriage (5.7%), boy-girl problems (5.5%), and personal inadequacy (5.2%). For females, the six largest problem areas were marriage (13.1%), problem pregnancy (9.9%), finance (9%), parent-child relationships (8.6%), physical-medical problems (5.9%), and personal inadequacy (5.4%).

The primary nature of crisis also varied by race. Of the 670 clients for whom race was indicated, and excluding those for whom the problem was either not identified or "other," the following were the four largest problem areas for each race: (1) black: marriage (21%), finance (18%), chronic behavior disturbance (8%), and physical-medical problems (7%); (2) white: marriage (11%), parent-child relationships (8%), chronic behavior disturbance (7%), and finance (7%).

SUMMARY

The foregoing narrative and statistical description of the SCIS in Gainesville has been presented to give an idea of the type of new agency which was created as a result of the earlier study of 10 different programs. The motives of the initiator and the attitudes and philosophy which have formed the basis of the service program have been elaborated. The SCIS is still considered an "experimental" program; new ideas are being tried out continually, and old ones are being evaluated in relation to experience in the community. The history of the SCIS reflects a continually encountered principle of community service, namely, that the needs and dictates of the local community will force specific structures and events to occur. Directors and managers of individual programs always must be prepared to compromise their own systems and relinquish some of the control if the program is to grow and develop and if its potential value to the community is to be realized.

The independent, community-supported crisis intervention system capable of responding to any and all human problems with immediate and active assistance appropriate to the unique needs of the crisis is beginning to become a reality. The model is simple and straightforward. All it takes to make it happen is leadership and imagination to set the example. Once started, the system will prove itself in any community; it has the dynamic power of an idea whose time has come.

12
THE FOUR-PHASE PROCESS OF CRISIS INTERVENTION

In his discussions of the techniques utilized by crisis workers, especially in the intervention of suicide cases, Farberow (1967) has highlighted *activity* as a behavior which distinguishes crisis interveners from more conventional therapists. The effective crisis worker is distinctly more active in behalf of the client than is the psychotherapist. Caplan (1961, 1964) and others have provided the rationale for this activity by describing a crisis as a time when the patient finds himself much more dependent upon the external sources of support available to him than at any other time in his life. Thus, in crisis intervention services, it is necessary always to distinguish between what may be called the *situational dependency* of the crisis process and the *characterological dependency* of the inadequate or immature personality. One is a condition of normal living processes, whereas the other is a condition of psychopathological deficits in the personality.

It is not the purpose of this chapter to discuss the differences between these two types of dependency or to set forth guidelines for making the differentiation. The important point is that in suicide prevention and crisis intervention centers there are a large number of both types of dependency represented in the cases presented by the clients. It is necessary and appropriate, therefore, for such programs to have some systematic means of dealing with the dependency aspects of their cases. In other words, a crisis service must address itself to the question: "How *active* shall our program be with a client in crisis?"

There are various ways of answering this question. As a matter of fact, the degree of agency activity that is built into the clinical service program is one of the most salient differences among suicide prevention centers studied in the project reported in Part II of this book. For example, one way to answer the question of how active an agency should be is to leave it to the professional consultants who give their direction (often in the form of passive permission) to the program directors. Many programs have been organized on the premise that all that should happen in a suicide prevention center is that people should be on duty *to receive phone calls* from persons in distress. During these client-initiated calls, the worker is supposed to perform his crisis intervention functions, and only in this way does he have any contact with the person in distress. In the early days of establishing suicide prevention services, it was felt by most local professionals that the volunteers would be violating the "right to privacy" of the callers if contacts were initiated by the volunteer at a later time.

A second method for determining how active a center should be has been to sample the feelings of the crisis workers themselves and to modify or even originate procedures on this basis. For example, in many of the centers just mentioned where the professional consultant set the rules, the volunteers became anxious over not knowing what happened to cases with which they had become involved on the telephone. When a seriously suicidal person called during the evening, it often was not enough for the worker that, during the conversation, the caller sounded less disturbed or maybe even promised not to take any lethal action. The caller may have agreed to seek another agency the next day. Still, many crisis workers found themselves waking up the next morning and searching the newspaper or tuning in the early morning local news on the radio to find out whether a suicide had been discovered. The "no news is good news" aphorism is of little comfort under these conditions. How much easier, and more reassuring, it would be simply to call the client back in the morning and ask how he is! Many volunteers began to do just that. The amazing thing was that they found that they hadn't invaded anyone's privacy at all. Instead, they nearly always found the client to be most grateful, appreciative, and convinced (if he hadn't been before) that the volunteer and the crisis center really did care what happened to him. So, many decisions about center activity have developed from enterprising volunteers who exercised their own good judgment and tried out new procedures within the context of being helpful to clients.

A third method for determining how active a center should be in its crisis work is to survey the other existing agencies in the community and to negotiate the role and procedures which the established agencies will accept for the new crisis service. This usually is facilitated by having a board of directors composed of executives or representatives from the established helping services. Sociologists use the term "domain" for the functional territory which an agency may occupy within the network of service systems. An agency will be granted a domain within which to operate its program for only so long, and up to the point where its domain is still perceived as not encroaching upon established domains. Anyone who has tried to negotiate a system for suicide prevention and crisis intervention with suicide attempters in hospital emergency rooms has encountered this phenomenon with clarity and intensity. It takes long discussions, patience, diplomacy, and several positive experiences from some activities to become accepted in a community. This method of determining activity of a center involves continually testing the limits which are allowable for the domain that the crisis service wants to occupy. In contrast to meeting the needs of the community, this is a process of getting the community to permit the center to meet its own needs. Many directors of crisis programs find themselves caught on the horns of this dilemma; they usually feel very annoyed by being in this situation, yet they are reluctant to extricate themselves from it.

The three methods of deciding how active to be in crisis intervention which are described above may be viewed on a continuum. The first method generally results in the most inactive, answer-the-telephone-only type of programs. Each succeeding method adds more activity to the centers' procedures. For the purpose of establishing a contrast, it is possible to skip many intervening steps on the continuum and to move to the other extreme, which yields the maximum amount of activity during the crisis intervention process. This leads to the identification of a method for determining activity level which is based upon applying the *minimum difference test* to each individual case. The system is based upon the following steps.

Question

What is the most serious outcome or consequence of this case which might possibly result from taking no action at all?

The answer to this question sets the *goal* for the intervention: to behave so as to prevent this consequence from occurring. This enables one to plan the activity to be taken in the case.

Question

What activity should be instituted in order to be reasonably certain that the worst consequence will not occur?

Once the action plan is developed according to this implicit criterion in each case, the individual volunteer or the center can then begin to implement the plan.

Evaluation

Was the action adequate? How sufficient was the action which was taken? Should more have been done, or less?

Every action plan developed by a crisis worker should be evaluated with respect to its effectiveness and its appropriateness. Ideally, this should be done with each case. However, it is certainly necessary for maintaining quality control to have supervisors, senior volunteers, or some member of the crisis center staff periodically review the action plans developed for individual clients.

Criterion

Assume that despite the action plan, the worst possible consequence identified in question 1 above does, in fact, occur!

Test of the Action

What the center actually did to prevent the worst possible consequence is of *no importance* in and of itself. What matters is the *difference* between that which *actually* was done and that which *might* have been done.

Planning Action

Act in every case so that this difference between that which is done and that which might be done is kept as small as possible.

By repeatedly applying this minimum difference test to the evaluation of action plans, with reference to the events subsequent to the intervention, where these events are known, the Suicide and Crisis Intervention Service in Gainesville, Florida, has progressively developed a model for crisis intervention activity. This model conceptualizes the behavior of the center in four distinct categories, or phases, of the intervention process. It highlights the fact that crisis intervention is not a single event, but a dynamic process through which the client and the center move together toward a resolution of the issue which brought about the first contact. The remainder of this chapter is devoted to an elaboration of the four-phase process of crisis intervention.

PHASE I—THE OPENING OF A CASE

Naturally, nothing can begin until an initial contact is made between the crisis service and the client. Usually, this contact is made through the advertised telephone service, which is staffed 24 hours a day. This is by no means the only method for achieving contact with people in crisis. For example, some centers are beginning to advertise the office address along with the telephone number, thereby stimulating a walk-in contact. In some communities, the crisis service has arrangements with law enforcement agencies whereby the service is notified of every suicide attempt; then the center initiates a contact with the attempter either immediately in the hospital emergency room or later at his home. Whatever the source of the initial contact, the opening of a case always involves certain basic procedures.

Litman et al. (1965) have outlined the three essential functions of crisis workers. Although their treatment of these functions was relative to the telephone intervention, the same behaviors are relevant and necessary in any type of first contact. They include: (1) establishing the communication, (2) assessing the client's condition, especially his lethality, and (3) developing a plan of action for the client.

Establishing Communication

When the initial contact occurs via the telephone, the crisis worker has the problem of establishing sufficient trust and rapport between the client and the service, so that the client will not hang up and break the communication before some helping relationship can be established. A broader definition of establishing the communication has been developed. It includes the criterion that the communication is not established until the worker has obtained the name, telephone number, or other identifying information sufficient to permit a recontact initiated by the center whenever the communication is broken and for whatever reason. The conversation may be terminated by a mechanical malfunction in the telephone equipment or because the worker and the client mutually agree that maximum benefit has been obtained at that point. However, if the worker can use what information he has to relocate the client and renew a conversation, then the communication has been established. When the communication is established according to this criterion, then a crisis case exists upon which some effective intervention may be possible. Such a definition automatically excludes all "John Doe" cases. Hence, a center may chart the course of its increasing effectiveness by keeping a monthly record of the number of "John Doe" or "first name only" cases. As the number of such cases declines, the center increases its potential for making crisis interventions.

Assessing the Client's Condition

In determining what type of case a client presents, the worker must first make a determination as to whether or not the threat of suicide is present. This means that the volunteer not only must learn whether some life-threatening action has already been taken, but he must uncover the existence of serious contemplations by the client. Usually, this determination is best made by careful and sensitive listening rather than by direct interrogation, although the latter is sometimes necessary and, in such cases, never should be avoided.

The base rate data from nearly all suicide prevention and crisis intervention services indicate that even threatened suicide will be a factor in only 15–20 percent of the contacts. The number of cases in which an actual attempt is in progress will be much less. In those 80–85 percent of the cases in which suicide is not currently being contemplated as an alternative solution to the presenting crisis, the worker still must determine the nature of the crisis. This type of assessment is often more involved than the mere attaching of a category label. For example, a woman who calls the center in the wake of a threatened separation and possible divorce may be incorrectly classified as a "marital crisis" case. For this woman, the marriage may have been chronically disordered and a continual battleground, in which there were frequent separations and other traumas. She may have found a fairly adequate means of coping with the chronic disorder in her home. However, if the husband has now left permanently, or if her perception of his intention to return has changed from previous events, her crisis really may be a legal one. She needs an attorney to represent her and to provide the crisis-resolving information with respect to her rights and the course of her behavior. Her crisis may be a financial one, in which she knows that her husband cannot pay sufficient support despite legal rulings of his obligation. Therefore, her problem is to find employment in a field of her competency. Her crisis may be one of personal identity. If she has been holding this unstable marriage together by determination "for the sake of the children," she may now perceive herself as inadequate both as a woman and as a mother. She may feel guilty because she truly wants the divorce to take place for her own self- (not selfish) fulfillment. Thus, assessing the client's condition may mean much more than finding a broad category into which to place the case. It means sensitive diagnosis of where the client is in his present feelings about the problem being presented.

Assessing the client's condition does not and should not involve making pseudopsychiatric diagnoses of psychotic or psychoneurotic conditions. Of course, one does not have to be a professional practitioner to detect just plain craziness in a client's talk, and these are times when the professional consultants may be useful. However, to define this craziness as a form or manifestation of schizophrenia or manic psychosis is well beyond the role of the crisis worker. Furthermore, assessing the client's condition does not and should not involve the development of psychodynamic etiologies to explain the present feeling state. As Caplan (1964) has indicated, these antecedent conditions are useless in helping the person to resolve the present acute crisis, because the crisis is not a manifestation of a neurotic illness in the first place. Therefore, to assess the client's condition, a worker need only be a sensitive listener, as well as an asker of appropriate questions about present feelings. Neither professional psychological skills nor dime-store, amateur psychological sophistication are relevant or appropriate.

Finally, a function of the client assessment which is usually very difficult to perform during phase I relates to making the determination of whether a case is one of acute crisis or one of chronic maladjustment and characterological dependency. This usually can be done only during phase II and phase III, but some initial clues may be gathered during the case opening. Certainly, every crisis worker should be aware that both types of cases exist, since any one worker may be having his initial contact with a chronic caller. If an enthusiastic volunteer begins a new case opening procedure every time a chronic caller contacts the center, the result will be a frustrated client, a confused crisis center staff, and probably an embarrassed volunteer.

Developing a Plan of Action

An effective crisis intervention service will have established a large number of functional relationships with helping services in the community. It will have developed a catalog of local resources which will serve in all types of personal distress situations. These resources will range all the way from public agencies to private citizens in the ghetto who will provide food and shelter for transients or migrant laborers. The plan of action developed in phase I necessarily will incorporate the identification of some additional service which may be called upon to aid in the present crisis. The plan may involve a potential "transfer" to this other resource for continued treatment or involvement.

In many cases, it may be that the crisis center itself is the only reasonable source of help needed in the present crisis, or that the crisis center should become the manager of the case. This is especially true in cases of suicide death, where the crisis service is available to aid the survivors in their grief over this most difficult of all bereavement problems. Similarly, if it appears that a person in crisis is hampered in his resolution of this problem by an existing failure to come to grips with a previous suicide in the family, this may be a case which the crisis service staff can handle with more knowledge and understanding than any other agency or practitioner in the community. Thus, it is perfectly reasonable that a crisis service may transfer certain cases to itself as it grows and develops stature and expertise as one of the helping agencies in the community.

A final word about phase I is appropriate to point out that some case opening work may be performed by some means other than on the telephone. Whereas the usual procedure for opening a case is via this method, some centers have found that more efficient assessment and action planning can be accomplished on a face-to-face basis. Thus, they have initiated outreach programs, such as the CARE Team, described in a later chapter, to go to the scene and engage the client in the completion of the case opening. Similarly, it is reasonable, where physical facilities permit, to invite clients into the office for interviews for the purpose of really getting to work on the action plan. Such a system leaves no doubt in the mind of the client about the sincerity of the service in its desire to be of help. It also causes the client to take an initial step and to make a personal commitment towards the solution of his problem. Such mobilization is often very helpful in getting the process started.

Wherever and however it is accomplished, phase I of the crisis intervention process is completed when the client is identified, his condition is assessed and understood, and a plan of action has been developed for dealing with the condition. At this point, the case is opened. What is to become of it depends entirely upon the extent to which the following phases of the process are followed. The case may be terminated at this point, or it may be carried through to an effective conclusion.

PHASE II–THE MANAGEMENT OF A CASE

After the action plan has been developed, the obvious next step is to begin to implement it. When a call comes in initially at night, and the action plan involves the utilization of community resources which are not open 24 hours a day, it is obviously necessary to wait until the next morning to go to work on the case. Some type of contract must be initiated with the caller so that he expects another volunteer on the day shift to contact him and carry through with the plan. The case manager, who is often not the one who originally opened the case, probably will contact the other agency if a transfer is planned and facilitate the changeover. He then would contact the client and report on the time and date when an appointment had been arranged or relay whatever information is relevant to the client's crisis. It is during the management phase of the intervention that the crisis center makes use of the technology for resolving crises which Caplan has described (1964). This is the time when the client is helped to confront the reality of his situation, but is enabled to do so in manageable doses. This is the time when necessary information is sought and conveyed, and when blame for the event is appropriately attributed. Above all, this is the time when the crisis center helps the client to accept help.

There are a few basic guidelines for the management of crisis cases. They may be very obvious, but they should be mentioned because they are easily over-looked. The first guideline relates to the dependency problem. The management of a case should proceed in such a way that the client is helped to be dependent as long as he needs to be, but only to the extent that he needs to be. There is nothing helpful to be gained in crisis resolution by treating the person like a child. Similarly, consequences may occur from denying the client a chance to lean temporarily on the support of the center. Thus, in some cases, it may be necessary for the crisis worker to provide the transportation and the comfort of his personal presence when the client keeps the appointment at the transfer agency. In other cases, helping only to secure the appointment may suffice, and the client can use his own resources to keep the appointment once he knows that such an alternative exists. A person never should be denied the opportunity to use whatever resources he has.

A second guideline for case management is that it is a process through which the client and the center move jointly. Expectations are placed upon one another, and a ground rule should be that these expectations must be kept. For example, the center may ask a client to call in a report on how a particular action turned out. That expectation should be fulfilled by the client, and if it is not, the reasons why it was not should be explored. Similarly, when a client has reason to expect certain action on the part of the center, it should be faithfully fulfilled. This obviously places heavy demands upon the ability of the crisis workers to com-municate clearly to one another within the center and with the client.

Another guideline for case management is that it should always proceed as rapidly as possible. There is no excuse for a case's becoming lost in the system, although this may happen in almost any center. A crisis will resolve itself in a matter of a few weeks, and possibly the client will be left with fewer healthy coping mechanisms as a result of just letting a crisis heal itself. If the crisis center does nothing to improve on this spontaneous remission phenomenon, it has little justification for being in existence. Arbitrary time periods probably are not very helpful, but it is difficult to see how any crisis case, if managed actively, would take more than three–four weeks to resolve.

It was mentioned earlier that the crisis center frequently may need to distinguish between the situational dependency of acute crisis cases and the characterological dependency of chronically maladaptive persons. One of the ways in which this assessment is made is by observing the resistance which clients show to participating in and following the plans worked out for their problem-solving.

Alcoholics particularly are very difficult to engage in phase II crisis work. When it appears that the client is deriving his satisfactions primarily from periodic contact with the center, which is always available to come to his aid, either on the telephone or more directly, it should be obvious that the case is not an acute crisis, and this model for center involvement is not applicable. The extent to which crisis services wish to support chronic problem callers is a matter which each program must decide for itself. Some suggestions for handling such cases have been made by Hoff (1971) and Brockopp (1970a).

A final guideline for crisis management is that no one crisis worker should take over a case to manage it solely by himself. This is especially important in the great majority of centers which utilize nonprofessional volunteers as the staff. Rarely is any worker on duty frequently enough to manage a case actively, and when the volunteer begins to do his crisis work from home, complications are likely to arise. Rather, it is generally a more helpful procedure for the client to understand that his relationship is with a total center which is capable of assisting him at any time of the day or night, and not with just one or two individual workers. The way in which this is best accomplished is for the center to make extensive use of significant others in the client's own life. These people also should be available to the client, and they come under the heading of his own personal resources. Some centers consider the identification of significant others to be an integral part of establishing the communication with the client in phase I. These people always should be included in the case management work of phase II.

The end point of phase II is defined easily. It has been reached when the action plan has been implemented, or when the crisis has been resolved by the client's taking specific actions to come to grips with his situation. This may mean that a transfer is completed, or it may mean that the client handles things on his own, with active direction from the crisis worker, and achieves resolution. Thus, self-report by the client that things are now back in good order will signal the end of the management phase. It is important to note that forcing a transfer to another agency may be more harmful than helpful if the crisis can be resolved by the client's own resources. With effective case management, the center will know when one or the other of these things has occurred and will be able to move on to phase III.

PHASE III—THE CLOSING OF A CASE

Unless specific methods and technologies are introduced into the closing of crisis cases, they are very apt to be closed by default. The simplest method for closing a case is to note that a transfer has been effected and to place the file folder in a different file drawer from the one containing the active cases. This action may be clear to the crisis center staff, but it frequently leaves the client with a lack of certainty regarding the conclusion of his relationship with the center.

Once the action plan has been implemented and the case management can be terminated, certain specific actions are necessary so that the client, the center, the significant others, and the transfer agency, if there is one, know exactly what is the status of the case. In order to provide such clarification, at least two, and sometimes three calls must be initiated by the crisis center workers. One call, of course, must be made to the client. The client is told that from the point of view of the center, it looks as if his situation is now being resolved. The client naturally is given the largest share of credit for having accomplished this end by keeping appointments and otherwise utilizing the services of the center. He is told that the center is still interested in him and wants to be of further assistance if necessary, but that for the present, this seems unnecessary. The client is told also that because the center is still interested in how he will be getting along, someone will be getting back in touch with him in a few weeks or months. This piece of information is given in such a manner that the client has a feeling that he can refuse such follow-up if he likes, but experience has shown that this rarely ever happens.

Similar messages are given to the significant others and to the therapist or other responsible case worker at the transfer agency. In effect, this formal case closing process enables a proper termination to be made, in such a way that the client can feel that he has grown from the crisis intervention experience. With his crisis resolved, his situational dependency is over, and this change is analogous to the feeling of accomplishment one gets from being able to discard a pair of crutches which were only temporarily necessary. Clients deserve the right to have this feeling of success. They also need to have a definite ending to their relationship with the center so that they are not left wondering why contacts have ceased.

It is amazing that so much technology and attention has been devoted to the opening phase of crisis cases and that so little attention is paid, in most centers, to the formal closing. Of course, if a crisis center does not concern itself with active phase II management, or if it doesn't even perform a thorough job of phase I opening, then it will have no need to develop its skills at formal closing. Unfortunately, it appears that many centers have not found the need to conceptualize case closing for these very reasons.

It is important to note that the groundwork for phase IV of the process is already laid during phase III. It is in keeping with the concept of crisis intervention as a dynamic, flowing process that one phase moves along and blends into another, even though they may be separated distinctly in time.

PHASE IV—THE FOLLOW-UP OF A CASE

The final phase of crisis intervention is perhaps the most important of all. It presents the opportunity for the center to learn two very important types of information. First, through follow-up, the center can learn whether or not the client is still functioning well in the transfer situation which had been implemented during the final stages of phase II. If the transfer was inappropriate, or if the client is no longer following through with the arrangements made in his interest, the center may not be aware of it without a follow-up call. Secondly, it is only through follow-up that a center can learn about its own effectiveness in the handling of cases. It is a characteristic of modern community helping services that some type of program evaluation is instituted. Program evaluation of suicide prevention and crisis intervention services cannot be conducted in any manner other than by recontacting the clients and learning how they are currently adjusting. That is the primary function of phase IV.

The usual procedure which is followed is for the center to contact each client automatically between six and eight weeks after the formal case closing and to attempt to elicit certain basic information. Among the questions asked are the following:

1. How is the client currently feeling in relation to the crisis which caused him to contact the center in the first place?

2. What effect, if any, did the activity of the crisis workers have in helping the client to attain his current level of adjustment with regard to the presenting problem?

3. Was a transfer to another agency effected, and if so, is it still a helpful source of support for him?

4. How does the client feel toward the crisis center and its program?

A number of individual questions may be asked to arrive at these broad answers; and, with experience, volunteers can learn to conduct follow-up interviews with the same level of sensitivity that they use in case opening procedures.

Observations made in the WE CARE center in Orlando and at the Suicide and Crisis Intervention Service in Gainesville (Marcus, 1971) have shown that clients are very grateful for the follow-up procedure, provided that the calls are made within two months of case closing. The data from these studies also show areas in which the center may not be performing its functions as well as it may believe that it is doing so. For example, in the Gainesville SCIS, it was learned that fewer than 50 percent of the clients actually were transferred to another agency, despite explicit policy statements of the center that transfer should be a primary goal of case management. Such data offer the possibility of determining why such procedures are not being followed or may lead to the realization that certain procedures are in need of modification. It is to be admitted candidly that phase IV of the process is intended, in the short run, to aid the center rather than the client. However, in some instances, it may be ascertained that further case work is necessary, and this can then be promptly instituted. In the long run, any changes in program design and procedures which result from data gained on follow-up are in the best interests of the community at large, and the potential clients yet to be served may be seen as benefiting from the conscientious collection of such information.

MEASURES OF CRISIS INTERVENTION CASE OUTCOME

Zelenka, Marcus, and Bercun (1971) have commented upon the advantage of using the four-phase concept for the purposes of determining the outcomes of crisis work. For example, the extent to which phase I activity has been performed adequately can be assessed with the Fowler Technical Effectiveness Scale (Fowler and McGee, 1973). This scale is designed to measure how well the volunteer performs the case opening functions of establishing the communication, assessing the client's condition, and developing an action plan. Various measures of center activity, such as the number of contacts or the number of individual client actions accomplished per unit of time, may be developed to serve as measures of the phase II effectiveness. Phase IV, as already noted, is designed primarily for evaluating the center's role in helping a client to resolve a crisis over an extended period of time. Therefore, this model not only serves to structure the crisis center program so as to ensure the maximum amount of intervention activity, but it also provides a necessary vehicle for continual observation and assessment of the center and its personnel. The time is coming when all suicide and crisis centers will be called upon to develop and maintain quantifiable standards of center operation. When this goal becomes a reality, the center which adopts and follows this four-phase process will be greatly facilitated in its effort to demonstrate the quality of the service it is rendering to the public.

13

THE NON-PROFESSIONAL VOLUNTEER CRISIS WORKER

"The lay volunteer was the single most important discovery in the fifty year history of the [suicide prevention] movement. Nothing else of any significance happened until he came into the picture." (Dublin, 1969)

It was proposed in an earlier chapter that the volunteer, nonprofessional crisis worker has been the sine qua non which has permitted the suicide prevention and crisis intervention systems to grow, develop, and spread throughout the country. The history and rationale of utilizing volunteers has been discussed in several chapters throughout this book. However, in this chapter, attention is focused more intensively on the volunteer workers and their place in crisis centers. The critical questions and issues arising from their role are discussed in detail. Building upon the results of studying other programs, the Gainesville Suicide and Crisis Intervention Service has attempted to observe systematically and to record its practices and experiences with volunteer workers, especially in the areas of recruiting, screening, training, utilization of various levels of personnel, and finally, the problems of morale within the volunteer group. This chapter attempts to review these experiences from the Gainesville program, in the belief that they will be relevant for other programs as well.

RECRUITING VOLUNTEER CRISIS WORKERS

In Chapter 6, the three primary methods used in volunteer recruiting were discussed in some detail. The method of mass advertising was adopted in Gainesville because of its dual advantage in reaching many people and simultaneously advertising the existence of the center for potential clients. It must be understood that recruiting and screening are inseparable processes. Each method of recruiting has its own relative screening method, the use of which is predetermined when the recruiting method is selected. However, the two functions are discussed separately in this chapter.

The mass advertising method, and its companion screening system, was first used in starting the Crisis Call Center in Nashville, Tennessee. The exact details of its origin are unclear at this point, but it must have been the product of planning by the team of psychological consultants from George Peabody College and Meharry Medical College. Basically, the method is very simple. It calls for the center director to establish liaison with all of the radio, television, and newspaper services in the community. Announcements that the crisis center is seeking new volunteers can be made in a number of ways. The usual method is a brief public service spot on radio and television. News articles initiated by formal press releases also may be used, as well as feature articles in the newspaper or appearances on daytime television talk shows. When good interagency relationships exist between the crisis center and the local news media, as they must for successful advertising of the service program, the many possibilities for mass advertising for volunteer workers will become apparent.

The mass advertising method sometimes is criticized because it may attract undesirable people who might be harmful to clients. However, that problem is resolved by screening and supervision after recruiting. Actually, the major difficulty with the method is that it is very easy for the center director or volunteer coordinator to overlook the absolute necessity of directing the advertising message to all of the populations to be served by the center's service program. Experiences in the recruiting of volunteer workers in Gainesville have revealed certain problems which have not previously been observed and discussed. For example, it has proven fallacious to assume that mass advertising on radio and in the newspaper reaches all segments of the community equally, or that all segments of the community respond similarly to messages which reach them. The Gainesville center continually has designed and presented its service program as one intended for the entire community. General crisis services have been developed for the permanently established community resident, as well as the university and junior college student, and for the black laborer as well as the family of the university professor or businessman. Yet, despite this wide range of people seeking services from the program, problems have arisen in the range of persons seeking to offer volunteer time to provide the services. These problems are primarily in relation to students and black citizens as volunteers.

Students as Volunteers

In a university community, students constitute the most available and potentially valuable manpower resource. Volunteering time and service to assist persons in need of befriending fits compatibly into the social-action-oriented life style of young people in America in the late 1960's and 1970's. Volunteering in crisis centers provides a meaningful and satisfying way to "do your thing" for many university students. Therefore, advertising for volunteers is always effective when it is placed in student newspapers, on bulletin boards in student lounges and class building hallways, or on radio stations which design their programming for the student culture.

Becoming a volunteer at the crisis center can also meet the students' needs in other ways. It has been discovered that some university professors teaching social science classes at the freshman and sophomore levels have been requiring their students to move out into the community and experience some social process as a form of augmenting the classroom curriculum. Many students have made application to become volunteers at the crisis center merely to satisfy the requirements for a particular course in which they are currently enrolled. Sometimes, the requirement explicitly states a number of hours to be served in some practicum capacity; sometimes, it is merely the student's way of collecting experiences to incorporate into the writing of a term paper assignment. Obviously, care must be taken continually by the volunteer coordinator to determine the boundaries of a student applicant's interest. Where term paper data is the goal, the issues of confidentiality of client case material must be encountered directly and explicitly. Where the applicant is seeking to satisfy the course requirements, the tendency to discuss confidential information in class, or among peers in social settings, must be actively discouraged. There is a tendency to sensationalize one's involvement in a suicide prevention or crisis intervention service initially, but this tendency appears to have an inverse relationship with the amount of personal involvement in the program and length of service with it.

To the students, another value of volunteering is that the crisis center duty shift may afford them an opportunity to study and prepare for class assignments. This is particularly true of students who take night watch duty during the week nights or early daytime shifts on the weekends. Such times usually are not very busy for the telephone worker, and studying in the office may well meet both the student's needs and the center's needs simultaneously. However, there is an obvious point of potential conflict here, and it must be made explicitly clear that the center's needs must take precedence. The telephone must be answered. Follow-up calls which the client may be expecting must be made. Routine duties must be performed, even if there is a midterm examination the next day. Further, group studying by peers, some of whom are not crisis center volunteers, must be prevented. The telephone room must be maintained as a confidential place that is not accessible to persons without explicit authorization to be there for the purpose of rendering service to clients. If a student should find that he is unable to study as anticipated during his duty shift, he may lose interest in the program and may find volunteering more of a burden than an asset. Some students have found themselves enjoined by their parents to terminate their volunteer service if their grades go down. Thus, their role in the program is cut short and a replacement must be found.

In many ways, students are not independent agents who are free to make and to fulfill a commitment of volunteer service to the crisis center. Their lives are governed by an academic calendar; they have daily schedules over which they have little or no control. Yet the crisis center may develop a dependency upon students and may expect a student to satisfy this dependency when he is powerless to do so. Students not only have unusual schedules during examination week, but their daily schedules change every 10–14 weeks. Students leave the community for holidays, sometimes for several weeks, or for several months during the summer. The crisis center must continue to operate during these times and must have people on duty at the telephones. The Christmas season is especially dangerous because of the high incidence of personal problems during that period, and it coincides with the time when there are the fewest student volunteers available for duty.

Obviously, the only possible answer is to make absolutely certain that nonstudent volunteers are recruited as actively as students, unless the program is such that it can cease to exist when the students are unavailable. Some crisis counseling services on university campuses direct their service program exclusively to the student population. Their problems in this regard are quite different. The center can take a recess when the academic quarter ends. However, the student volunteers must be available during the examination period to assist their clients who are unusually stressed and may call for help. A program which directs its services to the entire community cannot survive if it fails to recruit a substantial portion of its workers from among those who will agree to be available during times when student volunteers are inaccessible. This has been a constant struggle for the Suicide and Crisis Intervention Service in Gainesville.

It is also quite possible that many of the nonstudent callers to the crisis center will not accept assistance offered by a young person. Especially if the caller has markedly conservative values, he may automatically misperceive the student volunteer as a member of the "hippie" culture. By contrast, an automatic paranoia for anyone over 30 years of age is not necessarily a problem for young clients. Experience has shown that the kind of "middle-aged housewives" who volunteer for service are generally quite liberal in their attitudes, or at least tolerant in their expressions. Thus, they are able to make themselves acceptable to young people with problems more readily than the student can be acceptable to older clients.

It must be explicitly stated that the intent of this preceding section is *not* to discourage the use of students as volunteers in a crisis intervention service. It is absolutely true that students have been among both the best and the worst volunteers in the Gainesville program. Whether performance is measured by assessments of actual clinical performance with cases or by variables such as dependability, involvement, and longevity of service, students have always ranked among the highest as well as among the lowest of the volunteer staff. It is intended only that the experiences of the Gainesville center with university students may be made available to other center directors in order that they may recruit and utilize this major manpower resource with full knowledge of the special problems which students will present to the service delivery organization.

Recruiting Black Volunteers

The Gainesville center has experienced a major difficulty in recruiting black citizens, student or otherwise, from the mass advertising method. Announcements have been made on the radio station which is the favorite of the black community, and even special appeals for black volunteers made by black disc jockeys have had little result. It was not until a black worker was added to the paid staff for the specific purpose of recruiting black people that volunteer applicants were found. Efforts to uncover the reasons for this failure of mass advertising to attract blacks have revealed some interesting findings. Foremost among them is the fact that volunteering is not a part of the black culture to the same extent that it is a part of the middle-class white society. In many black families, both the male and female are employed. Their leisure time is reserved for personal recreation or for pursuing family interests. Furthermore, many blacks seem to be suspicious of the volunteer role, which they sometimes see as phony altruism, or the "do-gooder" game. In short, the concept of volunteerism often needs redefining for black people by someone whom they can trust to understand their initial reluctance. This cannot be done by the radio announcer reading a prepared statement in 10 or 20 seconds.

It has also been discovered that many blacks who heard the call for volunteers consciously rejected the thought of volunteering for service in "a white man's agency." Most of them did not believe that the crisis center provided any service for blacks. They were not aware that their black brothers and sisters actually were calling as clients. Of course, it was true that the proportion of black clients was, in fact, underrepresented for their proportion of the total community population. However, this is also true for university faculty families, and faculty wives volunteer very readily. Black people were afraid that there would not be any calls from other blacks, and that they might be rejected by white callers or find themselves unable to be of help to them.

Thus, in recruiting black workers, it has been necessary to deviate from the typical mass advertising approach and to carry the message directly to the population to be recruited. The message will have to define volunteering as a way of being of help to soul brothers, as well as a means of expressing the new black involvement in society generally. The message also will have to convey the real facts about utilization of the service by black citizens and about potentials for new service programs for blacks if their fellows will contribute time and energy to the volunteer staff. This message can be carried to all blacks indiscriminately. That is, it is not necessary to retreat to the nomination or group membership methods of recruiting. The vehicle for the advertising, however, must be another black person, rather than the impersonal news media.

Although the CARE Team method for delivering crisis services by face-to-face contact at the scene of the crisis is discussed in detail in another chapter, it is appropriate to add here that both students and blacks are especially necessary in effective CARE Team interventions with their own peer groups. The present state of relationships between the black and white segments of communities varies greatly from place to place. In Gainesville, relationships are such that, for the most part, a black client is willing to accept help from a white if he can ascertain that the white person is honest and is genuinely trying to be understanding.

However, the development of a helping relationship proceeds faster and more easily when both the client and the helper are of the same race. White clients have accepted and will continue to accept help from black CARE Team workers also, but the variables related to a successful intervention in such cases appear to be very complex and ambiguous. Finally, where the client is a member of the youth counter-culture, and especially if drugs are involved in the problem, a student intervener whose personal grooming and attire suggest an identification with the counter-culture is an invaluable asset.

In summary, it may be reiterated that the recruitment of volunteer crisis workers may be expected to proceed with greatest efficiency if the mass advertising method is used. However, for purposes of efficient organizational management and for most effective service to clients, the advertising must be consciously directed to reach all of the segments of the population which are to be recipients of the service. Representatives of all groups receiving service must be recruited to provide the service, even though some worker groups present special problems to which the agency must be able and willing to accommodate itself.

SCREENING OF VOLUNTEER CRISIS WORKERS

As clearly described above, the mass advertising method of recruiting predetermines the screening system to be followed. Again, the method was developed for use in the Nashville Crisis Call Center and has been used subsequently and with great success in Jacksonville, Florida, as well as in Gainesville. The screening process is best described as a series of progressively more difficult obstacles which applicants are asked to overcome. The method is designed to ensure that opportunity is given for persons to drop out at each hurdle. The hurdles, then, serve as successive choice points at which the applicant reassesses his motivation and determination to enter into the volunteer role. At each point, he learns something more about the program and, hopefully, about his potential suitability for service in it. The following is a description of each of the steps of the screening process used in the Gainesville center.

Requesting an Application

Naturally, the first step in responding to the advertising is to contact the center for information about how to become a volunteer. This is done primarily by telephone, although written requests and drop-in visits to the office are not uncommon. The prospective applicant is sent an application form which is called a Personal Data Sheet. Basically, it asks for demographic information, but it also includes some questions asking the applicant to think about why he wants to do such volunteer work and why he thinks he might be good at doing it. Other questions relate to the applicant's own history with suicide and with mental health problems and/or treatment. The applicant is told to return the application to the office, and that he will be contacted after it is received.

Application Received

Most people who request the application will complete it and return it to the crisis center office. However, there are a few for whom their interest in the program is so limited that they fail to take this simple second step. Perhaps they are put off by the questions on suicide and mental illness, or perhaps they are troubled by their own self-assessment of why they want to be volunteers. Whatever the reason, there are dropouts at this first choice point.

Personal Interview with Coordinator

When the completed application has been received, the Volunteer Coordinator schedules an appointment with the applicant for a personal interview in the office. This interview revolves around the material on the application, especially previous suicidal and mental health problems. The applicant's motivation and potential availability are discussed candidly, and his role as a research subject is explained. (Chapter 16 discusses the Center for Crisis Intervention Research and its relationship to the volunteers and the crisis service program.) At this interview, the applicant is told that if he is accepted into the program after training, he will be expected to make a six-month commitment to serve as a volunteer, taking at least one duty shift per week. This is an extremely important point to emphasize. Some crisis centers have extracted a one-year contract from their volunteers, but university communities are pushing it pretty far to get even six months. This requirement was added to the Gainesville program because of the many workers who, because they were students, were able or willing to stay only a very short time. If applicants are unable to commit at least six months to service in the center, their training and screening is more costly than beneficial to the center and to its clients. Naturally, unexpected interruptions such as sickness, injury, moving out of town, and other events which could not reasonably have been foretold at the time of application are valid exceptions to the six-month commitment. The personal interview is not intended to be an especially stressful one, but it does afford the opportunity for the applicant and the coordinator to get serious about the business of being a volunteer worker. Its primary function is to make certain expectations explicit and to give the applicant more information with which he can face the next dropout-continue choice point.

Psychological Tests

Once the personal interview is completed, the applicant is scheduled to return to the office for a second session, at which time he takes a battery of psychological tests. These tests often are administered in a group, rather than individually. On rare occasions, they have been given to the applicant to take home to complete, but this is a complicated and ill-advised procedure to employ regularly. The testing is not performed at the same time as the personal interview because the purpose is to provide an additional discrete step in the process. The tests employed in the Gainesville center typically have been the California Personality

Inventory, the Philosophy of Human Nature Scale, and the Myers-Briggs Type Indicator. Occasionally, a new test is added to the battery for some special research project which is in progress at the time. Efforts have been made to use only those instruments which can classify or describe nonclinical populations and which do so in terms which do not imply traits or conditions of psychopathology. Nevertheless, the taking of psychological tests can be a threatening matter, and a number of applicants pick this point for dropping out of the screening process. Any applicant, whether he remains in the program or leaves it prior to training, is granted the right to return for a feedback session on the meaning of his test scores if he wishes such information. The data and their interpretation are given by a psychology student or research team member with satisfactory competence in test interpretation or by one of the professional members of the agency staff.

Beginning the Training Program

After testing is completed, the applicant may be entered on the waiting list for the next training class and will be contacted when it begins. Most applicants at least begin training, although they may drop out prior to its completion. Every applicant is told that he is required to attend every session or to make up the material by listening to a tape recording of the session if unexpected circumstances prevent his attendance in person. The nature of the training program is discussed in a later section of this chapter. It is designed to be the first time in the screening process that excessive time commitments are demanded of the applicants. Training also serves as an eye-opening experience for some few applicants who believe that they already know all they need to know in order to help people with problems. When it becomes clear that there are specific right and wrong ways to be a crisis worker and that performance standards will be applied to their work, those without a desire to learn will drop out rather quickly.

Completion of Training

Those trainees who attend all of the sessions and come into the office for some practical experience observing an active worker on duty are considered to have completed training. There are always dropouts during training, and this attrition is to be desired rather than avoided. Those trainees who have completed training are given the opportunity to begin service in the crisis center and are scheduled for a regular duty shift. Initially, their shifts are scheduled either jointly with a more experienced worker or during the weekday hours, when the full-time staff is present to offer supervision and/or immediate consultation.

Beginning Service

There is usually some attrition between the end of training and the beginning of regular duty as a volunteer worker. Experience has shown that the attrition is greatest if the newly trained volunteers are not scheduled immediately for their own shift. If the end of training happens to coincide with the end of an academic quarter or with the start of a vacation term, so that there may be two or three weeks intervening between the end of training and the start of service, there will be more workers who fail to return for regular duty.

The data in Table 1 show the relative effectiveness of each of the hurdles in screening people out of the program. It should be remembered that this is a self-screening process. All those who complete each step are entitled to move on to the next one. Only at the final phase, after beginning service, may a volunteer be removed by the crisis center staff, after consultation with the worker about his performance or his behavior and its consequences for the total program. Even after the beginning of service, there are frequent dropouts. This represents one of the greatest problems for any crisis center and is discussed in a later section of this chapter. The data in the table were collected from the first 404 applicants for volunteer service, spanning a period from October, 1969, through August, 1971.

It is evident from these data that the greatest number of dropouts occur early in the screening process, either from not keeping the individual interview appointment or from not returning to take the psychological test battery. This is seen as a desirable outcome, since it separates those persons who are not committed prior to that point in training when they would have been exposed to the crisis center operation, and possibly to some of its confidential case materials. Once a person begins training, he is generally in a position to know a great deal about the program, although trainees are not granted access to case files until they begin service. Attrition after the beginning of training can be viewed as the most costly separation for the center; yet it appears that those who are separated late appear to be the most hazardous to clients, because of the latter's personal needs and insensitivities.

Table 1 Results of screening applicants for the Gainesville crisis center

Screening step	No. completing this step	% of total applicants
1. Request application	404	100.0
2. Return application	401	99.2
3. Initial interview	305	75.5
4. Psychological tests	263	65.1
5. Begin training	225	55.7
6. Complete training	211	52.2
7. Begin service	195	48.3

Early in the Gainesville Crisis Center history, an additional step had been inserted between the psychological testing and the initiation of training. This was a personal interview with a professional person not associated with the center. Usually these screeners were social workers or psychologists in local agencies or guidance counselors at the Community Junior College. This was designed and perceived correctly as a stress event for the volunteers, although none actually were eliminated by the interview unless they chose to drop out voluntarily. The difficulty with this step was that the applicants, through no fault of their own, were not always able to get their screening appointments prior to the start of the next training class. Therefore, the Volunteer Coordinator tended to let them proceed to enter training without the interview, with the implicit assumption that it eventually would be conducted. This failed to be the case; many applicants in training simply avoided this step and were permitted through negligence to do so. Further, because the screening process has been the subject of concentrated investigation in the research program of the center, all applicants were being accepted if they wanted to proceed. This left the professional screeners with a feeling of futility when persons whom they felt were undesirable were permitted to start training despite the screener's recommendation to the contrary. Consequently, the outside screener step was eliminated in the process and was replaced by an interview with one of the center staff members early in the training phase.

It should be noted that the foregoing description of the screening process has carefully avoided using the term "selection." Screening implies selection. However, selection, or the decision by responsible staff members to keep volunteers or to eliminate them, has been avoided intentionally until after they were on the job. This has been for research reasons, primarily to prevent a constriction in the range of variables which were eventually to be analyzed by multivariate statistical procedures. In order to provide the most powerful tests of the prediction of later performance, a wide range of scores on each variable is necessary. To select only those applicants who appeared to be potentially good workers on some a priori basis would have destroyed the prospects of successfully developing prediction and selection techniques. Furthermore, one may question whether selection—other than the self-selection employed in this screening method—is a relevant issue in community crisis centers. Personnel selection procedures depend upon the assumption that there are more applicants for the positions than there are positions to be filled. Selection is invalidated by manpower shortages, except in cases of very obvious deficiency in the applicant. Crisis centers nearly always have openings, and would take more volunteers if they could get them. More is said about this problem later in this chapter.

TRAINING OF VOLUNTEER CRISIS WORKERS

The training program in the Gainesville crisis center has been a constantly varying one. Whereas several centers around the country have developed systematic and standardized training procedures involving required readings, films, lectures, practical experience, and supervised role-playing, the Gainesville center has continuously modified its training package. There are a number of reasons for this. Basically, the assumption has been that training curricula and methods have not been adequately studied, and while every center has a method which it finds satisfactory for its own purposes, none can be said to be superior on the basis of any empirical research data. A thorough investigation of training technology should be the focus of a major research program, but prior to that time, some criteria and methods of evaluating workers on the outcomes of training, i.e., on-the-job performance, must be developed.

Furthermore, experience has shown that each volunteer training class had some very helpful and possibly relevant suggestions to feed back to the staff regarding its just-completed training experience. Efforts have been made to incorporate these into each succeeding training program. It is absolutely essential, however, that some kind of training be routinely administered before the volunteers begin to work. The details of *what* to teach and *how* to teach it are still quite undetermined. It might be noted that the Bay Area Association for Suicide Prevention, which is an association of crisis programs in the San Francisco area, has made the approval of a satisfactory training program one of the prerequisites for membership. Consequently, the member centers have devoted a great deal of attention to their training programs and have exchanged material and methodologies with one another. Probably the most carefully developed training systems are available from the Peninsula Suicide Prevention Center in San Mateo, the Alameda County Suicide Prevention Center in Berkeley, and the San Francisco Suicide Prevention Center.

Despite the lack of systematic study of training procedures in Gainesville, a few observations should be made from the experiences gained in nine separate training classes held over a two-year period. The following comments represent the current thinking about training in this center.

Didactic versus Experiential Training

It is our firm belief that didactic technologies, such as assigned readings of published research or theoretical position papers, and lectures from professional experts, are probably useless during preservice training. Such material may be very valuable for in-service training or for refresher courses for volunteers once they have had some actual experience on the telephone. Prior to that time, they have no real events with which to associate the didactic material, and without these associations, the learnings will be lost. What the volunteers need most is the chance to practice their native sensitivities and the covertly rehearsed responses which they have already worked out in fantasy during their anticipation of becoming a volunteer. This means that they must be given a chance to role-play telephone answering, interviewing, and caring for people in crisis. Then their behavior can be observed, both by themselves and by others, and reacted to by both peers and staff trainers. Such feedback of their own performance is more valuable than all the published literature on crisis theory and suicidology. This position is based squarely upon the rationale for using volunteers in the first place: that people have the capacity within themselves to help other people. Volunteers probably bring with them most of what is relevant and necessary for becoming outstanding crisis workers. What the training program should provide is the chance to discover and develop the skills which they already have.

Local Center Culture

Each crisis center has its own organizational culture with which the volunteers must become familiar and into which they must be allowed entry. This culture consists primarily of the local policies and procedures which naturally vary from one center to another. Such mores are determined from both the biases of the center officials, especially professionals who may be in positions of authority, and the cumulative history of the center's operation. Some of the cultural norms are the results of unique environmental circumstances provided by the community in which the center is located. Especially important in this regard are those policies and procedures which the center has had to adopt in order to satisfy the demands of its funding sources. These things should be thoroughly presented to all trainees and understood by them. For example, in the Gainesville center, one of the directors is convinced that the most viable role for community crisis services lies in its potential service in association with law enforcement agencies. As the city and county police agencies increase in their utilization of the crisis center and their dependency upon it, a very powerful source of influence is developed with the city and county government when requests are made for public funds to finance the program. Consequently, a very critical area of training in this center environment is the set of procedures for how to respond when a call comes from a law enforcement agency. A volunteer is never in as much danger of being relieved of his duty as when he fails to place the full resources of the center at the disposal of a law enforcement officer.

Of course, the most important local considerations are those related to the available resources other than the crisis center and the rules for getting clients into appropriate contact with other helping services. Even the best and most experienced volunteer in the Gainesville center would be largely impotent to open and manage a case in some other center without knowing the local resources of that community.

The crisis center culture also involves interpersonal patterns of communication and exercise of authority to which the new trainees must be exposed. The role of each staff member, his relative authority for the service program, and his ability or freedom to make decisions which affect their behavior in the center, must be made explicitly clear to new trainees. They should have the opportunity to meet, hear from, and talk to each of the staff members during their training. Just having an interview during the screening process will not suffice, for that will not tell the volunteer where the other person is in matters related to client service. Such awareness can be transmitted only during training classes.

It is especially important that this culture be transmitted throughout the training, and the best method found to date is for this transmission to be carried out by currently active, experienced volunteers. The staff, especially the center director and/or volunteer coordinator, are the least capable of doing it. Their own interpretations, biases, and control needs are too much a part of the culture for them to describe it accurately, unless, of course, they are exceptionally open and nondefensive people. Most center staff persons with a personal stake in the operation of the program cannot meet this qualification. Therefore, it has been found to be very effective to bring five or six current volunteers into the training program and have each of them lead small group discussions with between seven and 10 new trainees. These small groups take up at least half of each training session. They are essentially without a prearranged agenda and usually begin by focusing on the trainees' current feelings about their upcoming role in crisis intervention service. The leaders should take every opportunity of acquainting their groups with "the way things are" in the center.

Awareness of Self

Experience has shown that the methods which have been perceived as most helpful and most highly valued by the trainees have been those which enabled them to take a close look at their own motivations for serving, their response tendencies under various types of client-presented stresses, and their feelings of personal adequacy for the helping relationship. Group methods arising from applied behavioral science techniques are obviously most helpful for this type of training. Direct, hostile encounter or deep self-disclosure are not necessary conditions for developing self-awareness. Staff training personnel should be alert to ward off such behaviors by more "sophisticated" encounter groupers if they are perceived as threatening and possibly hazardous for other trainees. It is entirely possible for trainees to experience the positive aspects of self in relation to their fellow trainees. This opportunity should be provided during training, because it will have beneficial effects in aiding the comfort and confidence of the volunteer when he goes to work on the telephones at the conclusion of training. It must be understood that volunteers bring with them a large quantity of self-doubt. They are eager to help others, and the better volunteers are eager to be taught how to help others in the ways which the center has established. However, they have a deeply ingrained anxiety about how effective they are. The more rules and policies the center has, the more the volunteers will doubt their ability to learn to follow all of them. The more confidence and self-assurance they see in experienced or professional staff members, the more they may doubt their relative adequacy to be helpers. It is a paradox that the abilities of supervisors which offer a source of security for volunteers can, at the same time, be the yardstick by which they devalue themselves and feel even more anxious in relation to clients.

The coordinator must be aware of this problem, and use his own competence as a source of support rather than threat.

The experiences of the Gainesville center have revealed that no matter what training program is presented, the trainees will have criticisms of it. One group asks for less lecturing and more role-playing; the next says that too much time is spent in discussion and not enough is devoted to "being taught" what to do. Films and video tapes are desired by groups that don't see them and are rated as irrelevant by those to which they are shown. In short, trainees feel insecure and full of anxiety at the end of training no matter how the training has been done. These feelings are performance-inhibiting factors which must be effectively disposed of before the volunteer becomes a full-time worker. The only way to do this effectively is to provide a forum for experiencing one's feelings and becoming aware of oneself as an appropriately anxious person, among other anxious peers. Ideally, this forum should continue throughout the duration of the training program.

Continuous In-Service Training Opportunities

It already has been noted that certain theoretical and research-based material should be presented after the volunteer has begun service. Most volunteers will express a desire for this training, and some method must be found to provide it. Weekly or biweekly seminars with staff members have worked effectively for a time, but the content must be determined by the perceived needs of the volunteers rather than on some a priori basis and directed by the staff. Some centers require active volunteers to attend periodically some training sessions for new groups in order to take a "refresher course" if they are to continue as workers. Whatever procedures are employed, a continual in-service training program should be a part of every crisis center. A note of caution is necessary, however. Not every volunteer will take advantage of in-service training. Some may not need to, while others definitely should. Whether or not in-service training is required or permitted on an ad lib voluntary basis must be decided on the basis of local center policy. Every center should have some basis upon which to evaluate its workers. Even if the evaluation is a subjective one and lacking in demonstrated reliability, it should be used as a basis for providing in-service training to those who are seen to need it most. Furthermore, the Gainesville experience has shown that volunteers will ask for in-service training opportunities as a means of expressing their generalized anxiety or their overall morale problems. Such demands may merely reflect a need for the workers to be attended to at times when the staff may seem preoccupied with research, fund raising, or other pressing organizational problems. To set up in-service training specifically to meet these demands will probably be a failure. Volunteers will not attend the training meetings they have asked for if their request was really a veiled demand for something else. The only solution is to keep a constant finger on the pulse of volunteer morale and to provide in-service training as a regular, continuous aspect of the program rather than as an emergency reaction to unrest.

An additional aspect of the role of in-service training in a volunteer crisis center has been discussed by McGee and Jennings (1973). They point out that a lack of continual training and supervision will itself result in a decrease in volunteer morale. Unlike professional persons who rarely are supervised after they leave training settings, the volunteer is quite uncomfortable in his anxiety over knowing how to do "the right thing" with clients. Their need for in-service training and case supervision affords the crisis center system a built-in quality control mechanism. Full advantage should be taken of this fortunate circumstance.

Several suicide prevention centers and crisis programs have found that they benefit most from having graded levels of volunteer workers. Varah (1965) was one of the first directors to build a hierarchy of personnel into his Samaritans system. New volunteers in the program begin at the lowest of three grades and remain there until the organization can see some evidence in their work that they possess some of the "Samaritan qualities." Once this is demonstrated, volunteers may be promoted to the second grade. Most of them remain in this class indefinitely. However, a distinct minority are selected by unanimous election to become members of The Company of Samaritans. This highest level represents the core group of highly esteemed workers whose performance and dedication embody all of the qualities and virtues considered to be ideal for maintaining the program. Obviously, the system of promotion through the three grades in the Samaritans is not based upon amount of involvement or activity in the program, but on the evaluation of the abstract features of personality and ability. Varah describes what it means to be admitted to The Company of Samaritans:

> One who is elected will have been judged to be loving and wise, charitable rather than sentimental, neither hard nor soft, utterly discreet and loyal, sufficiently humble to be surprised at being selected, but accepting the decision realistically and without question, sufficiently conscientious to "reclassify" himself or herself in case of any failure to maintain the standard or because changed circumstances interfere with the work, and so devoted to the Company that if all the rest were to be traveling on a chartered plane that crashed, the one remaining would build it up again from the beginning. (p. 36)

Similarly, the Jacksonville Suicide Prevention Center developed a system for distributing actual responsibility for the service across several different persons. The front line volunteer is the worker on duty on the telephone for a period of four to six hours per week. Each of the volunteers is responsible during his shift to a Senior Volunteer, whose duty lasts for 24 hours. Each Senior is responsible for passing along critical information about currently active cases and for making case management assignments from one shift to another during his day of responsibility. A Senior Volunteer may be on duty one day every week, or sometimes every two weeks. Although he is the primary supervisor for the actual telephone workers, he has additional resources available to him as well. Each week, a new person assumes the role of Assistant Coordinator. This individual is responsible for everything that happens in the center during that week. He supervises the Senior Volunteers, and may, if necessary, take a telephone shift to fill in for a volunteer who cannot keep his shift assignment.

All of these higher-level persons started out as regular telephone volunteers and were promoted through the ranks, first to Senior Volunteer and then to Assistant Coordinator. There are many advantages to this system. The first is that it leaves the paid staff coordinator or director free to attend to nonclinical administrative details. The director is able to turn attention to public relations, advertising, recruiting, training, and the many other things which must be handled constantly in a volunteer organization. Another distinct advantage of this multiple-level design is that it provides an opportunity for volunteers to make an increasing commitment to the program if they wish to. Those who really want to move the center along will become involved more than the typical volunteer who faithfully takes a duty shift per week. If there are positions of increased responsibility and recognition, the volunteer is thus rewarded for developing his additional commitment. There are, to be sure, certain qualifications which Seniors and Assistant Coordinators must meet, but observations suggest that the major difference between the person who stays on the telephone for six or eight months and the one who moves up to increased responsibility during the same period of time is primarily in terms of their personal commitment to the program. Both are very likely to be intelligent, sensitive people whose maturity and personal adjustment render them popular among their peers and appreciated by their coordinator. Those lacking these basic traits generally do not remain with the program at any level for very long. But the workers who have either the time or the inclination to make their role in the crisis center a significant part of their citizenship in the community will move up to a higher level of service and responsibility.

There may be some problems for the director when some persons are selected for promotions and others are overlooked. A similar problem is encountered when special awards or honors are bestowed at the annual meeting. Actually, since there are usually more promotions to be made than there are awards to be given, this system tends to prevent some of the jealousies that arise without it.

In some programs, it may be successful to charge the working volunteers with the responsibility of picking their own leaders and supervisors. Promotion may thus become a means by which the workers express their own feelings of affection for one another. The director may be wise to maintain a consultation or even a veto role in such a procedure, however, thus preventing the elections from deteriorating into popularity contests. Promotion clearly should represent a recognition of leadership ability, competence in the clinical services, and special interest and dedication to the goals of the total system.

In the Gainesville Suicide and Crisis Intervention Service, the multiple-level system has been developed in a manner which is tied more to the four-phase process of crisis intervention than to the supervision function which characterizes the Jacksonville design. In Gainesville, there is a distinction between trainees and permanent workers. During the terminal phases of training, the trainees are permitted in the telephone room to begin taking telephone duty under the supervision of an experienced worker. During this trial apprenticeship period, the center does not consider them to be permanent workers and will not be depending on them to take duty shifts by themselves. Once this training is completed, the trainee progresses to the level of Clinical Associate (C.A.) if he desires to make a six-month commitment to take at least one shift per week in the crisis center. The C.A.'s are the backbone of the program. They are the front-line workers, without whom the telephone would not be answered.

While serving as a C.A. for a few months (the exact length of time needed is quite subjectively determined), the worker will have ample opportunity to reveal whether he is willing and/or able to assume increased involvement in the center. If it is evident that he does wish to commit himself, there are at least three ways in which he can assume additional responsibility. All of these higher-level positions are promotions from the role of C.A., although the person may still take regular telephone duty as C.A. as well. For example, it is required that if a person moves up to the CARE Team, he must continue to serve one duty shift a week on the telephone. There are several reasons for this, but it is primarily to prevent the development of the CARE Team at the expense of the basic telephone service. It has been discovered that nearly every volunteer would welcome an opportunity to serve on the CARE Team, since that is the unit that goes right to the scene of a crisis "whenever and wherever it occurs." If all the telephone C.A.'s who expressed a desire were allowed to make their commitment in the form of CARE Team service, the telephone service would disappear.

A special CARE Team responsibility which represents a promotion for the more reliable and dependable members is the promotion to Consultant. The Consultant serves as the Captain of the CARE Team during its shift, and he also is responsible primarily for the decisions made in case management during his duty. CARE Teams generally function during the evening and weekend hours, when the office staff is not on duty. Becoming a Consultant is clearly a sign of special skill and involvement in the program.

Finally, the most advanced level of CARE Team activity is the Death Investigation Team. This is the group which undertakes psychological autopsies for the state attorney's office, on request from the county medical examiner. Technically, the psychological autopsy is a service rendered by behavioral scientists to the medical pathologist. It is a professional responsibility and should not be undertaken without leadership and assistance from a professional behavioral science or mental health specialist. There are several reasons for this remnant of professional chauvinism in the crisis center culture. First, there is the need to know and understand the psychological dynamics of life styles, personality traits, habit patterns, and symptoms of psychopathology. Secondly, in the death investigation which is requested by the medical examiner, there are medical-legal issues of confidentiality and disclosure of any information prematurely or inappropriately which can have extensive legal complications. Maturity and good judgment are required to perform under these conditions. Finally, the role of the death investigator following an unequivocal suicide is less that of the behavioral scientist studying mode of death and more that of the counselor guiding the bereavement crisis of the survivor victims. One must be extremely capable as a counselor to handle this delicate situation with skillful crisis work.

There are some volunteers who do not want to work on CARE Team assignments or who are unable because of family responsibilities to be available during evenings and weekends. Such C.A.'s who nevertheless wish to make an additional commitment to the center may be promoted to the level of Crisis Counselor (C.C.). The C.C.'s rarely continue to take regular C.A. telephone duty. However, they work in the center from four to six hours per week in the role of case management specialist. It is their task to assume responsibility for a portion of the active caseload, and, by initiating telephone calls to clients or significant others, to ascertain that the action plan developed during the opening (phase I) period is brought to full implementation. When this has been accomplished, the C.C. is then responsible for closing (phase III) the case and preparing the records so that the follow-up (phase IV) contact can be made eight weeks later. Consequently, the C.C. has a major responsibility for seeing that the system really functions as it is intended to for the good of the clients. C.C.'s have the routine, sometimes boring, and always difficult duty of plodding through case records and keeping up on the current status of active clients. Yet, they prevent the program from deteriorating into nothing more than a telephone answering and referral service. When a seriously disturbed or suicidal client is followed steadily and consistently for weeks until some other alternative is found, and he emerges without resorting to self-destruction, it is the C.C. who is the unsung hero. The C.A. and the CARE Team may play the dramatic roles of insightful detective and rescue workers. Yet it all goes for naught when, two or three days later, the client makes a fatal, self-inflicted injury because the center failed to persist in its case management function. It is the especially concerned C.A. who is promoted to C.C. who has the opportunity to do those menial tasks which may be truly suicide preventive.

The trainees, C.A.'s, C.C.'s, and CARE Team members in the Gainesville center are all nonprofessional volunteers. There are also four paid staff persons and two secretaries who operate the program. Two psychologists from the University, neither of whom has any salary from the crisis center budget, serve as consultants. Both have a University role in the supervision of graduate students from a variety of disciplines who are taking practicum or internship training in the center. Two of the staff personnel are responsible primarily for the recruitment and training of the volunteer applicants. A third serves as supervisor of the case management function, coordinating the work of the C.C.'s, and the fourth is responsible for community organization and public relations functions.

It is important to note that in the first few months of the Gainesville center operation, one person was employed as a public relations specialist. Her role was exclusively that of keeping fresh copy available for the radio stations to use in public service announcements and developing feature stories for the local news-papers. The value of employing a person to fulfill this role cannot be overempha-sized. For example, after the center had been in operation for only six months, a survey performed by students in the College of Journalism and Communications determined that 80 percent of a sample of persons having telephones listed in the local directory were aware of the existence of the crisis center and knew, from local advertising, that it was a resource for persons with suicidal impulses. Further, an analysis of the Gainesville caseload, compared with that of another major suicide prevention program in the state, completely justifies the value of the public relations specialist. In its first four months of service, the Gainesville center had received more new case (first time) calls than the other center had received during the entire 12 months of its fourth year of operation. Gainesville's center serves a population of approximately 105,000, whereas the other center serves a toll-free telephone area with over 400,000 population. It is certain that program managers would greatly increase the impact of their agencies if they would appoint a volunteer team or hire a staff member to perform the public relations function on a continuing basis.

MAINTAINING MORALE WITHIN A VOLUNTEER SYSTEM

This discussion of volunteer workers would not be complete if the greatest single problem for program directors were overlooked. Universally, the most obvious questions concerning the management of a volunteer program are those which receive most or all of the director's attention. Issues of recruitment, selection, training, and scheduling of volunteers are so obviously important that most programs have neglected to worry about organizational maintenance strategies. The crisis center director who has not been faced with serious morale problems among the workers either has not been in operation very long or is not using volunteers to provide the service. It is of great importance not only to be prepared for such problems, but to have some idea what causes them and how they can be alleviated. The adage that to be forewarned is to be forearmed was never more true.

The primary issue which affects volunteer morale, in the experience of the Gainesville center, is the question of role relationship between volunteers and paid staff. It does not matter whether the staff members are nonprofessionals, profes-sional crisis workers, or professional mental health specialists. The important issue is that the staff is usually present in the office to open and manage cases at least a part of each working day, and the volunteer is in the office only three to five hours per week. This being the case, the question is: Whose center is it? Who works for whom? Both paid staff and volunteers are certain to have different answers to these questions, or at least they are certain to behave as if they had opposing points of view.

The staff members generally tend to feel that they run the center service program. Their greater familiarity with individual cases and with problems arising between the center and other resources in the community makes it natural for the staff to see the need for changes in policy and procedures, or for the staff to feel more knowledgeable about specific cases. The staff is clearly in a decision-making role where administrative matters are concerned. It is very easy to slip into the habit of making decisions which affect the lives of volunteers while they are in the office without consulting the volunteers first. Volunteers tend to resent this practice; they feel that they should make some of the decisions about their role in the program. Those who are on duty in the evenings, on night watch, and during weekends have the center all to themselves. They tend to feel that the telephone room is their own special place, and they take pride in keeping it organized, orderly, and efficient. These feelings may be quite incongruent with coming to work and finding that the staff has made a decision which has effected a new procedure for them to accept unquestioningly. The obvious solution to this problem can turn out to be no solution at all.

Coordinating Committee

Both the staff and some volunteer representatives in the Gainesville center have concluded that the volunteers need a representative body called a "coordinating committee." The purposes of this group are sometimes seen largely as those of a labor union, to negotiate with the staff for anything which would make the volunteer's time in the center more pleasant. In its ideal state, the coordinating committee could become a channel of communication, serving to create a forum for the staff to explore and explain ideas for organizational changes. When the committee fully understands the rationale behind the changes, they could carry the messages to the rest of the volunteers and interpret them for everyone's understanding. Of course, this would have to be a two-way process, and messages or requests from the volunteers to the staff would be interpreted similarly to the staff. Thus, the committee would become both a channel and a method for including volunteers in decision-making processes within the center.

However, what usually happens to the coordinating committee is something like the following. First, they meet at a time when there is excessive stress within the system. Such periods may occur after the suicide death of a client, or after a period of unsuccessful negotiations with the United Way for increased funding. The tension level of the center always increases as the number of calls increases, or as the number of available volunteers decreases. In any event, there is stress in the system, so the coordinating committee meets. They decide that there is a clear and obvious morale problem. Soon they discover that they do not even know all of the volunteers who work shifts not adjacent to their own. Perhaps what is needed is a good social function at which the volunteers could "get to know the staff better," or "relax and enjoy one another," or "get to meet other volunteers." So the solution to the morale problem becomes a party, and the coordinating committee becomes a social committee. Needless to say, this fails to meet the needs of most of the volunteers, and it fails completely to attack the original problem. After the party is over and the coordinating committee begins to look for its next agenda (the idea of having the committee being still a valid one), it becomes difficult to proceed. Other activities begin to take priority, and soon only a few members remain to do all the work. Even the most dedicated volunteers soon tire of this. Further, as a member loses confidence in the role of the coordinating committee, he is very likely to drop out of the center altogether. Of course, it is not considered appropriate for a member of the staff to sit in on the meetings as a member of the committee, for that would negate the very purpose of the group.

The only solution to the continuing dilemma over control of the center is to make very certain that the staff runs the program, but that the workers have a continuously functioning vehicle for adding their input to decision making. It is the staff which is in a position to know the full-time practical realities of the center's role in the community with other agencies and with clients. The staff must make the decisions necessary to keep that role alive and functioning at its maximum level. The point of view that it is really the volunteers who run the center and that the staff members are there merely in order to serve as "consultants" denies the reality of the organization. In the first place, job titles such as "director" defy the consultant role. When a director tries to act like something other than a director, it is immediately phony, and the volunteers will sense the incongruity and react with anxiety to it.

When a volunteer applicant first comes to the center, certain aspects of the culture must be made clear. These include the fact that the staff is in a managerial position and has certain expectations for the volunteer, if he decides to join the group. These expectations, involving participation in training before and during service, taking of duty shifts, length of service, confidentiality, etc., should be very explicit. One of the expectations should be that the volunteer commits himself to a regularly scheduled meeting of all workers in the center at least once per month. Twice per month is desirable for the first four months after training has ended, but it can be less after experience in the center increases. One of the purposes of these biweekly or monthly meetings is to permit communication between the staff and the volunteers. Questions can be raised, feelings can be expressed, anxieties and ambiguities can be reduced, and the staff can reveal that they truly are interested in the volunteers as people who are performing a valuable service under excessive pressures. Just because the staff maintain the directorate role is no reason for them to give up being understanding, sensitive, and concerned human beings. Just because a volunteer is *giving* his time freely is no reason to assume that he gives up the need for structure, direction, and limit setting.

In short, the experience of the Gainesville crisis center has shown that a perpetual morale problem among the volunteers results from the unclear role relationships and role expectations between staff and volunteers. These very critical factors must be made clear and must be clarified continually if morale issues are to be kept at a controllable level.

Another observation may be made briefly. Morale problems must be accepted by the staff and by the volunteers as a given fact in this type of anxiety-producing work. In the rest of this chapter, other specific sources of discontent will be discussed. All of them take a toll on worker morale. Thus, if morale problems are understood as a natural aspect of the program, no one need be too discouraged or react with panic when it becomes impossible to deny the low morale any longer. Tensions within the center are like the ringing of the telephone—they are certain to happen, and they will increase in frequency and in intensity in proportion to the level of involvement the center is taking in its community role. A volunteer staff can be a very happy staff, but if they are not having to work at it continuously, it is probably a good indication that they are either not getting very many calls or that they are finding ways to remain uninvolved with their clients.

Special Morale Problems

The previous discussion of role relationships is a general and pervasive problem. There are, in addition, a few specific issues which cause tension in the system, and they deserve brief attention.

The first specific problem to come to mind relates to the problems of a *communication* system. The coordinating committee has been suggested already as a means of communication between staff and volunteers concerning major problems. However, in the routine, daily need to pass information along from one volunteer to another, a less complex system is necessary. The Gainesville center has created a special bulletin board with a small envelope for each duty shift during the week. Messages for a particular person can be placed in the envelope for the shift that he is working. This method serves primarily for the case manager and C.C.'s to leave notes for the C.A. to make calls to specific clients during a prearranged period of time.

Of course, the client files are the most appropriate way of communicating clinical aspects of the individual casework. It is of great importance that the workers understand the value of using the files both for reading recent entries and for leaving new entries for subsequent workers.

A system of mailboxes for volunteers to receive messages about center operations, announcements of meetings, etc., is an absolute necessity. The same area should have a suggestion box, as well as boxes for each member of the staff, so that both personal and anonymous messages can be returned from the workers to the directors. It must be remembered that there are some volunteers working nights or weekends who may be a part of the center for several weeks without ever meeting some of the staff members, except perhaps for a brief talk they might have made in the training course. Consequently, they may underevaluate the significance of general notices which a staff member pins to a bulletin board. Further, volunteers lose interest in a general bulletin board if they see the same messages there time after time. Some staff or coordinating committee member must adopt the bulletin board specifically as his own responsibility. He must see that old messages are removed, that only vital messages of timely importance are there, and that messages are arranged physically in some rational order. For example, important clinical messages relating to the current lethality of a client should not be mixed up with messages advertising for roommates or announcing puppies to be given away. Communication within the center, including the proper use of bulletin boards, is a continuous responsibility for someone to assume. Failure to do so surely will result in confused, poorly informed, and unhappy volunteer workers.

Another problem which may create tensions within the volunteer group and between volunteers and staff members relates to the *differential commitment and involvement* which is certain to be present within the system. Volunteers will be very alert and vigilant to notice a lack of uniformity among the staff members in terms of goals, policies, involvement, and general attitude towards the program. If a volunteer perceives himself to be more involved than some of the staff, there is bound to be trouble. Similarly, if a staff member shifts his role, for example, from clinical service to research, the volunteers may have less contact with him in their duties. They will begin to perceive him as no longer interested in the service program or their role in it. When one group of volunteers, for example, the CARE Team, becomes keenly aware that its peers are barely keeping their obligation to keep the telephone shifts covered, there will be tensions within the volunteer group. There is no simple solution to these problems. The staff, by the very nature of their involvement must be, and should be, more personally committed than the volunteers. There always will be those staff members for whom working in the crisis center is a source of employment and regular income, while for others it is a way of life. There never will be a means by which personal commitment can be demanded or contracted. Most centers are currently requiring that the workers agree to sign up for a minimum period of service, usually between six months and a year after training. But that is no guarantee that the worker will not fulfill this commitment by perfunctory and uninvolved performance. The best way to assure the development and maintenance of adequate commitment is to build in rewards and recognitions for it. Promotion to a high level of responsibility is one method, but nothing will ever replace the director who is sensitive and aware of the volunteer and gives him a genuinely warm "thank you" for being there. Public praise for exceptionally well-handled casework not only rewards involved workers, but also develops role models and incentives for continued improvement.

A further morale problem, very much related to the last one, is the tendency for volunteers to "burn out." It has been observed that some workers not only are especially good on the telephone, but are willing to take on extra duty when necessary. Usually, it happens that such a C.A. will be promoted to the C.C. role, and perhaps will even start to work on the CARE Team. Such people are almost as visible around the center as the staff. There are two problems with these over-involved persons. First, the more a person is willing to do, the more will be asked of him. When it is necessary to get a replacement at the last minute for someone who does not show up for his shift, the tendency is to call first upon the persons who are most likely to agree to come in. Consequently, involved persons get excessive requests to continue to exhibit their involvement. Secondly, the more a person becomes involved in the center as a volunteer, the greater will be the costs in other areas of his life. Either school grades or family responsibilities are bound to suffer, and eventually, the pressures will be great for a disengagement. Some-times it occurs that the pressures to leave the center are internal to the volunteer himself. It is bound to happen that superinvolved people are especially aware and proud of the contribution that they are making. It is very difficult for the director to remember that these people need even more reward and recognition than the ordinary worker. Consequently, the more involvement a person has, the less relative appreciation he is likely to receive. A point will be reached when he must resolve this dissonance by resigning from the center. When a highly involved worker must leave the center, experience has repeatedly shown that, like giving up tobacco or alcohol, he must quit altogether. There is no such thing as "just cutting down."

The withdrawal of an especially overinvolved worker has notable conse-quences among the other volunteers. Usually, they too have looked to these people for role models and for leadership. When such a person leaves, it is not uncommon for two or three others to leave at the same time. It causes all workers to reassess their own feelings for the work and the validity it has for them.

In short, the overinvolved volunteer is a great asset to the center, but he is potentially an even greater liability. It becomes necessary for the director to monitor cautiously the degree of involvement of all the workers. He must assist some people to increase their involvement to an optimum level. He also must help others to set explicit limits on their involvement in order to prevent them from experiencing the burn-out phenomenon.

THE ROLE OF THE VOLUNTEER COORDINATOR

As a means of summarizing this long chapter, it is relevant to point out that the many duties and responsibilities discussed in recruiting, screening, and training volunteers, and in maintaining their efficiency after they get on the job, belong exclusively to a single person who has no other duties to perform. The coordina-tion of all volunteer manpower problems and issues is a full-time job in a crisis center. Clearly, certain details, such as scheduling of duty shifts, can be delegated to a responsible aide or clerk. Yet, the task of coordinating volunteers is a person-to-person job. It involves the keeping of extensive records religiously, and, by contrast, it involves the interpersonal sensitivity of a counselor or therapist. The coordinator needs to be a boss to some workers, a parent to others, and an emotional sounding board to others. He needs to be all of these things to each person at different times. Probably no task performed by the crisis center staff is more vital to its internal organization and harmony than those assigned to the volunteer coordinator. He must be the most self-confident of all the volunteers, for they will look to him for role modeling and security. He must be the most visible person in the center, for when they want to see him, they need him then, not later. He must be the most insightful and sensitive person on the staff, for when the volunteer is anxious and afraid, he will expect him to know it and make him comfortable. He must be among the most skillful clinicians, for when the volunteer does a good job, he will expect the coordinator to identify it and give him a pat on the back. When the volunteer does a bad job, he knows it himself, and he will expect the coordinator to gently, but quickly, provide constructive feedback which suggests alternative ways of handling the cases. Most of all, what the volunteer needs from the coordinator is someone who will pay attention to him and let him know that he is important. There is nothing more deadly for a volunteer than to miss one or two duty shifts and then to have the fact overlooked by the center. First of all, he may feel guilty for missing his shift. Secondly, if nobody calls to find out why, or to stress the importance of punctuality and responsibility, the volunteer wonders if he was even missed. If his failure to function in ways which he knows are required does not receive responses from the center, he soon comes to believe that his presence or absence in the system is of little consequence. When this happens, the volunteer drops out, six-month contract or not. Therefore, the very first duty of the volunteer coordinator each day is to see who did not keep a shift assignment the preceding day and to contact the worker to inquire as to his health, etc. This prevents the build-up of guilt in the worker and lets him know that he was in fact missed. Similarly, when another volunteer has come in for extra duty to make up the missed shift, it is the coordinator's role to provide immediate recognition of that fact and see that it is recorded, so that he may be relieved of his own shift later.

In the recruiting function, the volunteer coordinator is the first person to meet the applicants and to orient them to the total program. His friendly or cold nature will be interpreted as a reflection of the interest the center takes in people generally. He will explain and interpret the expectations of the center for its volunteers. His firmness or his hedging manner will convey the degree of sincerity and genuineness of these expectations. In the screening phase, it is the volunteer coordinator who helps each applicant to evaluate his commitment at each step of the way and assists him in making the stay-or-drop-out decision at each choice point. The applicant learns that the volunteer coordinator is a person to whom he can turn when help or understanding is needed.

During training, the volunteer coordinator is the person who has the greatest influence on changing the applicant from an uninformed general citizen to a skilled crisis worker. He has the chance to demonstrate what the center staff can offer to the community. Confidence in the knowledge and skill of the coordinator and an appreciation for the enthusiasm with which he approaches different clinical problems and procedures will be the major factor in stimulating the new trainees toward achieving similar skills. The perception that the trainees have of the volunteer coordinator during training will set the limits for their own achievement expectation and for their confidence that the center actually can perform its alleged role in the community.

The manner in which the volunteer coordinator functions in the center will be the critical factor in maintaining or eliminating the ever-present morale problems among the volunteer group. He must interpret the staff motivations to the workers and must be their voice in the staff meetings.

It is unfortunate that there are no formulas for identifying the person who would be an effective coordinator of a volunteer program. It is probable that any one of a large number of people in a volunteer organization could perform the role quite well. The important thing is for the coordinator to have no other responsibilities within the center beyond the full-time concern for managing the interests of the volunteers. He must be free from clinical case management, administrative responsibilities, and public relations chores. As much as possible, he must be free from research responsibilities, although the records that he keeps probably represent a gold mine of important data for research in the social and applied behavioral sciences.

In general, the volunteer coordinator is the keystone of the center. He sets the pace for the whole organization of volunteers, and the crucial nature of his role is such that he can be the weakest link in the chain. The success attained by the volunteer coordinator in performing his duties is the yardstick by which the success of the overall center operation may be measured.

14
THE
CARE TEAM

A study of the service programs of suicide prevention and crisis intervention centers reveals a marked inconsistency in the attitudes of program planners and managers toward the practice of having face-to-face contact with clients. As early as 1960, FRIENDS in Miami were unafraid of the usual taboos, and the lack of constraining control over their program by professional mental health specialists freed them from the conservatism which has prevented most programs from engaging in such practices. Members of FRIENDS frequently would meet callers for a cup of coffee or take them to hospital emergency rooms, but the practice was left up to the discretion of individual members and was not the subject of any organizational policy or procedure.

In the Orlando WE CARE program, the first director issued a blanket policy statement which clearly prevented face-to-face contact between callers and volunteers. Later, she became the one to break the rule. As others saw the benefit of going to the caller, they also began to ignore the rule. Gradually, it became a standard but still unwritten procedure for some volunteers to meet clients at the hospital or in coffee shops. Office visits by appointment or by walk-in clients generally have been discouraged by WE CARE, but routine hospital visits to contact and follow up on suicide attempt cases became the basis for the demonstration grant which financed the program during 1968 and 1969.

The two health department-related Emergency Mental Health Services in St. Petersburg and Atlanta have long followed a "go-and-see" policy. Both of them have always utilized professional social workers or nurses for this role, rather than the nonprofessional volunteer. Knoxville's new community mental health center program was the first service among the 10 centers studied in the Southeast to utilize the volunteer on a Community Intervention Team. As a rule, the programs in the United States have maintained either an ambiguous or a clearly negative position regarding the volunteer in face-to-face contact. It has been primarily the professional consultants and managers who decreed a "thou shalt not" policy, often despite the pleas of volunteers and nonprofessional program coordinators. Such a position often reveals an underlying ambivalence about the nonprofessional which suggests that the threatened professional is compromising as far as he will go by agreeing to let the volunteer answer the telephone. Only a very few volunteer programs have imposed this restriction on themselves. In such cases, the policy is presented in such a way as to reveal that the volunteers feel inadequately trained and prepared for direct intervention and are content to hide behind the telephone. One center director reported that her workers would all quit if they were required to see callers personally.

It has been interesting to speculate about the prevalence of this reluctance in the crisis programs across the country. On the one hand, suicidologists generally have agreed that the very least service that a suicide prevention center must be able to perform is that of effective *rescue*, or intervention, in cases of attempted suicide. It is possible to overcome the resistance of professionals, and some volunteers have successfully done so because they have seen the need and experienced the satisfaction of being of personal service to a person in crisis. Yet most centers have not adopted the practice as a general policy, nor have the directors attempted to develop and export an outreach service. Why not?

Speculating about this reticence, in the context of comments made by many volunteers and center directors, leads to the conclusion that everyone is interested in the idea, but very few have been willing to venture into such a potentially controversial program. It is apparent that many programs are willing to follow aggressive leadership and consider an outreach program if it is developed and documented elsewhere. No one has been willing to assume that leadership. Consequently, when the Suicide and Crisis Intervention Service was established in December, 1969, one of its explicit goals was to become a leader in the development of a service technology which could be described and exported to those crisis centers which were willing to "put content into the contact" (Dublin, 1968). The purpose of this chapter is to describe that system after 18 months of operation.

RATIONALE FOR THE CARE TEAM

Why should a crisis intervention service develop a mobile go-to-the-scene CARE Team? There are several reasons. The primary rationale stems from the exhortation of Louis Dublin at the organizational meeting of the American Association of Suicidology. Appearing on the symposium with the other distinguished pioneers in suicidology, Dublin challenged the center directors present to go beyond the telephone contact and add the *content* of real human involvement. In his usually persuasive manner, Dublin emphasized the point over and over until the phrase, "Put Content into the Contact," became one of the many statements for which he is so well remembered. Dublin's influence on the formation of policy in the Gainesville program was such that a face-to-face contact team was an inevitable aspect of the new service.

Secondly; the general philosophy of the Gainesville program outlined in Chapter 11 made the CARE Team a natural element. If one is going to respond to a request for assistance " . . . whenever and wherever it occurs," it is obvious that more than the telephone must be involved. If activity, rather than passivity, characterizes the crisis intervention, then going to the scene of a crisis is manda-tory. If the crisis intervention service is capable of demonstrating an innovative method of delivering a helping service not modeled after the traditional mental health services, then getting out of the office and into the living rooms and streets of the community is the sine qua non behavior. A helper on call at all hours to meet the client's need, when and where the client demands, is the best example of an alternative to traditional mental health practice.

Finally, a concern for quality control demands a mobile outreach service. Hansell (1968) has drawn a relationship between the quality of crisis intervention service and its proximity to the point where the problem was experienced. He suggests that the quality of intervention may be measured in feet, where the value of the service is an inverse function of the distance between the point where it is rendered and the place where the crisis occurred. A crisis intervention service is thus challenged to make a major investment in the outreach portion of its program. Failure to do so may be interpreted as substantial evidence that the service does not really mean business, that its name is a sham, rather than a genuine commitment to the public it seeks to serve. When the day comes in which standards are set for crisis centers to meet for purposes of certification or licensing, it is certain that a CARE Team service will be expected.

FUNCTIONS OF THE CARE TEAM

There is a crisis intervention organization operating in Sydney, Australia, under the name of LIFELINE. This group has spawned the development of the CON-TACT programs in the United States, under the leadership of the CONTACT Teleministry, Inc. The LIFELINE and CONTACT programs have instituted what they call a "Trouble Team," whose function is to respond to anyone in trouble, as needed. During the formulation of the service in Gainesville, the initial intent was to borrow that name and to develop the functions of the team around the concept of "being there when trouble exists." However, on deeper study, the proposed functions of the service took on a new name, and the CARE Team was created.

The purpose of the CARE Team is to make *Contact* with clients, to make an *Assessment* of the situation, to provide *Relief* and sometimes *Rescue*, and to securely *Engage* the client in the crisis intervention process. Hence, the name stands for the functions it performs; its goals are to live up to its name.

Contact

A telephone conversation frequently does not provide a genuine contact. The very least that is necessary to enter into a helping relationship with a client is the ability to recontact him if the initial communication is broken. As long as a caller can hang up without giving his name or telephone number, there is no possibility of entering into a crisis intervention process as discussed in the last chapter. However, once contact is made in a face-to-face manner, the communication is established, and the probability that this communication can be maintained is enhanced considerably.

Furthermore, the CARE Team is used to make a contact with those clients who never call the center themselves. These cases are primarily the suicide attempters whose cry for help is to the community at large. The prevailing practice in hospital emergency rooms throughout the nation is to "treat and release" all cases of self-inflicted injury or self-poisoning where the patient is ambulatory following emergency care. Even those hospitals which provide residency training in psychiatry may request a psychiatric consultation, refer to the outpatient service, and release the patient after gastric lavage or minor surgery. In one unusual, but nevertheless illustrative, instance, a man was released from the emergency room of a Gainesville hospital after having shot himself in the head with a .22-calibre pistol. The bullet had creased the exterior of the cranium without penetration or fracture; consequently, the scalp wounds at the point of entry and exit required only minor suturing, sterile dressing, and bandaging. The patient was to be released to return to his solitary room in a "flop house" hotel. However, on learning this, the captain of the Patrol Division of the Sheriff's office brought the patient directly to the Crisis Center, where the CARE Team could begin an intervention with him. As a result of this instance, both the County Sheriff and the City Police began to notify the CARE Team immediately when they learned of a suicide attempt case from any of the three hospital emergency rooms. This notification enables the Crisis Center to make a contact with clients even though they do not call the center directly. As long as one views a suicide attempt as a cry for help rather than as a manipulative gesture, it does not matter how directly or indirectly the cry is sounded. In all such instances, intervention is required, and the CARE Team enables *contact* to occur. Thus, no cry for help can go unheeded by the community.

Assessment

Generally, it is the job of the telephone worker to make the assessment of the client's lethality and the type of personal problem which has precipitated the present crisis. The most important assessment to be made of each new case concerns the question of whether or not the client is currently suicidal. If suicide is a factor, the degree of lethality must be assessed. If not, the precipitating problem still must be ascertained if the Crisis Center is to be helpful. Sometimes this becomes a complicated task, and if the telephones are busy during a particular shift, there may not be time to get all the information necessary to develop an action plan and initiate phase II management of the case. In such cases, an office interview or a contact in the person's home may elicit the necessary information upon which to formulate the action plan and effect a transfer.

A further aspect of assessment is making the distinction between cases of genuine acute crisis and those cases of chronic maladjustment and dependency. Such assessment may be simple in cases of alcoholic callers, but more frequently, it requires the sensitized ear of an experienced crisis worker who can use both visual as well as auditory cues. Thus, it is an important function of the CARE Team to supplement and improve upon the assessment initiated by the telephone worker if an efficient job of crisis intervention is to be carried out.

Relief

There are many forms that this CARE Team function can take. The most obvious, of course, is that of providing emotional support and comfort to the person in distress. Such support comes primarily from knowing unequivocally that someone else, particularly a stranger, really cares enough to try to help. The Gainesville CARE Team has adopted several mottoes from time to time, but the one which has been most descriptive of its creed is, simply, "Give a damn!" Nothing conveys the caring of a crisis center as much as having people actually *being there* when a client feels hopeless and alienated.

Sometimes relief comes from providing transportation to sources of immediate help. The CARE Team which actually takes a person to another agency can often secure faster and more careful attention than the same client would get if he walked in off the street. This is partly a reflection of the quality of interagency relationships which a crisis center can develop. When the welfare or employment service personnel see a new client who has been brought in by the crisis center CARE Team, they automatically know that some preliminary evaluation, problem diagnosis, and planning has already gone into the case. There is a set response to find the new case appropriate for receiving the services of that agency. It is harder to refuse service to one's colleagues in the helping services than it is to a client who may not be very enlightened about community resources. The sooner a client can be put in touch with another helping service, the sooner relief for his crisis can occur. This is a role of the CARE Team.

When the other helping agency happens to be a hospital emergency room, the relief can take the form of an actual rescue in a case of attempted suicide. Frequently, rescue demands quasi-illegal actions, such as breaking and entering if the client has lost consciousness while the CARE Team is en route. This type of action causes extensive anxiety in agencies which do not have CARE Teams. However, it is entered into only when the responsibility for the decision can be shared with other members of the crisis center staff. More can be said about these issues later.

Not only does the CARE Team offer relief by reducing the perturbation of the client, but it is often possible to lower his lethality as well. In cases of suicide threats, a typical CARE Team approach is to remove firearms, pills, or alcohol. Sometimes this may be done with the explicit consent of the client, but it is not always possible. In some cases, outright deception is necessary until the weapons have been confiscated and turned over to a relative or significant other person. Whenever the means of self-destruction are removed from immediate accessibility, the lethality of the potential victim has been reduced. Obviously, when this is the motive, theft or other illegal acts are impossible to substantiate, and any reasonable person would acknowledge such removal of possessions to be an appropriate act under the circumstances.

Engagement

It was pointed out earlier that the process of making a direct contact with the client is an aid to involving him in the crisis intervention process. It is especially important in any crisis situation to structure the next few hours of the person's life. How is he going to spend the weekend? What steps are to be taken when the community agencies reopen on Monday morning? How will he respond when a predicted event actually occurs? These are all things which the careful crisis worker will try to anticipate and plan for in helping a client over the first few difficult hours after a crisis has occurred in his life. Included within the structuring of the later activities should be periodic times for future contact with the center. If the client has an appointment to be evaluated by the intake worker of a mental health clinic the next day, the center will contact him and reassure him once more that it is important to keep that appointment. If he has a job interview, he should contact the center and inform a worker, who will be very interested, whether or not he got the job. If he does not call by a certain time, the center will contact him to learn the results of the interview.

If the case involves a suicide threat of moderate lethality, the CARE Team may both offer relief and secure an engagement by entering into a serious contract with the client. The terms of this contract are simple and explicit: the client agrees to take no harmful or self-destructive action without calling the center first. In exchange for this promise, the CARE Team agrees to perform some action appropriate to the situation which the client has asked for or has need of. The ease with which this contract can be established is a further assessment of the seriousness of the client's suicidal intention. Once it is achieved, however, the client has been firmly engaged in the crisis intervention effort. After more than 500 CARE Team visits, the Gainesville center has found that rarely does a client fail to honor a contract which was entered into at the request of the CARE Team. The contract involving homicidal threats, threats to flee from the scene, cooperation of clients under custody of law enforcement agencies, and any number of behaviors which the client may fail to realize would not ultimately be in his own best interests. Whenever such a potential exists, the need for the CARE Team to engage the client becomes even more important than in the usual acute crisis case. Records of the CARE Team activity on a sample of 250 cases reveal the character of the CARE Team's functioning. Table 1 shows the relative frequency of accomplishment of some specific goal of the CARE Team unit.

PERSONNEL ON THE CARE TEAM

Each CARE Team unit includes two people, never more, because too many people at the scene of a problem can create more confusion than help. In rare circum-

Table 1 Relative frequency of accomplishing some specific goals of the CARE Team unit

	Number	Percent
Rescue in an actual suicide attempt	17	7.0
Provided emotional support	170	70.2
Provided emotional support for significant other	107	44.2
Facilitated entry into other helping agency	73	30.2
Calmed immediate emotional state of client and/or significant other	128	52.9
Developed concrete action plan	133	55.0
Reestablished communication with significant others	47	19.4
Firmly engaged client in crisis intervention plan	80	33.1
Provided immediate treatment or other support	88	36.4
Alienated client, aroused hostility toward SCIS	6	2.5

stances, one person may go alone, but such action is not often advisable. As a general rule, it is important for both members of the CARE Team to be experienced crisis workers, so that each may have the benefit of the other's judgment and opinions about the client.

The CARE Team is considered a very special line of duty in the crisis center, and its members are treated as if they are special people. The CARE Team is consciously held up as an "elite society" within the crisis center in order to make membership on the team a matter of pride, dedication, envy, and an honor worth trying to achieve. The original image of the CARE Team was built by admitting only graduate students in psychology and clinical psychology interns to the unit, along with members of the center staff. Gradually, as the original members were no longer able to serve, their places were filled with regular telephone volunteers who had proven their ability and dedication to the total program. It was always the intention eventually to make the CARE Team totally nonprofessional in its personnel in order to maximize the ability of any other crisis center in the country to adopt the program, with or without a university in the community.

To become a member of the CARE Team, a telephone volunteer must have demonstrated satisfactory performance in the crisis intervention procedure. Such evidence is obtained from the Technical Effectiveness ratings (Fowler and McGee, 1973) and Clinical Effectiveness ratings (Knickerbocker and McGee, 1973) of their telephone interviews. Additionally, subjective factors, such as the impression that the application has made on the staff who supervised his casework, are taken into account. Once they have made application to the center director, applicants are permitted to sign up for duty with one of the staff consultants for a period of time until they can demonstrate under supervision in the field what kind of judgments and action plans they are capable of utilizing. Dependability and reliability are crucial factors in a CARE Team member, and no one is ever selected who has failed to demonstrate dedication and commitment to the crisis center as a telephone worker.

The two people on duty during each CARE Team shift are not generally of equal experience. Always, one is considered the "consultant," while the other is the "backup" member. The consultant is the captain and quarterback of the CARE Team. His job is also to be available as consultant to the telephone workers on duty during his shift. The consultant may be called by the telephone crisis worker several times when no CARE Team is necessary. It is always the consultant, not the telephone worker, who decides when a CARE Team is to go into action. Often the consultant utilizes the opinion of the telephone worker in making his decision, but the responsibility for action or inaction remains with him.

It is also the consultant's duty to be sure that he has a backup member standing by to go with him if necessary, and to notify each new telephone shift of the team's availability. The CARE Teams are scheduled from 4:00 p.m.–7:00 a.m. during the weekdays, and from 7:00 a.m.–7:00 p.m. and 7:00 p.m.–7:00 a.m. on weekends. Members of the center staff serve CARE Team functions during the regular working days. When the CARE Team is on duty, the consultant is theoretically the person in charge of the entire crisis center service operation. He always has access to consultation from one of the staff if he needs to broaden the base of responsibility for a specific decision, but it should be evident that the selection of consultants from the ranks of experienced and proven backup members is a matter which must be given careful consideration.

Public Image of the Members

The most difficult problem of the CARE Team personnel is related to the image that they cast on the public. Any crisis center which serves the multiple aspects of its community must be able to work on all sides of the street at one time. One cannot be too extreme in his dress, general appearance, or attitudes if he is to be equally effective with the drug users in the counter-culture, the elderly, establishment-oriented citizens, the black ghetto family, and the professional or upper-class suburbanites. The manner of dress which grants one easy entry to the student living area may be offensive in the hospital emergency room or the police headquarters. There is not time to ascertain what kind of a person to send to a crisis scene when the CARE Team is needed. A CARE Team must be prepared for any eventuality by maintaining moderation and general appropriateness at all times. One can wear long hair and a beard and still be neatly groomed, but one cannot be a "freak" and be on the CARE Team. One can dress comfortably and informally, but one cannot go barefooted on the CARE Team.

There is no evidence as yet that having a black member facilitates the role of the CARE Team in a black family disturbance or other intervention. An effort is being made to gather information on this question. It is evident on a strictly subjective, cursory level of observation, however, that one can appear too young to be effective with middle-aged people. The converse is not true. Middle-aged CARE Team members are the kind of people whose liberal and modern attitudes make them acceptable to young people much more readily than young people, no matter how they try, can be accepted by the older generation.

Training

There has been no special training program developed for CARE Team members other than the on-the-job experience or apprenticeship training which the member goes through in the process of selection. The CARE Team has monthly meetings, at which time special problems are discussed, and new procedures may be introduced. Theoretically, it should be possible to develop performance criteria and measures of individual performance appropriate to CARE Team activity. When this is accomplished, predictive instruments may be developed for selection, and training programs may be devised to satisfy these criteria. For the present, however, these techniques are barely beginning to be available for the telephone worker, and there is still much work left to do in this area first.

PRACTICAL ASPECTS OF CARE TEAM OPERATION

The most important single benefit to the CARE Team is the availability of two-way mobile radio equipment. It is possible to apply to the Federal Communications Commission for a radio license under the provisions for special emergency radio systems. It is also quite possible to use Citizen's Band radio equipment but, of course, there is less privacy with such a system. The Gainesville crisis center has been facilitated in the development of the CARE Team by the local Board of County Commissioners, who have granted the agency permission to use its federally assigned General Government Frequency. This is only a temporary arrangement for developmental purposes, but currently, plans are being negotiated with the police department to share one channel of its new four-channel UHF system. Obviously, use of the radio system maximizes the efficiency with which a CARE Team can be directed to a location within the community which may be difficult to locate. However, it also facilitates involving other services,

Table 2 Frequency of specific uses of the radio system by CARE Teams on a sample of 90 cases

Use	No. of times
CARE Team contacted originally by radio	7
Used en route for directions to address	23
Used en route for briefing on the case	45
Used to transmit directions to office	44
Used because no telephone at the scene	15
Used to request emergency help	2
Used to keep office informed on case	63

such as notifying the hospital if a suicide attempt victim is being transported, or asking for police or ambulance support on a case. Recorded data show that the radio is used in 37% of CARE Team contacts. Table 2 shows the various uses of the radio system in a sample of 90 cases. When the statement was made that efficient communication and rapid transportation are the two most important needs of a crisis center (Chapter 11), it was primarily the operation of the CARE Team which was being considered.

The CARE Team not only carries a portable two-way radio, but it also has a specially outfitted kit of materials and supplies which frequently comes in very handy. Included in this kit are such items as a flashlight; a small first aid kit; maps of the city, county, and university campus; directories of all motels and major apartment buildings, showing the location of individual rooms; simple tools; notepaper; and case report forms.

Some of the most frequently raised questions about the CARE Team involve questions of liability, insurance protection, legal rights and liabilities, and the personal danger to CARE Team members. These questions can be answered only through experience; truthful answers based on someone else's experience seldom dispel misconceptions and anxieties. There never has been any instance of any person attacked or harmed in any way while serving as a crisis worker. There have been times when the CARE Team was unwanted at a particular place, and good judgment was needed to leave before the client's anger was aroused. However, a reasonably mature consultant can determine easily when his presence is no longer useful. The dangers are minimum, if not nonexistent. As to the liabilities from a legal point of view, they have never been tested. There are frequent threats, but never have any litigations been initiated. Part of the CARE Team's role is to calm irate persons with an assurance of the desire to be of help. When this is successfully done, there can be no legal problems.

The Gainesville center's CARE Team was used by police on an occasion to gain entry into a home where a woman was believed to have already overdosed herself. By explicit direction, the policeman advised the CARE Team consultant to enter the house by forcing the back door and then to admit him through the front door. The rules regarding forcible entry and search and seizure change when the police arrive on the scene. The usual procedure is for the CARE Team to make certain of its reasons for concern and then to act accordingly. It is always necessary to notify and invite the police to the scene. Never has there been any problem with any client, relative, or law enforcement officer for operating on what was deemed clearly as the best interests of the client. A safe rule to follow is to recognize that the laws have been written to protect the public from invasion of their property and possessions. The laws were not intended to permit people to die unnecessarily after they had called a friend or a crisis center for help. Therefore, when the CARE Team has knowledge of someone's possibly being in trouble and unable to respond when help is offered, the thing to do is to act immediately and then worry about protecting the CARE Team later. Naturally, this requires sound judgment exercised by and shared with responsible people who themselves are in good standing with the legally sanctioned agencies of the community. The same CARE Team that makes psychological autopsy death investigations for the state attorney's office is the one which may be called upon to enter a home to prevent a death. It is not likely that the state attorney will prosecute a case against that CARE Team.

Another guideline is to ask, "Who am I really worrying about?" If one has no justifiable reason to worry about the potential danger to the client, then he should not be there at the scene. If he does have a genuine concern about the client, but is inhibited by worry over his own needs, then he has no business being on the CARE Team. It is possible to use mature judgment and deliberate caution rather than to act with foolish, reckless abandon. Under such conditions, one simply kicks down the door and asks later who is going to pay for it. Table 3 shows a breakdown of specific activities undertaken by the CARE Team in a sample of 250 contacts.

In responding to questions of legal sanction and liability, it is well to remember that these questions nearly always are raised by people who would rather not see a CARE Team functioning. These are issues which have been used repeatedly to stop rather than facilitate an outreach program. If one intends to wait until he has satisfied all of the alarmist warnings of those who would like to stymie a CARE Team, he would be better advised to become content with having his crisis program hide behind the telephone. If one wishes to operate a CARE Team program for maximum crisis intervention service, he would be best advised to start the program, and, by so doing, demonstrate that the questions need never have been raised in the first place.

Table 3 Frequency of specific actions taken by the CARE Team in a sample of 250 cases

Specific actions of CARE Team	Number	Percent
Premises searched for lethal weapons or drugs	29	12.0
Firearms removed	3	1.2
Pills, other weapons removed	17	7.1
Forcible entry	4	1.7
Law enforcement agency called to support CARE Team	20	8.3
Client taken out for a meal	7	2.9
Suicide contract made with client	48	19.9
Transportation provided	68	28.2
Ambulance called	9	3.7
Significant others contacted	98	40.7
Premises searched for suicide note	10	4.1
Death investigation begun	5	2.1
Specific actions planned for next few hours	120	49.8
Future contact with SCIS arranged	168	69.7
Auto disabled	9	3.7
Other	12	5.0

SOME EXAMPLES OF CARE TEAM ACTIONS

Suicide Attempts

Generally, notification of a suicide attempt comes to the crisis center from one of the law enforcement agencies. By state law in Florida, the police authority is required to investigate self-inflicted injuries and overdoses to verify that no criminal action was involved. It is a "nonproductive" report, since no follow-up by the police is ever involved in such cases. However, the emergency room clerk notifies the police when a suicide attempt case arrives at the hospital. By arrangement with the police and sheriff, the CARE Team is called by the dispatcher at the same time he sends a patrol car to the hospital. Usually, the CARE Team meets the officer in the emergency room and learns the patient's identity, address, and some of the details of the event from him.

In keeping with a concern for the patient's rights of privacy, as well as the medical ethics related to involving other people in the treatment process, the patient is always given the opportunity to refuse contact with the CARE Team. In most instances, it is the police officer who notifies the patient that the CARE Team is on the scene and advises the patient that it would be desirable to let the crisis center try to help him work out the problem which caused the attempt. Nearly always, the patient accepts the opportunity to receive help, and an initial contact is made before the patient is released. If there are relatives or friends who have accompanied the patient to the hospital, they are also seen by one of the CARE Team members. It is often possible to engage an ambivalent client by forming a secure engagement with the other family members. When a patient refuses contact with the CARE Team in the emergency room, he is visited at home within 12 hours after release. This visit is to give the patient one more chance to accept the help he asked for by the attempt, and to give the CARE Team one more chance to break through the ambivalence. If this fails, the client is not harassed further, but contact will be maintained with a significant other person, if possible.

Contact with the family is especially important since they, too, have problems about the attempt. Husbands or wives have feelings of anger and guilt, parents have feelings of embarrassment, and friends or roommates generally are confused and worried over how to take care of the patient when he is released. All of these concerns must be handled as if they were just as important as the problem experienced by the patient. A typical question which, when asked in an honest and genuine manner, always will stimulate the cooperation of a significant other, is simply, "Has anyone bothered to care how you feel about this?" Rarely has the emergency room staff wanted anything more from the significant other than the patient's name and address and a signature to authorize treatment.

If these feelings are not given relief early, the adjustment of the patient and the significant other, especially if it is a married couple, is going to become worse instead of better. The suicide attempt communication will have had no effect (Shagoury, 1971). Here is an excellent example of how the CARE Team, by responding to suicide attempts immediately, may be performing a suicide *prevention* function.

Sometimes, suicide attempts are called to the crisis center by the victim himself, or by relatives and friends who discover the victim in the process of making the attempt. In such instances, the action is dependent upon whether or not the client has lost consciousness, when any pills were ingested, and what they were. Where time is not critical, the CARE Team will go to the client's house and make an assessment on the scene before rushing into a decision to transport him to the hospital. Many times, it has been found that clients have not taken the amount or the type of drug which the significant other reports. Too hasty action in such cases causes unnecessary embarrassment, expense for the ambulance, and hostility on the part of the client.

On the other hand, in some instances, the CARE Team has arrived and found the caller already nearly unconscious or perhaps already passed out by the time entry can be gained. In such cases, the CARE Team transports the client to the hospital immediately without waiting even an additional 15 minutes for an ambulance. The CARE Team kits contain disposable mouth-to-mouth resuscitators for such cases. Here again, no concern is felt over questions of liability and insurance protection when the client's life may be at stake.

Family Disturbances

In a number of recent articles, Bard (1969, 1970, 1971) has described the utilization of crisis intervention concepts by New York City policemen in the development of a team of Family Crisis Intervention Specialists. Efforts at promoting a similar program in the Gainesville Police Department resulted in an agreement whereby the crisis center CARE Team would provide the manpower to be utilized by the police in their interventions on signal 22 calls involving a family dispute. In such cases, calls are received from the police when they respond to a signal 22, and where the family agrees to see a member of the CARE Team immediately. The CARE team attempts to arrive before the police are forced to leave the scene, but as soon after receiving the call as possible.

The procedures for handling family disturbances involve talking to the two disputants separately and then bringing them together to tell their own sides of the dispute. Every effort is made to negotiate and mediate a communication between the parties, where this is possible. Many times, when alcohol is involved and one of the disputants is heavily intoxicated, effective communication is impossible for the present. It often happens that one of the disputants has left the scene prior to the CARE Team's arrival, but it is nevertheless useful for the remaining party to be engaged in a crisis resolution. Future contacts between the crisis center and the family are arranged, and regular phase II management is begun as long as the family will continue to participate.

In most of the signal 22 cases, the family has very weak and sometimes no stable family ties. Many are short-term, common law relationships. Most occur in the black neighborhoods where fighting among couples, especially on Friday and Saturday nights, is a normal part of the life style. Alcohol plays a part in over 50 percent of the cases. Therefore, the family disturbance cases are, for the most part, not successful in the sense of the usual criteria for crisis intervention. In such cases, the resulting benefit is delayed and secondary. It has been observed that nearly every family involved in a signal 22 call is a family without resources. They are without resources for one of two reasons: either they have already tried every other institutionalized agency in the community and there are none left for them to use, or they don't know about the existence of the agencies which might be of help to them. In either case, the CARE Team and the crisis center represent a potential way of breaking up the immobilization of the family in the face of troubles. Many times, families have called the crisis center when future problems occurred. Even if there was no immediate source of direct help, the caller was able to find a degree of emotional support and understanding. The signal 22 program undertaken by the CARE Team has resulted in a marked increase in utilization of the center by the black community. Radio and newspaper advertising is abstract and meaningless to many black families, but personal experience and word-of-mouth contact with the actual services performed for the community have led many black citizens to seek help from the center when they did not do so prior to the start of the signal 22 program.

It should be mentioned that the family disturbance case is the one which is the most dangerous for policemen, in the sense that more officers are killed in the line of duty while responding to a family dispute than in any other line of police work. This fact has certain basic psychological roots, all of which tend to make the CARE Team not only more appropriate, but clearly safer in such cases. In the first place, many people involved in a dispute use the police as a "big weapon" to wield at the other disputant. If the police are called by the wife, and they come ostensibly to "protect" her against the husband, it is seen as a severe blow to the already aggravated male ego. At the sight of a police uniform and gun, and particularly if he is drinking and impulsive, many males in such "put down" positions will react violently. The CARE Team carries no guns and wears no symbols of authority over anyone. They go only to help, and to help each party equally. The wife may have called for help to subdue her husband, but the CARE Team goes with a set to respond to his feelings about the matter as well as hers. The dynamics of the situation are very different under the CARE Team type of intervention from what they are with the police. Not only are the police less likely to become victims, but the intervention is more likely to be psychologically helpful to both disputants.

Suicide Threat Calls

In many cases of suicide threats phoned in to the center, it is necessary for the CARE Team to make an on-the-scene assessment of the lethality. Many clients can sound very lethal when in fact they actually have little intention of dying at the moment. Such threats may be considered trial balloons, sent aloft to determine whether or not anyone in the community really cares. The response of the CARE Team demonstrates that there is in fact a group of people who care, and a new resource is provided. Many times, these threats are voiced repeatedly by an alcohol-dependent woman who, in the regular pattern of nightly intoxication, calls the center to get someone to come sit with her. Obviously, the CARE Team cannot continue to play this dependency-gratifying role once it becomes established that this is the pattern. However, other avenues can be approached, such as a contract to come only if the person will agree to initiate alcoholic rehabilitation at the half-way house. Repeated CARE Team calls to alcohol-dependent threateners have led the county judge to place a person under involuntary confinement until he can be sobered up and placed on the Antabuse program at the mental health center. Such treatment is court-ordered for drunks considered "dangerous to others," as indicated by drunken driving or public disturbance arrests. Drunks who are considered "dangerous to self," as evidenced by repeated suicide threats and CARE Team interventions, receive the same court-sanctioned intervention.

In deciding whether or not to activate the CARE Team, the consultant generally declines to go out on cases which are well known to be chronic and noncooperative alcoholics. Where the case is a new one, and the person's pattern is not known to the center, the CARE Team usually will respond, even if drinking is involved. A suicide threat without alcohol involved will cause the center to put every possible technique to work to identify the location of the caller and get the CARE Team on the way. The general rule for making the go or no-go decision is to decide how much risk one is willing to assume that the person might be found dead later. If the risk is unknown, or high, the consultant will go; if it is low enough that he is willing to risk being wrong, he may decline to go. It must be recognized by everyone that sometimes mistakes are going to be made. The tendency is to make the mistake in the direction of overreacting rather than underreacting.

Juvenile Runaways

The management of juvenile runaway cases presents some very special difficulties for the crisis center, and the CARE Team generally is responsible for handling the delicate issues involved. To begin with, the crisis center must walk a very thin line which includes sincere efforts to help the juvenile, while at the same time keeping itself in a position of credibility with the law enforcement agencies. The center will not turn a juvenile over to the authorities for the purpose of having him "busted" and sent home. Neither will the center harbor a juvenile fugitive from the law enforcement agencies. To resolve this paradox, a set of specific procedures has been implemented.

The best approach to a juvenile runaway, and the only one which is consistent with the adolescent's psychological needs when he gets to the crisis center, is to negotiate his reentry into the home setting. It takes some time to gain an adolescent runaway's confidence, but it can be done. He usually will accept the invitation to call his home and put his parents at ease concerning his safety and well-being. Once this is done, the CARE Team consultant can talk to the parents and fully explain the center's position.

Basically, the center wants the parents' explicit permission to care for the runaway in Gainesville until arrangements can be made to return the child home without force. It is much easier for a runaway to reenter the home scene when the parents have sent money for a bus ticket than when he is taken across country "in custody" and locked up in the juvenile detention shelter as soon as he gets home. In the meantime, the parents, knowing the whereabouts of the child, can notify the hometown police to cancel a teletype bulletin ordering local authorities to pick up the fugitive. As long as there is no teletype—which is just as official as a warrant for arrest—the crisis center can provide shelter and food and a wide variety of other emotional supports.

If the runaway will not agree to cooperate with the center and make contact with the family, then the crisis center is unable to be of *any assistance* whatever until it has been ascertained that no teletype pick-up order has been received in local law enforcement stations. It becomes the consultant's duty to check with the police and sheriff to learn whether or not there is a pick-up order out on a runaway answering the client's description. If a teletype order is pending, then the runaway is advised that the center will offer him no refuge unless he contacts the parents, and the order is withdrawn. If he refuses, he is allowed to leave, against sincere advice, but the center will not participate in his fugitive status.

Occasionally, it happens that checking for a possible teletype will result in a juvenile officer's coming to the center in the belief that he will apprehend a fugitive. However, the runaways have already left on their own, with no assistance from the CARE Team, and it can be said honestly that their whereabouts are not known.

This procedure has resulted in several advantages for client service. In the first place, the word has gotten out among the youth culture that the crisis center will help a runaway get home and will help him negotiate his way back in. The older young people, who generally harbor the underage fugitives for a while, have learned that the center will take the runaway off their hands when their position "gets too hot." The police have learned that the center is effective in getting the runaways back to the families, which is everyone's goal anyway, and they trust the center's procedure as not inimical to their own operations.

It is sometimes asked why the CARE Team does not automatically take the runaway to the police or contact the parents even without the client's permission. It is, to be certain, a difficult matter to see 12- or 13-year-old adolescents on the road hundreds of miles from home, subject to the varieties of victimization which they may agree to in exchange for food and lodging. At the same time, the crisis center never can ascertain, nor should it make a judgment about, the quality of home life from which the child is running. An automatic policy for sending the child home without first mediating a reentry negotiation with the family, and perhaps even the hometown juvenile authorities, would tend to leave out a concern for the welfare of the runaway client himself. In most of the cases, a genuinely warm consultant can win the runaway's confidence, and the CARE Team can engage both the child and the family in an agreement to seek some help for their problems when they are all back together.

General CARE Team Services

Every suicide prevention center is, by the demands of its caseload, forced to operate as a general crisis intervention service. Table 4 shows the types of cases to which the CARE Team responded in a sample of 250 contacts. Depending upon the extent of unmet needs in the community, the requests for general assistance

Table 4 Frequency of contact by CARE Team on different types of problems in 250 cases

Type of case involved	Number	Percent
Marital problem	71	29.5
Other family problem	52	21.6
Chronic alcoholic	31	12.9
Drug abuse case	15	6.2
Welfare, basic support case	12	5.0
Need immediate food, lodging	12	5.0
Juvenile runaway	6	2.5
Legal, criminal problem	19	7.9
Transportation	11	4.6
Vocational problem	13	5.4
Student, school adjustment	8	3.3
Homosexual problem	2	.8
Acute psychotic	17	7.1
Personal loneliness, alienation	84	34.9
Military, draft problem	3	1.2
Medical attention needed	29	12.0
Other	46	19.1

may be very great. It may be observed that the community agencies partition off areas of service for themselves, and they tend not to provide services which fall outside of their domain. The longer an agency exists, or the more it is controlled by external forces, such as state departments in distant cities, the easier it is for it to find ways of refusing service to specific clients. There are residency, financial distress, or physical disability requirements. Many people in genuine, acute need fall in the cracks between the institutionalized agencies. They come to the crisis center. If they have not been in town long, or if they have a residence elsewhere, most agencies are willing to give them a few dollars so they can move on and become someone else's case. The crisis center has no way to dispose of a client other than by helping him to resolve his problem.

Therefore, the CARE Team may be called upon to provide transportation, locate housing, get drugs for sick children, deliver a small contribution of cash—in short, to perform any of a thousand different unique functions demanded by the person or family in crisis.

The question of responding to drug abuse cases, where a client may be experiencing a bad "trip" on LSD or "freaked out" on "speed," has been deliberately avoided thus far in this discussion. The CARE Team is not known generally as a drug treatment unit. This is primarily because there is a formally licensed drug abuse treatment and education center, called the Corner Drug Store, in the community. The crisis center is in close contact with that program. If a call is received at the crisis center involving a drug case, the CARE Team will go, but usually will take a member of the Corner Drug Store staff with them to actually manage the case. It is the feeling of the CARE Team consultants that the talk-down of a bad "acid trip" is accomplished best by someone who really knows the drug scene from the inside. There are few CARE Team members who do, whereas the Corner Drug Store staff are more emotionally, intellectually, and experientially equipped to be effective with such cases.

Every crisis center will find itself called upon to provide services which other agencies could provide better if they would. Where the other agencies in fact meet their responsibilities, the CARE Team role is to provide the contact between the client and the other service. Where there are no agencies to fill the need, the crisis center and the CARE Team are called upon to be imaginative, creative, and supportive. In the end, it is this first-hand, personal contact with the people in need which identifies the directions for the community to move in developing new services and restructuring existing ones.

COMMUNITY REACTIONS TO THE CARE TEAM

It is probably not difficult for any crisis center worker to anticipate what kinds of reactions the CARE Team has experienced in different sections of the community. In brief, the reactions are negative from the medical enterprise, including the hospital personnel, generally neutral from the mental health professionals, and highly positive from the law enforcement field. Church groups, welfare offices, and the Salvation Army are generally positive in their attitudes, depending upon whether the clients involved are cooperative in accepting the help the agency has to offer. The attitude of the general public, the potential and active clients, is overwhelmingly positive. Comments such as, "I had no idea there was anyone who would come out to see me on a holiday," are typical of the appreciation people express.

Medical Reactions

Part of the difficulty with the CARE Team-physician interaction is a matter of definition. Most of the patients who are taken to the emergency room with a drug overdose or a wrist cut do not have their own private physician. They are treated by the internist or surgeon on call, or by the emergency room medical staff, if there is one. Most of these physicians have no orientation in or understanding of suicidology as a clinical specialty. They define a suicide attempt as a case where death would have occurred without medical intervention. The rest of the cases are manipulative gestures, not suicide attempts. They lose patience with the CARE Team's concern for the patient and for their effort to comfort the family.

Additional problems occur because of the issue of medical ethics and confidentiality. They are afraid of violating patient rights by admitting nonmedical people to the emergency room treatment area, even when the medical treatment has been completed and the patient is merely "being observed." One must be continuously cognizant that to function in the medical house, he must do so on invitation and according to the rules of the medical establishment. If the crisis center and its CARE Team are nonmedical units, they may have some difficulty finding acceptance. There is nothing to prevent them from contacting the clients later, however, and providing response to the cry for help.

On occasion, the CARE Team has encountered a really positive ally in an emergency room nurse or physician. In such cases, the CARE Team consultant has been asked to stay with the patient during and after treatment to free the hospital personnel for other duties. Certain psychiatric residents always will invite the CARE Team consultant into the interview room with them as they talk to the patients. Some of the local private physicians will refer their own patients to the crisis center and will involve the CARE Team directly if they are present when a patient makes an attempt. However, these are personal, individual matters, and they rarely become the basis for instituting policy or procedures. In general, the medical field is opposed to any routine treatment or evaluation procedure which involves nonmedical personnel.

The most characteristic use which the emergency room personnel have made of the CARE Team directly is in terms of *removing* the patient. When treatment and observation are over, and there are no family or friends, the crisis center will often receive a call to take the patient home. If the case involved a wound such that the patient's clothes were ruined or destroyed in the course of preparing him for treatment, the CARE Team will be asked to round up some clothing. Generally, it is in getting rid of a treated patient that the hospital will ask for CARE Team assistance.

Mental Health Professional Reactions

The local mental health clinic has found the CARE Team concept very useful and has tended to want to copy it in serving the outlying rural areas of the service area. It is possible, through the CARE Team system, to set up a series of small emergency satellite units much more economically than multiple outpatient clinics. These could be staffed by public health nurses and school guidance counselors, activated by the local police or sheriff's office, and served by traveling consultants out of the primary mental health center. The feasibility of the model in its own domain has led the mental health clinic to look favorably on and become supportive of the CARE Team in the central city community.

On a few occasions, mental health practitioners, generally of nonmedical disciplines, use the CARE Team as a resource when they are unable to locate a patient or when they have to be away from the city. Their clients are instructed to call the CARE Team if a need arises, and the team is alerted to the possibility of such a call. Naturally, response is always assured when a referral is initiated by one of the psychotherapists in the community.

The CARE Team frequently has contact with the psychiatrists who rotate on duty in the community general hospital. There again, acceptance and collaboration are functions of the individual personalities involved. However, there is definite evidence that both psychiatrist and CARE Team have found their roles mutually enhanced by the other, and it is merely a matter of deciding to be helpful to one another which determines what the character of the relationship will be.

Law Enforcement Reactions

As has been true of suicide and crisis intervention services in general in many communities, it is the law enforcement agency which is most helpful and most appreciative of the CARE Team. There is no limit to the service which the police or sheriff will extend to the Gainesville group. The suggestion that a client may have attempted to drive her car into a lake (because she had threatened to a relative to do so) will bring sheriff's patrolmen from all parts of the county until the client is located. The sheriff will contact the CARE Team whenever he needs to talk a disturbed person into giving himself up and seeking help.

Because of the closeness of the relationship between the crisis center CARE Team and the law enforcement agencies, there is hope that the CARE Team may eventually become a unit of the Community Service Division of the local Police Department. This would mean that administrative management and financial support for the CARE Team units would come from city police funds, possibly through a grant under the Law Enforcement Assistance Act. If such an arrangement can be developed on a pilot basis, it will be ample demonstration of the feasibility and the viability of the concepts which have formed the basic service structure of the crisis center and its CARE Team.

15
THE DEATH
INVESTIGATION
TEAM

Probably the most valuable of all the technologies developed by the Los Angeles Suicide Prevention Center has been the psychological autopsy (Curphey, 1961; Klugman, 1970; Litman, Curphey et al., 1963). The major function of this procedure usually has been considered to be the providing of psychological data from which to infer the attitude or intention of the deceased about his own death just prior to its occurrence. Such information can be provided only by the behavioral scientist; it is not apparent in the anatomical findings of the autopsy surgeon or the chemical analyses of the toxicologist. An investigation into the background of the deceased, especially his usual life style and any recent changes therein, often leads to conclusions as to the mode of death in equivocal cases. Such information naturally is important to the official agencies concerned with death certification, including the department of vital statistics, the law enforcement agency having jurisdiction in the area, and the insurance company. However, there are distinct advantages to the survivors in having as much accurate information as possible about the death. Such information is, to them, the basic ingredient of their bereavement crisis resolution. They need the facts to mourn in the most appropriate and healthy manner. Consequently, the by-products of the psychological autopsy investigation have essential primary prevention benefits to the community and represent one of the most important services which a suicide prevention and crisis intervention center can render to its community.

The SCIS in Gainesville began to provide death investigation services after it had been in operation about one year. The history of its activity has been a most interesting one and involves some issues which other centers should consider as they plan these services in their own communities. This chapter reviews this history, describes the functions of the Death Investigation Team as a special unit of the CARE Team discussed in the preceding chapter, and gives some examples of its service to the community.

HISTORY OF THE DEATH INVESTIGATION SERVICE

When the SCIS first was founded in the community, one member of the Board of Directors was an attorney who had been active as an officer in the Mental Health

Association. He was an Assistant State Attorney and had a professional role to play in the investigation of violent deaths. Therefore, his natural interest in the suicide prevention service led him to provide the necessary legal services for writing a charter and by-laws and otherwise satisfying the legal requirements for incorporating the agency. Shortly after the program officially began, the SCIS director asked for a conference with the State Attorney and discussed with him the role of the suicidologist in the investigation of equivocal deaths. He was interested and eagerly accepted reprints of the most relevant literature in the field. He promised to review it with other members of the State Attorney's staff and to contact the SCIS later. There was never a follow-up contact.

After approximately nine months, the local Bar Association president appointed three members of the association to serve as volunteer legal consultants to ths SCIS as a token of their interest in and support of the program. One of these consultants was a practicing attorney who was also on the State Attorney's staff part time. Once more, the same discussions were held with the State Attorney concerning the psychological autopsy. He expressed interest, but cautiously avoided giving any indication that the service was desired. There was no further effort at negotiating for several more months.

After a new psychiatrist-director of the county Mental Health Services arrived in the community, there was a major breakthrough in the relationships with the State Attorney's office. The psychiatrist was familiar with the literature in suicidology and knew of the value of the psychological autopsy when performed by suicide prevention center personnel. Therefore, he arranged a conference between the SCIS director, the County Medical Examiner, and the State Attorney's office. At that meeting, some very interesting problems emerged. The purposes and procedures of the psychological autopsy were discussed, and the value of the service was appreciated immediately by the Medical Examiner. He made certain that the State Attorney agreed, and a procedure was established whereby the Medical Examiner would contact the crisis center and request death investigations as part of his routine role in the investigation of violent deaths. At this point, the Assistant State Attorney inquired how much the service was going to cost his office. This question came as a complete surprise to the SCIS director, who had never discussed a fee simply because no fee was ever considered as a relevant part of the activity. Death investigations had always been seen by SCIS as a service rendered by one community agency for another.

As the issue was discussed, it was explained that the State Attorney's office would have been using the service since it had been first proposed except for the fact that they had a limited budget and could not afford additional fees. Thus, it had been the assumption that a fee would be charged that had been interfering with the negotiations for over a year, and this issue had never previously surfaced. As it was discussed further, and the SCIS director declined any interest in a fee, the Medical Examiner began to take a serious interest in the arrangements. It was his opinion that a fee must be charged on every case; otherwise, he felt, it would not be a professional service, and the County had no right to expect professional services without paying appropriately for them. He received a fee for his services, and he felt that the SCIS, working as his aide, should also receive a fee for its service. The argument had merit, and it served to make the SCIS dilemma more complex.

Consequently, it was agreed that a modest fee of $100 per case would be charged, although this was far lower than usual professional fees charged by psychologists in private consultation practice. A thorough investigation might require three or four days of work for two or three people, and $100 is thus a minimum fee; for the State Attorney, however, it was a large sum.

After these negotiations, death investigations were requested by the Medical Examiner on all suicide and equivocal deaths. They were performed by the members of the SCIS staff along with clinical psychology interns serving a training rotation at the crisis center. After eight reports had been filed, the Medical Examiner inquired whether the SCIS was receiving its proper fee. Actually, no money had been received for any of the investigations, but since it was not an issue for the crisis center, no inquiry had been made. Consequently, the Medical Examiner, who really cared about the fee, investigated and determined that the fault lay in the fact that no formal statements had been rendered by the crisis center. Although it had been included in the Medical Examiner's statement to the State Attorney, an invoice from the SCIS was also necessary. The SCIS director was instructed to send his statement to the Medical Examiner with the investigation report. Soon thereafter, payment was received for all eight previously submitted reports.

Almost immediately thereafter, two major changes occurred in the procedures which had been established. The first was that the State Attorney's staff began not to refer some deaths to the Medical Examiner for study. Where the immediately obvious visual evidence justified a conclusion of unequivocal suicide, there was no referral to the Medical Examiner. Previously, every death, whether obvious suicide or not, had been investigated with autopsy and toxicology studies. The second change in procedures occurred because the law enforcement officers had become accustomed to working with the SCIS Death Investigation Team. They began to call the SCIS immediately after the body was discovered, rather than wait for the team to arrive after referral by the Medical Examiner. The investigators from the County Sheriff's office call the crisis center as they are en route to the scene. Consequently, when the Medical Examiner had referred the last few cases, the SCIS team was already on the job. The Medical Examiner began to let the police and the Sheriff's office make the referrals, confident that the SCIS would be present and that he would get a report. This procedure worked quite well for several months, until changes occurred in the personnel of the two law enforcement agencies. Both the criminal investigation division of the Sheriff's office and the detective division of the city Police Department appointed new Captains in charge of the units. As a result, the routine procedures negotiated with previous captains were interrupted. The center staff was not being notified of deaths and learned about them in the newspaper and on the radio stations one or two days after the fact. When inquiries were made, it was determined that the new Captain of Detectives had investigated the SCIS role in death investigations and had learned that although it had been helpful to his officers, the reports had been costing the State Attorney $100 each, and that he objected to the fee. The Captain therefore determined that it was not going to be he or his men who were responsible for the State Attorney's receiving a bill that he did not want to pay. Once more, new negotiations were held to resolve this issue. It was agreed once and for all that no fees would be charged, and that the services of the SCIS team would be requested by the law enforcement agencies whenever they felt they would be useful to the officers or to the families of the deceased. The State Attorney, the Medical Examiner, and the police agency having jurisdiction in the case would all receive a copy of the investigation report.

RATIONALE FOR THE DEATH INVESTIGATION TEAM

There are two primary purposes for the involvement of the SCIS in death investigations. These are (1) the psychological autopsy function, and (2) the opportunity for bereavement crisis counseling with the survivors of sudden and violent deaths.

Psychological Autopsy

There is an extensive literature on the psychological autopsy procedure. Briefly, it is a source of information about the deceased which reveals the psychological data often necessary for drawing conclusions as to whether suicide, accident, or homicide was the more likely mode of death. Occasionally, even natural deaths may look like suicide until more information about the deceased is sifted for behavioral and psychodynamic facts. Finally, the suicidology literature offers a body of knowledge concerning suicide notes which may be very valuable for the police investigators. Evidence technicians can determine if handwriting is that of the deceased, but content analysis of suicide notes reveals whether the note was most likely a genuine or a fake (Shneidman and Farberow, 1957), or whether it is the type of note usually left by persons of the age and sex of the deceased (Darbonne, 1969; Frederick, 1969). Analysis of the contents of the suicide note often gives valuable information for rendering support to the survivors.

Bereavement Counseling of Survivors

Cain and Fast (1966a, b) have discussed the legacy of suicide as it affects marital partners and children whose parents commit suicide. The emotional suffering in these two groups is documented clearly by these authors. The implications of their reports demand the expertise of trained crisis intervention workers, knowledgeable in the dynamics of suicide, immediately after the death is discovered.

The primary prevention of future suicides, and of mental health casualties general-ly, in these survivors may be dependent to an undeterminable degree upon immediate intervention. Its role in cases which are contacted immediately has convinced the SCIS staff of the value of and need for the Death Investigation Team. The necessity for *immediate* contact, simultaneously with contact of the police officer, is due to the very short latent period before unhealthy psycho-logical defenses of denial, avoidance, shame, guilt, and withdrawal from communi-cation begin to take their toll in the survivors' adjustment process. A matter of two or three hours will make the difference in whether or not a satisfactory entry can be achieved.

An excellent example of the value of the SCIS team has been predicted by Cain and Fast (1966b) in their report on the effect of a suicide on the spouse of the deceased. Their study revealed that many of the 45 surviving marital partners experienced emotional stress at the time of the suicide because of the official investigations. They frequently reported stress as a result of unpleasant experi-ences with the investigating police officers and detectives, who had a duty to perform for the community and whose special training and skills were in the area of gathering technical evidence rather than in giving emotional support. In cases which are truly suicides, the surviving partner already knows that it is not a homicide. The very presence of the police performing their role naturally implies that they are not so certain. They must even ask direct questions about the quality of the relationship between the partners, which usually has not been a mutually supportive one. To some partners, most of whom are already beginning to feel resentment and hostility toward the deceased mate, such questioning provides the opportunity to refocus this hostility toward the investigating officers for their implication that a homicide motive is worth investigating. Further unpleasant experiences may be encountered with others who are doing their duty without fully understanding the psychological dynamics of the situation. The insurance agent or claims attorney is another example. The local press may be less than cordial in their efforts to get uncensored material, especially if the deceased was a prominent person or if the death had a sensational quality, as in the case of drug abusers.

The stresses experienced by the survivors call for expert crisis intervention for two reasons. First, the Death Investigation Team can substantially assist the police to actually perform their role more completely and effectively by explaining it to the family and orienting them about the policeman's function. Most families have not had extensive prior contact with police investigators and are uncertain why they must go through drawers, private papers, and other personal effects. The crisis workers can provide a valuable service both to the survivor and to the policeman by explaining these procedures and giving assurances that they are proper procedures. Cooperation of the survivors with the police has been facili-tated notably by the Death Investigation Team on several occasions. Secondly, the presence of crisis workers can establish a relationship between the survivors and a helping resource which can alleviate the most destructive emotional reactions to suicide almost before they begin. In both of their studies, Cain and Fast (1966a, b) pointed to the roles of guilt and communication breakdown in the subsequent emotional disorders which followed suicide deaths. Surviving parents wonder what to tell the children about the deceased parent and about the death itself. Spouses wonder what role they had, or what preventive measures they should have taken. Crisis workers who understand the psychological nature of the unique experience, and who *have the time* to help the survivors to work it out, can offer exactly the type of response which the police officer cannot make, even though he may want to. The crisis worker is in a position to encourage communication and can prepare the survivors for the talking they must do about the event. He can prepare the survivors also for the gossip, the accusations, and the stigma which they will eventually feel. He can interpret the shame, guilt, resentment, and denial which are natural consequences. In short, the immediate presence of suicidologists at the death scene aids both the police in their work and the survivors in their most difficult bereavement crisis.

EXAMPLES OF THE DEATH INVESTIGATION TEAM'S WORK

A few examples from the case histories with which the SCIS team has been involved will highlight some of the points made above.

Assistance to the Family

Where the survivors live in another city and hear the news of the son's or daughter's suicide by telephone, there is a very special need for the crisis center involvement. In a number of instances, the Sheriff's investigator has asked the crisis center staff actually to make the call notifying the survivors, but the Death Investigation Team will contact the family immediately, even when they are notified initially by the police agency. The purpose of this contact is to offer immediate support and to give the family another chance to ask whatever questions they want answered. It is frequently impossible to give them answers at the moment, but it gives the team a knowledge of specific answers that the family will be wanting so that they can be prepared to deal with these issues. The Death Investigation Team worker will instruct the family how to find the crisis center office and will ask them to make contact there as soon as they arrive in town. Then the team will escort them to the police agency, the university offices, if the deceased was a student, the hospital, and all other places where business must be conducted in the process of closing out a life. The Death Investigation Team, because it knows the local scene and has been through these events many times, knows who should be contacted and can make the arrangements in the manner which is easiest for the family. It is certain that no family gets to town to claim the deceased without spending necessary time with the police and other concerned parties who have an official interest in the death. Because of this service, the University Dean of

Student Affairs has instructed his staff to contact the crisis center in the event of any student death. The activity of the Death Investigation Team is the clearest example of the ombudsman role of any service that the crisis center provides.

In one instance, the deceased shot himself at approximately 7:30 p.m. one Sunday. His roommates did not know the address of his parents, and it was nearly 10:00 p.m. before the father finally was contacted in another state. The crisis worker gave him the news and answered those questions that she could appropriately respond to at the time, and then made arrangements for meeting him as soon as he came to Gainesville. He arrived at about 3:00 a.m. the next day, along with the grandparents, who met him at the crisis center office. For the next 15 hours, the crisis worker and the family went through the initial grief reactions, managed the business affairs with the hospital, mortuary, police department, apartment manager, and the bank. When he was ready to return home, the father had had a chance to explore many of his feelings about the son's death, and was prepared for dealing with the residual feelings which were certain to arise in the next few days. He had made arrangements for the crisis center to sell the son's automobile and dispose of his books and clothes and had learned what procedures he needed to follow to close the bank accounts. Many families have an immediate aversion to their child's property following a suicide. They do not want to see his clothes, ride in his automobile, or think about what to do with these personal effects. The Death Investigation Team must use a delicate diplomacy to prevent these avoidance reactions from generalizing and forming the roots of unhealthy grief work. Perhaps most important, the family knew where they could call for future needs as new issues and questions arose, and they did subsequently call with two additional requests for help. This family found their son's death as grievous as does any family; they mourned as deeply. However, they also mourned more appropriately than many because they were actively assisted in the difficult task of grief work. They were encouraged to cry openly, to ask questions about their relationships, to wonder about the answers to questions which they could not even ask, and to permit one another to alternately grieve and then console the others. They were not allowed denial, avoidance, or inactivity. Both parents felt the reality of their loss and went about their business alternately in a manner programmed by the crisis worker team. The Death Investigation Team worked continuously for 26 hours for this family, whose response to the help justified the loss of sleep.

Two other instances of specific help offered to families are relevant. In cases where the State Attorney and Medical Examiner are conducting an investigation, the information compiled has a medical-legal secrecy associated with it. No one can release any specific data until they are cleared by the State Attorney's office. This regulation runs counter to the basic psychological needs that the family has for getting the full facts to use in their crisis work. They are angered at not being given information by the Medical Examiner or the detectives. The crisis center team has a role in helping the family with this problem. While it cannot provide the classified information, it nevertheless can structure the family's lack of information. It can tell them how they will be given information, and approximately when. Further, the team can help the family to explore their feelings and knowledge of the deceased, and often to arrive at the correct answers themselves, which is better grief work anyway.

In one death, the survivors learned of the event in a most inappropriate manner. One of the local radio stations routinely monitors the police and sheriff radio frequencies. Since they know the radio codes, the news announcers broadcast the news of the suicide while the body was still in the house. While on his way home from work, a son heard over his car radio that his mother was dead from suicide. He arrived at her house just as her body was being removed. In this case, the son's anger was as intense as it was justified. The crisis center not only helped him to express his hostility, but also prepared a public appeal to the media to try to prevent future occurrences of this type of reporting.

Assistance to Significant Others

There are many important people in a death scene who are not members of the immediate family of the deceased. In cases of student deaths, these significant others are the fellow dormitory, fraternity, or sorority house residents. They too have many questions and are very prone to guilt and shame. In one instance, the deceased was a girl who had made many suicide threats; in fact, some said she talked of her death incessantly. Many of her friends had learned not to take her seriously because it was "just her way." Each, in her own way, had taken a turn at consoling the girl and helping her through one or more interpersonal traumas with her boyfriend or her parents. Each had felt the frustration of her inability to take suggestions. When they came back to school from a weekend and found that she had died, they were totally unprepared for it. This was a case in which the Death Investigation Team from the crisis center was especially helpful in talking to the friends and encouraging them to cooperate with the University Police while they conducted their search and investigation. An open discussion was held in the dormitory on the Sunday night that the girl died, then again on Wednesday evening, and a third session was held two weeks later. The purpose of these group sessions was to let the friends openly face their feelings and to ask questions of one another. Most importantly, they were helped to express their disapproval and resentment over what their friend *had done to them* by her suicide. Such feelings are natural, and when they are left unverbalized, a meaningful part of a relationship remains hidden and unavailable for the person to explore. It can become like a cancerous growth which eats away at the emotional life, and may, if unresolved, distort a person's responses to life and death issues for the rest of his life. These feelings were handled effectively by these friends with the help of the Death Investigation Team.

In another case, in which the deceased either fell or jumped from the roof of the fraternity house, there was a need for a psychological autopsy in a completely equivocal death, as well as the need for comfort to the survivors and assistance to the police. In this instance, it became apparent that not only the deceased, but many of his friends, were "high" on marijuana on the night that he died. Since there was a lot of "smoking" in the house, the fraternity brothers became immediately suspicious and totally uncooperative with the police. They even found an alumnus in law school to brief them on their legal rights to avoid answering questions. As this response emerged, the Death Investigation Team, aided by a volunteer in the crisis center who was a member of the fraternity, met with the group and completed much of the investigation without the threat which police officers had introduced into the situation. Even though they knew that the information elicited was going to be given to the police, the fraternity members were less inhibited. They eventually understood that it was the death that was the object of the investigation, not the drug usage or possession. Also, these brothers revealed an intense need to view the death as an accident rather than as a suicide. They openly admitted to screening out any information which might imply suicide. Consequently, their attitudes and fears about suicide were explored. It was determined that many of them were harboring some folklore and myths about suicide and insanity, masculine weakness, impotency, and social stigma which they interpreted as reflecting very poorly on their fraternity as a group.

Some very general discussions about suicide and suicidal people led to a relaxation of their worries and fears that the group would be forever stigmatized on campus. This was another case in which the law enforcement agency did its investigation, and the survivors, who had little positive regard for the investigation, were able to satisfy their emotional needs surrounding it.

Assistance to Police and Medical Examiner

In another example of an equivocal death in which a student jumped from the top of a dormitory after cutting his wrists and arms deeply, the crisis center Death Investigation Team was able to acquire some information which clearly pointed to an accidental death rather than a bona fide suicide. In this case, the student was "tripping" on LSD at the time of his death. He had taken LSD on several prior occasions, but he always did his "tripping" alone. He was a leader in the dormitory, was a good student, had many friends who admired him, had no problems with a girlfriend or parents, and had never been known to be depressed or dissatisfied with his life. However, on this particular evening, he had shared a purchase of LSD with two other men in the dormitory. The other two were with friends when they "dropped the acid," and because it apparently had been heavily "cut" with some unknown contaminant, they also experienced severe toxic reactions unlike the usual LSD euphoria. They were restrained forcibly by their companions. However, the third "tripper" experienced his toxic reactions alone, and as a manifestation of his terror and panic, he began to cut himself. After letting much blood drain into his waste basket, he went to the roof and jumped off. Before he died in the emergency room, he was conscious enough to talk to the attendants, and he verified the "acid" experience. Only when the information about the other two "trippers" came to light under unofficial investigation several days later was it evident that this death occurred accidentally as the deceased was engaged in what was, for him, fairly typical behavior. Without any history or present symptoms of suicidal intent, the death clearly should have been certified as an accident. The State Attorney, Police Department, and Medical Examiner were apprised of this opinion by the Death Investigation Team.

The role of the crisis center in suicide deaths is equally beneficial in the case of accidental deaths. Realizing this, the county Sheriff's office and the University Dean of Student Affairs' office both have called the crisis center in cases of accidental drowning in lakes and sinkholes in the Gainesville area. Frequently, deaths occur as a result of improperly trained or equipped scuba divers in underwater caves. In an effort to aid and support the survivors in their anticipatory grief, the crisis center staff will be present at the scene while the searchers are recovering the body. During this time, the survivors are prepared for the eventual truth, their time is structured, and arrangements are made for future contact with the center. Because of the CARE Team's mobile radio, calls can be made to the office to keep others informed at home or to handle arrangements which the family wants to make for notifying relatives in distant cities. Merely by being on the scene, with no motive other than to help the bereaved, the crisis center team is able to provide a wide variety of immediate supports.

The Death Investigation Team has its roots in a desire to provide assistance to local law enforcement agencies by applying a specialized technology of social science. It likewise grows out of an interest in providing accurate death certification and as a mission to provide necessary and appropriate crisis service to bereaved citizens of the community. The Death Investigation Team is called into action by the law enforcement agency. It is available as a resource because the law enforcement agencies have discovered its benefit. It may be the one service which is most difficult for a new program to establish in its community until adequate relationships have been developed with the police agencies. However, once the police see the crisis center as capable of staying out of the way when official police work must be done, and when they see the center staff meeting the emotional needs of the survivors in a manner for which they themselves have neither the time nor the training, the police agencies will be the first to request that the crisis center perform these services, and they will be the greatest source of support for the venture.

16
THE CENTER FOR CRISIS INTERVENTION RESEARCH

A discussion of the Suicide and Crisis Intervention Service in Gainesville would not be complete without at least a partial introduction to the research program which originally made the service unit possible. Although the relationship between the crisis service and the research team may be unique in the Gainesville setting, there are nevertheless some experiences which may be useful to other crisis center directors or investigators.

During the implementation of the WE CARE demonstration grant which was intended to develop the CARE Team approach to following up suicide attempters in the Orlando, Florida, hospitals, it was discovered that numerous complications exist when an outside investigator attempts to superimpose a set of procedures, necessitated by a research design, onto the operating patterns of a group of volunteer crisis workers. Volunteers who join a program for service purposes and suddenly find that a research methodology is directing their activity and decision-making tend to become resentful and uncooperative. Therefore, it became evident that the only way to study volunteer crisis work was to create a laboratory primarily for that purpose. The Center for Crisis Intervention Research was conceived to be such a laboratory. It was sponsored originally by a four-year research grant from the Center for Studies of Suicide Prevention at the National Institute of Mental Health.

Naturally, the research laboratory must have a volunteer pool from which to draw its research subjects, and the volunteers must have a crisis center in which to work. Thus, the Center for Crisis Intervention Research entered into a period of program development with the local community to create the Board of Directors which became the Suicide and Crisis Intervention Service, Inc. Two "sister agencies" were established, one under the public auspices of the Department of Clinical Psychology at the University of Florida, and the other under the private control of an incorporated Board of Directors composed of civic leaders and officials. There was, of course, more than an informal relationship between the two. The director and principal investigator of the research program was also the first director of the crisis center, although he did not sit as a member of the Board of Directors. Moreover, the charter and the articles of incorporation of the crisis center specifically designated that providing a facility for the Center for Crisis Intervention Research to perform its studies was to be one of the purposes of the corporation. Furthermore, the charter explicitly stated that the policies and procedures to be developed for the operation of the crisis center would take into account the requirements of any research which was currently being conducted in the research center, but that in the event of an unresolvable conflict of interests, the crisis center Board of Directors would have final jurisdiction.

Every effort has been made to keep the volunteer workers fully apprised of what relationships exist among themselves, the staff, the research team, and the studies in progress. When volunteers are first recruited and have their initial interview with the Volunteer Coordinator, they are told of the research program and its relationship to the crisis service. They are told that, if they are accepted into the program after training, they will become research subjects, and that their performance on duty will be recorded and analyzed as the basic data. They are told further thay they may from time to time be asked to participate in additional projects which may be introduced, that they have the right to full information about the individual projects, and that they retain the right to refuse to serve in such projects without prejudice if they so desire. That option has rarely been exercised by any of the volunteers. In order to complete the legal and ethical responsibilities to human research subjects, each volunteer is required to sign a Statement of Informed Consent at the time he enters the program as an applicant for volunteer positions.

Volunteer Attitudes Toward Research

It would be in error to conclude that the arrangements discussed above have eliminated all problems between the volunteers and the research team. In fact, the research program is a frequent scapegoat onto which the workers displace their anxieties and their morale problems. When the caseload increases and the tensions begin to build among the case management staff and the volunteers, the research team comes in for their share of criticism. Either they seem to be sitting around unoccupied when there is an emergency CARE Team call or a walk-in client to be seen, or their data-coding sheets are an inconvenience for the overworked and busy volunteers. The people and procedures which can be identified as "just for research" tend to serve as a safety valve for the crisis workers to get some pressures "off the chest." In this regard, the research program is both a liability and an asset to the operation of the crisis center.

It has been an aid to the volunteers to be reminded from time to time that in matters of clinical service decisions, research procedures are always secondary to client welfare. Thus, workers who see themselves as primarily interested in what is good for the crisis caller are continually reinforced and encouraged to meet client needs first and to take care of their research commitments when they can. This practice has made the research forms, coding and record keeping, and call taping much more acceptable to the volunteers. They rarely overlook the research procedures, and when they do, it is not out of resistance or refusal to cooperate. Another factor which has been an aid to worker participation is that the callers and other clients have never been used as research subjects. There is never a research project in which some clients are chosen randomly to receive a particular service, while others are given a different type or degree of response. There is every reason to believe that volunteers would react very negatively to such procedures.

Finally, it should be emphasized also that the volunteers on duty have never been subjected to performance evaluations without their knowledge. There is a tendency in some centers to periodically "test" the volunteers by placing a fake call to the office and recording their unsuspecting response. This information is of no value unless it can be related back to the worker either as praise for a well-done job or as constructive feedback with suggestions for improvement. Once they learn that they have been fooled by a fake call, volunteers naturally become suspicious and cautious later. If they should mistake a real call for another "test" and begin to concentrate on their own needs rather than on those of the client, they could make serious errors in judgment. If the volunteers can be oriented to accept these fake calls as necessary for the clinical program, they may be less resentful. It is certain, however, that they will not agree to being subjected to what they perceive as the "fun and games" of researchers when they are on duty for serious business; if the calls are just for research purposes, they will incite quite negative reactions.

RESEARCH GOALS AND PROCEDURES
IN THE CENTER FOR CRISIS INTERVENTION RESEARCH

The rationale for developing the research unit derives from the fact that in 1969, over 80 percent of the crisis programs in the country were utilizing the nonprofessional volunteer as their source of manpower. Yet, there were no guidelines on how to select good crisis workers from among the applicants recruited and no criteria for determining who was actually functioning well once they were on the job. The purpose of this research program was to study volunteers intensively in order to provide answers to these important issues. The methods employed in the laboratory are discussed for the relevance that they may have in other centers.

Psychological Tests as Screening Instruments

The role of the psychological tests as one step in the overall screening program was discussed in Chapter 14. In addition to providing a choice point for the applicants, the test data serve to develop an item pool for predicting later performance criteria after training is completed. Furthermore, they can be reasonably expected to predict such behaviors as dropping out of the program during training or failing to serve at least six months following training. Therefore, test data have been recorded for over 500 volunteer applicants. These data will be analyzed in a variety of multivariate designs to determine which of the many relevant service dimensions can be predicted from screening instruments.

The tests selected for use in this research have been chosen specifically because they do not purport to measure clinical syndromes or traits usually associated with psychopathology. Although the individual scales of instruments like the Minnesota Multiphasic Personality Inventory (MMPI) need not be used in their usual clinical manner, the items themselves suggest pathological attitudes or behavior which tend to cause concern in the nonclinical subjects taking the test for volunteer screening purposes. Furthermore, since it is a wise and ethical policy to give volunteers access to an interpretation of their test scores, tests such as the MMPI are difficult to interpret to normal subjects. Consequently, only instruments which measure differences in personality traits or styles along nonpathological dimensions have been included. The California Psychological Inventory, the Myers-Briggs Type Indicator, and the Philosophy of Human Nature Scale serve very well for this screening purpose.

It must be emphasized that volunteers who are asked to take psychological tests for either research or screening purposes have certain rights associated with the tests. These rights must be observed and protected. The possibility for skillful and appropriate feedback of scores must be provided, even if no selection decision is being made from the data. Furthermore, the test scores must be held in complete confidence by the research team. Worker names and identification must be removed and replaced by code numbers. Care must be taken to see that none of the research team permit test scores to be talked about, shared with research groups outside of the center, or otherwise carelessly used unless the identity of the individual volunteer is thoroughly obliterated. Failure to observe this simple confidentiality will raise suspicion and righteous resentment among volunteers. Even if the applicant has long since left the program and is not known to current workers, he naturally will wonder how his own data will be treated in the future. It is a necessary precaution to see that all volunteer records are kept as confidential as the volunteers are required to keep client data. The members of the research team are in a position to set the example and should go out of their way to establish and reinforce the norm that confidentiality is an absolute requirement in the crisis center.

Tape Recording of Telephone Calls

The establishment of on-the-job performance criteria necessitates systematic observations of the volunteers' performance. Such observations can be made only if some record is made for evaluation after the client-related behavior has terminated. This requirement necessitates the tape recording of telephone calls to the center, and this procedure requires an extensive discussion.

In the beginning, it must be made clear that taping of calls in the Gainesville program is primarily, but not exclusively, for research purposes. There are also very important clinical and training reasons for taping calls, and the practice should be followed in every well-run crisis center, even if there is no research in progress. For example, it is sometimes necessary to identify a highly lethal caller who is unwilling to give his complete identity to the volunteer. If the caller has called previously in a less lethal state, or if he indicates that he is in treatment at a local agency, someone usually can be found who can identify his voice from the tape, and rescue efforts can be initiated. Furthermore, when volunteers listen to their own performance and have access to a supervisor who will sit down and listen to the tape with them, the quality of performance is certain to increase.

However, the taping of telephone calls presents a number of legal and ethical problems which must be dealt with adequately. First, there is the problem of maintaining credibility and good relationships with the local telephone officials. Different telephone companies or different regional officials within one company have varying views on taping procedures. However, as of January 1, 1970, the former Federal Communications Commission Tariffs which specifically prohibited attaching customer-owned equipment to the telephone lines were revoked. It is now no longer a federal violation to install personal equipment to telephone lines, providing that the local telephone company installs the proper terminals for the foreign equipment. It is also necessary that the equipment installed be electronically compatible with the telephone circuits and that it causes no interference with the lines. This can be ensured by the installation of a "phone patch," which isolates the recording equipment from the circuit so that no resistances are created which send aberrant signals back through the lines to central switching equipment. Of course, taping with the use of induction coil devices or a microphone to pick up signals from a speaker across an air space in no way interferes with the telephone lines, and it thus perfectly acceptable to the telephone company. The problem is that such methods universally give a poor quality, or at least an inconsistent quality of reproduction. The induction coils are very sensitive to 60-cycle interference from power transformers, fluorescent light tubes, and other electrical appliances. Recording across an air space naturally picks up unwanted room noise from other conversations, passing motor vehicles, typewriters, and an unlimited variety of other sources of interference. Taping via direct connections to the telephone circuits through isolating phone patches is the only satisfactory way to make records.

Any center director who installs taping equipment would be wise to consult with the local telephone company representative, who may already be a member of his Board of Directors. In one major crisis center, that in Buffalo, New York, the director assured the telephone company that the taping was necessary for adequate clinical service, and that the telephone subscribers would be protected by the ethical responsibilities of the director and his associates. Consequently, the telephone company executive agreed to install the standard telephone equipment for taping, but he voluntarily *removed* the beeping signal which the company routinely requires in taping devices. Local regulations and the interpretation of regulations vary dramatically from place to place, both between and within telephone systems. However, even though it is not likely that too many centers will have the same degree of cooperation which the Buffalo program found, it is still a desirable effort to take the local telephone officials into confidence regarding the taping procedures.

The question of the legality of tapping phone lines and taping conversations is frequently brought up. Federal laws are explicit in this regard, and there are no known state laws which are at variance with them. According to Public Law 90-351, Title 3, Section 2511, Subsection (2) (D), the law does not prohibit the recording of a conversation if the person making the recording is either a party to the conversation or has obtained the permission of one party in the conversation. This exclusion makes it possible for crisis centers to tape incoming calls, since it is technically the volunteer on duty who is making the tape and is, of course, participating in the conversation. However, in order to ensure that the volunteer always gives his consent to the taping, the center director should install a switch by which the recording device can be deactivated if the volunteer does not wish to be routinely recorded. If this violates center policy in some way, it should be dealt with independently between the director and the worker.

The issue of informing the caller that he is being taped also must be handled if it becomes an issue. Generally speaking, most callers may be expected to object, just on principle, to having their calls taped. Therefore, the standard beeping signal is never included in taping devices used in crisis centers. However, if the caller spontaneously asks if the call is being taped, the volunteer must be able to answer the question without hesitation. To hedge on the issue surely will be identified by the caller as a form of deception, and the opportunity to be of help may be lost. Whether or not the volunteer should lie openly about the matter and automatically deny the taping is a matter which should be decided by the conscience of each center staff. In the Gainesville center, volunteers are told never to lie about it, as a matter of policy. Depending on how serious the case sounds, and on the basis of the volunteer's confidence that he can hold the caller on the line, he can either admit the taping and try to deal with the caller's feelings about it or he can turn off the tape and honestly respond in the negative. In such cases, however, the tape must be left off unless it is specifically determined that the caller does not object to it. In all cases, the tape is considered less important than the ability to establish a permanent communication with the caller, and if it must be sacrificed to help the client, the tape must be turned off.

The other very important question concerning taping of calls relates to making tapes without specific informed consent. This issue cannot be handled easily, but it can be rationalized by directors and investigators who carefully and zealously guard the tape library. Basic procedures must be established which totally forbid the playing of tapes for training groups or other audiences unless they are completely edited to remove all possible identifying information. Tape libraries must be securely locked, and their accessibility must be limited to specifically authorized persons. Every precaution must be taken to make absolutely certain that what the caller does not know can never hurt him in any way. If the procedures for safeguarding the tapes and the client's right to privacy are adequate, taping without informed consent may not violate moral and ethical restraints. Where the purpose of the taping is legitimate research, or training for higher-quality performance and service, it becomes necessary to balance one good against another. These issues probably should be decided on the local level by each center director. However, because of the importance of the issues involved, the American Association of Suicidology charged a special ad hoc committee with the responsibility of developing guidelines for taping in suicide and crisis centers. The recommendations of that committee should be consulted for a rationale for developing local taping policies.

THE PROBLEM OF PERFORMANCE CRITERIA

Without question, the challenge of identifying and measuring some universal criteria for crisis worker performance has been the central focus of the Center for Crisis Intervention Research. The evaluation of individual community programs and the development of standards for certification of services cannot proceed to the point of a functional reality until the performance of each and every crisis worker can be assessed in terms of specific behaviors which are clearly relevant to client care. Consequently, it is in this area where the majority of research energy was invested for the first four years of the Center's existence. It is not possible to report on the results of the individual research projects conducted in the Center in this account. They must be the subject of a separate volume. However, a brief discussion of the major directions of the efforts is in order.

The Rating of Technical Effectiveness

There are certain behaviors which are so taken for granted that for many years they went unnoticed as criteria of volunteer performance. Among these are the three basic functions of the telephone crisis worker which were identified long ago by Litman, Farberow et al. (1965). In retrospect, it is surprising that nearly every one of the centers studied in part II of this book had been exposed to this classic paper. Yet, none of the directors could put these concepts into words in describing their best workers. Sometimes the answer to a problem is so obvious that it escapes detection. That was clearly the case with evaluating the technical ability of crisis workers.

The three behaviors which nearly every crisis worker has been taught at some time in the training for volunteer service are: (1) he must secure the communication with the caller, (2) he must make an assessment of the caller's condition, and (3) he must develop a plan of action for the caller to follow. The rating of volunteer performance on the basis of these standards has been referred to as the

Technical Effectiveness evaluation. It was developed as a simple check list by Fowler and McGee (1973). This instrument has been shown to be highly reliable and easily administered, even by one rater. It could become a universal yardstick for every telephone worker in suicide prevention or crisis intervention services. However, while technical effectiveness is a necessary trait for every worker, it cannot be considered sufficient. A volunteer can mechanically interrogate a client until all of the information necessary for a perfect score has been obtained, and still have failed to establish a relationship through which either he, or the service as a whole, can be of any assistance. In addition to technical skill, certain clinical skills also are required of the telephone worker.

The Rating of Clinical Effectiveness

Suicide prevention and crisis services are by no means the only agencies which have utilized persons with less than professional mental health training. The literature in the area of counseling and psychotherapy has reported abundant evidence that such relatively untrained people as hospital aides, neighborhood youth program workers, housewives, and parents are capable of providing the conditions of a therapeutic relationship equally as well as, and sometimes better than, the professional therapist. Among the professional therapists, it is evident that it is the quality of the relationship established, rather than the theoretical understanding or the clinical knowledge of the therapist, which affects the client's outcome the most. A series of investigations by Truax and Carkhuff (1967) and their associates have demonstrated that nonprofessional persons can create these therapeutic relationships very well. Moreover, these investigators have developed scales which may be used by trained raters to evaluate the extent to which therapists provide the facilitative conditions of accurate empathy, warmth or caring, and genuineness. The combination of these skills has been used repeatedly to measure the Clinical Effectiveness of the volunteer crisis workers in studies by Knickerbocker (1972), Belanger (1972), Ansel (1972), and Galvin (1973).

The Measurement of Personal Involvement

The running of screening and training programs is one of the most expensive activities that a crisis center administration must face. The cost in terms of time and energy is nearly prohibitive unless a center has a person available for these duties full-time. Therefore, it is imperative that those applicants who will remain for a substantial period of time be identified and those who are prone to early dropout must be eliminated. A volunteer who exhibits high scores on technical and clinical effectiveness measures may be helpful to clients while he is on the job, but he will surely be a liability to the center unless he also has a measure of personal commitment and involvement with the program.

Such traits are instilled primarily after the worker has finished training. The critical role of the volunteer coordinator for determining that these morale factors are satisfied has been discussed in a previous chapter. However, it is possible to rank volunteers along a dimension of involvement by systematically observing such data as the number of duty shifts taken during a given period of time, the total length of time of active service, the number of extra, unscheduled shifts filled, or the number of shifts missed for various reasons, attendance at in-service training meetings, and extra time spent in the center. Such data require an extensive bookkeeping system, but the end result is a compilation of facts which will clearly sort out those workers who are dedicated to fulfilling the goals of the program from those who are willing only to fulfill a minimum required commitment.

The systematic evaluation of technical effectiveness, clinical effectiveness, and involvement with the center's program has been shown to produce reliable and feasible measures of the critical volunteer performance variables. These variables are as universally applicable in crisis services as any behavior could be.

THE PROBLEM OF OUTCOME CRITERIA

The tendency exists to validate worker performance against some criterion related to the product or output of the work. In the case of crisis intervention services, this takes the form of relating measures of volunteer performance, such as technical and clinical effectiveness, to the effect that such behaviors have on client change or outcome. However, upon deeper reflection, it is immediately evident that the outcome of client cases is subject to many different influences. Everyone familiar with the area of research in psychotherapy knows that no consistent evidence ever has been presented to substantiate the benefits of psychotherapy in terms of the outcomes of treatment with patients. With crisis intervention services, the outcome estimates are far more confounded by extraneous factors.

The first of these is simply the fact that rarely does a crisis intervention service permit individual workers to treat their own private caseloads. Even where the crisis service is the emergency unit of a community mental health center, the continuity of care principle is not applicable to the emergency program personnel. Consequently, during the management of any crisis case, it is highly probable that not one, but several crisis workers will be involved with the client. Whose performance, then, should be correlated to case outcome? The volunteer who opened the case may have been the key person, for if good work was done at opening, it increases the possibility that the client will stay with the program long enough to receive benefit. However, it can happen that the opening was handled very poorly, and that it was for that reason that supervisors or other staff personnel became actively involved and salvaged the client's relationship with the system.

An even more difficult problem arises for centers in which a key goal is that of transferring clients to other sources of continuing help in the community. If a transfer is made successfully to a professional mental health agency or practitioner, and then the client recovers from his suicidal tendencies, it hardly can be the center's success. A crisis service has no right to claim credit which belongs to the relationship developed between the client and his therapist. At the same time, every crisis center has experienced the dreadful fact that cases that they have transferred to professional resources have proceeded to complete their self-destructive intentions. Should the crisis service accept the blame for treatment failure if a suicide follows its transfer plan? Such responsibility hardly is justified. Therefore, it is imperative that the crisis service avoid focusing attention on any outcome variables which are subject to influences not completely under the active management and control of the center personnel. However significant they may be, long-term outcomes such as recovery or death cannot serve as criteria for crisis intervention worker performance.

The chapter on the four-phase process of crisis intervention suggests that outcome should be assessed at each of the four phases. This means that the center is evaluating itself in a dynamic manner, taking stock of its effectiveness with each client at sequential points in its casework. Such a system of repeated observation will substantially reduce the problem of outcome criteria against which to validate both individual worker performance and the system as a whole.

RESEARCH ACTIVITIES IN COMMUNITY CRISIS SERVICES

It has been indicated already that research activities can be disruptive to the operation of crisis intervention systems, especially where the investigators are not intimately associated with the internal administration of the center. However, this is not the only problem with research programs in community agencies. It is also true that they are quite expensive, requiring people and equipment which usually must be supplied from grants or other special budget allocations. Inasmuch as community crisis services generally have a difficult time securing funds sufficient for the adequate operation of the service program, it is difficult to imagine how most centers could finance a research unit as well. To do so surely would drain the valuable resources needed for the delivery of crisis services. Therefore, it seems evident that basic research in suicidology and crisis intervention can be centered in only a few of the larger crisis programs. Centers such as the Emergency Mental Health Service in Atlanta, the Suicide Prevention-Crisis Service in Buffalo, Suicide Prevention, Incorporated, in St. Louis, and, of course, the Los Angeles Suicide Prevention Center, have been well supported by local governmental agencies or by federal research and training grants to universities in the area. It may be that the development of even a dozen major research centers throughout the country would represent the maximum resources which the suicidology profession might hope to develop. To envision such a network of research programs, limited though it would be, immediately raises a number of issues.

Foremost among these problems is the matter of funding suicidology research. It is increasingly evident that the availability of federal research dollars through the NIMH will fluctuate markedly from time to time, depending upon current priorities, and thus cannot be depended upon for continuous support. There is a pressing need for the solicitation of private funds from foundations and industrial interests. It is a peculiar thing that the vast financial resources of the nation's life insurance companies never have been tapped for funds to support suicide prevention research or service. Even Louis Dublin, who served many years as an executive of the Metropolitan Life Insurance Company, was unable to gather financial support from his own company or from the Life Insurance Institute to finance local service or research programs. Yet, the insurance industry is among the hardest hit by suicide deaths, from a strictly financial standpoint.

It is challenging to speculate what it might take to develop such resources for suicide research. Certainly, there is one avenue which must be considered and which may prove fruitful. That is the enhancement of the American Association of Suicidology as a viable organization with a home office base and a team of financial consultants. It might take two or three years to successfully launch a campaign to endow the association as a base for research activity. However, organizations such as the American Cancer Society, the National Mental Health Association, and many others too numerous to name have found it possible to support basic research out of private dollars. Suicide and crisis intervention must have the same solid base of research support.

A second question also must be confronted. Assuming that a financial base is developed, how should the resources be allocated? Economically speaking, it would be reasonable to establish a few major centers where investigators interested in suicidology might assemble to pursue their work. This would keep overhead costs to a minimum; it certainly would cost more in the long run to fund small projects everywhere throughout the nation. It usually takes three to six months to set up a research activity of any magnitude at all, and if the grant is only for two years, up to 25 percent of the time and money are not utilized productively. Then what becomes of the facilities and equipment when the project is over? It is obviously advantageous to continue to support major centers which are already equipped and functioning.

However, there are distinct problems in such an approach. The need for continual review is paramount, so that programs thus supported do not decline in their output because of limited competition for funds. Procedures must be instituted to provide opportunity for new investigators to receive research stipends, summer appointments, or sabbatical privileges in these key centers in order to prevent the distribution of research funds to only a few established investigators.

Further, a system for agreements and understandings would be needed to distribute the research activities in some focused way with respect to type of research. It would be wasteful, for example, to fund three or four centers to develop biochemical and psychophysiological laboratories. It is not necessary to have more than one center devote its research talents to the epidemiology and demography of high-risk populations. It would seem to make the most sense to create specialized centers where depth rather than breadth of talent would be developed. Yet, what procedures would be satisfactory deciding factors about what type of research should be performed where? Excessive control over research enterprises violates the basic conditions under which behavioral scientists can function most effectively.

It is highly probable that with thoughtful planning and consideration of the many issues, such problems could be resolved to the satisfaction of most investigators and to the benefit of the consumers of basic research knowledge. The critical issues remain the development of private funding, and the initiative of the American Association of Suicidology to undertake the challenge.

What role would the local community crisis services be expected to play in such an organization of major research centers? First, of course, they would be the proving grounds for the findings coming from the research centers. Funds should be made available to pay local centers for their assistance in demonstrating new technologies. For example, volunteer training programs might be developed by a center with a concentration of talent in adult education. These training packages then could be put to work in several community centers, and some remuneration might be provided to aid the local services in meeting their operational costs.

Furthermore, the local centers should—especially if they are organized around the community model for providing services (discussed in Chapter 2)—keep an eye on their own program effectiveness. Program evaluation research should be a concern of every program director, even if he lacks the local resources to plan computer programming, data coding, and record keeping. The major research centers would have teams of consultants available to the local communities to assist them in performing their own necessary evaluation research. Thus, each agency would be aided in collecting the type of statistical evidence of successful intervention which is necessary to seek its own support from United Way or local government sources.

In short, the future of research in community crisis intervention systems would not remove investigation from the local scene, but would tend to support and enhance it. It would assure only that the greatest gains would be realized from the utilization of basic research energies and resources in the biological and behavioral sciences by creating and continually supporting major bases of investigation.

EPILOG

17
THE DELIVERY OF CRISIS INTERVENTION SERVICES IN THE DECADE AHEAD

The suicide prevention movement was barely beyond its infancy before it spawned such a broad spectrum of service models that many bore no resemblance to others, and very few were in any way like the original Los Angeles center. The preceding chapters have attempted to trace this early history, cite individual center programs, abstract the critical organizational and programmatic elements from 10 early programs, and finally, describe in detail the operation of one program which was built upon the experiences and problems encountered in others. Evidence collected from actual empirical studies, as well as by observation, site visits, and continued involvement with several programs, leads to the conclusion that there was much less variability among suicide and crisis programs in 1972 than there was in 1967. Generalized models began to emerge around 1970, and the programs most deviant from these models began to drop out of existence. One model for suicide and crisis programming which appears to have survived has been described in Chapter 2 as the community model for crisis services. It is now appropriate to project some thoughts and expectations into the future and to wonder about the form which these programs will assume in the decade of 1970–1980.

There have been previous efforts at this crystal-ball gazing. Two notable ones were by McGee et al. (1973) and Brockopp (1970). The former was a report of the Committee on the Delivery of Suicide and Crisis Services, convened as part of the NIMH Task Force on Suicide Prevention in the Seventies in Phoenix, Arizona, in January, 1970. This committee reviewed the current scene and, in a series of propositions, suggested the areas which should receive major consideration during the 1970's. It was an effort commissioned by the Chief of the Center for Studies of Suicide Prevention to advise him as he attempted to chart the course of a national suicide prevention program. That the Task Force was to be essentially an exercise in futility could not have been foreseen at the time of its meeting. However, the fact of its impotence has been demonstrated amply by the fact that its proceedings were not published for nearly three years. More significant, of course, is the fact that the Center for Studies of Suicide Prevention itself proved to have no viable future as a national impetus and support base for suicide research, training, or programming.

The second set of predictions about suicide and crisis services in the 1970's was stimulated partially by the Task Force. Brockopp was a member of the Committee on the Delivery of Services and wrote his own observations and ideas as a working paper for the committee. It was published subsequently in the *Crisis Intervention Bulletin* of the Buffalo, New York crisis center.

The latest attempt to take a comprehensive look at suicide prevention in the decade ahead was developed by Farberow (1972) as he convened a panel of suicidologists at the fifth annual meeting of the American Association of Suicidology in Detroit in March, 1972. The content of this final chapter was prepared for that panel under the title of *Clinical Services in the Decade Ahead.*

A GENERAL OVERVIEW

Litman (1971) has suggested the broad goal or mission for suicide prevention and crisis intervention services in the 1970's. It was his advice that:

> Possibly the most important role of suicide prevention centers in the 1970's will be to give a base line of support for unusual, imaginative and innovative outreach and treatment programs that are beyond the scope of present standard practices in conventional agencies. (page 162)

Litman is not explicit in indicating what are the "conventional agencies" about which he is speaking. One easily can interpret his remarks as intending a contrast between future programs and current suicide prevention services. Or, one may just as easily infer that he is speaking of the clinics and other professional agencies which constitute the "conventional" mental health system. In either event, it is abundantly clear that community suicide prevention and crisis intervention programs are very different from mental health agencies in 1972. It is also evident that the crisis services of 1980 may be equally unlike those of 1972. Whether this change will move them into closer similarity with the mental health agency or further into contrast with it is a matter of speculation and prejudice.

However, the purpose of this discussion is to accept Litman's position uncritically and to focus attention on some of the directions which imaginative and innovative programming may take. The crucial issues for the future evolvement of the crisis center movement may be categorized as follows:

1. Organization and structure of service systems
2. Populations to be served

3. Quality control for service systems
4. Philosophy of crisis services as agents of human needs

The basic premise upon which development must proceed is that suicide prevention and crisis intervention programs are dynamic, evolving agencies, rather than static, formal, and institutionalized ones. Even a minimum of experience in such a program leads to the conclusion that the former nature is demanded by the type of work. Responding to crisis situations, especially those requiring emergency rescue in cases of suicide attempt, requires the utmost in flexibility and freedom from the constraints and restrictions which characterize bureaucratic policy or procedural formalities. Furthermore, suicide prevention and crisis intervention centers are too new on the scene of community helping agencies to have yet formulated stagnating practices.

Therefore, one must expect that the present scene will evolve dynamically because it must, via constantly changing systems and procedures. Only by deliberate and conscious effort on the part of program leadership can a crisis center fall victim to the institutionalized rigidity which characterizes all of the other helping agencies and systems in our communities. One example may suffice to make the point. It relates to the concept of *eligibility for service.* Such a restriction is unheard of in a crisis service. The credo of a crisis intervention system which operates any type of comprehensive program must be that it "participates in the solution of any human problem whenever and wherever it occurs." Any person may expect to receive assistance without any concern over where he lives, how long he has lived there, what kind of problem he has, or whether a physician has agreed to refer him. He may receive service even when there is no one to sign papers granting "permission to treat" or promising to be responsible for the cost. He may receive service whether or not he has a "sickness," and his sickness does not have to be of only specified kinds. His income and his number of dependents are irrelevant to his receiving assistance. He does not even have to have his own telephone or be considering suicide. As soon as a service becomes institutionalized under some formal structure (like the mental health centers), there are immediately some people who are not eligible for service. Crisis services cannot function to their limitless potential when there are eligibility requirements for their clients.

ORGANIZATION AND STRUCTURE OF SERVICE SYSTEMS

Telephone Services

The telephone always has been, and probably will continue to be, the core of suicide and crisis services. However, it is evident that the telephone system will undergo at least two distinct changes in the future. First, it must be vastly improved, and secondly, it must cease to be the *only* method used for delivering crisis services. The fact that there are eight different telephone answering procedures in use, and that in five out of 76 calls it was not possible to get any answer to the call (McGee, Richard, and Bercun, 1972), indicates that substantial changes must be made in the telephone systems. There is an implicit contract between a center director and the public, and it may be a serious ethical issue when the responsibility for the execution of this contract is delegated to someone not under the control of the agency director, i.e., a commercial telephone answering service or another community agency. One of the observable trends is that new centers are covering the telephone 24 hours a day with their own personnel in their own offices. By the end of the 1970's, this will be the general rule, rather than the exception.

In addition to its improvement, the telephone system will become only one of several delivery methods in use by crisis centers. The end of the 1960's saw the development of a new breed of crisis program, which included a mobile CARE Team or some other form of go-to-the-scene outreach activity. Even though such procedures had been put into operation by professional personnel in St. Peters- burg, Florida, and in Atlanta, Georgia, the more innovative programs, such as WE CARE in Orlando, Florida, began to use their trained volunteer workers for face-to-face crisis counseling. By 1972, several programs which had been reluctant to start CARE Team operations were beginning to experiment with the idea. It was only a matter of months before the CARE Team (Chapter 14) became an integral part of the Crisis Call Center in Nashville, Tennessee, and the Suicide Prevention Center in Jacksonville, Florida. Others are still hiding behind the telephone and thinking of a wide range of excuses why they should not venture out into this significant service area. As experience grows, these excuses must fall by the wayside, and there will be an increasing utilization of the telephone as only the *first* step in the crisis therapy process, rather than as the only means of helping contact.

Not only practical experience, but theoretical issues as well demand this development. Hansell (1968) clearly advocated outreach service when he argued that the quality of service rendered may be measured in the number of feet which describe the distance between the point where a problem occurs and the place where service is rendered. The shorter the distance in feet, Hansell said, the greater will be the quality of crisis service. One might add that quality service is measured also in minutes elapsing between the emergence of the problem and the arrival of a helper. Such notions seriously challenge (and should discourage) the practice of providing service in the clinic, by appointment, at the place and time convenient to the helping person.

Volunteer Crisis Workers

The most telling arguments in favor of the volunteer as the person to provide services in crisis intervention agencies have been presented by McGee and Jennings (1973). The practice needs no further justification or defense, since the 1972 directory of suicide prevention and crisis intervention agencies published by the

American Association of Suicidology shows that 87 percent of the 185 programs use nonprofessional volunteers as their crisis worker personnel. Further, the ratio of volunteers to professionals engaged in crisis work, as reflected in this directory, is three to one. There can be only a continuing increase in the utilization of trained volunteers in local programs. Furthermore, the 1972 meeting of the American Association of Suicidology was marked historically as the one at which the volunteers achieved a prominent place in the heretofore primarily *professional* association. The volunteer made possible the development of the suicide prevention center movement in the 1960's, and it will be the volunteer who moves into a position of major responsibility for guiding and directing the total crisis intervention movement in the 1970's.

The one great change which should be evident by 1980 is a matter of semantics. There may be a variety of new terms entering the vocabulary of crisis intervention center personnel to refer to the unpaid workers. Terms such as "Clinical Associate," "Crisis Counselor," "Intervener," etc., may acquire widespread popularity. However, what the workers are called probably matters less than what they are *not called*. It is apparent that the distinction between *professional* and *nonprofessional* is functionally useless and survives only because of chauvinistic and status-conscious considerations. By the end of this decade, these terms will be used rarely, if at all. Rather, it may be expected that all who engage in crisis intervention will be considered *professional* persons. Some will conduct scientific research or engage in graduate training at university or professional school levels. Others will engage in direct intervention on the telephone and in face-to-face counseling. Some will be psychologists and some will be housewives or businessmen; *they all will be considered professionals in the field of suicide prevention and crisis intervention.*

Community Mental Health Centers

The relationship between suicide prevention and crisis intervention agencies and community mental health centers continues to be a most perplexing and ambiguous one. The NIMH Task Force Committee on Delivery of Crisis Services (McGee et al., 1973) recognized that one form which crisis services might take would be that of the emergency component of community mental health centers. This was one of a half-dozen organizational models discussed. The committee further indicated its belief that there is no necessary requirement that crisis intervention services be administratively affiliated with the community mental health system or operated under its authority as long as they maintain open channels of communication and collaborative clinical practices. It is mandatory only that crisis services be willing to work alongside the mental health program in order that both services might render maximum assistance to the community.

There are several distinct advantages which might accrue from a formal and administrative affiliation with the mental health program. One of these is clearly financial. Community mental health centers still have priority for federal funding, but they must have local funding in some proportion as well. This means that there are personnel lines and operational budgets which might well include the local suicide prevention and crisis intervention service as the emergency component. Further, affiliation with the mental health program may benefit a program in terms of increased legitimization with the community power structure, especially the medical community. Finally, since the publication (by the NIMH) of the *Criteria for Defining Community Mental Health Centers' Emergency Services* (1971), there exists the distinct possibility that the crisis intervention service will enable the mental health program to have at least a minimally adequate emergency program. These guidelines call for program practices which are characteristic of suicide prevention and crisis intervention programs, but which never have been characteristic of mental health clinics. Thus, the merger may add substantially to the quality of mental health service, enabling it to meet the standards set by the NIMH.

On the other hand, there are potentially severe consequences for the crisis intervention service if it takes the administrative course of dissolving itself as an independent organization and merging administratively with the mental health center. The greatest hazard comes from the uncertainty of what the mental health program will become five, six, or seven years hence, when the federal funds are scheduled to give way to total local support. Experience has shown already that where local sources of money are not adequate to make up the deficits caused by the regressing federal participation, the program managers retreat to those forms of service with which they are most comfortable, which they know best how to perform, and which render the greatest revenue from patient fee structures. Hence, what may remain is an excellent inpatient service and an augmented outpatient clinic. The emergency service, always underrated and underemphasized by mental health professionals, retreats to the hospital emergency room. Elaborate telephone and outreach systems are seen as unnecessary luxuries when the money gets tight. The crisis intervention center may find itself the major loser in such a situation. It is a gamble which should be avoided at all costs.

Furthermore, those crisis intervention programs which have moved under the mental health system find that they are extremely limited in their autonomy to provide the kind of service that they want to provide. The go-to-the-scene approach of the outreach program is generally inconsistent with the mental health practice of treatment once a week by appointment. Wherever centers have struggled against pressures to develop a CARE Team, it has been the mental health professionals on the board or among the consultant staff who have opposed the program. The message which, since 1965, has been coming from most mental health professionals in the community is that the crisis intervention service is incompatible with the professional model of rendering mental health care.

There are two alternatives which may offer some hope for resolving this uncertainty. Either one, or the two in combination, already has proved effective in the Gainesville, Florida center. The first alternative is to maintain a strong, independent corporation to operate the crisis intervention center and, using that corporation, to enter into formal contracts with other agencies, including the mental health system, to provide whatever services the contractor may wish. In this manner, the crisis intervention service actually may be the agency which provides the community mental health center with the emergency service that it is required to have. The crisis intervention service provides the service for a fee, and both the mental health program and the crisis intervention center gain from the engagement. Further, the community gains by having a much better emergency service upon which to rely when necessary. At any time, the terms of the contract may be renegotiated if the money becomes inadequate or if the quality of service deteriorates. It is apparent already that where a strong crisis intervention system exists in a community conjointly with a strong mental health center, both will benefit from a contractural relationship between them. In such cases, administrative merger of the two is both unnecessary and unwise. However, if the mental health program is faltering, easily threatened, and infiltrated with morale problems among its staff, it may seize upon the crisis intervention service as a predator devours its prey. Obviously, neither will benefit from this arrangement. Where the crisis service sees itself as weak, financially unstable, and dependent upon the stronger mental health program, a merger will mean that the crisis intervention service is quietly laid to rest, and the mental health program will neither suffer from the merger nor reap the benefit of incorporating the crisis intervention service into its larger program.

A second alternative involves a reconceptualization of the crisis intervention service as something other than a mental health program. A marriage between the two may be satisfactory under the complementarity hypothesis which says that "opposites attract" and that the best marriage consists of partners who are distinctly dissimilar to one another. If the crisis intervention service and the mental health program both can see the crisis intervention service as a unique system, rather than as one which specializes in providing a specific form of mental health care or which provides mental health care in a partial, tangential, or inferior way, then the marriage may work. Each system will be called upon to provide its own unique service to the community without defensiveness or threat. Under such a reconceptualization, it is just as functional for the mental health program to affiliate with the crisis intervention service as it is for the crisis intervention service to become a component of the mental health program. Realistically, of course, the funding structure sets limits which require that the mental health program attract the crisis intervention center into its system, rather than vice-versa.

This second alternative of reconceptualizing the crisis intervention service as a nonmental health program is discussed further under another topic heading.

Development of Special Programs

There have been a number of other services which have emerged in recent months and which obviously have taken their lead from the suicide prevention and crisis intervention service methods. These are special interest programs which relate only to a particular segment of the social scene. Teenage hot lines primarily providing junior and senior high school students with places to call to talk about adolescent development problems are perhaps the best example. There is another recent development, called "Switchboard," which exists in many communities to serve the special needs of the youth culture. It specializes in abortion referral, temporary "crash pads" for transient young people moving through town, some legal counseling, and drug-related assistance. The telephone services for drug abuse treatment and for lonely, elderly, or shut-in populations are other examples of special interest programs not designed to provide general crisis intervention service. Many of them are not in operation around the clock or on every day of the week. There are other programs which offer primarily religious counseling as the solution to problems of alcohol, divorce, and even suicide, but generally they attract relatively few subscribers.

All of these special service programs have in common the fact that they do not affiliate with any other systems that already exist in the community. They are essentially on their own, although they compete for the same sources of local money. One rarely finds a teen hot line developing in a collaborative manner with the existing suicide prevention program. In some communities which have both a crisis intervention center and a teen hot line, a Switchboard group will start a third telephone service without seeking to affiliate with the existing programs. Thus, these special services tend to obfuscate the roles of other programs and confuse the community by providing duplicate services. Fragmentation, rather than mutually supportive collaboration, is the rule.

The decade ahead undoubtedly will see the continued development of these new and specialized forms of service. Many of them may have advantages and they should be observed carefully, rather than uncritically dismissed, because of the overall contribution they might make. However, unless there is a tendency to integrate functionally into the network of helping services, they may not be expected to survive very long. By the end of the 1970's, they may have run their course.

NEW POPULATIONS TO BE SERVED BY CRISIS PROGRAMS

Despite the fact that the words "suicide prevention" are still found in the names of many crisis intervention programs, there are relatively few which actively engage in service to some of the most important populations which are affected by suicide. Two of these populations are suicide attempters and survivors of suicide victims. Both of them are groups which must be served regularly and routinely by crisis intervention programs by the end of the 1970's. There are some precedents already in actual operation which suggest the feasibility of automatic referral of suicide attempters to the crisis intervention center's suicide counselors. Most of these referrals come from the law enforcement agencies, which usually make an investigation of all self-inflicted injuries and self-poisonings. Immediate contact while the patient is still in the emergency room, or as quickly thereafter as possible, is a necessary procedure to ensure that a cry for help does not go unanswered just because it was not made via the usual telephone channels. Naturally, such programs require extensive negotiation and collaborative attitudes among the hospital, the physicians, and the crisis intervention service. Initially, the crisis intervention service is in the role of an outsider, since it is not present to provide a medical service. But with time, patience, good public relations, and a determination to proceed and let the results of its work speak for themselves, the crisis intervention center will find itself being called into the emergency room by the medical community, rather than excluded. That has been a clearly demonstrated fact in the Gainesville, Florida community.

Murphy and his colleagues (1971) developed an extensive form for police reporting of suicide attempts in the St. Louis area. This was primarily for statistical and research purposes, since very little is known about the incidence of self-inflicted injury. However, a similar form might be used, not for research interests, but for providing clinical services. Data supplied by the law enforcement agency can be followed up by the crisis intervention center as it seeks to enter into a helpful engagement with the person with respect to the problem which precipitated the attempt. By the end of this decade, such service should be a daily activity in the larger suicide prevention and crisis intervention programs of the country.

Similarly, the survivors of suicide victims are a distinctly overlooked population. Theirs is the most difficult of all bereavement crises, and it takes a crisis worker who understands and can communicate the underlying dynamics of suicide to help the family deal with the issues. It also takes someone who knows the needs of the bereaved, which every crisis worker should understand. The entry of crisis workers into the family is a difficult one, and usually can be accomplished best under some official auspices. Again, the law enforcement agencies, and sometimes the medical examiner, are the most appropriate sources. The value of immediate, knowledgeable support for survivors in a case of suicide is one of the greatest services that a crisis intervention center can offer and may be one of the most effective means of preventing future suicides within the family of survivors. Before the end of this decade, this population must become the focus of one of the special services of every crisis intervention center which has any involvement with suicide prevention.

Nonsuicide Populations

There are some other groups which may prove to be appropriate for crisis intervention service, although there are limited data at this time on the feasibility of providing such services. One of these groups is comprised of disputants in family disturbances. Usually, families which fight so vigorously or with such physical violence that the police are called to quiet the disturbance are found among the low-income white and black families of disadvantaged neighborhoods of the cities. Bard (1969, 1970) and Bard and Berkowitz (1967) have shown that special details of police officers can be trained for family crisis intervention. Many police departments cannot afford the luxury of special units for social service, rather than criminal, functions. Therefore, the suicide prevention and crisis intervention center may be a valuable resource to augment the police department. Preliminary investigations at the Gainesville center suggest that this is a very promising approach, and one which not only provides a service to families in stress, but serves to free the policeman from a hazardous and distasteful non-police function. It may be two or three years before satisfactory empirical data can be gathered to document the clinical value of this service, but if it proves as beneficial as early results suggest, it is a program which all general crisis intervention centers should be prepared to adopt.

Another nonsuicidal population which rarely receives service from present crisis intervention centers lives outside the city in rural areas. Generally, suicide prevention programs are primarily urban agencies. Residents of rural areas also find themselves in personal crises and need the services which city dwellers have. Problems of spatial location of centers, low-population density for outreach team coverage, party line telephones, and inaccessibility of private pay telephone booths all present problems which must be encountered and solved, but as this is accomplished, crises intervention service to rural clients can and should be developed.

Finally, there have been some efforts, like the family disturbance interventions, to extend the service of crisis intervention centers to populations not actually in an acute crisis. For example, the problems of the skid-row alcoholic have been the subject of a special program described by Russell (1970) in Buffalo, New York. The Night People of the Buffalo program made themselves available for the skid-row residents in a storefront office. There are no actual data on the effectiveness of this program, but it represents an example of the extension of service to a heretofore untouched population. There are a number of such populations which imaginative and innovative outreach programs can and will identify during the remainder of this decade. New technologies and new theoretical approaches may be needed, but the many unserved segments of the community will be finding someone who cares about their needs in the crisis intervention programs of 1980.

Disaster Recovery

When the Susquehanna River overflowed its banks in Eastern Pennsylvania in June of 1972, creating, in Wilkes-Barre, the greatest natural disaster in American history, a new role was born for crisis intervention services. In responding to the flood recovery needs of the community, the federal government provided nearly $1,000,000 for a crisis intervention program under the name of Project Outreach.

After a year of service to the flood victims, the paraprofessional crisis workers had firmly established crisis intervention as a major service delivery system in disaster recovery.

Independently, and without communication among themselves, crisis intervention-oriented professionals engaged in innovative services elsewhere in the nation during 1972. Teams of workers responded to family crises when a Korean War vintage jet aircraft failed to execute a take-off and crashed into an ice cream parlor in Sacramento, California. A crisis intervention program was attempted when two commuter trains of the Illinois Central Railroad crashed during morning rush hours in downtown Chicago. Other crisis intervention programs were developed in response to floods in Corning, New York, and in the Buffalo Creek Mine disaster in West Virginia. By the end of 1973, it had become evident that some mechanism for delivering crisis intervention services following a natural or manmade disaster was both possible and necessary to maximize recovery effectiveness.

The possibility exists, and will be actively developed during this decade, that a national disaster preparedness program will be mobilized in which the crisis intervention centers and services of the country will affiliate with the American National Red Cross, the Civil Defense Authority, or a similar agency, and provide a stand-by corps of trained personnel for immediate service when disaster strikes. Such activities are far removed from the telephone services originally conceived in the early 1960's, but if they do in fact materialize, they will signify the relevance and importance of crisis intervention services in the lives of people experiencing acute stress.

QUALITY CONTROL FOR CRISIS INTERVENTION SERVICES

The biggest and probably the most significant change in the suicide prevention and crisis intervention services will be in the establishment of standards for the certification of individual programs. It is unclear at this point who will make the site visits and issue the official certification of accreditation. The American Association of Suicidology will become the agency to set the standards for quality service, although there is still much deliberation to be done before such standards are ready to be applied universally. It is clear that there are relatively few centers in the country today which could meet various sets of standards which have been in use in some areas (Motto, 1969; Ross and Motto, 1971). The Samaritans in England have been certifying their branches for several years, and the programs associated with CONTACT Teleministry, Inc., are certified by the parent corporation for having met established standards. This must be a universal practice for crisis programs by the end of this decade.

One system which holds promise would consist of a collaborative action between the American Association of Suicidology (AAS) and individual state governments. For example, AAS standards could be applied by state departments of health, bureaus of licensing boards, or similar certifying agencies. There are now a number of states which license drug abuse treatment and education centers. A similar mechanism should be developed for suicide prevention and crisis intervention services. By the end of this decade, anyone who calls a crisis intervention service should be as certain of receiving quality service as he is when he receives service in a general hospital. Hospital accreditation may be the model for crisis intervention services to follow. Agencies which do not wish to be held accountable through external evaluation by the state on the basis of professional standards set by the AAS should not be listed in official directories and should not be eligible for grant funds or for any state or federal support under mental health or law enforcement programs.

PHILOSOPHY OF CRISIS SERVICES AS AGENTS OF HUMAN NEEDS

By the end of the present decade, there will be a new concept of the role which crisis intervention centers have with their clients. Presently, the concept is that of a telephone service which responds on a 24-hour-a-day basis, to anyone who calls in with a problem. The crisis worker is seen as one who listens, who is empathic and understanding, and who makes suggestions of where the caller might go to find someone who will help with the presenting problem. The crisis intervention center could become the "helping someone" itself, as long as the help needed is personal emotional support. In this way, the crisis intervention service would begin to play an ombudsman role in behalf of clients, running interference in their behalf and cushioning their distraught interaction with the environmental factors associated with the stress. For example, a woman has to go to court on a series of bad-check charges. The crisis intervention center does not act as her attorney, but should send a representative to go to court with her, to talk with the attorney, the prosecutor, and the judge. The crisis worker would provide assurance that someone will help the woman to secure employment to pay off her bad checks and fines. The ombudsman might request a delay in sentencing so that the woman can go to work rather than to jail. He would then provide both personal counseling and assistance in securing job interviews, help to gather significant others who may be able to help, and assure both the community and the client that someone does in fact care about the client's emotional stress as well as her social behavior. This is far more than a telephone answering service function. Crisis intervention centers which provide this kind of help are not hiding behind the telephone.

Furthermore, this is not the service of the mental health system. There is no health or mental health issue in such a case. It is a legal and economic issue, with personal stress factors. During the 1970's, the crisis intervention center may be the major agency to dispel one of the worst types of chauvinism and bigotry currently prevalent in our communities. This is the notion that any kind of problem which causes people to worry or to be upset is automatically a case of psychological maladjustment of psychiatric illness. This professional chauvinism also concludes that anything good for the alleviation of human misery or discomfort either is a health problem or is rendered under the auspices of the church. A more realistic view is that people have other needs besides medical, psychological, or religious ones; they have basic human needs, among which are food, shelter, and personal contentment.

It cannot be denied that the mental health system, including its professional practitioners, its institutions, and its pharmacological agents, does produce a measure of personal contentment in persons whose problems or illnesses are responsive to such ministrations. There are other people whose needs for emotional satisfaction are met very adequately by the formal church in which they are believers. Yet there are many people with problems of living for whom neither church, psychiatrist, physician, nor any other agency is an available or relevant source. Such people fall into the cracks between existing agencies. The crisis intervention services of 1980 must be prepared to assume the role of catching these community citizens and offering them a unique service related to their individual needs. To do so will not mean that the crisis intervention center is trying to provide mental health services any more than it is providing public transportation, general welfare, educational, or employment services. At times, it may provide all of these, but none is its special mission.

As a final comment on the nature as well as the future of crises intervention services, it would be well to recognize a very simple fact and to build towards the day when the operation of crisis intervention services reflects this fact:

Every community needs a school, a police department, a radio station, and a newspaper, a bus depot or railroad terminal, a minister, a public hotel and restaurant, a fire department, a hospital, a bank, an attorney, a grocery and pharmacy, a welfare office, a psychiatrist or a mental health clinic, a public park, a utility department, a post office, a gas station, mechanics, plumbers, barbers, a local government, and a crisis intervention service. In the course of its work in behalf of clients, the crisis intervention center will have to function collaboratively with any and all of the other community helping resources and businesses. It must be prepared to stand side by side with them, *but it is neither a substitute for, nor a component part of, any one of them.*

When the day arrives that every suicide prevention and crisis intervention service functions in its community as one individual member of the total spectrum of service agencies, it will have come into its own fulfillment. Its future will be assured, but most of all its unique service will be available to the citizens who experience problems of living and have needs which would be unmet if the crisis intervention program were not there.

LITERATURE CITED

Altrocchi, J., and L. Batton. 1968. Suicide prevention in an underpopulated area. Paper read at the meeting of the American Association of Suicidology, Chicago, March 1968.

Altrocchi, J., and V. Gutman. 1968. Suicide prevention in an underpopulated area. Paper read at the meeting of the Southeastern Psychological Association, Roanoke, Va., April 1968.

Altrocchi, J., C. Spielberger, and C. Eisdorfer. 1965. Mental health consultation with groups. *Community Mental Health Journal*, 1: 127–134.

Ansel, E. L. 1972. Correlates of volunteer performance in a suicide prevention/crisis intervention service. Unpublished dissertation, University of Florida, Gainesville, Fla.

Ballard, W. C. 1963. *The Emergency Mental Health Service.* Pinellas County Health Department, St. Petersburg, Fla.

Bard, M. 1969. Family intervention police teams as a community mental health resource. *Journal of Criminal Law, Criminology and Police Science*, 60: 247–250.

Bard, M. 1970. *Training Police as Specialists in Family Crisis Intervention.* National Institute of Law Enforcement and Criminal Justice, U.S. Government Printing Office, Washington, D.C.

Bard, M. 1971. The role of law enforcement in the helping system. *Community Mental Health Journal*, 7: 151–160.

Bard, M., and B. Berkowitz. 1967. Training police as specialists in family crisis intervention. *Community Mental Health Journal*, 3: 315–317.

Belanger, R. R. 1972. CPI predictors of clinical effectiveness of volunteers in a suicide and crisis intervention service. Unpublished dissertation, University of Florida, Gainesville, Fla.

Brockopp, G. 1970a. The chronic caller to a suicide prevention center: Therapeutic management. In: *Crisis Intervention*, Vol. 2. Suicide Prevention and Crisis Service, Buffalo, N. Y.

Brockopp, G. 1970b. Seven predictions for suicide prevention in the seventies. In: *Crisis Intervention*, Vol. 2. Suicide Prevention and Crisis Service, Buffalo, N. Y.

Cain, A. C., and I. Fast. 1966a. The legacy of suicide: Observations on the pathogenic impact of suicide upon marital partners. *Psychiatry*, 29: 406–411.

Cain, A. C., and I. Fast. 1966b. Children's disturbed reactions to parent suicide. *Americcan Journal of Orthopsychiatry*, 36: 873–880.

Cameron, W. R. 1961. County psychiatric emergency services. *Public Health Reports*, 76: 357–360.

Cameron, W. R. 1962. How to set up a county psychiatric emergency service. *American Journal of Public Health*, 52: 16–19.

Cameron, W. R. 1965. The emergency mental health service. Paper read at the Conference on Emergency Mental Health Service, Regional Office IV, USPHS. Atlanta, August 1965.

Cameron, W. R. 1967. Emergency mental health services—their organization in typical counties. Paper read at the Annual Meeting, Division of Community Services, State Department of Mental Health, Birmingham, Ala., June 1967.

Cameron, W. R., and V. Walters. 1965. The emergency mental health service: An important contribution to preventive medicine. *Southern Medical Journal*, 58: 1375–1379.

Caplan, G. 1961. *An Approach to Community Mental Health.* Grune & Stratton, New York.

Caplan, G. 1964. *Principles of Preventive Psychiatry.* Basic Books, New York.

Caplan, G. 1970. *The Theory and Practice of Mental Health Consultation.* Basic Books, New York.

Case, S., and C. J. Hoffman. 1962. *Springboards to Community Action: A Guide for Community Improvement and Resource Development.* Pamphlet No. 18. Colorado State University Extension Service, Ft. Collins, Colo.

Curphey, T. 1961. The role of the social scientist in the medico-legal certification of death from suicide. In: N. L. Farberow and E. S. Shneidman (Eds.), *The Cry For Help.* McGraw-Hill, New York.

Darbonne, A. R. 1969. Study of psychological content in the communications of suicidal individuals. *Journal of Consulting and Clinical Psychology*, 33: 590–596.

Dublin, L. I. 1963. *Suicide: A Sociological and Statistical Study.* Ronald Press, New York.

Dublin, L. I. 1965. Suicide: A public health problem. *American Journal of Public Health*, 55: 12–15.

Dublin, L. I. 1968. On suicide: 1968. Presented at the meeting of the American Association of Suicidology, Chicago, March 1968.

Dublin, L. I. 1969. Suicide prevention. In: E. S. Shneidman (Ed.), *On the Nature of Suicide.* Jossey-Bass, San Francisco.

Dublin, L. I., and B. Bunzel. 1933. *To Be or Not to Be.* Harrison Smith and Robert Haas, New York.

Farberow, N. L. 1966. The selection and training of nonprofessional personnel for the therapeutic roles in suicide prevention. Presented at the meeting of the Southeastern Psychological Association, New Orleans, April 1966.

Farberow, N. L. 1967. Crisis, disaster, and suicide: Theory and therapy. In: E. S. Shneidman (Ed.), *Essays in Self-Destruction.* Science House, New York.

Farberow, N. L. 1968. Suicide prevention: A view from the bridge. *Community Mental Health Journal*, 4: 469–474.

Farberow, N. L. 1969. *Bibliography on Suicide and Suicide Prevention.* U. S. Public Health Service Publication No. 1970. National Institute of Mental Health, Chevy Chase, Md.

Farberow, N. L. 1970. Ten years of suicide prevention—past and future. *Bulletin of Suicidology*, No. 6, 6–11.

Farberow, N. L. 1972. The decade ahead. Symposium presented at the meeting of the American Association of Suicidology, Detroit.

Farberow, N. L., S. M. Heilig, and R. E. Litman. 1968. *Techniques in Crisis Intervention: A Training Manual.* Los Angeles Suicide Prevention Center, Los Angeles.

Farberow, N. L., and E. S. Shneidman. 1961. *The Cry For Help.* McGraw-Hill, New York.

Farberow, N. L., E. S. Shneidman, R. E. Litman, C. I. Wold, S. M. Heilig, and J. Kramer. 1966. Suicide prevention around the clock. *American Journal of Orthopsychiatry*, 36: 551–558.

Fowler, D. E., and R. K. McGee, 1973. Assessing the performance of telephone crisis workers: The development of a technical effectiveness scale. In: D. Lester and G. Brockopp (Eds.), *Crisis Intervention and Counseling by Telephone.* Charles C Thomas, Springfield, Ill.

Frederick, C. J. 1969. Suicide notes: A survey and evaluation. *Bulletin of Suicidology*, March 1969, 17–26.

Galvin, M. D. 1973. A comparative study of psychological type and facilitative conditions in professional and paraprofessional psychotherapists. Unpublished dissertation, University of Florida, Gainesville, Fla.

Hansell, N. 1968. Casualty management method: An aspect of mental health technology in transition. *Archives of General Psychiatry*, 19: 281–289.

Haughton, A. 1967. Intra- and inter-community coordination of emergency services. In: R. K. McGee (Ed.), *Planning Emergency Services for Comprehensive Community Mental Health Centers*. University of Florida, Department of Clinical Psychology, Gainesville, Fla.

Heilig, S. M. 1967. Manpower: Utilization of non-professional crisis workers. In: R. K. McGee (Ed.), *Planning Emergency Services for Comprehensive Community Mental Health Centers*. University of Florida, Department of Clinical Psychology, Gainesville, Fla.

Heilig, S. M. 1970. Training in suicide prevention. *Bulletin of Suicidology*, No. 6, 41–44.

Heilig, S. M., N. L. Farberow, R. E. Litman, and E. S. Shneidman. 1968. The role of nonprofessional volunteers in a suicide prevention center. *Community Mental Health Journal*, 4: 287–295.

Hillman, J. 1964. *Suicide and the Soul*. Harper & Row, New York.

Hoff, L. A. 1971. Handling of problem calls. Paper read at the meeting of the American Association of Suicidology, Washington, D.C., March 1971.

Joint Commission on Mental Illness and Health. 1961. *Action for Mental Health*. Science Editions, New York.

Kalis, B. L. 1970. Crisis theory: Its relevance for community psychology and directions for development. In: D. Adelson and B. L. Kalis (Eds.), *Community Psychology and Mental Health*. Chandler Publishing, Scranton, Pa.

Klein, D. C. 1968. *Community Dynamics and Mental Health*. John Wiley & Sons, New York.

Klugman, D. J. 1970. The behavioral scientist in the medical examiner-coroner's office. *Bulletin of Suicidology*, No. 6, 45–49.

Knickerbocker, D. A. 1972. Lay volunteer and professional trainee therapeutic functioning and outcomes in a suicide and crisis intervention service. Unpublished dissertation, University of Florida, Gainesville, Fla.

Knickerbocker, D. A., and R. K. McGee. 1973. Clinical effectiveness of volunteer crisis workers on the telephone. In: D. Lester and G. Brockopp (Eds.), *Crisis Intervention and Counseling by Telephone*. Charles C Thomas, Springfield, Ill.

Kobler, J. 1948. Suicides can be prevented. *The Saturday Evening Post*, March 27, p. 20.

Kramer, J. 1964. A history and resume of the first year's operation of the clinical associates' (night watch) program of the suicide prevention center. Unpublished manuscript, Los Angeles Suicide Prevention Center, Los Angeles.

Lester, D. 1970. Steps toward the evaluation of a suicide prevention center. Parts 1–4. In: *Crisis Intervention*, Vol. 2. Suicide Prevention and Crisis Service, Buffalo, N.Y.

Litman, R. E. 1963. Emergency response to potential suicide. *Journal of the Michigan State Medical Society*, 62: 68–72.

Litman, R. E. 1971. Suicide prevention: Evaluating effectiveness. *Life-Threatening Behavior*, 1: 155–162.

Litman, R. E., T. Curphey, E. S. Shneidman, N. L. Farberow, and N. D. Tabachnick. 1963. Investigation of equivocal suicides. *Journal of the American Medical Association*, 184: 924–929.

Litman, R. E., and N. L. Farberow. 1961. Emergency evaluation of self-destructive potentiality. In: N. L. Farberow and E. S. Shneidman (Eds.), *The Cry For Help*. McGraw-Hill, New
York.

Litman, R. E., N. L. Farberow, E. S. Shneidman, S. M. Heilig, and J. A. Kramer. 1965.
Suicide-prevention telephone service. *Journal of the American Medical Association*, 192:
107–111.

McGee, R. K. 1965. The suicide prevention center as a model for community mental health
programs. *Community Mental Health Journal*, 1: 162–170.

McGee, R. K. 1967a. A community approach to crisis intervention. In: R. K. McGee (Ed.),
Planning Emergency Services for Comprehensive Community Mental Health Centers. University of Florida, Department of Clinical Psychology, Gainesville, Fla.

McGee, R. K. (Ed.). 1967b. *Planning Emergency Services for Comprehensive Community
Mental Health Centers*. University of Florida, Department of Clinical Psychology, Gainesville,
Fla.

McGee, R. K. 1968. Community mental health concepts as demonstrated by suicide prevention programs in Florida. *Community Mental Health Journal*, 4: 144–152.

McGee, R. K. 1971a. Suicide prevention programs and mental health associations. *Mental
Hygiene*, 55: 60–67.

McGee, R. K. 1971b. Development of "We Care, Inc." In: J. Zusman and D. L. Davidson
(Eds.), *Organizing the Community to Prevent Suicide*. Charles C Thomas, Springfield, Ill.

McGee, R. K., D. Berg, G. W. Brockopp, J. R. Harris, A. B. Haughton, D. Rachlis, H. Tomes,
and L. A. Hoff. 1973. The delivery of suicide and crisis intervention services. In: H. L. P.
Resnik and B. Hathorne (Eds.), *Suicide Prevention in the Seventies*. U. S. Government
Printing Office, Washington, D. C.

McGee, R. K., and B. Jennings, 1973. Ascending to "lower levels:" The case for nonprofessional crisis workers. In: D. Lester and G. Brockopp (Eds.), *Crisis Intervention and Counseling
by Telephone*. Charles C Thomas, Springfield, Ill.

McGee, R. K., and J. P. McGee. 1968. A total community response to the cry for help: We
Care, Inc., of Orlando, Florida. In: H. L. P. Resnik (Ed.), *Suicidal Behaviors*. Little, Brown &
Co., Boston.

McGee, R. K., and J. P. McGee. 1970. Profile of a pioneer: Louis I. Dublin (1882–1969).
Bulletin of Suicidology, No. 7, 5–8.

McGee, R. K., W. C. Richard, and C. Bercun. 1972. A survey of telephone answering services
in suicide prevention and crisis intervention agencies. *Life-Threatening Behavior*, 2: 42–47.

Marcus, S. J. 1971. A follow-up study of the suicide and crisis intervention service. Unpublished thesis, University of Florida, Gainesville, Fla.

Motto, J. 1969. Development of standards for suicide prevention centers. *Bulletin of Suicidology*, March 1969, 33–37.

Murphey, G. E., W. W. Clendenin, H. S. Darvish, and E. Robins. 1971. The role of the police
in suicide prevention. *Life-Threatening Behavior*, 1: 96–105.

National Center for Health Statistics. 1967. *Suicide in the United States, 1950–1964*. U. S.
Public Health Service Publication No. 1000, Series 20, No. 5, Washington, D. C.

National Institute of Mental Health. 1971. Criteria for defining community mental health
centers' emergency services. *Bulletin of Suicidology*, No. 8, 4–6.

Perlin, S., and C. W. Schmidt. 1969. Fellowship program in suicidology: A first report. *Bulletin of Suicidology*, March 1969, 38–42.

Pokorny, A. D. 1968. Myths about suicide. In: H. L. P. Resnik (Ed.), *Suicidal Behaviors*. Little, Brown & Co., Boston.

Randell, J. H. 1970. A nightwatch program in a suicide prevention center. *Bulletin of Suicidology*, No. 6, 50–55.

Rioch, M. J. 1964. Evaluations of mental health counselors after two years employment and implications for counseling psychology. Symposium presented at the meeting of the American Psychological Association, Los Angeles, September 1964.

Rioch, M. J., C. Elkes, A. A. Flint, D. Usdansky, R. G. Newman, and E. Siber. 1963. National Institute of Mental Health pilot study of training mental health counselors. *American Journal of Orthopsychiatry*, 33(4): 678–689.

Ross, C. P., and J. A. Motto. 1971. Implementation of standards for suicide prevention centers. *Bulletin of Suicidology*, No. 8, 18–21.

Russell, J. 1970. Using clergymen as night people counselors. *Crisis Intervention*, Vol. 2. Suicide Prevention and Crisis Service, Buffalo, N. Y.

Seiden, R. H. 1969. Suicide among youth: A review of the literature, 1900–1967. U. S. Public Health Service Publication No. 1971 (supplement). National Institute of Mental Health, Chevy Chase, Md.

Shagoury, J. B. 1971. A study of marital communications and attitudes toward suicide in suicidal and non-suicidal individuals. Unpublished dissertation, University of Florida, Gainesville, Fla.

Shneidman, E. S. 1963a. Suicide. In: N. L. Farberow (Ed.), *Taboo Topics*. Atherton Press, New York.

Shneidman, E. S. 1963b. Orientations toward death. In: R. W. White (Ed.), *The Study of Lives*. Atherton Press, New York.

Shneidman, E. S. 1964. Pioneer in suicidology. *Contemporary Psychology* 9: 370–371.

Shneidman, E. S. 1967. The National Institute of Mental Health Center for Studies of Suicide Prevention. *Bulletin of Suicidology*, July 1967, 2–7.

Shneidman, E. S., and N. L. Farberow. 1957a. *Clues to Suicide*. McGraw-Hill, New York.

Shneidman, E. S., and N. L. Farberow. 1957b. Appendix: Genuine and simulated suicide notes. In: E. S. Shneidman and N. L. Farberow (Eds.), *Clues to Suicide*. McGraw-Hill, New York.

Shneidman, E. S., and N. L. Farberow. 1965. The Los Angeles Suicide Prevention Center: A demonstration of public health feasibilities. *American Journal of Public Health*, 55: 21–26.

Sower, C., J. Holland, K. Tiedke, and W. Freeman. 1957. *Community Involvement*. The Free Press, Glencoe, Ill.

Tabachnick, N. D., and N. L. Farberow. 1961. The assessment of self-destructive potentiality. In: N. L. Farberow and E. S. Shneidman (Eds.), *The Cry For Help*. McGraw-Hill, New York.

Truax, C. B., and R. R. Carkhuff. 1967. *Toward Effective Counseling and Psychotherapy: Training and Practice*. Aldine, Chicago.

Varah, C. 1965. *The Samaritans*. Macmillan, New York.

Weisman, A. D., and R. Kastenbaum. 1968. The psychological autopsy: A study of the terminal phase of life. *Community Mental Health Journal*, Monograph Series No. 4.

Whittemore, K. R. 1970. *Ten Centers.* Kenneth R. Whittemore, Atlanta.

Yolles, S. 1967. The tragedy of suicide in the United States. In: L. Yochelson (Ed.), *Symposium on Suicide.* George Washington University, Washington, D. C.

Zelenka, M., S. J. Marcus, and C. Bercun. 1971. Assessing case outcome in crisis intervention programs. Presented at the meeting of the American Association of Suicidology, Washington, D. C., March 1971.

INDEX OF NAMES

SUBJECT INDEX

Technical effectiveness, 208, 242,
  273–275
Telephone counseling, 97–98
Telephone service, 5–6, 83, 87–95,
  283–284
  commercial answering services, 89–
    92, 94, 284
  directory listings, 92–93
  evaluation of, 93–95, 156
  future developments, 283–284
  ideal system, 92
  number of lines, 87–88
  use of "hold" button, 88–89
Transfer, 98, 202, 205–207

V

VITA, 9
Volunteer coordinator, 215, 218, 222,
  232–234
Volunteers
  and the AAS, 19, 285
  as the "real professional," 112, 285
  black, 212–214, 243
  college student, 210–212
  commitment of, 231–232, 274–275
  criteria for performance of, 109,
    242, 273–275
  levels of responsibility, 223–227,
    241–242

limitations of, 112, 181
management of, 110, 227–234
morale of, 67, 87, 107, 110, 172–
  173, 223, 227–232
nonprofessional, 6, 108–112, 153
professional, 78–79, 104, 112
recruiting of, 44, 66, 108–109,
  209–210
relations with professionals, 103,
  105–107, 112, 235, 254–255
screening and selection of, 75, 108–
  109, 209, 214–218, 269–270
self-awareness, 221–222
significance of, 6–7, 33–34, 39, 181
supervision of, 110–112, 223–224,
  232–234
training of, 7, 111–112, 218–227,
  234, 243
unacceptable traits in, 109–110

W

Walk-in counseling, 86, 102
WE CARE Suicide Prevention Center,
  12–15, 43, 48, 55–60, 61, 62,
  72, 75, 84, 86, 87, 89, 90, 92,
  98, 99, 100, 102, 103, 105, 115,
  125–126, 128, 132, 155–163,
  170, 171, 173, 175, 176, 191–
  192, 207, 235, 267